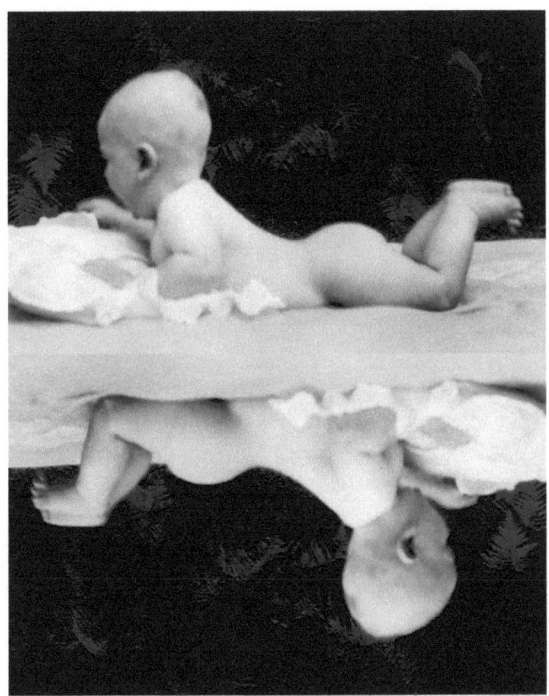

Tim Dry age two months

Tim Dry

Falling Upwards
Scenes From a Life

Camera Journal
Cambridge, 2020

Falling Upwards
Scenes from a Life
© Tim Dry, 2012, 2013 and 2020

ISBN: 978-1-9997231-6-3

Tim Dry is identified as the author of this book.
The moral rights of the author have been asserted.

Published by Camera Journal, Cambridge
A sub-division of Buffalo Books
camerajournal@hotmail.com

Book design by Paul Sutton

All rights reserved. No part of this publication may be reproduced
or transmitted in any form or by any means
electronic, mechanical, photocopying, recording, print on demand or
otherwise, without the prior written permission of the author.
This book shall not, by way of trade or otherwise, be lent, re-sold,
hired out or otherwise circulated without the publisher's prior consent
in any form of binding or cover other than that in which it is published.

Also by Tim Dry:

*Continuum: The Star Wars Phenomenon
As Experienced from the Inside* (Kindle only)
Ricochet – a novella (Paperback and Kindle)

Also by Camera Journal

Understanding Gary Numan by Paul Sutton
Paul Dufficey, The Art of Collage
To Each His Own Dolce Vita by John Francis Lane
Six English Filmmakers by Paul Sutton
Dracula by Ken Russell

Acknowledgments

I'd like to thank Barbie Wilde,
Actress (*Hellbound: Hellraiser II, Death Wish 3*)
and Author (*The Venus Complex, Voices of the Damned*)
for her help in this venture.
Also, Steven Cook for the cover design.
And Sean Crawford for the best times of my life so far.

This life is dedicated with all my love to:

Samuel William Donald Dry, 1906 - 1987
Peggie Joyce Dry, 1921 – 2003
Gena Ann Dry, 1963 – 2010
David William Dry, 1934 – 2011

'Into this house we're born
Into this world we're thrown.
Like a dog without a bone.
An actor all alone.
Riders on the storm.'

Jim Morrison, 1970

Preface

And the movie begins like this:

An aerial shot of a Victorian lodge house situated at the end of a lane on the outskirts of a medium-sized, characterless suburban town in Surrey. The house sits in its own modest grounds and has black-painted beams and gables. It is quaintly named Wiggie Lodge and was once, in grander times, the gatehouse to the Manor that now lies in ruins at the far end of the unmade-up road, just beyond the red brick, ivy clad railway arch. Roses grow in profusion along the south wall of the house; cherry, oak and horse chestnut trees cast their elegant shade over the flowerbeds that bloom in chaotic primary colours. There is a British Racing Green Humber 'Super Snipe' parked on the gravel driveway, the bonnet warm to the touch. It has whitewall tires and a wooden dashboard. The driver's door is open and the interior smells of warm leather, 'Old Spice' aftershave, and tobacco. The seat behind the varnished wooden steering wheel is still indented from the recent presence of its owner. Facing the front of the saloon car, a few feet away, is a dishevelled-looking and slightly lopsided garage with pale grey walls made of asbestos and faced with rust-coloured wooden doors.

Still looking down, the camera pans over the tall hedge that needs a trim and onto the rectangular lawn, which is dusted by the small white faces of daisies, and aromatic with the timeless fragrance of newly-mown shavings of grass. Staring up is a two-year-old boy. He is wearing a white woollen top with baggy powder blue shorts encasing chubby legs, white socks and a pair of shiny red leather sandals. A white sun hat is perched haphazardly on his head and he has some strawberry jam smudged around his mouth. He raises a pudgy arm, squints, and tentatively waves to the camera. It is high summer in 1954 and he is me.

A tall man with receding swept back, greying hair and a face like a less villainous Basil Rathbone sweeps me up into his strong hairy arms. He smiles at me and then to the camera, the sunlight full on his face, shaded by heavy eyebrows. My father wears a white open-necked shirt with rolled up sleeves, a cravat, grey, baggy, pleated trousers and dark brown suede shoes. He has a lit cigarette in the corner of his mouth. We are joined by a beautiful woman in her early thirties. Her hair is wavy, chestnut-coloured, cut fairly short and highlighted by the sun. Before the War she was screen-tested at Denham film studios and was hailed as a potential English Ingrid Bergman. But then the air raids started, life shifted to a darker place for a few years and the dreams had to fade. She's happy now though, and it shows in her greeting. Mum is dressed in a long, full skirt with a pattern of geometric shapes in different colours on a dark background, white sandals, a peach-coloured woollen top and a dark blue scarf tied loosely around her neck.

She kisses my sticky cheek and slips one arm around her husband's waist. Seen from the air my parents and I stand casting long shadows on the grass, as we all wave to the camera above our heads. Zoom in to a close-up of the shiny red surface of the baby sandals I was wearing. The colour fills the screen and then triggers zygotic memories of: the blood-coloured lip paint on the white face of a Mime; the flow of crimson from my nose as I get nutted in the face by a skinhead in 1969; red Lady Esquire-dyed zip up boots in Brighton in 1972. The ruby twin-set and lips of the girl embracing an elegant suitor in the Jack Vetriano painting on my living room wall. The flush on my face as I remove my Robo Cop Helmet in Hamburg in 1994. The bright scarlet of the tail coats that Tik and Tok used to wear. The colour of my Holborn flat in 1977 and the cherry-picker military jacket that I bought at Portobello Market. A swirl of red Grenadine in a Mai Tai cocktail in a bar in 1980, the glowing tip of one more late night cigarette at Malaga airport twenty-two years later. But firstly, all I can see and focus on is the dark, vamp-red lipstick on the voluptuous mouth of a movie star.

Chapter 1- Does My Ego Look Big In This?

Joan Collins turned over to face me in our bed this morning, kissed me on the forehead with breath still perfumed by last night's champagne and whispered: "Good morning darling. I love you. I have to go to work now. I'll see you tonight". I grunted a sleepy response, turned over and then woke up. Bugger! At least this time the dream was based in some kind of reality. I've awoken on my own in a hotel room in Luxembourg. It's March 1993 and I'm out here working on Steven Berkoff's cinematic directorial debut, *Decadence*. It's based on his stage play of the same name, and there are about nine of us character-actors fleshing out the bare bones of his two-hander theatrical tour-de-force for the screen. I was excited by the prospect of working with Mr. Berkoff, as I'd been an admirer of his stage work and his dangerous persona for a long time. I think his use of language, the audacity of morphing almost Shakespearean verbals into East End yob speak, is inspired. Like myself he was originally trained in mime and he uses that foundation brilliantly in all of his stage plays. That was a great source of inspiration to me in my post Tik and Tok wilderness years. It made me realise that maybe you didn't have to do Rep for thirty years and have a RADA accent to be a proper 'Actor'. I naively thought I could emulate his accumulation of physical and linguistic skills and use them for my own ends. Most of the time I was wrong but I did have fun using one of Les the Hitman's speeches from the stage version of *Decadence* as an audition piece of my own. It starts with:

"What a turnabout / what a double choke to suffer slagging from the slut I poke / you think I am not waiting, choosing well before consigning adenoids to hell / don't make me piss my pants / don't make me laugh / death takes it's time / it stalks a lonely path. Conditions must be good / the hour right / don't mess it up and make me rush it / right!" © Steven Berkoff (1980)

Of course the source of Berkoff's vehement power was forged as a son of Russian Jewish immigrants born into poverty in the pre-war East End, and not as a middle-class, too-polite misfit from suburban Surrey. My gurning face, massive body-language and preposterous faux-cockney accent never landed me more than a single job, but it was worth attempting it just to see the blank horror plastered over theatre director's faces when I'd stand before them and deliver the above at high volume as they cower behind the desk. "NEXT!" "Oh, but don't you want to see my Richard the Third?" (unspoken) "No, we fucking don't. Piss off!"

The irony is that I did audition in front of Mr. B. himself for the film, but this time with an improvisation that utilized an equally exaggerated Sloane Ranger vocal mannerism that he seemed to enjoy enough for me to get the job. None of us are required to do that much in the movie, basically we're just window dressing for our two stars. We'll pop-out a few rhyming couplets when Steven deigns to write them for us, and do a bit of freeze-frame stillness in panning camera shots. For reasons known only to himself Mr. B. has chosen to cast, and subsequently given room to, the inexplicably popular entertainer Christopher Biggins who hams and cackles his way through far too many scenes. I mean, Christopher Biggins? Where's the edge? Christophers Lee, Lloyd or Walken, yes, definitely, but our camp little Butlin's redcoat orphan doesn't cut it for us at all. Until our Joan makes her own way to the set on day two. Of course! She and Chris go way back into the murky mists of fag-haggery. Icons like Ms. Collins always surround themselves with queens, as it's safe and un-threatening. And they can swap nail-care tips and info on the newest moisturizers with impunity. There is another major 'Friend Of Dorothy' in the cast. His name is Edward, and he, Joan and Christopher form themselves into a security blanket trio of campness that gets her through the arduous tasks of a no-budget movie and Berkoff's Hitlerian-but-charming directorial style with a degree of comfort. That odd little round bump in the middle of Mr. B.'s forehead would start to pulsate and glow redly when his temper started to rise, like a warning light on the dashboard of an alien spacecraft.

Joan Collins is a living legend. She is quite possibly the last of the true Hollywood Divas and Rank Starlet girls from fifties England, and she's suffered with grace, humour and charm the slings and arrows of Tinseltown's fickle infatuations. She deserves her place in the Pantheon for prospering against all odds, undergoing massive shoulder-pads in the eighties, and being married to Anthony Newley. We all discreetly checked behind her ears for evidence of surgical uplift, when one by one we casually stood at her side in between-take inaction, but nothing was manifest. And who really gives a tuck anyway? She's a survivor and that's laudable in itself. She'd quietly play Travel Scrabble when not needed, or gossip with her two girlfriends, and close her eyes to the gawping stares of the Luxembourgian Extras drafted in for the nightclub scenes. What was weird for me about working with Ms. Collins was how much she resembled my then wife Rosie. If I squinted and ignored the thirty-year age gap between them it was quite uncanny. Bizarrely, Rosie was up for a part in the movie, a whip-wielding dominatrix who delivers a sneering monologue, straight to camera, about the shortcomings of men but, in the end, a possibly threatened Joan decided to do that scene herself.

Steven Berkoff is that schizophrenic mix of despotic auteur and sensitive, insecure artist that is endearing yet vaguely unnerving. One moment he's berating the beleaguered camera crew, or an actor, for not following his impromptu directions instinctively,

the next he chums up with us in the bar and asks: "Is everything all right? You happy? Do you think it's going well?" Having that fearsome, black-clad, chrome-dome physiognomy, that is so familiar from stage and film, in proximity, standing in the same space as me, is worth the price of admission in itself. I become a maladroit twerp whenever he speaks to or looks at me. He's been there. He knows what it's like to be rejected, humiliated and chastened by the shallow whores of show business. Doesn't he?

Decadence looked stunningly stylish in its camerawork and art direction but it didn't really work as a film. The rhyming dialogue succeeds brilliantly on stage for two actors and no props but, cinematically, the concept is impractical. The response from the audience at the premiere in January 1994 bore that out. Deep down I think Mr. B. knew it but his ego wouldn't let him admit it.

Back in the glory days, when I seemed to have money to spend on creative ventures, I decided to put on my own production of a one-man play written by Steven Berkoff called *Harry's Christmas*. My fiancée Rosie said that she'd willingly direct it and I agreed with pride and excitement. We booked the Fringe venue The Etcetera Theatre in Camden for a two-week slot covering late December 1989 to early January 1990. Fringe Theatre is a strange beast. After weeks of rehearsal in a hall somewhere, marking-out exits and entrances, doing dialogue run-throughs and costume fittings, you end up performing the play in an area no larger than your living room. The audience is so close that not only do you generously spray them with saliva, if you get a bit carried away in your performance, but you can smell on their breath what they had for supper. You almost want to ask them if they'd like a coffee or some nibbles, and direct them to the lavatory. Invariably the 'theatre' is a black-painted room with no windows above a sticky-floored Pub in North or South London and, because there's no sound-proofing, you'll suddenly hear someone below ordering, "Three pints of Stella, mate!" just as you go into a death-scene; a hushed quiet-worded moment abruptly now contains the extra line: "Oh and a packet of cheese and onion crisps. Cheers!". Although I expected the worst of my ego from being told what to do by my lover, it actually was a very creative and non-confrontational experience. She guided, cajoled, seduced and encouraged me into giving what I think is the very best performance of my entire career. I know I could not have done it without her.

We designed the lighting, the music, and made all the props ourselves, from the sofa and table, right down to the very Christmas cards that poor Harry displays in his isolated, lonely little flat. We devised a stage-set of seven 8-foot-high screens, hinged together and painted in a style reminiscent of *The Cabinet of Dr. Caligari*, that allowed maximum flexibility and portability. Harry's character is similar to my own in times of weak, self-indulgence and is very obviously made up of a large percentage of Mr. Berkoff's own vulnerabilities and anger.

The whole piece was cathartic to perform and very painful to watch. We weren't expecting large audiences and massive press coverage but we got enough of both to feel justified in our little venture. For me it was the only time that I've actually poured myself, without self-consciousness or restraint, into a role presented on stage to the public.

Chapter 2 – The Magic Hour

A magical and inexplicable event took place in the summer of 1961 when I was nine years old. Nicky Clarke, my friend of the same age, and I were on the swings in a little playground on the cleared area of a grassy knoll in the Castle Grounds in Reigate, Surrey. These grounds are the remnants of a medieval castle that once dominated the town. There's not much of it left now, just a gateway and a small cairn of stones in the centre of neatly manicured paths and flowerbeds. It's a polite and tranquil place. Reigate is the Good Cop to Redhill's Bad Cop. Situated next to each other underneath the North Downs; they are suburban chalk and cheese. Redhill is a featureless, monochrome town completely lacking in character. It developed from its origins as a coach stop on the way from London to Brighton with an indecent, sprawling haste. Reigate is a genteel market town with wealthy inhabitants, nice buildings and charm. It even has an art school, which will, in a mere nine years time, tremble at my imminent arrival. Nicky and I attend Reigate St. Mary's Preparatory School For Boys and we're just over a third into our five-year stay. My friend has white blonde hair and very pale skin. He's smaller than I am and quite frail in demeanor. We're not really that close. We go to the same school, hang around together some times and share enough interests to get along.

The time is about the hour of twilight in early August. The sky has reached that wonderful deep gradated turquoise, with the trees beginning to change to silhouettes. The street lamps have just come on, dappling the view with amber like a Maxfield Parrish painting. The air is still and heady with the smells of summer. Directors of Photography call this time The Magic Hour. Nicky is sitting to my left. We're aimlessly gliding slowly back and forth, our feet carving soft tracks in the dry bare soil under each swing. Nothing is happening, we're not talking. Just two slow and quite possibly bored pendulums. Silence. I look up into the sky, for no reason, and something is there in the air above me. A black disc of indeterminate size is just there. I don't know how close or how far away it is. I have no feelings at all at this point. I'm just staring upwards, observing. It doesn't move or change dimension or do anything. It just is.

I have an overwhelming feeling of timelessness, not exhilarating or recognized, more an indefinable lasting moment. I hear silence and there is nothing else to focus on. I have no peripheral vision. The disc has always been there and is benignly unthreatening. Did I see an impression of blurred light that could have been the edge windows of a spinning vehicle? After all this time I find it almost impossible to say. I don't want my imagination or my wish fulfillment to interfere. Why did I choose that particular moment to raise my gaze? Was it already there? WHY was it there? After I don't know how long it just wasn't. As if it never had been. Ever.

There was nothing *Close Encounters* about this singularly mind-changing moment. No purple and grey clouds illuminated from within, folding back on themselves in mysterious organic formation. No deep synthesized bass-notes or choral fanfare of contact. Nothing at all. Just a motionless black disc hung against the darkening blue of a summer's evening. You have to remember that I am nine years old and we are halfway through 1961. The majority of people are not familiar with, or even aware of, the concepts and realities of UFOs, Extra-Terrestrial life, Alien contact and all the paraphernalia of the paranormal that we nowadays almost take for granted. We were on our own. I looked across at Nicky, who was sitting in the same position as me on his hard wooden seat, and said, in what I think I remember as a tremulously hopeful voice: "Did you see that?"

(A long, thought-gathering pause ...) "Yes." (Trying to adjust back to what was only a moment ago our reality ...) "What do you think it was?"

"I don't know." It's hard to write young boy-speak at any time, especially at this time. I felt as if something inside me had shifted a little; that life from now on would be imbued with a secret. A glimpse of some 'otherness' that we would never be able to fit into our growing lives. To my amazement we found ourselves unable to say anything else apart from "Let's go." I think we felt vaguely guilty, as if we'd been privy to something illicit. We made our individual ways back to our homes and never mentioned it to anybody else or, bafflingly, to each other. In fact, I think our friendship started to deteriorate from then on, as we buried our enigmatic moment deep within ourselves.

So what was it? When I was walking home I remember thinking that it must have been some kind of kite, or balloon, or even a plane. I don't know how long the moment lasted. It could have been seconds or several minutes. I'm not convinced by any of those excuses. How silly I was, desperately trying to rationalize and explain it. It's impossible, especially when you're only nine. I do know without a doubt that it was most definitely circular, motionless, black and by its very presence not 'right'. I had no sense of it being harmful or threatening or communicative. I couldn't tell anyone about it and I found that hurtful but I knew, in my unformed way, that doing so could provoke some difficult judgments. The element that makes this experience so vital is that I was not expecting it, or looking for it, and I had certainly never heard about any other people's sightings. That all came quite a long while later, when it seemed that uncountable numbers had been visited in some way or were definitely anticipating the event.

Ten years further down the road to where I was then, I was on Glastonbury Tor in the middle of a Summer Solstice night, very very high on LSD, with a gathering of other spaced-out travelers desperately willing some manifestation to occur. It was some collective primal longing we shared. We'd surge from one side of the mystic hill to the other if someone spotted a car's headlights plowing through the distant mist, and sigh in unison as the mundane reality became unavoidable. We wanted something greater than just ourselves, some proof of Time and Space as being mutable and infinite. Well, I'm convinced I got my wish when I was too young to know what it was and sadly I don't really think it added to my life in a way that was cathartic or helpful. It was just... there.

Flash-forward twenty years... *Xtro* is the nadir of the British desire to compete in the Horror / Sci-Fi genre led by *Alien*, *E.T.*, *Close Encounters*, *Species*, *The Thing*, *Hellraiser* et. al. Though briefly banned as a would-be 'Video Nastie' it woefully lacks an inventive and gripping script, incisive direction, good lead actors and, let's face it, any redeeming features whatsoever. If, like the lyrics of the old Blue Mink song *Melting Pot*, you take a pinch of this, a pinch of that, you should hopefully end up with a simmering cauldron of riveting visual entertainment. But not in this case. The only good things in this movie are Tik and Tok (me and Sean Crawford) in their respective roles as 'Lizard-like Alien' and 'Action Man Come To Murderous Life'. Even Maryam D'Abo (who flickered briefly as a Bond-Girl in one of the tired Timothy Dalton episodes) retrospectively wiped it from her CV. Sean gets off lightly as a plastic-headed, robotic, bayonet-wielding G.I. Joe (albeit to well-deserved acclaim) who stabs to death an elderly lady in her apartment, but I, on the other hand, undergo hitherto unknown depths of discomfort and potentially life-threatening artistic suffering. "Oh Please!" I hear you derisively snort as you leaf through the safe confines of Halliwell's Bible and smugly page the contents of your Digi-Box.

OK, check this out: It's 3 a.m. in the depths of a wood in Buckinghamshire on a cold March night in 1982. I've already successfully shot most of my scenes as the reptilian Alien who comes to earth and bafflingly chooses to impregnate an ex-Page 3 girl named Susie Silvie (who was not in any way, shape or form an actress). They were bad enough to do, as some bright spark on the production had decreed that instead of being a 'vertical man in a rubber suit kind of monster' I would actually be on all-fours in a crab-like position, but the wrong way up and with the monster head on backwards!

So far, so very uncomfortable. But tonight I've been re-called at the behest of the 'Man Who'd Like To Call Himself A Director' to film just one more scene. A vision that obviously slid into his head whilst lolling around with other double-barrelled Jerkoffs after Bonging-Up in Dad's Chelsea pad, that would absolutely (toke) bring the whole (toke) thing to life, yeah? This involves me as the Alien emerging head first in slo-mo from a pool of brackish water. They've created said puddle somewhere in a clearing deep in the heartless and chilly forest, lit it and now the crew stamp their cold feet, exhale the breath of the privileged and warm and await my shivering arrival. I ease my body into the cold water and have my Xtro head applied. I then, against every instinct of my goose-pimpled body, submerge myself under the scummy surface and allow the contents of the pool to flood in through the eye and mouth sockets in the mask. I can just about make out the Director's distant and muffled shout of "ACTION!" and I slowly raise my head up from the swampy water. It's a revoltingly claustrophobic and genuinely frightening experience, as I could actually very easily drown doing this, and I realise that no one has had the foresight to prepare for that possibility. I do the action once again 'for luck' and that's it. There will be no more! Even if the world's largest hair is jammed in The Gate. You are not paying me enough to undergo this. Fuck you very much and goodnight. I'm home by six a.m. and I vow never, ever to do that kind of dangerous, underpaid wank ever again.

Chapter 3 - The Beatles

Back in 1963, like nearly every other kid in England, I was obsessed with The Beatles. They had seemingly overnight transformed the dull grey wasteland of post-War Britain into somewhere full of joy and infectious energy. Their charm and vibrantly memorable songs captivated an entire country's youth (and a large proportion of its adult population, too). In these sad days of mass-marketed and manufactured 'Pop Stars', it's nigh on impossible to imagine the changes that the Beatles ushered in. That a group of four scallies from Liverpool could so comprehensively cause a nation to fall in love is almost beyond belief.

In Pre-Fabs days all there was to listen, snog or dance to was Cliff Richard, Alma Cogan, Joe Brown and The Bruvvers, Tommy Steele, and that stable of strangely unexciting Larry Parnes acts who, ironically, all had dynamic and evocative surnames: Marty Wilde, Billy Fury, Vince Eager, Duffy Power, et al. It was all so bland and uninspiring. Already Cliff had changed from Elvis-Lite to a wholesome family entertainer and there really was no one to turn us on and give us a soundtrack to our pre-teen longings. And out of the blue arrived our saviors. Looking at The Beatles from this huge distance, I see how perfect their combination of four distinct characters within one entity was: The Hydra with four heads. And the songs leaped from radiograms, dansettes and radios with an almost indecent haste to be heard. Half a century later, if I put on With The Beatles, the exhilaration and energy rush of track one, side one, It Won't Be Long is so magnetic that I am instantly eleven years old again, sitting in the living room at home, transfixed and full of new joy. By the end of '64 Beatlemania had gone global. Everywhere you looked there they were: on our small, laughably inadequate, black and white TV's, on front pages of newspapers and magazines, pouring out from radios and, at last, on the silver screen in their first feature film *A Hard Days Night*.

They even had their own magazine, The Beatles Book (every month, price one shilling and sixpence) by Beat Publications Ltd. of Westbourne Grove, London and edited by one 'Johnny Dean'. (Doesn't sound like his real name does it?) I was also a member of The Official Beatles Fan Club, whose secretary was a lady named Anne Collingham (I wonder who, where and what she is now?) and, every month, I received my newsletter and other bits and pieces that I assumed she was personally sending to me. There was also Beatles chewing gum. In every packet there was a small black-and- white photo card with printed Beatle autographs. I thought they were real signatures at first, but no amount of saliva could cause the ink to smudge. After about a year's worth of jaw-breaking effort and swapping with fellow FabFans, I'd managed to accumulate the entire set of gum cards and a lifelong aversion to bright pink chewables. I never recalled actually throwing this now extremely valuable set away, but I obviously had in one of my periodic cathartic clear-outs. Bugger!

I had a small red plastic Beatle guitar that you couldn't actually play because the strings were nylon and the tuning pegs were molded plastic. You hung it on your bedroom wall by its plaited red, white and black cord, right next to the full-colour free poster of The Fabs in wacky striped Victorian bathing costumes from Rave magazine. The guitar had the same Moptop signatures as my gum cards but these were embossed in black plastic, along with cartoon faces of John, Paul, George and Ringo, on the front body of the 'instrument'. It's funny how the order of their names from '63 onwards was immutably the same, and no change of order was ever countenanced (except for the Yanks who seemed to find Ringo the most appealing). They also sold nylon Moptop wigs in Woolworths, but even at the age of eleven I knew that only the truly sad or the prematurely bald would actually consider owning one.

The best moment of my young life came in December of 1964 when Mum announced that she was taking me to The Beatles Christmas Show at Hammersmith Odeon in London. I was apoplectic with excitement for weeks beforehand and, come the day, I was so high I felt I was going to burst. The Fabs held these shows every winter and they were like the old variety bills that used to tour the UK, with all sorts of diverse acts and comedians appearing. It's bizarre that the biggest band in the world, ever, still chose to do this. At this stage in their career they had really gone way beyond just being a Pop Group and were well on their way to becoming Olympian Gods, whose every utterance was Gospel and whose every move was documented and reported. But one could still go and see them playing live in tiny provincial town halls or theatres up and down the length and breadth of Merrie Olde England.

Mum and I had seats in the circle of the cinema and Dad had a seat in a pub round the corner. His stoical bafflement was tempered in his inimitable fashion by at least three Large Scotch's and a probable intake of DNA infused bar-snacks: cocktail onions, tiny cubes of cheese on sticks and stale peanuts. The Odeon seemed gaspingly vast to my twelve-year old eyes, and was packed to the gills with hysterical young girls and their bemused chaperones. The Master of Ceremonies was the Jolly Gap-Toothed Scouser comedian, Jimmy Tarbuck, whose only function seemingly was to come out before and after the other acts' performances and say teasing little comments about the imminent presence of You Know Who to the audience. Any mention of J, P, G. and R. caused a monumental squeal from the girls and added to the mounting excitement. On the bill at these shows were the tiresomely wacky Freddie And The Dreamers, whose fifteen minutes must have surely been up by now, and, oddly enough, The Yardbirds, fresh from their first hit single *For Your Love*. (Their young lead guitarist Eric 'Slowhand' Clapton would in another eighteen months become the object of my nascent guitarist worship). Mr. Tarbuck finally stops his superfluous clit-teasing, with the barely able to stay seated and dry teenie-boppers, and simply says: "Ladies and Germs, The Beatles!"

The red curtains drew back and there they were! Actually there in the flesh! Four oh-so-familiar little marionettes barely visible on the distant stage. The noise from the audience is gargantuan and primal, unbelievably loud and quite terrifying. I look around me and all I can see are tearful, joyous, pre- and mid-teen girls plucking out their hair and sobbing the names of their favourite Fab. If you could bottle the collective Beatle energy and market it as a perfume every guy in the world would get laid consistently and forever. We've all seen the mania footage from concerts in the '60's, but to actually have been there right in the eye of the storm is something I shall never, ever forget.

Needless to say the laughably inadequate cinema P.A. is in no way up to the task of conveying a single audible note of the music. Even two years into the mania theatre owners still hadn't thought about the logistics and necessity of updating their sound amplification. Minuscule 100-watt P.A. speakers versus 3,000 full-on screaming teenagers? I don't think so! The whole country was caught on the hop by the express train momentum of The Beatles, no one over the age of thirty had any serious thoughts about the phenomenon sustaining itself, and they were woefully unprepared. Through the damp roar of the noise from the audience I could sporadically make out a recognizable riff or vocal line, but it really was impossible to feel the music in any way at all. But let's face it; the point was just to be there in front of them, we had the records at home. I remember at one point, John dropped his harmonica, which prompted another tidal wave of hysteria. He grinned and shrugged in that unforgettable way of his, so familiar from every piece of footage of him ever shown. An incessant hailstorm of hurled Jelly Babies bounced everywhere on the stage. Imagine enduring four years of that AND not ever being able to hear a note of what you're playing. It's no wonder they had to make that momentous decision in '66 to stop touring forever. Their all too brief set ended with John's throat-ripping version of Twist And Shout. I knew it was that song because it was the only time John was at the mike alone, in that curiously sexy bent-legged stance of his, whilst Paul and George would harmonize on the call and response backing vocals and the ascending "Aaaahs" of the coda.

And then they were gone.

Chapter 4 – Ms. Rosetti and Mr. El Pico

Inevitably I had to have a guitar. I was thirteen and, unluckily for my Dad, I had no interest in cricket bats or footballs. Mum's manky old tennis racquet was fine for practicing the moves of my heroes in front of my bedroom mirror (yes, it is a cliché and we all did it, didn't we?) but the time had come to make my undeniable need known to M and D. Naturally, I chose early December 1965 to announce my chosen calling. Ever keen to encourage me in anything that I might just conceivably be any good at, they very sweetly took me along to Redhill's sole music shop, Rhythm, to choose my weapon. Choices were limited on their parental budget, so we finally opted for a red sunburst semi-acoustic made by Egmond called a 'Rosetti'.

Just think, you spend all those years perfecting your Art as an eccentric and tortured Pre-Raphaelite painter and you end up having a cheap guitar named after you. Did they produce a model for tone-deaf aspiring musicians named a Van Gogh or, at the top of the range, a Beethoven? (yes, I know Dante Gabriel Rossetti spells his name with a double 's'). The deal done, I now had to wait until Christmas Day to receive my curvaceous fulfillment. The day finally came like a shagged-out snail trailing to the finishing line. I tore off the wrapping paper, ripped open the triangular cardboard container and clutched my gleaming six-stringed beauty aloft with unbounded joy. I marveled at her shiny sexy form with her bright scarlet finish, her glinting silver, and the perfection of her F-holes. (Jesus! I'm sure I've described many of the women in my life with exactly the same words and, back then, I hadn't even had my first full-on Stiffy!) I manfully struck a D Major chord to show my apprehensive parents that their son was shortly going to bestride the stages of England like a musical colossus. Needless to say the instrument was hideously out of tune. Oh, you mean you have to tune EACH string to the next? How dull! I'd imagined that guitars came already set up to enable one to windmill out Townshend-like power chords the moment you strapped it on.

I embarked on my life's first major learning curve. *Play in a Day* by Bert Weedon (no, really!) was my first port of call. The inanely grinning middle-aged man on the front cover, with improbable wavy hair, assured us that within a mere 24-hour span we would be able to lurch through such classics as Cum By Ya (unfortunately not in any way as suggestive as the title hints) and the patronizingly Christian vacant-smiled Youth Club favourite Michael, Row The Boat Ashore. I think I realized about here that one of the fundamental flaws in my character is that unless things progress EXACTLY as I want them to, I turn hideously truculent and pissed-off and regret even starting on whatever it is that I started. I mean, our Bert wasn't exactly Fab George or Eric C., was he? How dare I have to start at the very bottom? Ironically Beatle George himself said in one issue of Beat Instrumental that one of his first influences was, in fact, the very same Mr. Weedon. Does Bert have a granite-carved guitar-shaped tomb somewhere? I hope he does.

My best friend, Pete Miles, had been given a guitar at the same time as me and we'd sit together studiously learning the basics of chord structure and notation. We listened to early Donovan and Bob Dylan, Pete Seeger and Martin Carthy and imagined ourselves as strolling waist-coated troubadours turning up and playing for our supper in small Cornish villages. Peter was remarkably precocious in every way, and naturally enough managed to master the intricacies of fingerpicking eons before I did. And to top it all he was exceedingly good-looking too. But, in my mind, Mr. Miles deserves his place in Hell for the sole reason that he was THE BASTARD WHO STARTED ME SMOKING CIGARETTES! A fag in his hand or in his mouth looked so louche and so dangerous that I just had to follow. Forty years later I'm still falling for that cancerous bullshit.

I bought a little clip-on electric pickup for Ms. Rosetti so I could amplify my aspirations. To my joy, I discovered that with the aid of two matchsticks I could plug the guitar into the back inputs of one of Dad's old Bakelite radios. The sound it produced was dirty and nasty, yet not loud enough to disturb M & D downstairs on a Sunday half-asleep in front of Songs Of Praise. It was good enough for me to start trying to replicate the sexy raunch of my guitar heroes. To be honest I didn't really want to be Pete Seeger, but I did definitely want to be Pete Townshend (I had The Nose and that was a start). So much so that, in a fit of idolization angst, I smashed Ms. Rosetti to bits against the corner of my wardrobe while she was still plugged into the radio. What a complete and thoughtless pillock! Imagine trying to explain and justify that to the loving parents who'd forked-out for the instrument in the first place?

I have a half-brother, David, who is an architect. Back in the early sixties, he landed a job designing a new music club in London's Soho called The Marquee Club, for a

gent named Harold Pendleton. Originally located in Oxford Street it had, by 1966, moved to Wardour Street. In later decades, the club became a black-painted sticky-floored hellhole for Heavy Metal bands, but in the '60's it was undoubtedly THE place for up and coming and established groups to play. It was cool.

David was a cord or suede-jacketed Trad Jazz kind of guy in those days and R&B, Blues and Rock, didn't appeal to him. One of the perks given to him, as architect of The Marquee, was free membership and admittance to the club, and to any other events the organizers put on. The big one every summer was the Richmond Jazz and Blues Festival held on the athletic grounds of that splendidly elegant town on the Thames. I would go and stay with my brother and his then wife in their town house for that long August weekend. On the Friday, David would escort me to the Festival's backstage area and leave me to wander and worship. I could go wherever I wanted, completely hassle-free. I was a gangly 12-year old kid with a good connection. In those days, Festivals were not the colossal mega-events they are today. It was all rather quaintly parochial and naive. By 1964 the Festival had shifted the musical emphasis away from Jazz and more towards Blues-based pop and Rock. In '64 and '65, I saw, at close hand, The Rolling Stones (twice), The Who, The Yardbirds, Steampacket (featuring Rod Stewart sharing lead vocals with the magnificently camp Long John Baldry), The Pretty Things, The Spencer Davis Group (starring a 17 year old Stevie Winwood playing guitar and Hammond organ), Manfred Mann (twice), The Graham Bond Organization (with Jack Bruce and Ginger Baker in pre-Cream days) and many many others who would lay the entire foundation for British rock for years to come. Free! Backstage! Me!

I used to go back to Prep School after the summer holidays and guys in my class would chatter on about seeing The Stones or The Who on ITV's sole pop programme, Ready, Steady, Go! and I would say with justifiable pride that I had in fact seen all of them playing live a few weeks back AND I went backstage and got autographs! In a mind-numbingly stupid moment, I gave a girl, I was infatuated with, my autographs of Brian Jones, Keith Moon, Pete Townshend and Eric Clapton. I've often mused on what she did with them. We split up very shortly afterwards so she can't have been that impressed by my magnificent gesture.

In 1966, the Jazz and Blues Festival moved from Richmond to Windsor. That year I saw the first ever live gig by Cream. Eric had big sideburns and the haircut that Noel Gallagher has since appropriated, a glittering gold tuxedo, a white, open-necked shirt and tight black trousers. He played a beautiful maple-finish Gibson Les Paul and was just about as cool, talented and God-like as it is possible for a musician to be. Jack Bruce effortlessly managed the dual tasks of playing a six-string bass and the harmonica at the same time and Ginger was an inventive and perfectly syncopated orange-hued powerhouse behind his double bass drum kit. Their music was blindingly inventive and powerful, with very little of the endless virtuoso jamming that overtook them a while later.

By '67, a very noticeable shift had occurred in the music and in the look of the bands that played at that year's Festival. LSD had made its awesome presence felt but I was too young to know that then. Cream topped the bill on the Sunday, with Eric sporting his bubble perm and playing a Gibson SG that had been hand-painted by

The Fool (the stoned Dutch artists who decorated Lennon's Rolls Royce and, a year later, the exterior of the ill-fated Apple' store that The Beatles unwisely opened in London's Baker Street). Also on the bill were The Jeff Beck Group, The Move (who trashed everything in sight on the stage, ending up with singer, Carl Wayne, taking an axe to a TV set), Paul Jones, The Small Faces, Pink Floyd, The Crazy World of Arthur Brown (yep, complete with flaming headgear), Donovan, Pentangle, John Mayall, the first performance by Fleetwood Mac and a tediously frenetic Ten Years After. See what I mean about these unbelievable line-ups? For me, as a fifteen year old, it was three days of repeatedly smacking my gob with glee. The ticket price for the whole weekend was 30 shillings! (Or £1.50 these days).

Being born in 1952 meant that by the time the Swinging Sixties metamorphosed into The Summer Of Love I was only fifteen years old, still at school, and frustrated by my youth. It's amazing what a difference even a couple of years make at that stage in your life. If I'd been seventeen or eighteen in '67, I could have actually partaken of that brief but joyously naive celebration. I did however manage to give myself a home perm one weekend in an attempt to emulate my now-hippified rock heroes' hair. I strode into school on the Monday and, by the first break, was the object of derision of all who saw my crown of badly induced curls. All except for my rather fetching female English Lit. Teacher, who used to perch alluringly on her desk with the twin-set elegance of a Kim Novak. She said she found my new look quite appealing. (She was probably lying through her teeth in sympathy.) That cranial folly is high up on my personal scale of school humiliations, closely followed by the time I decided to apply an over enthusiastic quantity of Mum's fake-tan lotion the day before Autumn Term started. That 'tan-fastic' stuff not only turns your face the colour of a satsuma, it also stains the palms of your hands. And unless you're very skilled, or have the services of a domestic make-up artist, you will inevitably have a clear borderline running down the sides of your neck and chin, normal flesh tones on one side; Del Monte on the other. I was followed around all day by inquisitive, whiffy, little pre-pubes examining the frontiers of No Tan's Land. No amount of furious bathroom scrubbing removed the stain, and the fact that I looked like a member of some hennaed Bedouin tribe was little compensation.

Also, jostling for pole position on my graph of embarrassment is the time I had to have a septic fingernail removed from the middle finger of my left hand. This hurt and bled like hell. The feeling, as the ultra sensitive sub-nail pulpy skin was revealed and started to heal, was like having a Q-Tip inserted into your penis. But worse than that was the fact that I had to wear a huge, sausage-like bandage covering the whole digit for at least a week. Each school day was soundtracked by some bright spark (who assumed that he was the first one to think of it) crowing: "What's the matter? Didn't she open her legs? Hur, hur!"

I didn't know about giving someone The Finger back then. I wish I had, as I would have revenged myself on their merciless inanity by telling them all to "Fuck Off" just by raising my hand.

In 1967, Mum and I went to this very odd Aladdin's cave of second-hand goods in Croydon called The Swap Shop and we bought my first solid body electric guitar. It was white with a single pickup, made by Vox ("Wow, they make all the amps that

The Fabs use!") and called The Stroller. It cost £15. I acquired a little amp called an 'El Pico' from a gullible and trusting friend (also named Pete) who lent it to me, not realizing that he would more than likely never see it again. The noise that this tiny green and beige leatherette amp emitted was quite probably the best guitar sound I've ever achieved. Although it only produced a laughable five watts of power, it had all the crunch and feedback I wanted. If only it had been twenty times more powerful I could have bled myself to death from the eardrums. As it was I discovered that if I lay on the floor with my head right next to the speaker and left off the Sellotape, it really did sound (sort of) like a 100 watt Marshall stack. Sir Paul McCartney himself once said in some interview somewhere, that the very first guitar amp he ever owned was an 'El Pico'. If I'd possessed even a single cell of Maccas' talent we may have met, bonded, and lolled around together at one of his farms. Vegging-out on some of Linda's freshly prepared meatless nibbles and eulogizing about the wondrous aural qualities of our little etiolin and cream Hispanic sounding friends. Inevitably I had to have a group. I'd done pointless, meandering and masturbatory Jams with more gifted friends over the years, but the lure of male bonding in a Tap-like way proved to be too strong to resist any longer.

I carried on going to The Jazz and Blues Festival right up to 1970 when it had relocated, yet again, this time to a small village in Sussex called Plumpton. By this time the word 'Jazz' in the title was completely redundant and the musical emphasis was most definitely Rock with very little Blues. The festival ended up finding a secure home at Reading in Berkshire and resides there to this very day. I saw The Who perform *Tommy* in its entirety under the star-filled firmament of a late summer night. I saw the hideously unwieldy mistake that was Ginger Baker's Airforce (oh please!), Eclection (starring future 'Sailor' frontman, Georg Kajanus), Deep Purple, Black Sabbath, Jethro Tull, Pink Floyd again (with David Gilmour replacing poor confused Syd Barratt), Traffic, Yes and virtually every other big name band of that era.

Chapter 5 – Random Violence, Teenage Sex

Two incidents. In the first I'm walking up Redhill High Street on my way home from school. It must have been autumn or winter because I'm wearing my school scarf. I pass two nascent skinheads already known in the town as a duo to be avoided. One of them was named Bert Weller, a legendary Hard nut with a younger brother named Paul, who wasn't the Modfather of Pop that we know so well but a 'well 'ard' twerp with an older-sibling-veneration complex. He got his head run over by a speeding car as he lay paralytically drunk in the London-to-Brighton road late one night a few years later. Ouch! That's gonna hurt in the morning! I inadvertently glanced at the pair as I overtook them, blithely carried on up the main road and, as a shortcut home, stupidly headed into a quiet side road. Next thing I know I'm pushed up against someone's brick garden wall and Bert's right there in front of me with his chimp chum grinning away behind him. His Cro-Magnon head crowned with razor-cut stubble looms towards mine as he enquires: "Oi, you screwin' me?" Before I can even absorb the question, let alone attempt speech, he throws his head back and nuts me full in the face. I reel back and then for good measure he punches me hard and swiftly in the stomach. I bleed, I sway, and they stroll off laughing. It meant no more to them than casually swatting a fly or stepping on an ant. By now my scarf is soaked and crimson with blood, I could have wrung it out it was that bad. It didn't hurt, it just felt like I was stuck on a carousel that was spinning out of control, throbbing, and blurring my vision. I made it home and Mum went ballistic. After cleaning me up and ascertaining that it was worse than it looked, she went out into the garage. From the living room window I could see her rummaging around in Dad's odd and rusty display of car tools and retrieving a tyre-iron then mounting my old bicycle and roaring off down the drive and out into Frenches Road with pinched face and bloodlust in her eyes. Before I could hoarsely cry: "Mum! What are you - ?" she was gone in vengeful pursuit of my assailants. When people are really angry their mouths get all sphinctered-in and mean looking. Of course Bert and the Baboon were long gone, but the thought of them as the cowards they were, fleeing in terror from a well-built blonde woman roaring towards them on a boy's bike and brandishing a lethal weapon is one that assuaged my anger and fear. I guess in retrospect it's just as well she didn't catch up with them, as I know she definitely would have put them both into Intensive Care and herself into a female prison for a few years. Bless!

Here's incident two. But first a little setting of the scene. It's hard for today's young people to visualise that, from the late '60s through to almost the middle of the seventies, youth in my Suburban England was made up of tribes. Four to be precise. You were either: A Greaser. Unkempt guys in leather and denim riding powerful motorbikes and with a penchant for standing opposite each other in Youth Clubs doing their strange macho dance to the music of Gene Vincent, Eddie Cochran and young Elvis. Like to hang out in oily coffee bars with steamy windows talking abaht carburetors or the new Triumph 650cc bike. Prone to roaring around town with hair flying in the wind, wearing a cut-off denim sewn with patches over a leather biker jacket. A direct descendant from the mid-sixties Rockers. Ton Up Boys torn somewhere between Brando in *The Wild Ones* and Peter Fonda in *The Wild Angels*. Yep, they were pretty wild. Favoured drug? Booze or more specifically Beer. Destined pretty damn quick for a short violent youth followed by a life sentence of mortgage, kids and pensions.

A Straight. Basically dull, boring and sentenced to be a Drone for life. You weren't a threat, you had no interest in clothes or music but did like to do the Football Pools, play a bit of Soccer or Cricket and have a leisurely game of darts in the pub of a Friday or Saturday night. Industry, accountancy or banking would welcome you with open arms. Favoured drug? A bottle of Pale Ale and a nice cup of tea. Normal, safe and destined pretty damn quick for a life sentence of mortgage, kids and pensions.

A Mod (or latterly and more terrifyingly) a Skinhead. Feared because of their hatred of, and violent attacks upon, anyone who isn't one of their own. If you were an Officer, they were the sort of guys whom you'd put in the front row of the trenches. Brutal, powerful and ugly in their chosen uniform of shaved heads, huge DM boots, Levi jeans with braces rolled up a quarter inch at cuff and Ben Sherman shirts with short sleeves. A Crombie coat for winter tops off their malignant presence in nearly every town in England. Naturally they 'ated Blacks and Pakis (although hypocritically their chosen music was always West Indian or Jamaican in origin and form). Favoured drug? Amphetamines and booze. Destined pretty damn quick for a short violent youth followed by a life sentence of mortgage, kids and pensions.

A Hippie (aka a Head). Despised by both Greasers and Skinheads and frequently targeted for attack by either. Long hair, sometimes a beard or moustache and invariably clad in bright clothes of velvet, satin and Indian cotton. Possessors of an insatiable urge to sit cross legged and get really really wasted on grass or acid whilst listening to music in someone's pad. Gentle, artistic, inquisitive and peaceful. Not remotely aggressive or threatening. Favoured drug? Wow, this is good shit man! Destined pretty damn quick for a chilled out youth followed by a life sentence of exploration, artistic endeavour and internal and external travel.

And that really was it back then. Weird isn't it? You were a member of one of those four tribes because there was absolutely nothing else outside the quadrant. Homosexuals? No, not in those days or certainly not ever remotely visible. Blacks? Nope, not in Suburbia. So, who gets the brunt of all that small town violence and pent up frustration when spotted out on the street? I think you can guess the answer to that one. We lived in fear for quite a lot of the time but we were safe and strong when we were indoors and safely plotting to overthrow the universe.

It's now 1969 and I'm seventeen. And I'm caught in the void between leaving school and going to Art school. I am embryonic and can't wait to become a Hippie at last. My hair is medium long. I'm at a dance in a youth club in Caterham with R, my first love, her brother and a couple of others. We're watching a band playing some amateurish but not unexciting sub-Cream muso wank. "Get off! You're crap!" I shouted to myself. Suddenly, there's a tap on my shoulder. I turn round and a fist attached to a leather clad arm punches me full in the face. I stagger in my familiar humiliating fashion and see that my current assailant is Gaz Wyatt, the Über Greaser of most of my part of Surrey. He lived further up my road and I'd often seen him riding past with his blonde hair billowed back as he soared along on his BSA with its 'Ape Hanger' handlebars and tall extended mirrors. He did look cool and he knew it. I suppose a part of me envied him his panache because he'd focussed himself into becoming an object of respect and envy. He looked a bit like Daryl Hall of Hall and Oates and that could explain why I've felt a dislike for their music and their image ever since. He didn't say anything after the blow, just strutted away to do that strange Greaser dance with his cronies in another part of the hall. We left shortly afterwards and went back to R's parents place. She comforted me in the ways that she knew so well while I seethed inside.

The next week, I'm in the café above a shop in Redhill thinking about whys and wherefores when in walks big Gaz. I flinch men- tally as he comes up to where I'm sitting but, instead of pummelling me into a shivering heap down on the sugar-speckled lino floor, he says: "Alright? Listen I'm sorry I hit you the other day."

"Why did you do that?"

"Dunno, I just felt like it. Anyway, no hard feelings yeah? I grudgingly accept his inverted form of apology and then say: "Can you get me a bike?"

"Well, what you lookin' for?"

"I dunno. A 350 or something?"

"I'll have a think. I'll get back to you alright?"

"Yeah, thanks Gaz."

What the fuck am I doing? Well, in order to avoid a recurrence of Youth Club or street face smacking I decided to ingratiate myself, lower my eggshell ego, and join the enemy as a form of self- protection. I was not in any way shape or form a 'Greaser' but I managed to flirt with the imagery and the camaraderie well enough to be accepted by him and his ghastly mates. Thus ensuring that they would now leave me alone. At least until I could get to Art School and become the person that I hoped I really was. I hated myself for doing it but I was at that time lost and confused and tired of being frightened. I did buy a bike from Gaz a week or so later. A stonking great 350cc Matchless. It cost me the princely sum of £10 (and I had to save for that!). Black with Ape Hangers, the same extended chrome mirrors and somewhat disconcertingly no number plates. I couldn't ride it legally, because owning any bike over 250cc as a Learner meant you had to have a sidecar or a wheeled platform attached to the body and that was the just about the most uncool thing to be seen out with ever. Plus I couldn't really get to grips with the learning curve of actually riding the damn thing. So I kept it propped against the side of Dad's asbestos-walled and crooked garage, named it 'Horace', and would occasionally sit astride it and imagine myself cruising around downtown Redhill with the wind hurling back my hair as gaggles of teenage girls stood on street corners ogling and marvelling when I roared past. Oh what a ridiculous, sordid, yet marvellous aberration from my true character! I sold Horace to Frank Millard, my Art School chum the next year for £9. He never rode it either.

Let's talk about sex, baby ... "CUNT! FUCK! PRICK! BOLLOCKS! WANKER!" Strange isn't it, how these words that describe pleasurable body parts and actions have morphed into words of abuse to be used in anger? I wonder if our Indian brethren back in pre-Jingoist Empire days squirted insults at each other in quite the same way: "You look a right Yoni in that robe!" "Move that bull out of the way, you Lingam!" And were our Ancient Roman ancestors prone to such verbal ejaculations as: "Oi, Marcellus, you daft Phallus! Why don't you Coitus Off and annoy someone else?". "There I was, on my way to The Forum, minding my own business, when some flash Vulva in his new chariot nearly ran me over!" Unlikely isn't it? These one-bar aggressive sound-bites seem to be a peculiarly percussive Anglo-Saxon form of abuse. From some imaginary Paglia-lite social behaviour thesis comes this fictional quote: "On some Freudian level, the reliance on such terms of insult reflects a deep-seated, subconscious embarrassment about the sexual organs and the sexual act. Particularly from young adolescent males".

"You wot?" they grunt, squeezing the contents of profuse and livid spots onto their bathroom mirrors. The sexual act is the most enjoyable activity for every species on the planet (unless, of course, you're unlucky enough to be re-born as a male of the Black Widow spider genus, getting jiggy with a Film Noiresque female of the same breed) yet we use it to insult people. It's a real baffler, and I have absolutely no idea why I'm writing about it. Maybe it's just a fairly clumsy link into me recounting my own first sexual experiences? Intimate writing could be seen as proffering just a little bit more information than we need. It's a bit like posting a photograph of your naked self on the Internet. Do you apply a little Photoshop manipulation? Or even a touch of the old Oliver Reed in the nude-wrestling scene with Alan Bates from Ken Russell's *Women In Love* style self-enhancement? Will friends or even (gulp) family members be amused? Might they be embarrassed or envious? Possibly threatened or smugly un-threatened? Or do you just go head down for total yet discreet honesty and hope for the best? Because every one of us has had first sex, good sex, unexpected sex and sometimes bad sex and, in order to put a stop to all my pedantic questions, that's what I'm going to do.

'R' was my first sexual partner. That's not really surprising given that I was just fifteen when we started going out together, and she was only thirteen. God, it sounds so odd and a bit pervy: thirteen years old! Well if I'd been thirty years old at the time it would most definitely have been pervy but we were just kids who smooched a lot. R had large breasts, longish blonde hair, a beautiful wide sensual mouth and a warm and generous character. She was voluptuous in a slightly chubby way. She was my close friend's baby sister, at the same school but two years below us. She seemed to spend a fair amount of time following us around in that irritating way younger siblings sometimes do. I didn't really take too much notice of her until one ghastly pre-Christmas School Fair where she made her affections known by consistently tickling me. It was then that I observed her early development in the bosom department and my male hormones started to make themselves apparent. I asked her out (in whatever clumsy way that had previously worked for me) and she said 'yes' and lo and behold we were dating!

After a few months of furtively joyous cuddling and kissing, we progressed to being practitioners of light petting. This involved me cupping and squeezing her tits through her top, and a serious amount of licking tongues whenever and wherever we could. All that snogging is hard on the jaw and tongue muscles. After about two hours of it you lose most of the taste and sensation, and your mouth feels as if it has had the same bit of chewing gum on the go for a week. I finally got my hand inside R's bra whilst watching *The Fantastic Voyage* (oh how apt) at the Astoria cinema in Purley late one Saturday afternoon in 1967. It was a complicated maneuver that involved undoing enough but- tons on her top to gain access - a thrilling moment - that first touch of warm soft flesh. The illicit ingredient of being in a semi-public place made it even more exciting. On our next cinematic excuse for a fumble I managed to lever up her cumbersome brassiere to release its contents, and spent the next hour or so squeezing each unconfined breast in turn. Very erotic for me but probably uncomfortable for her. I was under the impression that when a girl got aroused sexually her breasts got hard, so I was confused by the fact that the nipples were erect but nothing else. I should have read my Henry Miller or D. H. Lawrence a little more attentively, but there was a whole load of other stuff in them that I didn't yet know about or understand and, after all, this was only 'first base'.

It got easier the more we practiced and the more movies we allegedly went to see. R would now wear tops that facilitated my fumblings. I became very enamored of the feel of her hard nipples under my fingers, and started to want full availability. And that would mean her taking off her top and her bra altogether! Our chance came at a friend of R's place one Saturday night, after watching the latest episode of *The Monkees* on a tiny black-and-white TV. In Katrina's sitting-room (her father was a very well-off M.P. and the house had many rooms) there was a curtained-off alcove, with some kind of sofa or dusty chaise lounge, where R and I would snog while her friend was groping naively with another pimply thruster. This time, my sweetheart took off her blouse and brassiere altogether and sat there coyly covering her naked breasts, whilst I sighed with awe and anticipation. I moved her hands away and held both of her unfettered beauties in my hands. I couldn't believe how full and warm they were. Her nipples were a light pink and looked somehow new and recently formed. The symmetry of shape and colour was breathtaking and she smelled comforting and subtly milky in the same way that babies do. I bent my head and took a roseate nipple in my mouth for the first time as a grown boy. It felt so good, so right, and so natural. She gave a small gasp of pleasure and her friend light years away on the other side of the curtain chimed in with a rhetorical "What you two up to in there?" and we just giggled and carried on regardless.

The next stage after much bosomy enjoyment was for us to progress down into the mysterious hidden realms of the underwear-clad zones. The idea of venturing to these secret places was thrilling yet daunting at the same time. Once we had explored the first true essences of adulthood there would be no turning back; innocence would be gone forever for both of us. And that was just finding 'her' and 'him', let alone entering into touching mutual ready organs with nervous digits. Oh for God's sake! I was hard and she was wet. So we did it. We reached out and touched each other. And thereafter kept on touching each other whenever and wherever we could: in the back of a car, after school in some cow-dung-dappled field, in a friend's bedroom, or at a bus-stop or train station. I used to sit with a secretive smile on a cold platform at Purley late at night after an evening with my adorable girl and wait for the connecting train to Redhill. I'd inhale repetitively the aroma of her pussy on my fingers. She smelled somehow alien and familiar all at once. I felt like a member of some secret olfactory society overseen by a small olive-green Jedi Knight of Testosterone that recognized naive acolytes only through smell: "Ah, Young One. Learned much you have from your fumblings in secret places. Venture forth you must into the land of full on Rumpy Pumpy. Use The Force, Tim. Trust its power." We'll never get it back, that first moment of someone else caressing you, masturbating you. We all crave tactile and sensual contact when we're early teenagers with our raging hormones and urges, and now, after seemingly endless months of mutual manual gratification, R and I needed to fuck. ASAP. Unfortunately, her Dad appeared to us to be an over-protective Paternal Fascist of the First Galactic Order, who merely lacked a black uniform, shiny helmet and terminal asthma for him to terrify us fully. So we were forced to plan our musky and illicit liaisons with a degree of precision and cunning.

The big moment of our First Fuck arrived in 1968 during a little sojourn for R and myself in my brother David's house in Richmond, whilst he and his wife were away. It was just the two of us on our own for the whole weekend, adrift in a big town house and wondering which room might be most suitable for our carnal needs. We opted for a spare bedroom with a small single bed, upon which we spread several towels in order to disguise the fluidic remnants of our fucking, especially as we'd decided to attempt this momentous event during her period for maximum safety. Well, everything went according to plan and we both wondered what all the fuss was about. The timing of the act and our complete inexperience meant that it wasn't quite the romantic or aesthetic experience we'd been expecting from films and books and, in some odd way, we were slightly disappointed by its mundanity. Almost our only thoughts afterwards were a kind of relieved 'Well, at least we've actually done IT.'

Of course, from this moment forward we were no longer nervous about actual fucking and, after only a few more practices, we got it down to a finely crude art and really started to get-off on the pleasure of it. Then we knew what the fuss was indeed all about! It didn't even cross our minds that Rachel was still two years under legal age, and the possible consequences of being caught in flagrante were too horrific to entertain, especially if her Dad were the one to find us at it. That would have permanently sent him over to The Dark Side. It's amazing how quickly one can re-arrange oneself if discovery is imminent. On several occasions Darth Dad was mere heartbeats away from seeing his daughters lips wrapped around my cock but, on his entrance to the living room, we'd be sitting there demurely looking at a book of poetry or some such hastily placed on our laps. Thank God I never had to stand up and salute the arrival of Pa from The Death Star, because 'he who must be obeyed' would have got there first. Once in my bedroom at home we were pre-coital and hands-on when, in a most unexpected and stiffy-reducing act, my Mother knocked and without waiting for a tight-throated "Hello?" came into the darkened room. Somehow, in a mere six-second-time span, we were fully dressed and chatting cheerfully about whatever came to mind. Luckily, because the lights were dimmed, Mum wouldn't have seen that my jeans were somehow now being worn inside out. Or would she? My whole family has always had a very open attitude about sex (and booze) and part of me thinks that Mum knew exactly what had been going on. She would have gone back downstairs to Dad, sat in his chair with another large whisky in his hand, and told him that we were at it upstairs. He would have smiled and said "Good!" Bless him. Strangely (or maybe cosmically) my father did actually look very much like Alec Guinness. He was the Obi Wan Kenobi of Redhill's used car salesmen, and he knew where his destiny lay.

I went out with R for five years on and off from the age of fifteen to nearly twenty. The 'off' came after two years of being together and it was a brief fling for each of us with friends at school. I don't remember much real fun or satisfaction being had by either of us by doing that, it was more like a means of testing how strong our feelings really were for each other. Five years is a long time to be in a relationship when you're that young. Maybe we wanted to see what it would be like with someone else to relieve a tiny hint of complacency or repetition? One of the good things about being a long-term couple was the amusement factor of hearing other boys my own age excitedly telling stories of furtive fumblings, hand jobs and tentative explorations of pussy. Since I'd actually been having full-on sex for at least a year, it made me feel just a little bit smug and Skywalker-like.

We had one major scare when R came to me during the school lunch break and told me that her period was late. We sat together at the distant end of the playing fields holding hands and trying to seriously think about what to do if the nightmare of underage pregnancy became a reality. We entertained a quaint notion of running away together and living in a little cottage down in Cornwall or somewhere to raise our child. I naively envisaged painting pictures of harbours, rocks, and the ocean, and hopefully selling them whilst she nursed and nurtured him or her. In reality, the grim truth of the potential situation was far too ghastly to properly consider, despite our little romantic notions, and we were both scared shitless.

Luckily for our future lives, Ms. Menstruation made her monthly visit in the next couple of days with profuse apologies for being tardy and blamed it on internal traffic. It was a narrow escape and, looking back, it does make me ponder on how one's future can unexpectedly shift in an instant to an altogether different destination. Who knows? I might just conceivably have made a settled and domestic life for us (albeit at a ludicrously premature age) and quite possibly developed the peace and inner strength that I now often lack. Because of the restless searching I still endure, and the shifting careers I have ended up choosing, I do sometimes wonder whether I might just have been happier... R and I drifted apart a year or so after I started Art School. I wish I had been wise enough to maintain contact throughout all the years from then till now. But is it really ever too late to try?

My time as a grammar student at Secondary Modern was limping to its painful end and I was due to start at art school in January. You can't imagine how glad I was to flee that cesspit of bigotry and malevolence and arrive in the welcoming arms of college with my hair proudly flapping in the gentle breeze of freedom. In the year above me at the art school was a lad named Nick, whom I'd last seen when we were at prep school together. His hair was not only raven-black and straight, but literally fell to the bottom of his spine. I was gutted! I knew that I could never compete (my inherited genes saw to that) but I determined to grow it as long as I possibly could with haste and impunity.

Chapter 6 - Art School

It's 1970, I'm eighteen and doing my Foundation Year at Reigate School Of Art (Malcolm McClaren was a student there for about a week and a half in the early seventies too, allegedly). I have a brand new best friend now. His name is Tony and he is worldly-wise in a way that I haven't achieved yet. I mean, he hitched up to Birmingham on his own last summer to see The Floyd at the Mothers' Club! He'd thumbed his way around Cornwall and slept on the shores of Tintagel and St. Ives, man! Apart from being a deviously manipulative control-freak, he was then a charming, dangerous, fun-loving and creative person. We immediately and foolishly formed an 'us against them' kind of club. We reacted against the duffel coat and 'Monkey Boot' clan at the college, who seemed so very ungainly to us, by going up to The Kensington Market in London, shoplifting as many pairs of crushed velvet and satin trousers, Victorian blouses and little singlets with a star printed on the front, as we could, and flaunting ourselves deliberately to wind up our fellow students. It made us very unpopular and I think we loved every minute of it. Art Schools were supposed to be seething hotbeds of exhilaratingly creative anarchists with great clothes sense, but by the time Tony and I made our way to one it was like a school for trainee accountants or corporate logo designers. I suggested that we form a band. There was no doubt that I would be The Guitarist, so therefore Tony had to swallow his pride and become The Drummer. There are likely to be tribes of one-legged tone-deaf pygmies deep in the Amazon Basin with more rhythmic aptitude than my dear friend, but no one could 'charisma you' like he could. We somehow roped in an acolyte of Tony's (yet another Pete) to attempt to play the bass guitar. In a series of excruciatingly painful sessions in the bedroom of Tony's Mum's council flat, I ended up teaching them how to play their instruments. After a few weeks we had to choose a name for ourselves. This is harder than it sounds. Your name has to sum up who you are and the overall vibe of your music and image. Think The Who, Led Zeppelin, Black Sabbath, Deep Purple, etc. We inexplicably opted for, and chose in all seriousness: Cosmic Stoat! We played two gigs (without I might add the benefit of an actual singer) and that was it. It would have been three gigs but, at the first one, all the main power fuses blew just before we were about to start our brief set (someone trying to tell us something?). For our first proper performance we were third on the bill below two other local bands, and we shot ourselves in our fake snake-skin-clad feet straight away by deciding to use fumigation pellets to generate a mysterious and smoky atmosphere. These pellets are the chemical things gardeners and people with small farms use to rid their land of unwanted bugs (or neighbours). Once ignited they produce a vast amount of greeny-grey smoke which is deeply unpleasant and probably toxic to inhale. The draft from Tony's ego behind his cheap drum kit meant that all the smoke drifted away from us and out into the hall. Through the evil haze we could see fellow teens holding their hands over their mouths, clutching handkerchiefs to their streaming eyes and stumbling blindly towards the fire exit. We were not in any conceivable way, shape or form, popular with anyone unlucky enough to have been there and narrowly avoided being beaten to bits by irate other musicians, and - horror of horrors - a smear of local greasers who had decided to drop in to 'have a laugh'. We snuck out the back way as unobtrusively as possible.

On our second gig the gargoyle-featured promoter, who was younger than we were, interrupted us in the midst of our fourth instrumental to say: "Would you mind stopping now - we'd like to play some music!" Egos crushed back inside our velvet pants, we slunk our individual ways back home in disgrace and silence. The day of The Stoat had slid by. Unnoticed by all except for a handful of pimply teens recovering in Redhill General Hospital from either temporary blindness or fumigation poisoning.

I did form another band a short while later (same bass player, different drummer) and we were so lacking in ambition we couldn't even be arsed to think of a name for ourselves. "Hey! What about (pause for unrequited effect) Mind Octopus?". "What?". " OK. Oh!! I know, I know... Gods Trousers!". "Er, sorry?". "Anyway. so it's D to B after the verse, right?" We'd rehearse once or twice a week in a local Church hall, again without the helpful presence of a singer. We were a power-trio without the power. However, I did have a 50-watt amp and a huge homemade speaker cabinet the size of a small wardrobe. This went some ways towards making me feel a little bit more assertive and ax-hero like. I used a wah-wah pedal and an overdrive box to get somewhere close to the sound I wanted, but it was all just a meandering mish-mash with no identity or energy. The drummer was a very gifted and very loud troglodyte (also named Tony) who swaggered with all the bullish and eventually self-destructive characteristics that a good rock drummer has to possess. We played one gig in a youth club somewhere to literally five people. Four of whom drifted away after the first number to play table tennis, leaving a bespectacled ten-year old staring up at us. His glasses were the comedy type that was held together by a grubby piece of Elastoplast. I became very angry at this humiliation and proceeded to smash my guitar on the wooden boards of the stage. No, I didn't look like Pete Townshend. Yes, I did look like a petulant wanker. This action gave the drummer such violent convulsions of laughter that he fell of his drum stool and lay on the floor red-faced and clutching his sides. The little four-eyed scrote seized his moment, jumped up on the stage and grabbed the remnants of my guitar and ran off with them! And that was the end of my involvement in making music until 1980.

Somewhere in the lofty environs of Fine Art, and a year or two older than me, resided a guy named Steve Niner. He was cool and his friends were cool too. He dressed in a ragged paint-splattered artistic way. He was 'Bowiesque' but with longer hair, and had a style that I admired and envied. His parents owned a farm outside Reigate and indulged him in whatever he desired. Steve may well have been a spoilt little rich kid underneath it all but so what? He brimmed with charm, humour, and a spirit that quested for adventure and knowledge. I am unquestionably heterosexual, but emotionally and spiritually I have become infatuated with every strong male figure that has been part of my journey so far. My life has grown to be what it is through and because of the influence of these men, and for what they gave me (and continue to give me) I am constantly grateful.

Steve and his friends, Andrew and Nick, had created a kind of local attempt at Surrealist Cabaret they named "The Cardboard Orgy Pop-Up Theatre", and held it every Friday and Saturday in the back room of The Greyhound Pub in Redhill. A dismal dive if you were in one of the two bars and hated playing pool with greasers and ex-cons but, if you chanced your way back to the room at the rear, it became the nearest we could get to the impromptu happenings and Arts Labs of the '60's. Bands would come and play in the tiny space. The claustrophobic volume and proximity were a high all on their own.

The most memorable (apart from Steve Hillage playing guitar with Khan, and a band named Egg with a keyboard player who was called David Stewart, but who wasn't the one from future Eurythmics) was a group from Crawley called BASTARD. Their set started with the singer being carried on stage in a coffin. He looked and acted like Aleister Crowley on amphetamines. He had a shaved head (which in 1972 was about as extreme as you could possibly get) and wore some mangy kind of monk's white robes. Midway through their heavy-as-it-got set he would kneel in front of the guitarist who clutched a fake cock to his groin, and simulate giving him head. After miming swallowing an unhealthy amount of dark jism shot straight into his open and ready mouth, he would produce a knife and cut the end off the thrusting dick and release gouts of fake blood that covered his face and bald head!

What you might call a 'seminal' influence on the more theatrical aspects of my career at least. I remember Steve and the other cast members of The Orgy on one occasion executing a performance-art piece that had them seated on the stage in chairs staring at the audience, exhorting them to do something, anything and then in frustration throwing money at them. A kind of 'guess you had to have been there moment.' The Greyhound was a shining little beacon piercing the gloom of Redhill's dull twilight, and people still fondly talk about the good times enjoyed there. It was ragged and ingenuous, but joyful and exciting.

One of my many regrets from this advanced viewpoint of age and a degree of wisdom is that I chose to do a Graphic Design course for a potential diploma in Art and Design and not Fine Art. Whilst I was sequestered in a kind of Nissen hut attempting to design the perfect label for a packet of processed cheese, guys with style, imagination and lack of fear, were throwing paint at canvases, photocopying images (like the famous one of the Viet Cong prisoner being shot in the head) and gluing them to bits of wood, painting slogans of inflammatory Dadaist intent on anything they could lay their hands on and generally having a free and sexy time. I used to slouch by the Fine Art hut burning with regret and jealousy. The people on their three year journey to 'nice secure design jobs in a publishing company in Tunbridge Wells' were as dull as dishwater but with less personality. So, with the aid of Tony, I started to become resentful and disruptive and we made ourselves pretty unpopular as a result.

I've always wanted to be a dangerously instinctive artist, but deep down I'm shackled with the invisible chains of so-so talent and a lack of courage. This has consistently caused a massive dichotomy within myself. I found that I was confused and lost at an age when I should have been vibrant and liberated. I always cared too much about what others thought of me, and doing what I thought was the right thing, to the detriment of following my heart. Inevitably I ended up doing the wrong things again and again, getting into trouble, and focusing my frustration and confusion on others' failings not my own. It would have been so easy in retrospect to have put my brush where my mouth was and changed courses, but that would have meant actually going for it rather than just complaining about it. So I left.

Early autumn, 1972. I'm guiltily still living at home with my confused and disgruntled parents and scraping a living making and selling painted, varnished, plywood brooches of characters from *Alice in Wonderland*, *Wind in the Willows*, *Winnie The Pooh* and *Rupert Bear* at the Portobello and Kensington Markets. I cut them out with a fretsaw, sand both sides, stick on a brooch pin and then paint them. It was Tony's idea not mine, but it's a good one. We've tapped into a 'nostalgic for our youth and would like to display it' vibe. But I seem to be stuck in a frustrating domestic loop, I'm starting to find the pressure of secretly-stoned bedroom life a little bit... inhibiting. M and D are as loving and reluctantly supportive as can be expected after seeing me blow what was supposed to be my career, but I'm Gulliver needing a new roof. And the song that keeps playing in my head is:

"I still don't know what I was waiting for / And my time was running wild
A million dead-end streets. And every time I thought I'd got it made It seemed the taste was not so sweet. / So I turned myself to face me.

But I've never caught a glimpse / Of how the others must see The Faker / I'm much too fast to take that test." David Bowie, *Changes* © 1971

Chapter 7 - A Ton of Karmic Wax

Brighton, Suffolk. Autumn 1972. I went upstairs to fetch something from my room. As I put my hand on the door, I noticed that it felt unnaturally warm, almost hot. I swung it open and fumbled for the light switch. The bulb came on, flickered for a few seconds then died. But in that strobe-like moment I saw that the whole of the room's interior was black and, where my rug used to be was now a circular cavity glowing redly like Lucifer's arsehole. In that sitcom way I shut the door, hoping that if I opened it again everything would be back to normal. It wasn't. I stood for a moment in a 'Wow, that was weird!' holding pattern and then hurtled downstairs to the parlour where Steve and Frank were sitting cross-legged and staring at Blake-like visions in the fireplace. "Er, guys?"

(A slow gathering of mental and visual focus.) "Yeah?".

"Something really, really weird has happened to my room...". "Wow..........".

(An eon of Space Time Continuum gently passes). "What?".

"I don't know. But I really think you'd better check it out with me. Oh, and bring a torch!". We surged upstairs in a non-urgent fashion. I opened the door and the three of us stood slack and wordless as only the very stoned can be in times of crisis and stared at the Dantesque scene before us. Everything in the remnants of my room was indeed black, and the middle of the floor really, until very recently, had been on fire. Now it was embered in red in the most evil-looking way. Somehow, even though the flames must have been high enough to melt the tuning pegs on my guitar, the fire had extinguished itself. There was no visible smoke or smell outside of the room, which is why we hadn't been aware of what was happening. Steve reeled back, looked intently at me and said: "It's Dave, man. It's his karmic revenge for me throwing him out".

"Do you think so?".

"It's gotta be. He's a Scorpio, man. Yeah... this is exactly the sort of thing he'd do".

"Oh.... Shit!".

"It's a very bad vibe . . .".

"Well, what are we going to do?".

I thought: "Well this is just great. I finally leave home, become a hippie, and move into a cool little house in Brighton and then some malevolent ex-lodger psychically destroys my room!". Luckily, on the night of the fire in my room, the wretched and woeful rug was crisped back to Floral Hell where it originated. Thanks Dave! Actually it transpired that the conflagration was not caused by Dave's vengeful astrologically motivated ego, but by an antiquated and unsteady Aladdin oil-heater that had been knocked over by a propped-up painting in front of the fireplace. How the fire burnt itself out so abruptly without causing any more damage than three or four charred floorboards is still like a mystery, yeah? How and why did I find myself in such a strangely charred new world? Well, it goes something like this ... (Cue swirly, dissolve camera effect to denote a journey back in time).

One day at The Greyhound, Steve says that his parents have bought him a small house in Brighton and he's just had to evict a rather satanic housemate named Dave. Would I and my gentle friend and co-explorer Frank be interested in moving down to Sussex to share the house with him? Would we? Fuck! Double Hallelujah's all round! The Oblivion Express is steaming at the station and these hirsute Cinderellas are packed and ready to board! I create a new look for myself to celebrate my departure. My hair is now long enough to hang down to my chest and I've hennaed it. This involves spending about an hour and a half with a disgusting pat of cow-shit green gunk slapped on your head. You have to stay motionless because if you move your cranium even slightly in any direction there's a very good chance that it will slide gracelessly down the back of your neck. Finally you wash it all off, which makes the sink look like an incontinent elk has just relieved itself all over it, dry it and find to your dismay that your hair doesn't look the slightest bit different! Until you step out into direct sunlight that is. Then your whole head looks like its bathed in bright orange light, and you have become a Belisha Beacon of Gingerness. People you don't know rush up to you in haste and hurl buckets of water over you and then say: "Shit, sorry. I thought your head was on fire!"

My outfit of choice clashes so violently with my hair when I'm outside that even I'm horrified: a red and black striped top, bright red leather boots (dyed courtesy of Lady Esquire) and black satin trousers rolled up at the cuffs and held up by red braces. In an attempt to look edgy and vaguely Rock 'n' Roll I sport black eyeliner and a hint of mascara. If I didn't still have the photographs I wouldn't believe it either. It's a miracle I didn't get beaten to death. At least when Tik and Tok looked at their weirdest we had an excuse and an outlet for looking very different.

And so began a very *Withnail and I* kind of lifestyle. Frank and I moved into the small converted workman's cottage that Steve now owned in a side street off the Lewes Road in Brighton. My room was on the top floor, next to our host's, overlooking what used to be a garden. This was now overgrown, untended and littered with territorial turds from the ugly tomcat next door and leftover props from the Cardboard Orgy shows. We only had an outside toilet at that time, an oddly Victorian experience singularly lacking in 'comfort and joy' in the run-up to Christmas. At night you'd stumble out by candlelight, yank open the ill-fitting wooden door and lower your cold pale arse onto the chilly wooden seat. On warmer evenings you could sit with the door open and empty yourself whilst gazing up at the stars, or at whatever lurked behind the neighbours' windows.

I painted the non-functioning fireplace in my room with a swirl of rainbow colours, the woodwork bright blue and the walls white. The floor was bare and the unsanded original timber gave you splinters if your bare feet came into contact with it. It was The World Of Interiors all right, but unfortunately it was my own interior. All my books were in piles along with what clothes I possessed, and my hand-painted electric guitar slouched in one corner. Like so many of us, my reading matter of the early '70's consisted primarily of: *Damian, Siddhartha* and *The Glass Bead Game* by Herman Hesse; an assortment of Von Danikens and Castenadas; *Zen and the Art of Motorcycle Maintenance*; *The Prophet*; Colin Wilson's *The Occult* and *The Outsider* and *The Centre of the Cyclone* by John C. Lilly. *Plus Be Here Now* Baba Ram Dass; a few Sword 'n'

Sorcery novels by Michael Moorcock, *Alice In Wonderland* and Pauwels and Bergiers' *The Morning of The Magicians*. And not forgetting *Dune, Stranger in a Strange Land, On The Road* and *The Magus*.

I hung a few cosmic pictures on the walls alongside blu-tacked postcards from the Tate or V&A shops of Pre-Raphaelite paintings of lovelorn and probably consumptive young women. Sparse illumination was provided by one of those white Japanese-looking globe lampshades made of wire and paper that were everywhere in those days. I needed to have a duvet and some kind of covering for the floor. Steve's parents either had very good taste or he had told them exactly what he wanted. What he got was a rust-coloured Habitat duvet and two large, slightly threadbare Moroccan rugs. What I got from dear but not cool M and D was a hideously twee quilt cover with little flowers all over it in brown and cream and the world's most inappropriate rug: a truly nightmarish circular thing with a tasseled edge, again with flowers but this time they were large abstract daisies, in purple, pink and violet. It was obviously designed for Laura Ashley or somesuch by a painfully out of touch and straight sado-masochist. I mean, what chance had I of impressing some horny Patchouli and cheesecloth wearing Hippie Babe with kit like that?

We did take a lot of acid during my seasons in Sussex. We had Purple Haze, Strawberry Fields, White Lightning and many other Lysergic variations. It was our little ritual to swallow a tab and set off into the surrounding countryside to walk, watch and marvel at the induced clarity. Ploughing through the gold and amber of fallen leaves, smelling the evocative wood-fire smoke of distant bonfires, and delighting in the shiny luster and deep rich colour of fallen horse chestnuts. Everything we focused on would be transparent and teeming with microscopic life; the same patterns visible in the sky, our skin, every blade of grass and the bark of every tree. Breathing and alive. The sudden enhancement and deepening of all colour and form. It made your heartbeat accelerate to feel the timeless and joyful 'oneness' of everything.

Coming back to the safety and warmth of the house in those autumn nights was magical. Fresh sap-sweet logs would be thrown onto the fire in the grate, and we'd sit for hours lost and entranced by the pictures in the flames with some gentle, spacily soothing, music drifting around us. Sometimes we'd lie warm-clothed on the beach at night and just gaze up at the infinite canopy above our heads, swarming with vast and unanswerable questions. Life seemed unhurried and stressless for a brief moment, and we savored it as much as we were able. We saw LSD as an extraordinary and generous tool for experiential learning; a means of increasing our perception and definition of an infinite, living universe of which we are all ultimately just a minute particle. Does that sound pretentious? I hope so, because at the very core of me I believe that, contrary to the force-fed stimuli and motives we endure daily, our primary goal as sentient beings is exactly the above. Of course acid is a short cut, an express train to somewhere new, and to fully realize ourselves we have to make it under our own steam. Maybe it's like athletes feeling they need steroids to enhance themselves? Deep down we know that the best victories come as a result of dedication, sacrifice and hard work. Sometimes we just need a little vacation, a daytrip to The Promised Land. But for me, the LSD experience wasn't always sweetness and light. It had, on two or three occasions there and then, taken me somewhere very frightening indeed. Obviously these 'bad trips' were self-induced at a subconscious level but, at the time, it felt like I was helplessly adrift in dark currents that swept me hither and thither at random.

In the summer of '71 I went along to a free concert in Hyde Park with a few friends and I stupidly bought some brown microdot acid from a person I thought I knew. It was a tiny little dark cube about the size of one of those liquorice breath-fresheners that used to be around back then. I carelessly swallowed it without thinking it through, a dumb thing to do at any time, especially as I was the only member of our little group that wanted any. I had undertaken quite a lot of acid trips already and they'd all been controllable and very pleasant and recognisable. But-I-want-my-sixties-now! I wanted to partake in something that I'd only just missed-out on!

Naively I thought I knew my way around the cosmic chessboard but I was to be proved wrong. David Bowie has another song from 1971 that encapsulates the questing, yearning need for self-love, wisdom and acceptance that we all still seek. It's entitled Quicksand. It's on his album *Hunky Dory*.

The harmless-looking tiny cube that I'd recklessly ingested was a lot stronger than the variants I'd taken before and it came on very quickly. After only fifteen minutes or so I found myself becoming emotionally separated from those I was with, cut-off from them as if they were behind oddly-transforming glass. My voice sounded distorted and distant, the words seemed to be heard way, way, after I'd actually said them. I thought they were laughing at me, and my body felt heavy and clumsy, elongated and somehow not part of 'I'. Seated on the grass in the midst of probably about 125,000 people I, Me, Mine had never felt more isolated or more alien in my life. Whatever I tried to visually focus on rippled away from me, the faces of those I looked at seemed to jump out of my vision as if they were under an invisible strobe light. I became scared and paranoid by the proximity of all the bodies around me, especially when a fight broke out in the crowd ahead and people surged away from the punching cavemen and started to swarm right towards me. All I could do was sit there and pray that they wouldn't trample me to death. I felt like I was in the front row of the Stones' gig at Altamont where the Hell's Angels ran amok, beating people at random, culminating in their murder of a young black man. My lysergic paranoia blossomed like a mushroom cloud. Then, magically, the crowd came back together and solidified afresh into its ant-like density. The sky overhead now looked ominous, full of bruised flesh and pain and it moved like a piece of time-lapse film. The music drifting across from the stage was swirling, discordant, and unlike anything I'd ever heard before. It sounded like I was hearing it rising up from the bottom of a deep and troubled ocean. In actual fact it was Jack Bruce (ex-Cream) and his band playing what were in reality some of his new and very inventively-structured compositions. How long had all this been going on? It felt like hours since I'd started this unpleasant solitary journey. My breathing was coarse and ragged, my heartbeat the same. From a vast distance I could hear someone's tiny voice saying: "Tim, are you alright?"

"Do you think he's OK? He looks... weird."

"Yeah, he's alright - Aren't you?". As the last two words suddenly leapt into loud proximal focus, I knew that actually I wasn't alright at all. Something was very wrong. But I couldn't remember what it was. Everytime my brain tried to tell me that I was feeling like this because I'd taken a drug, it was overidden by the sneering knowledge that I had actually, inexplicably, gone suddenly 'mad' and that I would never be able to get back to..... No! That's not right! It's because I've taken a.... I've gone mad! I'll never be able to get back to....There. Not Here. Now Here. Nowhere. I need help. Yes, that's what I need! At these free concerts there was always an ambulance and a few trained staff on hand in case of illness or trauma in the audience. I managed to eventually convey my need to be taken to that refuge IMMEDIATELY to my trusted friend, Pete Miles, and that was hard. Because externally, I wasn't really acting that strangely at all in their eyes. But inside I was writhing under the incessant onslaught of those gigantic, ghastly, circular thought-worms, plus a very real and new fear. How do you convey that without sounding like you've suddenly gone mad? No, it's OK Pete. It's because I've taken a...

    I knew somewhere in what little functioning neuro-mechanism I had left that taking Vitamin C could bring you down from a bad trip, and I managed to make this request apparent to the baffled and un-prepared ambulance men in a brief clear window before the soaring madness obscured it all again. They gave me orange squash! That was not going to work at all and now I had no safety net to fall into. I lay on the grass and started to pull a handful of it out and put it in my mouth. I had to make physical contact with the earth before I was sucked out into the void forever. Pete, Peter, good old shared-times Pete is now very alarmed by my need to eat the surface of Hyde Park and decides to kneel on my chest to try and restrain me. I swallow some grass and spit the remainder out onto my clothing. But suddenly Peter wasn't my trusted and loyal friend anymore, he was some malignant force pinning me down, pushing me back deep into the ground and enjoying it. He looked like a... Satyr. Yes, that's it! With his dark eyes and dark curly hair he now appeared aptly mythological, and he was grinning down at me. I felt betrayed, confused and very far from serenity and sanity. I begged him to stop but he wouldn't. I saw the new little fleshy horns nestled amongst his hair very clearly all of a sudden and his knees were cruelly bruising my flesh. He sweated and smelt like you'd imagine something half-human would do, and his power was dangerously primal and virile.

    My third eye roamed the barren universe looking for rescue. Then from nowhere came the sound of a flute, soothing, melodic and instinctively remembered. I turned my head to the right and saw a beautiful young man sitting at my side and smiling at me. His eyes were full of radiant love and in that timeless moment they were the most beguiling I'd ever seen. He played some more and the music entered my troubled soul and calmed me. Suddenly I knew that he was the embodiment of Christ-like love and I started to cry, great shuddering sobs wracked from the very depths of me for the first time ever in my life. The tears poured down my face as I tried to thank him. Peter eased his weight off me and I looked anew at my friend. He was back. He reached out his hand to me and gently pulled me upright. I laughed with relief and felt little jigsaw pieces of normality slowly, slowly forming around me. I turned to try and express my gratitude again to my musical saviour but he'd gone. I felt bereft but somehow replenished. I couldn't see him anywhere at all and

Pete couldn't understand what I was talking about ... what guy with a flute? I did see a tall, elegantly dressed man standing watching me some yards away, perhaps with an enigmatic smile playing on his face, but it was hard to be sure because the late afternoon sun was behind his head.

The very nature of all hallucinogenic drugs and especially LSD decrees that you do not attempt any action away from the safety of home that involves normal-life reflexes and responses. Above all what you should never do is get in your car and drive it, especially with passengers who are as lost and disorientated as you undoubtedly are. Even more dangerous is to have three wide-eyed participants in the back and a couple (Adrian and Penny) embracing, one on top of the other, in the front. I was not the driver in this incident but I was equally culpable by being there in the first place, and by being wedged into the back seat with two others. I didn't know where we were headed and nor did anyone else it seems. I think we were trying to get home after a little excursion somewhere else in Brighton, and were stupid enough to think that we could just hop in this car that friend Cano owned and find our way back.

Wrong! Very, very wrong. We are now in a snowstorm of constantly moving and shifting hallucinations and overly tactile real objects that don't seem to have any basis in reality. What's this round thing in my undulating hands? Is this a steering wheel I see before me? We drive up from Montpelier Square, down near the seafront, to a major crossroads and go straight over. There's a Cronenberg-like impact, the breaking of glass and a shuddery sound of hissing silence. We've come to rest in dazed bafflement by the side of the road and all is still, disquietingly still. Except for the steady, cinematic drip of blood from Penny's forehead, who still sits clutching her man in the front seat. It's funny how we sober up in an instant when something genuinely untoward happens, and we all did. We blink-out from the comparatively undamaged vehicle and stand slumped with confusion by the side of the road, until the inevitable arrival of the police. Somehow (and I still don't know how) we managed to get away with it. It was a very chastening experience that I never shall repeat, and luckily poor Penny's injuries were only skin-deep.

Because The House In St. Paul's Street was a cool and laid-back place to hang out, we had a neverending succession of differing visitors. He or she or they would just turn up unannounced, sit right down amongst our lives and pass the chillum and the time. It was (or seemed in the moment to be) quite tribal, a sort of peaceful gathering of like-minded heads around the campfire.

"Hey! If you need more heat - let's all go up to my room!" Maybe somebody would bring round a new album that we hadn't heard, or a book we should read, or just their own tales of travel and adventures. One day, a lady a few years older than we were, took me to my room, sucked and fucked me, dressed, and then chose to make us all supper.

A girl with deep unfathomable dark eyes sat naked on my bed and read my Tarot cards. Two young female students from a local girls' school sat in their weekend clothes and got very stoned and giggly on their first joints. We made a hash-cake for my 21st birthday. It was leaden, had the texture of a cork brick, and was virtually inedible, but it got me so stoned that I had to very quickly go and lie on my bed to 'Think About Things'. Midway through my antisocial internal wanderings, I slowly noticed a shifty looking guy named John with bad hair and a v-neck sweater sitting in front of me, staring into what he hoped were my eyes and telling me how he'd just been released from prison. Being caught with two ounces of Moroccan hash stashed inside his pants seemed to have bewildered him, and he had "absolutely no idea how they got there, Your Honour." He was OK, our John, he had a good heart and all he needed was somewhere to stay for a while and people who wouldn't judge him. We gave him some breathing space until he could go back to North Africa, pick up more supplies and then get nicked again. A few years later I cut out and kept a little article from a newspaper that had the title *Snake in the Pants Smuggler Fined*. Apparently a 'confused' youngish man had been apprehended at an airport after Customs Officials noticed a suspiciously large and mobile bulge in the front of his trousers. It did cross my mind that maybe John had given up on the dope smuggling lark and was now importing live reptiles into the UK inside his underwear. Did his flimsy defense state that he was "absolutely at a loss as to explain its presence, Your Worship"? I thought that was just about my all-time favourite headline, apart from the supremely enigmatic and unforgettable "Elephant Kills Clown Dressed as Peanut!"

Painfully inept 'musicians' would come by and settle into our incense-perfumed living space, produce flute or a guitar and imagine themselves as time-traveling troubadours (whilst I imagined them as deserved victims of The Inquisition). There are a large number of people who should be experimented on without anesthetic should they ever indulge in an urge to strike the bongos in public, and at some point in my hippie sojourn I must have met them all. I'm just thankful that our little oasis was never visited by apprentice didgeridoo or krumhorn players.

One particular flautist and his girlfriend came to stay for a patience-stretching eternity. His name was Mike and her name was Sue. Before we'd become fully aware of it, the duo were no longer our guests, they were now actually living with us! Excuse Me? Did I crash-out at the very moment when we said: "Sure. Of course you can move in here?".

Mike had one of those sort of beards that were constructed to cover-up a facial deformity ... the type that just about reveal a rather too red and moist pair of lips. His hair was a vast halo of frizzed and dry-looking stuff that against all odds continued to flourish, and seemed to conjoin with his beard to form a ski mask of fuzz. He wore round Lennon glasses, and would sit lotus-like in front of you playing his flute, and beam in what he thought was a benevolent and insightful way. After an hour or two of his inflicted therapy I for one, became just a tad twitchy. "Tim.....".

"Mmmm?".

"Relax, man!".

"Sorry?".

"Relax, man. You're too tense!".

"Er, No, I'm not ... (dismissive yet gentle snort) tense'!".

"Yeah you are, man. I can feel it ... Go with the flow, yeah?".

(Gritted-teeth internal voice says: "I was ... you ... twit") Of course the inevitable conclusion to confrontations like these is that tenseness settles around you like an unwanted cape. It's manifest in my voice and in my body language. Mike can now rest smugly back, smirk with renewed vigor and tell me that he was right. How I longed to snatch that flute from his self-righteous hands, gleefully shove it where he thought the sun shone, then say: "Hey, Mike... relax, man! You're too tense. Why don't you play us a tune?".

I know that he probably meant well but, at the time, I was too stressed to be sure. Mike's girlfriend, Sue, was American and wore the same kind of glasses. Instead of a beard she had opted for not shaving her legs. And as her sartorial proclivity was to wear long shapeless skirts in 'Earth' colours, white socks and army boots, her calves were revealed looking like the shanks of some semi- evolved simian. She fashioned her hair into two long pigtails that hung down to where I imagined her bra-free tits should be, and she'd picked up on and improved upon Mike's smug and misdirected chill-out technique. Unfortunately this all made Sue utterly un-feminine in my eyes and induced a guilty resentment in me every time she glided into view. Our mild breaking-point was finally reached the day Steve and I emerged downstairs to be confronted by a huge fishing net draped across the entire staircase and lounge. Sue had kindly taken it upon herself to re-decorate our inner sanctum! Not exactly a 'Changing Rooms' moment for us that's for sure, and so Mike and Sue were ushered out into an unsuspecting world that was the unwittingly recipient of their unique approach to body hair, Feng Shui and therapy.

Dennis was another unique and deranged individual who landed like an alien spore into our home. He was an already troubled and over-excitable young man who had made the mistake of taking acid in dangerous quantities... and he was already operating at a mental speed and agility beyond ours, and certainly way beyond the grasp of The Normal World. Dennis saw the Universe as a code that had to be broken in order to achieve a proper state of being, or indeed simply to make a cup of chamomile tea. This concept may well be a vision of reality that could make sense, but to the unprepared it becomes a dangerous and impractical method of self-destruction. Traffic lights informed Dennis when to move or act, by what we would define as a random pattern of signal that was being transmitted straight into his cerebral cortex. The Universe bafflingly told Dennis to uproot every plant in the gardens of certain houses in a Brighton side street. Quite why was never made clear, but it did lead to ugly confrontations that caused this sweet harmless boy to be incarcerated for a while. Dennis arrived one day ready for comfort and a degree of understanding. I don't remember how he found us, he just did. And we gave him what we could to help him. It's hard when someone is firing-off thoughts, concepts, glimpses and answers in a relentless torrent but at least we offered a place for him to just BE for a while. Our mistake was mentioning in a moment of practicality that our fridge wasn't working properly and we couldn't afford to have it professionally repaired. To Dennis this was like asking Einstein to solve a crossword puzzle in the Evening Argus. Before we could stutter, "Erm...", he had taken the entire refrigerator to bits (and there seemed to be a whole fishing-net full of bits) and cascaded them all over the flagstone floor of the kitchen. It really was a Monkey and The Typewriter situation and we seemed powerless to stop it. We lived for months with an Airfix Kit reconstruction of the internal organs of our sad little Fridgidair splayed at ground level for us to step over whilst ducking under The Net. What we needed of course was a domestic-sized traffic light to force Dennis into a coherent re-building program.

Steve was a staunch vegetarian during our time together, and so were most of those whose company we shared. I thought I'd give it a try out of curiosity and camaraderie - nothing to lose and possibly something to gain, or so I thought at the time. Back in '72, kids like us were not hip to the culinary adventurousness and sophistication that is all around us today. We seemed to possess only three main condiments to enhance any selection of the garden-stuff we managed to afford to buy: Miso, Tahini and Soy Sauce. We'd stagger back from Brighton's sole wholefood store, the wonderful Infinity Foods in the centre of town, with several pounds of dirt-encrusted carrots, onions, turnips, leeks and potatoes. We'd give them all a cursory scrub, shove the whole lot into our one big saucepan, lid it up, start simmering and hope for the best. We'd use a lot of chickpeas, lentils and kidney beans as well, flavoured with one or quite often all three of our exotic savouries mixed into the steaming swamp of over-cooked healthiness. We'd ladle huge mounds of this putty-coloured gunk onto plates, pass them around and pretend to make appreciative "Mmm - this is far out!" noises. The food was indeed 'far out', in fact it came as far out of your bum as is humanly possible in the shortest possible time. Just imagine a scene from a hippie remake of Dante's Inferno:

Exterior - Outside Toilet - Night

Six sweating, longhaired young space cadets queue with increasing desperation, dreading the departure of the previous occupant, but in gut-clenching need at the same time. No amount of strategic incense will cover the accumulating cumulus of whiff that hangs malignantly over the ruined garden. Even the turdular tomcat next door has retreated far, far away in horror. The neighbours are furiously packing their most essential possessions in order to make their hasty escape, whilst scenes of disaster movie volcanic eruptions play before their eyes: "SHE'S GONNA BLOW!". The antiquated Victorian plumbing and sewage system must surely be about to surrender to the irresistible force of The Lentil.

Needless to say, after six months of this I began to find excuses to sneak out of the house and run sobbing with relief into the welcoming arms of the local fish n' chip shop which sold SAVELOYS! These elegantly-named, bright orange-coloured, phallic meat vehicles satisfied my illicit carnivorous cravings for a brief guilty moment. You could buy nude ones or ones fried in an unholy batter that made it look like a leprous discarded male organ. I'd cram one or even two into my salivating mouth with Deep Throat lust and haste, frantically chew some gum to cover the breath-smell and saunter back covering my nervous satisfaction with: "Oh, Bummer! They were sold out of Exchange and Mart."

When not dreaming about generously-proportioned and needy Rossetti Babes clambering under my floral duvet, I'd envisage greasing-out with a bacon sandwich or even - gulp - a hamburger! *We don't serve Hippies* sign in Pub windows. "That's OK, we didn't want to eat one anyway."

We had a good friend named Gren, who was an American hippie from the first crop who had re-located to Brighton and who now owned a head shop called Ananda. He sold paraphernalia: rolling papers in textured perfumed variety; chillums made of stone and marble; a myriad pungent and sexy perfumes and incense; inlaid stash boxes from the exotic East; candles, many fine and tempting Indian artifacts; rice paper prints, posters, bowls, jewelry and, for a short while, hand-painted plywood brooches of childhood storybook characters (Well, I had to support my saveloy habit somehow). And Tiger Balm. This was a heavily mentholated unguent from the Orient that came in a little round red tin, imprinted in yellow on the lid with the image of that magnificent feline. It's a kind of Cosmic 'Deep Heat'. We used to annoint ourselves with a fingertip dab of it in the middle of our foreheads when we felt in need of soothing (we got through a lot of it). But the one mistake that you will never willingly repeat (unless you happen to be a rug designer for Dorothy Perkins) is to have a piss or a wank after massaging the stuff into your face and neglect to wash your hands. It is there on your fingertips and you will burn and writhe in an agony unlike any you have ever known... until perhaps in later domestic bliss you decide to prepare a dish using fresh chilli peppers for your loved one or friends and make the same negligent error.

Looking at the array of waxy cylinders on sale in Gren's shop one day, Steve and I made a foolish and regrettable decision: "Hey! Why don't we make our own range of candles?" We worked out that it'd be pretty easy to do. Just make molds from sections of plastic drainpipe cut to size, smear in a release-agent, add the wick, and then pour in molten wax in different colours! Cool!

Our first obstacle was finding somewhere to manufacture these illuminatory delights. A few none-too-subtle hints later, Gren very kindly offered us an empty room above Ananda. Much to his later regret and bemusement, I imagine. All we needed now was the actual wax to start building our melty-empire. In steps my older brother David. By now, he's become a successful architect in London and seems to be doing very nicely, thank you. So I don't feel too unreasonable about asking him to sponsor our business venture. Out of the goodness of his heart, David loans us the money to buy A TON OF WAX! Do you have any idea exactly how colossal that amount actually is? We'd obviously vastly over-estimated any possible supply and demand. We were saddled with about 500 boxes of heavy and colourless candle-wax that took up ninety percent of any available space in the tiny upstairs room. We could have actually built an extension to Steve's house with it all, or even made an igloo. (Not the most practical idea in the summer months maybe.) We ended up with a small range of different sized transparent candles with chunks of coloured and perfumed wax inside them. They looked pretty crude and amateurish, but we felt that just making plain coloured candles was far too 'straight, man'. Sometimes we'd overdo the perfume essence or combine several at once and cause an immediate evacuation of whatever room in which they were lit. Occasionally something odd would happen with the wick as it started to burn, and instead of a soothing and mellow illumination we'd create a rising haze of oily black smoke.

"Anybody got a candle? I can't see where we are!" Gren sold quite a few in his shop, all of our friends (and a lot of complete strangers) were given as many as they could find a home for. Every room in the house was stuffed with the damn things and we still had 497 boxes left. Let's face it, apart from candles there isn't really a huge amount of things left to make with wax is there? If we'd been a bit more adventurous we could have tried hands or heads as candles (very Vincent Price in *The House Of Wax*) when they start to melt down) but that would have involved far too much planning and effort. And so, to my lasting shame, and my brothers' long-term annoyance at our inept business approach, we just walked away from it all. Poor Gren was left with an upstairs room full of boxes and a floor covered in splashes and rivulets of hardened coloured wax. And I had accumulated a Karmic debt that to this day hasn't fully melted away. At the beginning of 1974, after little more than a year and a half of a full-on hippie lifestyle, I'd had enough and decided to move back to my parental home to try and work out what I wanted to do next in my life. I didn't realise that I'd end up being stuck there for another two and a half years.

Chapter 8 - Steeled by Dan

A room in a house in a town in suburbia. Four others and I are sitting in this room: two on chairs and three of us crossed-legged on the floor. My hair is shorter now. It reveals a brand new, sleeker kind of me that could possibly wander from teepee to terminally hip with ease. However, the Wavy Curse inherited from my Mother meant that in order to attain and retain a kind of Bowie-like, straight floppy fringe I had to Sellotape those strands to my forehead after washing them. I think my poor, long suffering M and D had long since reconciled themselves to their son's quest for Grail-like follicular perfection and were accustomed to the tearing sounds and mild yelps that would be heard from the bathroom each time I prepared to venture out onto the mean streets of Redhill of an evening.

But one splash of rain and my tortured yet forgiving hair would inevitably shrink by about an inch and a half and come to rest in a cubist formation of unnatural angles that upset the very foundations of my being. I'd also given up on the velvet or satin trousers, Victorian crepe blouses, velvet jackets and three-button Grandad vests look that I had previously favoured and replaced them with an inexplicably cheesy desire for a 'Man At Harry Fenton' look. Harry Fenton (the name says it all, doesn't it?) sold clothes for the younger discerning gent who doth lack a sense of irony. Even the name of this insignificant suburban chain reeks of Croydon and sharp lads who can't pronounce their "R's" properly, but back in '75, Mr. Fenton was the bees' middle joint of the leg.

A guy named 'John' is sculpting a particularly inventive form of spliff. This is known locally as The Trident. John is one of that unique breed of young men who, for whatever reasons, have been "Banged up at Her Majesty's Pleasure", but emerge a few months later wondering whether "Her Majesty's Pleasure" could have possibly involved HRH masturbating furiously behind a two-way mirror, whilst the "Johns" of this world partook of their daily exercise in the yard and sadistic screws cajoled them into ever more strenuous activities. These and other provocative questions meant that John had the demeanor of a 'geezer', but the soul of a hippie.

He and his bland, long-suffering, but spiritually generous wife 'Mary' were my hosts this particular evening. The Trident was an architectural labour of love. It consisted of three funnels, each containing a different breed of hashish, converging into a central tube. Structurally speaking it seemed at the time to epitomize an advanced level of joint engineering that only the very bored or the very fastidious attain. But what the fuck! We pass it around like you would an Arthurian relic on a BBC Antiques programme, after drawing deep into our twenty-something lungs the ridiculously mismatched yet very potent fumes of Moroccan, Red Leb and Afghan Black. The decor of this room is very typical of "heads" who rent a flat or house in the mid '70's. They aren't really allowed by tenancy terms to inflict their total domestic and spacey vision on their environment. So instead they have ghastly Landlord furniture and fittings left over from the utterly naff part of the '60's, mixed uneasily with a blue-tacked poster collection of Roger Dean album covers for bands like Yes, Greenslade and Osibisa, plus a few tantalizing oriental tidbits and a rug or two picked up by John in Thailand or somewhere else on the Hippie Trail.

By now (about fifteen minutes later) we are quite understandably VERY STONED, and in the absence of our hosts suddenly appearing with a tray of fearsomely effective alcoholic refreshments (or indeed anything at all following the Gladiatorial One's impact), I knee myself over to rummage through John's impressively eclectic vinyl collection. Choosing the right album for the right moment was a challenge we all enjoyed at this time in our lives. The mood of an entire evening could shift somewhere disturbing if the wrong choice was made. For example: in the midst of a tranquil and chilled space-out with silent friends contemplating the infinite mysteries of Time, Space and Eye-Floaters, DO NOT place on the turntable *666 The Mark of the Beast* by a Greek trio called Aphrodite's Child or *Inna Gadda Da Vida* by Iron Butterfly.

There was something wonderfully satisfying about the size and proportion of the 12" sleeve, perfect for skinning up a spliff as you balanced the square of cardboard on your knees, and also providing room for good-sized artwork and sleeve notes to be absorbed by. It's hard to re-create that feeling with the sharp, unforgiving angles of small plastic CD cases. I finally select an album by Steely Dan.

Can't Buy A Thrill has a sleazily stoned cover and is performed by an American ensemble of two main men and several session players. But it contains the most slinky, crafty, and perfectly played and balanced selection of music you could ever hope to hear when you're in the spaced arena like a Sellotape-free Kirk Douglas.

Do It Again is track one and it's a loping smooth ride through Border Town, Tex-Mex outness. We loll back in total surrender to consummate musicianship and the spliff's three-pronged calling card. I realize again that music has the unutterably wonderful ability to transcend time, place and upbringing. Here I am: a raw-fore-headed Fenton deep in someone else's home in Surrey, but at the same time I'm also in a stolen '64 Chevy with a Latino hooker moistening the seat vinyl next to me, as we ooze down to Mexico to fuck and Tequila our lives away. This track always takes me to Tarantino Land effortlessly and quickly. It's movie music and I love it.

Reelin' in the Years swiftly follows. Its double entendre title still seems clever and bait for us Trident fans. The track's slick labyrinthine and coiling melody line beckons you in to its lyrical storytelling:

"Your everlasting summer / You can see it fading fast So you grab a piece of something / That you think is going to last. / But you wouldn't even know a diamond If you held it in your hand/ The things you think are precious I can't understand / Are you reeling in the years? / Stowing away the time, Are you gathering up the tears? Have you had enough of mine?" © Walter Becker/Donald Fagan 1973.

Chapter 9 - A Book and a Bowie

In late summer 1976 I managed to make my escape from the confines of Redhill in Surrey (recently twinned with Dante's Seventh Circle of Hell) and I'm now living with my best friends, Nina Fortune and Trevor Wooldridge, in a rented detached house in Lingfield, Surrey. The rent is £35 per week. A couple of years earlier, with Nina and Trevor, and a small handful of artistic contributors, I produced and self-published a colouring book for kids and their stoner parents called *The Cosmic Colouring Book*.

It was very spacily drawn and heavily influenced by Surrealism, Tenniel's drawings for the original publication of Alice, Art Nouveau, Sci-Fi and Salvador Dali. It was designed to shift the somewhat old-fashioned genre of the colouring book into a more contemporary psychedelic area. It was well-received by bookshops and open-minded toyshops and we sold enough to almost cover the production costs. We even thought, "Sod it, let's send a copy to the Queen, she's got grandchildren and lots of relatives with kids!" And we actually had a very sweet letter from someone in HRH's organisation saying how nice it was to receive it. We shifted a fair amount of copies to Head Shops all over the country, especially in Brighton and Portobello Road and we had some flaky and interesting meetings with first-generation hippies who now owned publishing companies or book shops. Being somewhat idealistic dreamers, it was almost enough just to have created something that was actually out there and being owned and enjoyed.

We had started to make tentative plans for a follow up to be called *The Rainbow Picture Book* when, out of the blue, Nina and Trevor (they were the main contact for the project) received a phone call from Angie Bowie's PR woman, asking if we'd be free to get together and talk with her client about an idea Mrs. Bowie had. Apparently Angie had got hold of a copy of the colouring book for her and David's son 'Zowie' who then was about three years old. What is it with addled pop stars and the naming of their kids? You had Zowie Bowie, Rolan Bolan and 'Zak' Starkey. Zappa's sprogs were christened Dweezil and Moon Unit (what a spiteful Dad!), Grace Slick from Jefferson Airplane called her two China and God (drug use alert!). Of course the ironic twist for the new Millenium is Liam Gallagher's first born being annointed 'Lennon'. Anyway, Zowie enjoyed being messy and creative with felt-tips and his imagination, and his mum liked the contents of our book. Bloody Hell! Being an ardent Bowie-phile for many reasons (his music, vision, charm, intelligence, beauty and fearlessness for starters) this call was like getting the equivalent from one of the Apostles saying that "JC has seen your book, yeah? And he thinks it's really cool and he'd like to fix up a meet, if that's OK with you guys?"

Angie invited the three of us to the house in Chelsea that she and David were renting to discuss the plans and notions she was formulating. WHAT DO I WEAR? Let's face it, nothing I owned or wore in 1974 would, in any way, shape or form, be cutting edge or hip in the eyes of The Bowie Inner Circle, so I was lumbered with my best Harry Fenton Suburbo-Kit. We turned up at this big elegant town house in Oakley Street, off the King's Road, and were ushered into a world that we'd only ever fantasised about or seen in movies. Zowie's nanny opened the front door, a beautiful young black girl named Daniella with bleached short-cropped hair, alongside her equally pretty blonde boyfriend, a musician named Simon Fisher-Turner. We passed a sitting room with a silver-painted ceiling, dark maroon walls, Chinese rugs and an impressively extensive collection of original Art Nouveau pottery and glassware, and were led upstairs into the first floor guest area. I'm in David Bowie's house! This is way, way prior to the current profusion of voyeuristic celebrity stalker mags like "OK!", "HELLO!" or "WANK!" and none of us had ever glimpsed inside a real Rock Star's home. The 'party space' was a large split-level room running from the front of the house to the back, and was entirely painted white. The furniture was white, the carpets were white, and there was a sunken pit in the front half of the room that was lined in white fur and leather. Above the pit hung a huge brightly coloured Expressionist painting by one of the Bowies' painter friends. There was a proliferation of chrome and smoked glass objets d'art and mirrors, and shiny metal picture frames with photos of David then and now, David and Mick, David and Angie, Angie and Marianne, Mick and Angie, Marianne and David and so on.

One framed photograph on a table still sticks in my mind, it was a small black and white portrait of a man's cock with a lit match inserted into the hole in the tip. Whose was it? The raised level of the room housed two white leather sofas, a TV set unseen outside of *2001*, and a stereo system beamed straight in from sonic wet-dream land. The top two floors of the house were the master bedroom, Zowie's room, guest bedrooms and storage for all of David's old stage costumes. In my mind I saw myself as Peter Lorre, face filmed with nervous perspiration, gently holding the hem of a Ziggy suit, crooning: "Mmmm ... I want to... stroke them. Can I please stroke them?" Angie met us with the grace of a Senator's wife entertaining a delegation of hicks from Somewheresville. She was platinum blonde, stridently American, immaculately made up and exquisitely dressed. Her eyebrows had been removed and then re-drawn. Her body was terribly thin and her mouth was full, red and voluptuous. She was charm and theatricality incarnate and immediately put us at our ease with a succession of spliffs and some very fine chilled Chablis. I prayed to the God of Clumsiness that he would leave me unvisited for the duration of our stay. Luckily He did, because putting a colossally expensive pristine white carpet and me together is an inevitable and hard to remove accident just waiting to happen.

David unfortunately was still in L.A. recording *Young Americans* at the time of our first visit, but he did phone up Angie twice when we were there and talked to her for about 45 minutes each time. I could almost hear His Master's Voice! Cocaine does not provide you with small economic phone bills. Angie's reason for our presence in her home was that she was thinking of doing an illustrated book of the fairy story Undine. She was wondering if we'd like to illustrate it, using images of her as the water sprite. We said in unison: "Yes. Absolutely!" We subsequently went back to Oakley Street a few more times with roughs and proposals, which Angie and her circle liked, but her attention was shifting somewhere else. She was 'allegedly' up for the title role in a proposed movie of the Wonder Woman comic strip, and showed us a set of photos of herself in costume and character taken by Terry O'Neill. Peter Clifton, a friend of the Bowies who'd directed the Led Zeppelin movie *The Song Remains The Same*, was attempting to put together the ultimate Rock 'n' Roll TV spectacular featuring both Bowie and Led Zep (amongst others) playing live and being shot on video, and he was interested in us designing the stage sets. Unhesitatingly we did, and I have a Polaroid to prove it:

Sadly it never got off the ground. But at the very least we were ushered in to a world of possibility outside of our own parochial strivings, and briefly saw how it all fits together when and if you have connections on creative, business and chemical levels. Angie had a good and honest heart, and in the long slow run that is more important than gratification by default. It left me with a conviction that I had to leave my little domestic suburban cocoon and head out into Metropolitan life.

Stage-set. March '75.

Chapter 10 – Jimmy Cagney in White Face

July 1976. I am 24 years old and suffocating in the heat of the hottest summer since records began. I'm slowly drowning in the quicksand of frustrated ambition and desire. It's an odd time. Music is caught somewhere between Progressive and what will soon be known as Punk. As for me, I'm still playing Steely Dan, The Eagles, Todd Rundgren, Gong, Kraftwerk and Stevie Wonder. I saw an unusual band on In Concert on The Beeb. They were called Sailor and their non-electric decadent romanticism intrigues me. Their front man, Georg Kajanus, has an anchor marked on his face and wears a kind of Matelot costume. He looks cool and predatory in a retro-matinee idol way. Good smile and boudoir eyes. They have a song called Girls, Girls, Girls that somehow harks back and forth twixt Weimar and Roxy, suggesting a joyful love of Parisian low life. It is imbued with a cheeky, nautical, boys-on-the-town charm. He's someone I will actually meet and get to know some years later, but of course I don't know that then.

David Bowie is making some of the most edgy, inventive and challenging music of his career. Station To Station is out and is marvelled at. What a dark, powerful, sexy and mystical piece of work that is. Golden Years, in its slinky sensual way, seems to encapsulate all my lust and emotions. Its lyrics are those that I long to croon to the love of my life. Needless to say, in my life at this time, sex is hazy and inconsistent like a Spanish mirage. I have some, it's gone again. Is there NO ONE OUT THERE FOR ME? My lust for Nina is constantly unrequited and almost unbearable. She has an enviable penchant for being naked at any time of the day or night that suits her. She is only thirty-two but to me is was the ultimate 'older woman'. Absolutely uninhibited, naturally sexy in an earthy and irresistible way and most definitely barking mad. To my addled hand-stroked mind, she was the personification of everything I ever desired at that time.

I was her acolyte and her apprentice. She turned me on from groin to Third Eye. One late summer day the three of us drop acid and go walking. For me this was the last time I made this chemical journey. Somehow I sensed that things should start to change about here. I couldn't rationalise it then or now, but it really did seem like the end of an era. I spent the usual amount of trip-time staring at things and getting cosmically worked up. When not falling deeply and unrequitedly in love with several fully-grown trees, I'd want to get touchy-feely with my friends. Conversation as we knew it, Jim, was circular and somehow not satisfying. We sloped our way back to the house in a kind of "What do we want to listen to when we get back?" mode. And, after making sure that five-year old Julian (Nina's son) wasn't trying to jump out of a window in sympathy, we settled down to some serious 'carpet time'. Trevor had disappeared somewhere in the house, Nina took her clothes off, lay on the floor on her back and spontaneously masturbated in front of me. I was (sadly, in retrospect) too preoccupied to be turned-on by her actions and instead, for reasons that only became clearer a few years further on, opted to go and change into a Jester's outfit and lie on the leatherette sofa staring up at the ceiling, with unbidden and sudden tears in my eyes.

Later I went upstairs to spend a few decades staring at my face in the bathroom mirror. Why? Maybe, just like Robert Palmer, I was always Looking for Clues? For an instant I saw myself in a hotel in 1983, doing exactly the same thing, but then my hair was dyed black and I was wearing make up. Upon my gradual re-entry into the living room I heard The Eagles' music pouring from the hand-painted speakers. With their perfectly harmonised, somehow psychically apt, open-spaced music they seemed to say everything I longed to convey to the Naked One:

"I like the way / Your sparkling earrings lay / Against your skin so brown / And I want to sleep with you / In the desert tonight, With a billions stars all around / 'Cos I got a peaceful, easy feeling, / And I know you won't let me down / 'Cos I'm already standing on the ground. And I found out a long time ago, / What a woman can do to your soul / Ah, but she can't take you anywhere / You don't already know how to go". *Peaceful Easy Feeling* © The Eagles (1975)

Now call me old-fashioned, call me a retro-head or whatever, but this song captures my aeon of hormonal discontent like no other Bard Ballad in history. You will say, "Jesus, Tim?" I will shrug and say, "Well, you had to be there!" Anyway, more about my Pre-Raphaelite Unrequited One. She had eyes that saw right through you to the real you beyond and an olive-skinned body to worship in front of. Everything she wore, did and said, was somehow right in an addled, naturally spontaneous, way. In her face, I saw every muse for every artist I'd ever loved. I was helpless at her sandalled feet and three times in four years we slept together. And each time I was a semi-impotent awestruck child who only got the real hard-on after the moment had been and gone. Like a returning worm this thought kept coiling in my head: "I MUST DO - SOMETHING... THERE HAS TO BE MORE THAN THIS?"

"I'm just a small boy from a small family spare him his life and his warm sausages. Galileo!" Isn't that what the Mercurial Freddie said? So I got a job. It was numbingly dull and unfulfilling, but it paid my share of the rent. I was Graphic Designer for a publication entitled *Hotel International*. Yes, it really was as stimulating a read as you could ever hope to find, especially if you're a lone travel rep in your Novotel in Hartlepool. Boredom is like pubic lice of the soul. And then suddenly it came to me. Not like a divine jab in the head, but more like a nudging whisper: "Why don't you go to London and study Mime?"

"Excuse me?"

"Well, you've seen Lindsay Kemp's shows haven't you?"

"Er ... yes."

"And you've seen *The Rocky Horror Show* in that small theatre in the King's Road, with it's elements of mime and burlesque? And of course Bowie's stage shows?" (his show at the Epsom Town Hall, which opened with *The March* from *A Clockwork Orange* and *Hang On To Yourself*, seemed like The Second Coming to me. Curiously he encored with a cover of The Beatles *Love Me Do*). "Yeah. But ...".

"Wouldn't you like to leave this stuff behind and go off and do something unique and exciting?".

"Yes, I would actually. YES. I would really like to do that."

"Well then. Off you trot!". So I did.

Time Out had an advertisement in the back pages for evening classes in Mime, given by a guy named Desmond Jones. He promised us the technique originated by Étienne Decroux in pre-war Paris, which was most notably taught to Marcel Marceau and Jean-Louis Barrault. The course was held two evenings a week and, I think, each two-hour class was about £1.50. I caught the train from Purgatory up to Waterloo, walked over the bridge past the multicoloured geometric neon light display on the South Bank, into the glistening magic land of the lower West End and changed my life. I was hooked - by the hem of my knee length black tights - there will be no turning back! Rush me my copy of "Yep, Finally Got Off My Arse And Did It!"

Before I can mime picking an imaginary flower from an imaginary flowerbed, I am climbing the worn wooden stairs to fulfilment in a venue called The Dance Centre in London's Covent Garden. I still remember the smell of the place, a heady mixture of sweat and energetic muskiness. Amidst a class of maybe twenty equally novice explorers, I stumbled silently into a world and a life that I'd only previously fantasised about. I was a member of a club! We talked earnestly about Mime in the post-class pub in the same way, I imagine, that my artist heroes did about painting or photography. I tear up my return ticket to Palookaville with unbounded joy. I'm on board that invisible train to Mime Central. And what is so gratifying is that I'm actually good at this. Why wasn't Art School like this? Desmond is generous, encouraging and creative. He was a Footlights performer at Cambridge alongside the nascent Monty Python team. He drifted away from them, beyond the fringe, into the strange unknown waters of Physical Theatre. Over the next few months I become totally obsessed. I'm doing two classes a week and all day workshops at the weekends. It is definitely a form of magic, the ability to be able to create illusions and stories without words. It's all become a bit of a cliché now, the image of a stripe-shirted, white-faced asshole annoying you on the street, even I nurture fantasies about bludgeoning one of them to slo-mo death with an imaginary fence post, but, back then it was new and secretively unknown.

In late summer 1977, after living for six months with Tony on a houseboat moored at Swan Island Marina outside Twickenham, a lady friend of his gave me the opportunity I'd been looking for. I was lucky enough to obtain a large room to rent in a building in Lambs' Conduit Street, Holborn. The flat was owned by an actress named 'Billie' who had been one of Benny Hill's girls in his TV series, and that, plus a few other parts in sitcoms and dramas, had given her the means to purchase the property that today would be worth twenty times more than she paid back then. The rent was £15 per week and I took it on the spot when she showed me round. Two windows in my room looked down onto the genteel charm of the street below, which was busy during the day with office workers but virtually deserted after six p.m. There was a baker's shop opposite which sold huge and addictive wedges of homemade bread pudding, two wonderful legendary pubs, a couple of arts and craft shops and, round the corner, stood a quaint Welsh grocery store unchanged in nearly a hundred years.

I painted the walls of my new home bright red in homage to Turner's pad in Nic Roeg's trippy '60's masterpiece *Performance*. God, I was obsessed with that film. I didn't see it when it first came out but I caught it on its re-release in '77, and then saw it on an almost monthly basis in tiny little independent movie theatres like the Essential Cinema in Wardour Street; The Electric in Portobello Road; the Minema in Knightsbridge and the Paris Pullman in Fulham. There's something darkly enigmatic and evocative about the film that repeatedly lured me into its Borges-like hall of mirrors. The by-lines on the poster (underneath the two pictures of Jagger) said it all: This film is about madness. And sanity. Fantasy and reality. Death. And life. Vice. And versa.

The movie illustrates the strange merger of the dark underbelly of Kray-time violence and organised crime and the hedonistic decadence of sex, drugs and Rock 'n' Roll. Plus it was set in London as the '60's took that irreversible shift into the murky waters that led to Altamont, Rock Star deaths and loss of innocence. The journey of James Fox's doomed but penultimately redeemable young thug, Chas, adrift in a psychedelic cyclone at the hands of Turner (Jagger) and Pherber (the toweringly tumescence-provoking Anita Pallenberg) triggered something in me that I recognised from the past and that I would recognise again sometime in my future. "The only performance that makes it, that really makes it, that makes it all the way, is the one that achieves madness ... right? Am I right? You with me?" (years later I would meet Nic Roeg at a party hosted by Pamela Stephenson and Billy Connolly. We'd done a show with Pam. Nic was talking with Teresa Russell and George Harrison. I managed only a shy 'hello'. What can you say to people you are in awe of?).

So the walls of my room were blood red, the woodwork was black, and the lighting was diffused and evocative. I had my own eclectic collection of bits and pieces from the past few years, plus lots of ethnic cushions, rugs (no sadistic, flammable florals anymore) and throws bought from a wonderful shop on Goodge Street called Nice Irma's Floating Carpet. Irma's seemed to cater perfectly to ex-hippies like myself who needed their own film set.

Tim, the guy in the room next to mine, was a record collector of abundant dedication. Every available shelf surface in his tiny abode sagged under the weight of albums by obscure and magnificently named bands from the last twenty years or so. Tim went on to have (and quite possible still does have) his own record shop in Hanway Street, behind Tottenham Court Road, which was (is) vinyl heaven to edge-seeking audiophiles with a nostalgic mindset, a kind of Nick Hornby-esque home away from home or romper room. When Tim was away on one of his frequent record buying or DJ-ing trips he'd leave me in charge of his affectionate grey tomcat called Jake. Because this feline fellow was one ear short of a full set I just had to re-name him 'Vincent'. Barbara, my sweetheart of the time, extended his moniker to Vincent Van Go-Cat which enabled our Vinnie to justifiably scrabble endlessly under the bed for a paintbrush (or something at least) in order to express and somehow define how he saw the world. Unluckily for our Vince, the art-buying world wasn't yet ready for a one-eared depressive yet visionary cat with manic eyes and a bandage, who painted fish, mice and low-level landscapes in vivid, swirling colours. Oh, Saatchi's wherefore art thou?

One night earlier, only a few weeks into my tenancy, I was downstairs in landlady Billie's apartment, enjoying some wine, her company and a joint or two and watching her knit one of the jumpers that she sold in her own shop round the corner.

We're pleasantly mellowed out, she's wearing a Kimono as a dressing gown with nothing underneath and there's soothing music playing in her Japanese style bedroom cum sitting room. I catch repeated glimpses of part of one of her breasts as she reaches for glass or spliff, and I find it arousing. She says: "Is there anything else you'd like?" I take my balls by the horn and say for the hell of it: "Yes,

I'd like a fuck!" She places her unfinished knitting down onto the coffee table, stands up, opens her gown so it falls straight down either side of her breasts and wordlessly takes me by the hand to the bed. We make love with her on all fours, the Kimono pushed up over her raised buttocks, and her unleashed hair swaying down to the curve at the base of her spine. It was rude, rhythmic, virtually silent and reached a mutual conclusion with ease. After a quick wash we sat back down exactly where we'd started and she poured us both another glass of white wine, and that was it. She reminded me of Anita in *Performance*, the uninhibited and liberated seductress. How simple an act having sex actually is but how complicated we so often have to make it. This was the first time in my life it had been like that. It was a one-off and sadly never repeated, but it was a Golden Moment that I'll always cherish.

When you move into any large city, especially London, you're let loose into a vast teeming playground, full of history and vibrant life. Everything seems new and shiny with promise, to be stared at and explored. Just knowing that I actually now lived here was a high all on its own. I no longer had to scurry to get to Victoria station to catch the last train back home, or walk from Richmond station to the houseboat in Twickenham. I used to love strolling from the Holborn flat into the West End, sauntering past the Kubrick-like Brunswick Centre, and then through Russell Square, with a stop to gaze up at the sinisterly Orwellian buildings of the University College. Then I'd cross over the Hi-fi-shopped faintly squalid artery of Tottenham Court Road, down Percy Street, take a left into Rathbone Place, over Oxford Street and there I was - bang in the middle of Soho Square. This little grassy sanctum in the heart of Soho's media and sex shop matrix always gave me a lift when I walked through it then, and still does today. In summer months it teams with people strewn over the grass and sitting on the benches: the young, beautiful, black-clad and terminally hip media gunslingers with their schemes and debaucheries; shop girls and temps leisurely eating M&S sandwiches from triangular, plastic cartons; a token wino or two doing their unthreatening rounds; Lycra-shorted bicycle couriers with sunburnt hairy legs and hissing radio transmitters; and a few stressed-out business men in rumpled grey suits with attaché cases on their knees, who squint up at the sun and loosen their ties.

Charles the First used to come here hunting for deer when most of London was still fields, now film or casting directors hunt here for suitable faces and bodies for their next project. For me, on a purely subjective level, the films that define either the real or the imagined essence of London are: *Performance, Blow-Up, Frenzy, Breaking Glass, Jubilee, The Servant, The Ipcress File, Up The Junction, Poor Cow, Notting Hill, The Long Good Friday, Alfie, The Tall Guy, The Lavender Hill Mob, The Knack* and a strange black and white from the early '60's called *The Idol*, which starred John Leyton as a declining and troubled pop singer.

CHILDREN'S ROOM WITH A VIEW July 1976

THANKS to the kindness of two local artists, Tim Dry and Julian Bridle, the children of Andrew Reed ward in the Royal Earlswood Hospital, have a far brighter future.

Tim and Julian spent 80 hours painting the walls of the very large day room, transforming it into a beautiful colourful world in which the children can play and work.

The ward is "home" for ten mentally handicapped children in need of special training. They cover their new surroundings.

One wall shows a sunrise and mountains, another a desert with pyramids and palm trees, a third cliffs and a balloon and the fourth a starry night with moonlight flickering on the water.

The artists gave their work free, using bright and cheerful colours, lots of green and blue and yellow.

"The staff had reservations at first," said Tim, "But now they like it and two or three other wards are keen for us to do murals. We may paint the dining room too."

Tim and Julian, both 25, have been working together for two years. They both paint, design and illustrate. They were freelancing but Tim now is an art editor with Associated Newspapers, while Julian continues with interior design.

Along with friends from Reigate Art School and co-directors Nina Fortune and Trevor Wooldridge, Tim formed the company Mushroom Cloud. They've produced a children's book, which sold at Liberty's, and hope to bring out another "The Rainbow Picture Book" in October.

They design jewellery, including coloured bracelets and rings currently on sale at Kensington Market, and are working on book covers for science fantasy novels.

The aim of Mushroom Cloud is to give local artists a chance to do what they "really want to do".

Our picture shows: the new day room at Andrew Reed ward, Royal Earlswood Hospital, decorated free of charge by local artists Tim Dry and Julian Bridle.

TIM DRY
MIME

I take part in a few of Lindsay Kemp's workshops in a church hall in Fulham in mid-1977. Lindsay is an extravagantly camp and legendary performer who combines mime, dance, theatre and decadence in his productions like Flowers and Salome. He taught a young David Bowie the art of stage presentation back in the late '60's and was feted by Pop and Dance Royalty. Because I loved his work I went along to his classes. This was very different to the strict disciplines I was learning with Desmond and I quickly realised that in order to benefit properly from the experience you had to be a dancer, beautiful and preferably gay. Well, that meant I was excluded from the moment I walked in. I found my hungry gaze kept sweeping over a well-proportioned teenage brunette with a face like a young Liz Taylor, who was writhing around in a skintight leotard on the other side of the hall. I realise now that this heavenly beauty was the soon-to-be-mega Kate Bush, picking up the techniques that she would very shortly weave into a truly unique persona and talent. If only I'd had the confidence to approach her we could have been rolling and falling together out on the windy, windey moors to this day.

As a group we did a lot of slow-motion dying and re-birthing. We'd become sheaves of wheat, cruelly cut down by the scythe, only to slowly (very slowly) grow again. It was emotional. It was cathartic and liberating. I enjoyed it. Lindsay's memorable piece of advice to us was: "Always remember the overhead cameras, Daaarlings!" But the day of my humiliation was at hand! Mr. Kemp announced at the start of what I knew was going to be my last class that: "This is your chance to dance your way into Heaven! Impress St. Peter with your fabulous grace and beauty!"

Uh Oh. With nut-tightening dread, I see all the Sylphs enthusiastically scampering into one corner of the hall and forming a line. I shuffle to the very back of the queue. Lindsay stands like a balletic ring-master (ooh!) in the middle of the hideous chasm of open space, claps his hands and off they go one by one, leaping, spinning and flowing through the air with grace and joy. Lindsay, like a proud mother, exclaims praises of utmost fabulousness upon his golden children and flutters his expressive hands with encouragement. Being at the back of the line means that when my turn arrives with impossible speed, the entire class is standing flushed and breathless awaiting my moment. In the instant before I launch, I flash right back to being twelve-years old at grammar school, in the same position in the queue, waiting to vault over the wooden horse in the gym. It's EXACTLY the same feeling! Instead of a surly and butch PE Master in dubiously stained white shorts sneering at my spindly cowardice, I'm now faced with a world-famous Theatrical Master bemused by my reticence. I hurl myself forwards through space like an arthritic mule and land with a graceless thud that I can still hear in my head. Inexplicably I add a couple of swivelly mime movements to my trajectory freeze and then stride off. At the end of the ensuing horrified silence Lindsay declaims: "Well, Darling, I don't think St. Peter is going to be opening his gates to you just yet!"

I pack my tights, say an internal farewell to the girl who will soon be Kate Bush and hurry back to the safety of what I know and do best. Well, at least I gave it a shot. Thinking of Kate Bush as she was back in the late '70's (and I still do, believe me) reminds me of a little moment of foolishness that Barbie Wilde and I undertook in the spring of 1979. Kate, the leotard-wearing girl that I'd marvelled at in Mr.

Kemp's classes only a year-and-a-half previously, had embarked on her first and only tour of the UK and was playing The London Palladium for her sole gig in the capital. We couldn't get tickets for love nor money but knew that we just had to see the divine creature in the flesh performing her utterly unique music.

I'd become enthralled by her invention, beauty and talent. So, in a moment of madness, B and I decided to scale the fire escape at the back of the Palladium and thereby gain entrance to the theatre. Barbie's vertigo (do NOT ever travel by plane with this lady, I still have nail-scars in my arms) was kept in abeyance by her need to see Kate in action and my determined hectoring. Well, we made it up the ladder eventually and climbed through some kind of hatch into darkness. Upon acclimatisation we realised that we were on the lighting gantry directly above the stage! There she was right below us, writhing through Wow with headset microphone and sinuous movement. We gazed down like proud parents at our gorgeous baby until a hand grabbed my shoulder and a fearsomely gruff voice demanded to know what the fuck we thought we were doing.

The lighting technician walkie-talkied ahead and led us down stairs and ladders until we reached a backstage area where a stern-looking security guard in uniform waited for us. Barbie burst into tears and I seethed with embarrassment and guilt. Well, we were rightly castigated and threatened with arrest and were just offering up our wrists for the metaphorical cuffs when a soft girlish voice said: "Can I have my dressing room key, please?". We turned and right next to us was Ms. Bush, flushed, breathless and hopefully damp from completing her performance. She briefly smiled at us, shrugged in a kind of 'sorry, can't help' way and was gone. Fuck and double fuck! How tragically ironic that we should finally get to see her but under those circumstances. We felt like shameful arseholes as we were booted-out into Great Marlborough street. The two of us drowned our remorse by inexplicably going to see David Lynch's black and white debut oddity *Eraserhead* at a cinema in Panton Street.

I did actually meet Kate Bush under professional circumstances about three years after the 'Palladium Incident' and that's going to come up further into this book but, for now, it is 1977 and I'm a member of Desmond's Mime Company *Silents* and I need to introduce you properly to the 'Barbara' who will become 'Barbie Wilde'. With eight other acolyte I'm performing sporadically in Art Schools and Fringe Theatres. I look back on my previous life in Redhill as one would look back on that newly avoided vom patch on the pavement. I'm Jimmy Cagney in white face, "Made it, Ma, top of the world!" Bliss is compounded one day when, during a class improvisation, I meet Barbara. She is Canadian, cute as a button, twenty-two and single. My heart tremulously starts preparing Eagles songs and Bowie's *Golden Years* as the soundtrack for a possible seducto-croon moment. In this impro class we're playing comically against type, I look at her next to me in the mirrored dance studio and think: "I absolutely must get to know you as soon as is humanly possible!" Post class we are all secular and conversant in the nearest pub to Mime-Land. Barbara and I are talking about anything that comes into our heads: music, art and, for still mysterious reasons, herbs. Or as she endearingly pronounced them, 'erbs. One long look at her heart-shaped, beautiful face and I was mimetically floating somewhere above Trail, B.C. (her home town). She suggested herself back to my flat in Lamb's Conduit Street, where Barbie and I talked the whole night through about this, that, and everything. By the barely noticed light of what passes for dawn in London, I knew I was utterly infatuated. You see? Just occasionally, when we're ready, the universe smiles and says, "You shall go to the ball." But what to wear, Darling?

1977 saw London awash with Union Jacks and patriotic bunting. It was the Queen's Silver Jubilee and we were all supposed to be celebrating that momentous occasion. I was indifferent. I held no Royalist sympathies or gratitudes. The Queen and the rest of her inbred Germanic family were an abstract concept that held no sway over my day-to-day existence. Spotty gimps were turning themselves into angry spiky Punks.

Rat Scabies, the drummer of The Damned, was from my hometown. Only two years previously, when he was still named Chris Miller, we'd worked alongside each other at the Post Office sorting depot just outside of Redhill. We used to talk excitedly about live recordings by Humble Pie and Johnny Winter until we got the sack at the same time (Ha Ha, we got the sack from the Post Office!). Suddenly overnight, he was a credible 'Punk' who had, but a few months ago, trimmed his long, ginger hair into a ragged crop and hitched a ride on a swiftly moving Bandwagon up to London and Speed-Land. I was jealous and appalled at the same time. I must admit that Chris was always a wild boy. He used to turn up for work on an earlier job as a building-site labourer in a velvet suit and he became legendary in local pubs for consistently putting his head through somebody else's glass. Luckily the tentacles of suburbia couldn't reach me where I now was, in my role as a Mime Artist living in London, and I'm damned sure that Chris and the rest of his band felt the same. As far as I know there have only ever been a handful of people who've made something of themselves who were incarcerated in Redhill, and they are: Ronnie Biggs (Great Train Robber); Nick Hornby (author); Roy Lynes (organist on Status Quo's first few singles); Chris 'Rat Scabies' Miller; Dave Fenton, who flashed briefly with a band named The Vapors and their one massive hit *Turning Japanese*; Aleister Crowley (who for a short while lived in a house in The Grange opposite my parents' home); and me.

Jump cut forward to the snail end of winter 1979. Barbara and I have been touring our own Mime show, *Drawing In Space*, around the country for about a year or so. Des's somewhat curious indifference to two of his pupils putting together a collection of pieces and performing them rankled slightly. We played whatever gigs we could find, after letter or phone-call, in cultural armpits like Croydon or Bromley. The show was about an hour and a half long, including a short 'interval' (meaning that this is your cue to slink out and miss part two), enabling us to change into something less comfortable, namely another thirty minutes. Buried within the miasma of my own self-indulgence are a few quirky, innovative and unusual ideas, but to our mounting dismay most of the fourteen or so punters in each Arts Centre (Misnomer!) are really only enticed by the Mime tricks like the inexplicable glass box, previously undetected strong wind, comedy eating and death. Mind you, if I lived in Croydon, those representations would probably sum up the entire structure of my day-to-day life.

But there is only so much wind you can walk against, and although the occasional good review in a local paper or The Stage (if they could bear to lurch further than the local above-pub theatre) was complimentary, we knew we needed something different and exciting. It was starting to seem a little too po and white-faced for B and myself. We wanted, and stamped our little silent-slippered feet to have, Music - oh yes! Lights - mmm! Drama! And Glamorous Costumes!

And Fate, like a hyperactive and totally irresponsible Dark Angel, stepped in. Enter Mr. Robert Pereno. A legend before, during, and long after his own lunch-time. Robert and his voluptuous blonde girlfriend at that time, 'L.A.' (short for Lowri-Ann), found themselves, along with Barbara and myself, making the opening day of a King's Road shop called The Liberated Lady go with a memorable bang. B and I were in the window being Living Mannequins - "Fack me, I fought they was real!" said Arthur Scrotebag (63), as he passed by on his way to the local shop to purchase 20 'No.6' and a copy of the *Daily Mail*. In the meantime, the berserkly impromptu other couple jived and hurled each other about with careless abandon inside the shop. Many Lycra bathing suits with a tiger's scowling face on the front were sold, alongside alien vomit-pink leg warmers, T-shirts of big-knobbed cowboys and glittery, spandex tops.

Robert has the charm and danger that all true artists share. Unfortunately for those in his path it is not tempered by normal restraints or considerations. But hey, at least he wasn't BORING! After our joint displays were over we exchanged phone numbers and went our separate ways to our homes at either end of the King's Road, ours rented and barely paid for, theirs owned by his rich Italian mum. Oddly enough, the flat that Barbara and I lived in was in the same building as Vivienne Westwood's current shop, Seditionaries. On the day we moved in, by friend with van, we piled all of our meagre hippiesque belongings in the mutual hallway and ran excitedly around our very own second floor Chelsea Pad. Going back down to the hall to take upstairs more Heart and Todd albums, we met three black-spiked Punks rooting through our personals and saying in West Country accents: "Bit Faaackin weird innit, this shop? I mean, like where's the clothes, yeah? Where's Johnny Rotten?". Like Hugh Grant without the looks or follicular floppiness I stumble into, "Look, terribly sorry and all that, but these are our things. We're moving in!".

"You what? You fuckin' weird nutter!".

They dribble off into the shop proper. I feel hopelessly middle class, clumsy and unexciting. I dash upwards into our new flat and play Elvis Costello's *I Don't Want To Go To Chelsea* at nervously high volume. Sure enough, a mere chorus or two later, the downstairs neighbour, who it transpires is an 'Actor Darling', complains bitterly about my ironic comment on our new address. "You fuckin' weird nutter," I guiltily thought. Two months later I'm at home whilst B is in The States, wondering what having a colour TV must be like, when the phone rings. It's Robert. In his odd shorthand way, he tells me that this group he's got, which he's magnificently named 'SHOCK', are doing a gig the following week at this black funk club called Maunk-berry's. Would I like to come along and do a couple of Mime pieces as part of their act? With no time to think of dithering excuses I say, "Yes!"

I turn up and, after minimal pre-show direction, do two of what I hope are my most immediate and funny pieces. It works! I'm in a club full to the gills with white-clad funk boys and they really like what I've done! My gob is smacked, eels overrun my hovercraft and I hurtle back home to phone Stateside Barbara to share the news. Robert has offered me, and therefore us, entry into a world that we'd been looking for, but weren't able to locate on our own. Somewhere at this point in time Barbara has become 'Barbie'. I thought it was a name she hated, but apparently it's only the way that North Americans say: 'Baarwbieeee' that put her teeth on edge. In a typically ill-advised fashion I opt for Marcel Muscle as a stage name. You see, even at that early stage, I knew I was going to the ball and this time I knew exactly what I was going to wear. "Bring on Lycra! Bring on Spandex! Bring on all the Gods of late seventies Disco clothing! For we are destined to strut and fret our hours in these very garments!"

SHOCK now consists of Robert, L.A, Barbie, myself and a blonde dancer named Karen Sparks. For our first short show with this line up, we do a couple of rehearsals at the Empire Ballroom in Leicester Square. The venue is the Bali Hai Discotheque in Streatham and, yes, it was exactly as non-exotic and cheesy as you'd imagine, especially as the event was called 'A Jox Night Out'. Barbie and I perform two of our most accessible mime pieces amidst the frenetic and almost-choreographed dance routines. Then we do a kind of 'We Are Cute Mannequins' movement on either side of the others for the last number, a long disco track called *I Have A Destiny*. It's a strange little combo, a hybrid of dance, mime and burlesque, but it seems to be catching people's attention. We're in that Hot Gossip, 'Sponooch' entertainment area, pretty girls in suggestive and sexy Lycra costumes, a crazed and magnetic male axis, and the oddly compelling visual ingredient of Mime. Something is forming here and growing rapidly. It's very different to the silent precision of what B. and I have been doing for the last couple of years and it is exciting to be part of. She who was up until recently 'Barbara' is blossoming as 'Barbie' and I'm witnessing the organic creation of her new persona.

It becomes apparent very quickly that Robert seems to know everybody in London, from flippy-hand-shaked soul boys, debutantes and ex-Page 3 Girls, to club owners. They all love him and want to be in his company. His fearlessness and spontaneous creativity are very attractive. Even at this early stage, I'm jealous of the Pereno qualities that I don't seem to consistently possess and I realise, yet again, that I need a mentor-like male figure in my life in order for me to flourish. Robert is very good at tuning-in to the Zeitgeist, whether it's music, clubs or movers and shakers. This gives us a great advantage momentum-wise. Shock are being offered bookings at a rate of knots, in places that I'd never dreamt of entering, let alone performing in. Our act is taking shape, more routines, better music, Spandex (see?), masks, unexpected props and lots of make-up! We even acquired a manager somehow; a slightly seedy guy in his thirties, whose '15 Minutes' came as the drummer in a '60's band who had a hit with a cover of The Beatles' song *Ob-Bla-Di, Ob-Bla-Da*.

There used to be a large cocktail bar just up from The Lyceum in Covent Garden named Rumours and we find ourselves booked there as the cabaret on New Year's Eve 1979. A 'Golden Moment' bathed me as I sat in the dressing room, nursing a

Mai Tai. It's how I define one of those rare times when you are absolutely in the right place at the right time, when everything connects in a positive way and you are able to acknowledge it. We were about to enter a new decade, The '80's. Things were vibrant and exciting and anything seemed possible. I swirled the red Grenadine in my cocktail and grinned at myself.

August 1980

Chapter 11 - How I Lived Through the Blitz

After the exhilarating performance by Shock at the Rumours cocktail bar on the last night of the '70's, and a well-needed recovery day from Mai Tai madness, Barbie and I had to go back to working with Desmond's mime company on the second of January 1980 to do nine days of rehearsals for two shows at the Battersea Arts Centre. As much as we both loved Des and the company, it all seemed a little pedestrian and un-glamorous after our vivid, chaotic, and extravagant shows with Shock. B and I also had commitments to do two more *Drawing In Space* shows. In order to try and inject some well-needed pizzazz, we'd incorporated a piece that used as backing, The Human League's version of *You've Lost That Loving Feeling*. Ironically (in a retrospective Tik and Tok way) it was about two Robots who fall in love, short-circuit, and slowly wind down to stasis. Barbie and I wore bright-coloured cotton boiler suits, gloves, and those transparent creepy plastic face-masks you used to be able to buy from novelty shops. I think we also did a number to a funky Eric Clapton track (no, he did make at least one or even two in the late '70's, honest!), which I called *Writhe and Shine*. In this we were a domestic couple having a shaky time of it first thing in the morning, naturally, in that mimetically inevitable way, it ended up with a freeze-frame moment. This one was me with my dick caught in my zip and Barbie spilling boiling water over her tits. Hence the incredibly apt and amusing pun of a title. I've always been quite good at titles and sound-bites. For about five minutes I was seriously going to call this book (as a wanky in-joke for Byrne and Eno afficionados) 'My Life In The Gush of Boasts'.

The first proper 'queen', apart from Lindsay Kemp, that I met at this time was a guy named Michael (part Asian, part space-cadet) who was the manager of a tiny little club called The Alley in Mayfair. Robert, with his all-powerful social magnetism had inveigled this guy into giving Shock a residency at the club. Michael would sit cat-like curled on a stool at his bar, watch us rehearsing, and purr that we were 'fabuloussssss'. You have to try and imagine that at this point we were suddenly mingling with, and now becoming the 'Darlings!' of, the rich hedonists who were stuck in the social spirals of a London still getting-on-down to Disco and glitter. It really was like a nightclub scene from *The Bitch* or *The Stud* or a three-years out of date TV documentary, watching monied coked-out celebs, wannabe celebs and debs, in too much fake leopard skin and make-up boogieing to crap music in front of lots of full-length mirrors. I found this new scene repellent and intriguing at the same time. One day I'm on stage in whiteface doing a seriously silent piece of Mime to four men and a dog and the next day I'm on a dancefloor doing a variation of the same thing to four dogs and a man. Here, however, the man happens to look and dress like Omar Sharif and the four women are replicants of vintage Jackie Collins with a runny nose (and an out of touch dresser) warped into a newer style of cliché. Very weird and also very exciting in a kind of 'wow, what a contrast!' way. I didn't do cocaine, I just loved the smell of it, I was going with the flow. I loved and disapproved of myself. I was half-in and half-out of my skin at that time, one half of me wanted the purity of Art with its obligatory obscurity, and the other half wanted the sacrament of cash and social mobility.

Me: "Oh Lord, won't you buy me a Mercedez Benz?" Other Me: " No. Sorry!" Just to add to my dichotomy, on the 23rd of January, I got asked by Martin Baker (son of Stanley the actor) who'd overnight become a video director, to do some Pierrot-like background, mimey stuff in a promo for the Jon and Vangelis single, I Hear You Now. Even the duo themselves were schizophrenic, Jon Anderson has a high-pitched voice and is regrettably wearing big sleeves and too-long hair for 1980, and the mighty Vangelis is a souvlaki-fingered but dextrous Greek who oozes absolute passion and prodigious musical proficiency. The next day I'm with the other gang, Silents, at the Cockpit Theatre doing a lunchtime mime performance to the hushed and twitchy and, at one in the AM the next morning, I'm back in The Alley with the fabuloussss Shock, playing to the lushed and richer. Then a few days later I'm white-faced-up in a studio at LWT doing a comedy mime about spiders and bananas for a kids' TV show called *We'll Tell You A Story* (I even had a striped top on and therefore deserved an imaginary beating by my future self), followed by another late show at The Alley club. And this was just one week in the new and hectic trajectory. Is it any wonder I was a little flakey?

We got to know a singing duo named Biddie and Eve around this time. Like Shock they were an alternative cabaret act doing the rounds of the newer clubs and bars in London. They were great fun to be with. Biddie was a rake-thin bleached blond androgyne, and Eve was a big blousy redhead with a heart the size of Manhattan and a laugh to match. She made Bette Midler seem like a subdued wallflower. Their act was a fast-moving pastiche of every belting torch singer you've ever heard, very ritzy in a cheap sequins and tin-foil way. Their drummer was the future TV 'personality' Roland Rivron, which sounds like an anagram but probably isn't. Some of us went over for supper at Biddie's Battersea flat one evening; to my everlasting joy he had the best bathroom I've ever been in. It was painted vivid green, absolutely full of plants and fake vegetation with a few stuffed parrots and brightly-coloured little fake birds here and there amongst the leaves and fronds. Taped bird-song and jungle noises played when you pulled on the cord for the lights and, best of all, it was carpeted with fake grass! I could have spent hours in there. Biddie and Eve were working Saturday nights at a wine bar called Blitz in Covent Garden and we saw them do their act there several times. We didn't know it then, but that place was very shortly going to figure largely not only in our lives and careers, but also those of every clubber in London. Media feeding-frenzy was just around the corner...

In the meantime, Shock carried on with our residency at The Alley, as well as doing shows at a bizarre disco called Maximus in Leicester Square. Shame it's no longer there, would-be Russell Crowes would love it, two Centurions acted as bouncers on the door flanked by flaming torches in holders, and the interior was a full-on Roman spectacle of tack and pillar'd splendour. It's a pity the patrons weren't forced to wear suitably historic costumes to gain entrance, instead it was the usual fake leopard print kit for the women and more of the same Omar clones with far too much expensive cologne splashed over their perma-tanned faces.

We jettisoned our lacadaisical manager and were now being represented by a duo called SBM Management, who also looked after the dance troupe Hot Gossip. One of them was an erudite charming homosexual; the other was an unctuous little hetero who seemed only interested in the fantasy of getting into our girls' pants and to keep us gigging anywhere and everywhere. Oh and he used the word 'fabulous' far too much, managing to make it sound as slimy as his personality.

One of his first endeavours on our behalf was to book us as the cabaret on a Seaways cruise ship sailing to Esbjerg in Denmark. There are countless definitions of what Hell must actually be like, and believe me I've got a whole load of my own stashed in my internal memory bank, but this little jaunt added a new one. Imagine gorging yourself on a massive cold buffet of Scanda food (copious quantities of smoked and pickled fish, and meats and cheeses of every size, shape and colour) and then having to do your act as the ship starts to enter rough seas. Gravity's great sense of humour was amply illustrated by it hurling us around the dance floor at a 45-degree angle every five minutes. We all looked like mimes striving for verticality against an invisible wind, and as soon as our mercifully brief act slid to a halt, Robert and I rushed to get horizontal in our cabin. I always thought that people turning green with nausea was just a colourful metaphor but poor Pereno really achieved it. His face was the colour of mint ice cream and shiny with the effort of keeping at bay the imminent re-emergence of chunked-up herrings and that disturbing cheese that smells like an unclean bum-hole. If I hadn't been so close to the same state I may have seen the humour of it.

Oddly enough the Shock girls seemed immune to the condition, leaving Robert and I to groan and clench our way through the interminable passage across the cruel North Sea. I don't remember anything at all of our journey back to England, apart from a hazy image of the five of us and our luggage dejectedly sitting at a deserted railway station in the wilds of Norfolk.

Keith Macmillan, the video director for Kate Bush's first few promos (my favourite for erectile fantasy is the one he did for *Babooshka*) located Shock and asked us to appear in a video he was doing for the berserk German Pop Diva, Nina Hagen. Only after we'd agreed did we discover that we were all going to be playing masked and nearly naked African Mud people holding flaming torches. We were caked in this evil-looking grey clay from head to foot that weighed a ton once it had set, and cracked most painfully on hairy male body bits whenever one moved. Maybe Barbie and the other two Shockettes found the mud cleansing and beneficial for their skin? All we had to do in the filming was menacingly lurch in an ethnic stylee behind Nina as she mimed to her song *African Reggae*. God I wish had photos of us doing that job, especially for a possible "What did you do in The War Dad?" occasion. I like Nina Hagen. She is quite possibly barking mad but who cares? We need crazy, entertaining pop stars to keep us alive in these dull twilight days of manufactured, short-lived Frankenstein's monsters. She's still out there with her extravagant voice and style and making some great music. A couple of years ago she did a monstrously coiling dance track with Adamski called *Get Your Body*, which is her take on UFO's, alien abduction and male chauvinism. And she should know.

Barbie and I met this young, very pretty boy at Desmond's mime classes. His name was Sean Crawford and I liked him instantly. He was quirky and creative and used to wear a long tweed overcoat with a length of thick string as a belt which I found endearing. Although a babe-magnet in a Bowie sort of way, he was modest, un-cocky, and shy. He told us in one after-class pub session that he was developing a character called Plastic Joe who moved like a robot and was as unlike a human being as possible. Wow! That caught my attention and I knew that this boy was someday soon going to join Shock, especially since Robert and L.A were as intrigued as we were when we told them about him. Sean was working as a window display artist at a posh clothing for posh people store named Simpsons in Piccadilly, and he came out with a stunning idea to jazz up their somewhat dull frontage. For one-day only (and that day would be April 1st of course) he, myself, Barbie, Robert and L.A would be living mannequins in the window. The powers-that-be at Simpsons bought it with very little persuasion and, kitted out in various casual garments, we took it in turns to grace the long street-facing window.

It was a brilliant ploy and we drew crowds previously undreamt of to gawp at us doing our thing. We got a half-page in the *Evening News* out of it and saw for the first time that what we were doing was going to captivate the press. The headline was: 'An April 1st Dummy Run For Shoppers And Swimmers' (I never quite got the 'swimmers' bit). With the by-line: 'What A Blinking Lovely Model!' A Mr. Webster was quoted in the paper as saying: "They really are fantastic. I can't believe it!" It was exceedingly difficult not to laugh with all those goldfish faces pressing up against the glass and leaving little condensational mouth-marks of surprise and, as none of us had thought of wearing shades, after about ten unblinking minutes the tears started to stream down my face. Sean joined Shock the next day and we started rehearsing together as a six-piece. I apologise for not talking about the third girl in the group but Karen always felt she was not quite on the same level as the rest of us and we all knew her days were sadly numbered.

Robert found an amazing song called *Ricky's Hand* by an electro-artist named Frank Tovey who'd aptly re-christened himself Fad Gadget. He and Sean (as Plastic Joe) worked out a routine to it; a kind of Robotic S & M number that, for reasons known only to himself, involved Pereno clad in a woman's lycra bathing suit, with a full-head mask of Jayne Mansfield, being assaulted by this truncheon-wielding android. Sean had got one of his female admirers to knock up a one-piece black PVC uniform for Joe to wear and, with pancake make-up on his face, and his hands liberally covered with shiny gel, he looked terrifyingly convincing. A beautiful but malevolent creature programmed to punish. Instantly Shock became something darker and more edgy and, despite the efforts of the turdular half of our management to keep us nice, safe and a bit more family-orientated, we were heading slowly but surely into new areas of entertaining confrontation.

We still had Disco elements in our act but they were quickly being erased. Having three mime artists in the group now meant that our visual impact was stronger and less tacky. So bye bye Omar! To our joy, a columnist in some London rag described us as 'a most sordid cabaret' and that affirmed we were doing exactly the right thing. Whatever successes and kudos we gathered are to a large extent down to Robert's fearless approach to life and performance. His energy and restlessness were a fearsome combination that always stopped us getting stale or repetitive. Unfortunately for the rest of us, the downside to his personality was about to manifest...

In early May, we got an excited phone call from the oily one telling us that he'd got the group three weeks of nightclub gigs in Bangkok! The truth of the matter was that he'd cocked up a deal for Hot Gossip and to cover his mistake he'd offered them Shock as a cheaper replacement. But did we care? We hurtled around London getting armfuls of innoculations, taking our battered array of costumes to be dry-cleaned, buying extra props, bits of hopefully useful stage-stuff and inquiring about visas for Thailand (remarkably hassle-free). In about three days, we had to create, rehearse, and make backing tapes for a thirty-minute extension to our stage show. For us this seemed quite normal but it would have put the fear of God into lesser, more organised, outfits. Then, the day before we were due to leave, Sean told us that he hadn't actually got a valid passport! What? The Oleaginous One tried to exert what flimsy power he could with the authorities but they were having none of it. Sean was staying at home while the five of us flew off to Bangkok.

We had a day and a long plane journey to re-work our act. We stopped over in an hotel that I think was part of Cairo airport, and which seemed to be solely occupied by flies and dodgy-looking swarthy men, smoking untipped fags, sitting at tables under propellor blade ceiling fans. When one or all three of our Shock girls walked past with their bleached and coloured hair, make-up, mini skirts and tight tops, the tables lifted under the combined Egyptian erections.

Of course, in 1980 men like that would never have seen girls like this outside of the movies or whorehouses. Back onboard the plane next day, whilst trying to ignore Pereno's incessant fidgeting and chatter, I found myself staring out of the window at the desert below and marvelling at it's cruel and vast expanse. You'd see a thin, absolutely straight thread of black road far beneath that would suddenly shift off at peculiar angles to circumnavigate difficult terrain. An hour later I gaze down and we're still flying over the desert. After another hour I felt like saying to God: "Okay, I've done desert now. Can you show me something more interesting and varied please?" It was about then that the plane suddenly dropped about three hundred feet in two seconds. We all gasped, Barbie screamed and squeezed my arm so hard her fingers and thumb met in the middle of it, and I realised that The Big Fella or 'Him Upstairs' doesn't take kindly to criticism of His creations. We landed in Bangkok at some ungodly hour and somehow found our way to The Impala Hotel, our home for the next three weeks. An ugly but efficient modern edifice just off the Patpong Road.

The Chokchai, the club we were performing in, was on the top floor of an office block round a corner from the hotel. The owner was fat, greasy, and limping badly. Some local hood had shot him in the thigh a few days earlier over an unsettled debt. Such is life in Bangkok we thought; it's going to be an interesting stay. There was a permanent buffet of hot and cold Thai food in the dining room of the hotel, and we could gorge ourselves for free on my favourite cuisine. We learned from The-Burning-That-No-Amount-Of-Liquid-Will-Relieve to avoid any dish with evil circular slivers of red or green chillies floating in them. Every night, the hotel house band played cover versions of Western pop songs. Their grasp of English was tenuous at best and, as they'd obviously learned the lyrics phonetically from the vinyl, it led to some interesting and very amusing interpretations.

Karen and I had a dressing room stage left and Barbie, L.A and Robert shared the one on stage right. We rehearsed from 2 P.M and did our new show that night. It went OK. We were all so wasted from the journey that we just floated through it somehow. I realised after the second number that it was going to be seriously warm out on stage every night, and we'd finish each number drenched in sweat. My black plastic trousers could be wrung out into a bucket. After a few days they started to whiff alarmingly. Little green lizards would appear on the outside of the dressing room windows, and I'd marvel at their determination in climbing twenty two floors of a building to watch Westerners take their sodden kit off. I never saw Karen's tits the whole time she was in the group. She had the knack of changing costume modestly and discreetly. Whereas L.A's pert breasts and blonde pussy were flamboyantly displayed without a second thought.

Arab men in the audience would throw money onto the stage as a sign of appreciation, probably of the girls more than Robert and I (no, really?). After a few days of constant daytime swimming pool frolics I went deaf in my right ear. I tried Q-Tips to no avail; bought a little syringe that also failed; went to a Thai doctor who, after curing me of my inaudiblity, said "Didn't your Mother ever tell you never put anything smaller than your finger in your ear?" I thought of Richard Pryor's coked-out stage routine of the little monkey that liked to sit on his shoulder and stick it's Q-Tip like penis into his ear and fuck away making "Eeh, eeh, eeh" noises.

A young, good-looking Thai Policeman, Lieutenant Pierpon, befriended us. He took us to a Sex Club where the young female waitresses had numbers pinned to their skimpy tops and all had names like Apricot, Jasmine, or Kumquat. As we trouped in they squealed over to us, ignored Pereno and me, and excitedly sniffed at the three girls' skin. Mmm, Western Fresh! Then Apricot got on stage and smoked a cigarette through her vagina (it must be like kissing an old ashtray!), opened a Coke bottle with the same organ and finally ejected a peeled banana from her perfect de-nuded lower lips that shot over our heads with glistening velocity and hit the back wall!

Pierpon was obsessed with the Dirty Harry films of our man Clint. So much so that he'd bought himself a shiny, brand new Magnum handgun exactly like that used by his hero. He took us out into the country one day and showed us his pride and joy. It did look sexy and very powerful, glinting in the sun on its bed of cloth. He let us fire it too, very smooth action, just squeezing the trigger gently, let it do the work. I saw then how masturbatory an accessory a good gun can be. We shot at trees or was it bushes? I can't remember. It felt good.

Peirpon, Robert and I were in the hotel lobby one evening looking at a gaggle of exquisitely beautiful porcelain Thai girls in skin-tight satin dresses and immaculate make-up and coiffure. I'd never seen such magnificent exotic beauty in the flesh before. Our Lieutenant told us they were Hookers (doh!) and we could have one each if we so desired. It would be his treat. To my dying day I shall regret passing up on the offer, but I was still with Barbie, my lover, who slept innocently upstairs, and I couldn't betray her trust. The same went for Robert and L.A. too. I suppose a more adventurous and callous man would have done it anyway, after all they'd never find out would they? One night back at the hotel after the gig, Robert, L.A. and I found ourselves in a room with two Middle-Eastern guys wearing expensive grey suits, wide grins, and holding a black leather attache case on each of their laps. They'd obviously been in the audience for that evening's show and afterwards invited us in for a drink or so we thought. Shortly after our arrival one of them flicked open a case and revealed that it was packed to the brim with a gob-smackingly huge amount of grass. Pure Thai Stick, some of the best and most potent weed on the planet. They rolled a spliff, we all smoked it and fifteen years later I seemed to be still passing it to Robert. I got very paranoid after I'd asked one of them what would happen if the police burst in right now. He answered with a shrug and said they'd just pay them off. In my mind, the subtext of his casual statement was that the three of us would however be arrested and consequently spend the rest of our days reliving *Midnight Express*. Everytime I stood up and mumbled about "Having to, erm, go to bed. Right now!" they'd say "No, no, no" and insist that I stay and smoke some more. Eventually I shot upwards, bellowed good night, flung open the door and ran all the way back to what I hoped was our room. Barbie slept like a baby and I spent the remainder of the night clutching the sheets, waiting for those sinister shadows under the door to the corridor.

Somewhere around the end of Week One, Robert flipped completely. He's medically hyperactive. In England he'd go for a five-mile run everyday to counteract the onset of his disability. But in the humidity and energy-sapping heat of Bangkok he'd have been dead in five minutes if he'd tried running a mile. The poor boy lost it in the most demonstrative way. Our sympathy turned to apprehension then anger as he physically attacked L.A. in their dressing room after a performance. I rushed across just as he was going to do the same to Barbie and picked up a bit of wood and motioned as if to strike him with it. He collapsed and sat down panting. He was literally steaming like the winning horse at The Grand National. We tried to comfort him but he had gone somewhere else in his head. He then refused to have any verbal contact with any of us for the whole of the next week. "We're in Thailand but we're trapped with a madman. Help!" were the imaginary postcards we wrote and sent home in our heads.

We struggled through it somehow. But it was fucking weird doing our act with him plus all the socialising too, especially as I was still deaf in one ear. 'Silence is golden' so they say, but in my case it was a buzzing red colour. We did sightseeing trips to brightly coloured Buddhist temples and majestic places of serenity. I bought statues of the Buddha and a ceremonial sword which was confiscated at the airport. We sat on the backs of elephants, swam in the sea at Pattaya Beach, ate endless sticks of chicken and beef Satay at a barbecue full of corrupt policemen and gangsters; were taken to a brilliant Lady-Boy drag show at The Roma Bar, and to a brutal Kick Boxing tournament in a vast neon-lit stadium. We visited clubs called Bubbles and Bobby's Arms. Robert and I stupidly went to see the most sickening cinematic collection of real-life accidental death and deliberate dismemberment called *Faces of Death*, while the girls had dresses of sensual Thai silk made up very cheaply by a local tailor. We all avoided anybody with a grey suit and an attache case. We played 21 shows, lost weight, gained tans and sometimes got ferried about in those little motorised rickshaws called 'Phut Phuts'. It was a sexy, strange and stimulating visit. Returning to England with a contrite 'Plastic Joe' back in the fold and with Robert calmer and safe, we recommenced our working twice a week at The Alley club and whatever else came our way. Which all seemed a little mundane after our travels but our act was tight and almost polished. Sometime around here, Karen left Shock with our mutual best wishes and a sense of relief, for her destiny lay in greener and more suitable pastures. We got a lithe blonde dancer to fill the gap for a bit, but she was always only going to be a floating sixth member until we attracted the right girl to complete the sextet. Most of June was a club performances until the end of the month when one of those seismic shifts happened to us. We were contacted by a booking agent named Simon who worked for an agency called NEMS (the younger shabbier offspring of the Brian Epstein-founded organisation that handled The Fabs back in the '60's, but sadly there was no trace of them left). He would be arranging some gigs for us in the near future, more Rock 'n' Roll than Cabaret which suited us just fine, but which wouldn't be quite comfy and schmoozy enough for our so-called manager, Ian. He'd much rather we hung out with the disco nobs in Club Coke Land who amplified his tiny personality perfectly, as small men become giants after a swift 'chop 'n' sniff.' We also had a meeting with a couple called Kate and John Hudson who had a small record label called Spot Records based at Mayfair Sound Studios. They told us that they'd got this project on the go and that Major Record Company Giants RCA were going to take it on board. They'd recorded a cover version of the old Glitter Band track called *Angel Face* with two studio-based musicians (both drummers) and they needed a group to front it. Would we be interested? Do androids dream of electric sheep?

Barbie and L.A. sang backing vocals on the song but the lead vocals were handled by the guy who wrote it, the ex-Glitter Band guitarist Gerry Shephard (he with the star-shaped axe and improbable quiff). I don't remember how or through whom these connections were made, things just started to happen, I guess because we were hot and ready, full of energy, and utterly shameless. The first of the two musicians responsible for creating the *Angel Face* backing track was Rusty Egan, formerly the drummer of the band The Rich Kids formed by Midge Ure and ex-Sex Pistol, Glenn Matlock. Rusty was the fearless motormouth-about-town who almost single-handedly created a brand new club culture and music scene in London in 1979-80. He was DJ and mastermind behind clubs like Billy's, which only played Bowie, Kraftwerk, Georgio Moroder and Euro-centric electro music for wannabe Weimar decadents. His combination of charm, bullshit and 'Fuck it. Let's do it!' galvanised a sleepy metropolitan clubland still bemused after the slow entropy of Punk into creating something new and glamorous. His partner in these crimes of fashion was a young adventurous kid from Wales who'd moved up to town and re-invented himself as Steve Strange. He'd act as the arbiter of taste and was the petulant changeable doorman at the wine bar in Covent Garden that was his and Rusty's new foot-stamping ground, The Blitz. Nobody got in unless they met his weekly requirements of sartorial extravagance and style. It was a good combination, Rusty on the decks, schmoozing all and sundry and playing brilliant music, and the Celtic Chameleon at the door gleefully and bitchily turning away all those who didn't fit that night's costume Drama. And yes, that did on one legendary night include Mick Jagger, and on another Gary Numan. History tells us that both of our rejected stars continue to shine and our not-so-strange-underneath-it-all doorman ended up back in Wales, a few years later, with the twin back-monkeys of heroin addiction and sporadic kleptomania.

The second of our *Angel Face* musicians (or as one shortly to be written review titled it: *Angle Face*) was Richard Burgess, the drummer in a band of Twilight Zone progressive synthed-up jazzers called Landscape, whose quirky fifteen minutes of fame, and enviable Roland product-endorsement, lurked just around the corner. Somehow Rusty's percussive paganism and Richard's methodical yet inventive musicianship combined to make *Angel Face* a killer of a track. Play it today and the energy rush is palpably right back in your face... Syn-drums a go go! Sequencer syncopation! Backing vocal Vixen Violence! It's a 125 BPM time capsule of New Joy, and Sigue Sigue Sputnik weren't even born yet! Who really gave a monkey's if we hadn't played on it? We were absolutely the best people for the job. We made it our own. It was our calling card as we clawed our way upwards into somewhere brighter.

On the 24th of July 1980 (no, I don't have an enviably retentive memory, I do however have day-to-day diaries) something wonderful was born. A few days earlier Barbie had left to go back to The States for a week or so's break to see her parents and Shock were on vacation. Sean phoned me on this propitious Thursday and said: "Why don't you and I go busking tonight?" I was confused. We didn't play any songs. What could we do? An acapella rendition of every street singer's favourite, Streets of London? I don't think so! With no hesitation at all he said we'd pretend to be robots outside a very chic and expensive Knightsbridge restaurant called San Lorenzo (it's still chic and still expensive). I'm a good copier and I'd been watching Sean as 'Plastic Joe' for months. I knew I could do it pretty much as well as he could. It was a stunning idea but what would we wear? Sean had that dilemma already worked out: white-face make up and black shades, white dress shirts, black bow-ties and black tailcoats, trousers and shoes. For reasons I'm not sure of, we both had these outfits at home. We dashed out to buy white gloves from a strange little shop in Old Compton street which sold evening dress and accoutrements for the catering trade. We met up at his home in Knightsbridge, got made-up and dressed and, at about 10pm, walked round to the restaurant.

We took up position just to the side of the front entrance and assumed frozen show-room dummy poses. At the moment any diners left the eatery we'd jerk into robotic action. People were terrified at first, then entranced and delighted as they watched us emulate living machinery in front of their eyes. It really was an amazingly powerful feeling to enthrall these satiated socialites with our controlled and realistic movements. I think if Sean had looked like I do we would have kept the viewers in a state of fright but, because he was smaller and prettier, we balanced each other. A battered old top hat of his was at our feet on the pavement and every one who stopped to look threw loose change and a few pound notes into it. After about an hour or so we got out of character, grinned, waved bye bye and went back to his place like excited children. We had a total of £11 in cash! It doesn't sound a lot now but back in 1980 it was definitely a handy little sum for so little effort. We had just created something utterly unique, a little moment of truly inspired magic that still resonates in people's memories to this day. The next night we did the same activity outside of THE big celeb's nightclub 'Tramp' and got a total of £18. The following week we did a daytime quickie in the Piazza in Covent Garden (£11), South Molton street (£29!), 'Morton's' (£17), Covent Garden again (£17) and the opening night of 'Stringfellows' in Upper St. Martin's Lane (a measley £7). £110 in cash for the two of us in one week! It was more than we were making from gigs with Shock at the time.   We discussed what we should call this wonderful new duo. After a few minutes Sean said: "How about Tick and Tock?" I said: "Yes! That's perfect! But let's spell it Tik and Tok". And there you go, a moment's natural creativity and you've given something to people that lasts forever. I LOVE THAT! The good thing that came out of our poor showing outside Stringfellows was that we met two Italian brothers named Tony and Ozzie Rizzo who had their own hairdressing salon in Brook Street called 'Sanrizz'. There was a third brother, named Rikki, who also tended to people's coiffure. They were excited by the prospect of tampering with and glorifying our natural nondescript hairstyles. Sean (the lucky little bastard) was blessed with thick dark brown hair that was straight and shiny. The Gene Jenie was obviously on his side and granted him his every cranial desire. We were introduced to the joy and folly of fire-red 'Crazy Colour' hair-dye. This stuff worked vibrantly well but you had to bleach-out all the colour from the chosen area, which briefly leaves your hair a limp pissy kind of yellow.

We agreed to be models for Sanrizz at an up-coming major hairdressing event called The Oro International Hair Festival (wow! I wonder if The Crimpers will be playing?) These events are big news in the coiffure biz and Oro was taking over the whole of Wembley Conference Centre on the 29th of September. Auspiciously Tik and Tok were going to be The Rizzo's star turn. A female designer named Mezz began creating two Robot suits for us to wear, fashioned from copper-coloured metallic plastic. They were jointed like medieval armour and held together with press-studs. We had huge pointed shoulders and tubes and bits of circuitry adorned our arms and chests. They took about half an hour to get into but greatly facilitated our mechanical movement. Add to the costumes newly re-structured and coloured hair plus extravagant make-up and we were ready. This would be the first proper outing for the new and shiny Robotic Duo in front of a large audience and we knew it couldn't fail. It didn't. The whole place went beserk as we started up and we saw our future beckoning us with open arms.

Sometime around the beginning of August, Robert rushed in to a rehearsal and mentioned a stall he'd discovered in The Great Gear Market in King's Road which sold outrageous clothing. The concession was run by two truly over the top glamour babes from Birmingham named Jane Kahn and Patti Bell. Their clothes were fantasy wear for hedonists, an extraordinary jewelled and glittering mix of Japanese Kabuki, pantomime, ethnic and foppery. We were all smitten by their wares, especially Sean who immediately hit it off with Ms Kahn and pretty soon afterwards they embarked on a long, loving and visually extravagant relationship.

Because of our new contacts with Rusty and Mr. Strange we were introduced into this brand new club culture of music and, equally importantly, clothing and make-up. The press would pretty quickly christen the inhabitants of this short-lived moment 'The New Romantics' for they have an unerring need to classify and then capitalise on anything youthful and new, as it makes them appear hip and sells papers. Some bright Hack also coined the phrase 'Blitz Kids' because of the growing notoriety and popularity of the dynamic duo's Tuesday nights at The Blitz wine bar. And didn't they also triumphantly waffle on about 'Peacock Punks'?

To us inside the bubble it was just a whole load of creative and vibrant talent hanging-out in the same clubs and enjoying everything that came along. It was a very fruitful time for fashion, design, filmmaking, media and music. It was bright and optimistic and therefore the antithesis of Punk. And for it's brief duration it was great fun to be a part of. It was a vibe and an energy that echoed the first flowering of Swinging London back in the mid-60s, and although I'd been too young to have been there then I was most definitely right here, right now. We hung out dressed to kill and thrill in our proud new Kahn and Bell schmutter in clubs like Le Beat Route, Hell, Le Kilt and of course Blitz. Manning the cloakroom in the latter club was an androgynous and perfectly made-up lad named George O' Dowd, who favoured a look somewhere between Geisha and Nun and who had an un-noticed fondness for the contents of people's pockets. He also had a sharp tongue and a surly peroxide-blonde bitch of a best friend who called himself Marilyn. The two were in their element and were seen everywhere, invited or not (usually not, but their sheer effrontery got them into anything and anyone). George changed his name soon afterwards to Boy George, formed his own band, after being sacked from Bow Wow Wow for being too outrageous, and to everyone's surprise and pride went on to become a global superstar.

Watching the oft-shown Blitz Kids footage they regularly trot out on TV documentaries about the early '80's, you could say that we all look a bit silly, overdressed, and self-consciously vain and shallow. But you know what? I don't give a fuck! As dear old Oscar Wilde once said: "To love oneself is the beginning of a life-long romance". Maybe that's what the general public and the media in their frustrated, cynical and narrow-minded ways found fearful - we loved ourselves and didn't care what anyone thought about it. Out of this carnival of libidinous new expression came some of the best pop music ever. Take your pick of your fave tracks from:

The Human League, Soft Cell, Ultravox, Spandau Ballet, Duran Duran, Culture Club, Depeche Mode and ABC. For the more adventurous, you can choose from: The The, Killing Joke, Cabaret Voltaire, D.A.F, Bill Nelson, Suicide, Magazine, Kraftwerk, Vangelis, Bowie's *Scary Monsters*, Grace Jones, Talking Heads, Japan, early Psychedelic Furs, The Cure and Simple Minds. Ryuichi Sakamoto and The Yellow Magic Orchestra and Public Image's *Flowers Of Romance*. This is all music borne out of experimentation, youth, romance, fearless energy, drugs and new technology.

Chapter 12 - Angel Face

Tik and Tok briefly continued to go out busking in between Shock gigs but the novelty was wearing off. In September we started doing weekly (or whenever we were available) cabaret at a cocktail bar called Coconut Grove behind Oxford Street. We'd glide around the restaurant delighting and occasionally terrifying customers. It was £30 a night cash and we got free cocktails as well. We incorporated ourselves into Shock's stage show as robots to start off the act. For a short while we wore the plastic robot suits that Mezz made. Because they took so long to put on we just had to open the show then, after the first song ended, we'd run backstage and frantically rip off all the sections of armour, hoping we'd each pick up our own bits after the gig. We began to attract even more attention as a result; it gave Shock another facet that people could pick up on, much to Barbie's slowly growing disgruntlement, I think. But what was I to do? When that train comes along you grab hold, leap on board, and go where it takes you.

In Shock's case it took us up north to perform in clubs in Sunderland, Leeds and Edinburgh, then back down to London to have our picture taken for the *Angel Face* sleeve and publicity by a photographer named Ted Polhemus. His partner at that time was a well-endowed 'performance artiste' named Lynn whose act seemed to involve lashings of tomato ketchup and no clothing. Ted was a cool guy with a penchant for wearing black leather and bleaching his hair white. He looked Germanic and slightly pervy in an S & M way and went on to become a social commentator of sorts, writing books about youth culture and fashion. We began a weekly residency in a club called Wedgies (dumb name) in Chelsea run by mega-socialite Dai Llewellyn (brother of Roddy, who was principally famous for hanging-out with and allegedly shagging Princess Margaret).

This was Shock's dichotomy: one night we'd be performing to and socialising with our peers in New Romantic venues, the next we'd be doing the same act to Debutantes and rich high rollers in the King's Road. Luckily, Simon from NEMS came through with a support slot on a tour by a band called 'Famous Names' (formerly 'Writz') on a few dates around the UK. This was our first exposure to a Rock audience and it gave us a bit more cred as a live act who could work the sticky stages of music venues. Up the M1 again, in the back of a Transit, to suffer the ignomy of Motorway Service stations and College audiences. The robot suits came in handy at a show at Aberdeen University, which was packed to the gills with 3,000 drunken Scottish students. As the lights came up through the dry-ice revealing these two glittering, motionless androids objects came flying at us over the footlights and bounced-off our armour. Catcalls and insults followed, then as soon as we started to move and the music kicked in they cheered with delight. And when the three girls came gleefully dancing out onto the stage the whole place just erupted. We had them in the palm of our hands. So much so that after the gig we were trapped in our dressing room for an hour or more with hundreds of the little fuckers baying at us behind the doors and windows, demanding that we autograph their arses or whatever. We declined.

Famous Names were led by and were the brainchild of two of the sweetest, most genuine people I've ever met, Bev Sage and the tragically short-lived Steve Fairnie. They were Art School graduates with surreal humour, quirky songs, and a style all their own (Steve had a Chaplin-esque moustache and a pink and powder-blue checker-board suit for the stage). Their lighting designer was Pete Williams, who sported a magnificent Rockabilly quiff. He later changed his name to 'Willy Williams' and is now one of the world's most-in-demand lighting artists who is regularly employed by U2 and has designed for The Stones, David Bowie and R.E.M. (Bev and Steve would change their name to Techno Twins. I played a tearful Pierrot in the video for their chart-hit single *Falling in Love Again*). Part of me really enjoyed all this new activity because it was what all my musical heroes from the '60's and '70's did for years. It wasn't Rock 'n' Roll but it was close enough to it to savour the sights, sounds and smells.

Falling in Love Again

I don't remember exactly when, but it must have been around here that we found our permanent sixth member of the group. Her name was Carole Caplin. She was working in a Chelsea shop called 'Ace' until Pereno convinced her to leave and join us. She had a mass of red curly hair, a full sexy mouth, and legs that went on forever. She also never wore underwear, which might have horrified the other two girls but delighted us boys. She could dance well enough and she looked great which was all we wanted. Her personality fitted, she was uninhibited on stage and gave us another magnet for hormonal boys and men everywhere we went. History has been less than kind to poor Carole. She will be seen to have fairly appalling taste in men and to be far too gullible for her own good. I hope she finds what she's looking for away from the sordid glare of the spotlight.

With *Angel Face* in post-production, and sniffing the foetid breath of hungry press, RCA paid for our first proper photo session as the new six-piece Shock. In a studio in Covent Garden, against a backdrop of large shiny black vinyl tiles on screens arranged to resemble a mad scientist's laboratory, we disport ourselves in a configuration that summed-up our act and personae: Tik and Tok in their metallic-plastic Robot suits and white-face make-up with lightning streaks of red and blue greasepaint flank the others. We are inhuman yet custodial, energy contained but imminently demonstrative. Robert wears the costume of a Rake from a perverse Restoration Comedy, lace, ruffles and a sequined frock coat. His hair is dyed black with two swathes of white sneering-back from his forehead. His eyes are darkly-kohl'd and intense. To his right is L.A. clad in an ermin cloak and white silk mini-dress with black vinyl elbow-length gloves. Her hair is now platinum blonde with two streaks of black at the temples. She looks like a predatory version of Elsa Lanchester in *The Bride of Frankenstein* but sexier and pre-ravished. Barbie is sitting crossed-legged in front, clad in a witchy black ruched-silk Kahn and Bell Gothic dress and long wicked metallic finger extensions that we got in Bangkok. Her hair is bright aubergine and she stares, like Kate Bush's darker sister, enigmatically and sensually straight into the Lens. Lying on her back, full-length across two dial-festooned and plugged-in consoles of the type usually seen in Hospital cardiovascular units is Carole. She is contorted as if in electric ecstasy, her mane of flame-red curls flung back and her glistening mouth is red and ready. She is wearing a bikini made of gold metal, with proudly extended cones covering her breasts. How could anyone resist this combination? They didn't. Especially when you add to this picture a few selections from our self-written publicity: "SHOCK - a flamboyant, visual entertainment. A combination of mime, music, dance and extreme theatre... he first group without instruments - computerised, fashionable and elegant." "Ambitions for the future: to be stars in the video age, and CASH, CASH, CASH!" "They are all 18 years old with ridiculous hairstyles - and they all sleep in the same bed." A lot of people (including us) took this pretty seriously. Only a small part of it was untrue.

> "Got to get you ready fast / Who knows how long your looks will last?
> Look in the mirror - Believe that it's true,
> The face of an Angel - Is looking at you, Looking at you."
> *Angel Face* (c) Gerry Shephard/John Rossall, 1973.

In November, we met a couple named David and Kathy Rose who, strangely enough, weren't married then but had the same surname. Kathy had bought a pair of 'exotic' knickers from Barbie when Barbie was filling-in a little blank in our Shock schedule by being a salesgirl behind the counter of The Liberated Lady, The King's Road shop where she and I first met Robert and L.A. David was a photographer and aspiring video director. Kathy was his muse, a frequent model for his softcore photographic visions and the Producer of their nefarious schemes. They saw Shock a possible vehicle for David to manifest some of his visual ideas, and offered to do us a promo for *Angel Face* for free. We said 'Yes', like Del Monte people inevitably do when a window is opened for them, and we all went with their take on our single and us with glee. Basically the video was a moving picture enactment of the Shock publicity photo: Sean and I (as Tik and Tok) on plinths either side of the rest of the group, moving to the beat with our magnificent mechanismo. Robert, clad in his Glam Restoration outfit but this time with the complement of metallic gold greasepaint covering his face, is the MC from Hell. He mouths the song's lyrics and clutches a goblet made from a human skull. Black-garbed Barbie sneers at the camera with dangerous yet romantic sensuality whilst brandishing an ornate, be-jewelled dagger that is crowned with ram's horns. Carole flings the fiery curls of her cranial hair back and forth with rhythmic abandon, and manages to be barely contained by her miniscule lacy corset whilst moistly pouting straight down the lens. L.A, in her chosen role as a perverted Fairy Tale Princess, wears her white ermin frock, black vinyl gloves, and a thin layer of white clay covering her face. On the line from the song: "Who knows how long your looks will last?" she grins into camera and (lo and behold!) her visage seems to crack like the skin of a three-thousand year old Ursula Andress in She. Good clean fun for the kids really.

A week later David and Kathy filmed us live on stage as Shock did the first of many gigs at a place in Victoria called The Venue. I loved that redolent terrain, like so many other gigs in London it had once functioned as an Edwardian variety theatre, which had been closed down in the post-war years and then re-opened in the '70's as a rock 'n' roll locale. It came complete with a full-sized, raised stage, theatrical curtains, big lighting rig and P.A. system, and the obligatory sticky carpet in the bar and toilet areas. Pre or post-performance one could chill, curse and chat in the salubrious upstairs lounge. And we did on many occasions. Unfortunately in the late '80's it became derelict, then somehow underwent a metamorphosis into a branch of 'Bigun's Ribs' (how elegant a title is that?) and now it languishes unloved and unremembered as yet another brash brightly-lit but not unappealing adjunct of the Pizza and Pasta Empire 'ASK'. Where are the blue plaques when you need them, huh? Mr. Metropolitan Historian?

On the 15th of November, most of us struggled back, in our newly-narcoleptic fashion, to Mayfair Sound Studios to record two tracks for possible Shock-usage. Both were co-written by myself and Richard Burgess (now our main producer, since it seemed that Rusty's short attention span had been used up by co-creating *Angel Face*). I had the lyrical content and Mr B. had the musical manifestation. This double-act inevitably added more fuel to a growing schism within the group that we'll explore later. The songs were: *Dynamo Beat* and *Screen Me, I'm Yours*. In my head *Dynamo* was a full-on slab of 120 BPM Neuro-Techno that should have sounded like a mix of early Human League and D.A.F, edgy, a little secretive and rhythmically dark. But, sadly, our man from a different Landscape had crafted something so repellently inappropriate that to this very day I still shudder when I hear it's twee Flamenco-isms and bland beats. However, *Screen Me*, had possibilities, the subject matter decreed a sleazier vibe. It's about a man alone in front of his VCR endlessly re-playing movies of a celluloid siren who becomes real in his imagination. She comes through the screen to manifest herself and he falls desperately and futilely in love with her.

RCA had the idea that to promote *Angel Face*, Shock would make live appearances in as many nationwide branches of Our Price Records as possible. So off we trotted to suffer the indignities of the general public's abuse and indifference. The promo video was not shown on TV at all, and we wondered exactly what RCA were actually doing to sell our record. They produced a Shock poster, flyers and round stickers with our logo in red on a black background, which were nice to look at but not exactly useful. Without the audience generated from Radio and TV exposure the single was going to go nowhere. Basically the Record Company didn't really know how to market us at all. We weren't a group in the conventional 'send them out gigging in every toilet in the UK' manner, and no one seemed to be working on or interested in plugging our single. The 12" was being played to death in all the New Romantic clubs and it was always in the indie charts compiled by DJ's but people were not buying it in sufficient quantities to make an impact. We did three live shows at The Venue in the run up to Christmas, where we went down a storm to everyone's delight, a few more P.As, a little bit of press and that was it for 1980.

It had been a very exciting and energetic year, and we'd come a long way in a very short space of time. The changes we'd gone through were quite awesome in retrospect. I went home to see Mum and Dad for Christmas and that felt so strange after all my little adventures during the previous twelve months. Just stepping back into that cosy suburban womb for a brief respite was a dichotomy of Twilight Zone peculiarity.

1981 had formerly dawned un-noticed in the haze of several parties and too many amphetamines but at least we had a few days off to recuperate. Charles Fox, the theatrical costumiers, had a huge sale on the 6th of January and we and every Blitz kid in London went along to rummage through endless racks of period costumes and artifacts. It was kids in a sweetshop time and we all staggered away with bin bags full of outrageous gear at ludicrously low prices. Shock started work again on the 7th at the Embassy Club, followed by The Venue again, La Valbonne club (3 times), the Embassy once more, small clubs up in Glasgow, Edinburgh and Aberdeen, followed by The Lyceum in London on the 25th supporting Classix Nouveaux and Theatre of Hate. Thanks to the enthusiasm and generosity of a journo named Tony Mitchell, and against all odds, we did a big interview with the heavy metal-loving music paper Sounds which came out on the 24th of January. It carried the headline: "Shock Horror Probe!" Other allegedly clever and witty headlines we garnered around this time were: "A Shock To The System", "Future Shock", "Shock Value", and "Shock Are Electric!", "Shock Waves" and "Shock Of The New". You can see why the press loved us can't you? Especially when you saw what we looked like.

We did The Playboy Club on February 5th, which wasn't sexy at all and I think we managed to inadvertently set fire to the ceiling. Two days later we played our worst gig ever (in terms of technical ineptitude and audience indifference/hostility) at The Porter House in Retford. The New Romantic scene went overground on the 14th when Steve and Rusty hosted 'The People's Palace St. Valentine's Ball' at the Rainbow Theatre in London's Finsbury Park. From this moment on of course the whole movement went downhill, as the rest of the country appropriated the looks and styles that were pioneered in London over the previous two years. We shared that evening's stage with Ultravox (icily-flushed with the success of *Vienna*, then at No.2 in the charts); Depeche Mode (in the very week their first single was released and who were paid ten times less money than Shock); the androgynous Ronny; and Peter Godwin's band, Metro. The trouble with playing to an audience consisting of 'Peacock Punks' is that they're more interested in looking at themselves than at the performers on stage.

Chapter 13 – High Rise and Lowlands

The Dakota Building stands like a sinister Gothic castle on the corner of West 72nd Street and Central Park West. Polanski used it's brooding demeanor to demonic effect in *Rosemary's Baby*, but what brings tears to my eyes as I stand outside it is the murder of John Lennon, my first musical hero, who gave so much joy and vision to the world. How could it have ended like this? It seems only yesterday that I saw The Fabs playing their Christmas show at Hammersmith Odeon way back in 1964 when my world was naïve and unformed. Now all I can see is his blood bursting from exit wounds, all I can hear are the words: "Mr Lennon?" and the percussive brutality of five .38 bullets entering the back of a forty year old man returning to his home, late at night, from a recording session. It's March 1981. Shock are in New York for a 12-night residency at a large music venue called The Ritz. With our lighting man, Pete Williams, I've walked through Central Park, from the Barbizon Plaza hotel, and we're standing at the gates of the Dakota. Lennon's slaying was only three months ago and the flowers, candles, photographs and shocked, tearful hand-written messages of love and condolence still proliferate. We're silent, lost in our thoughts and memories. Darkness swirls like ink in water. One of the shows we're participating in is called 'Rock Against Depression'. The Customs men at JFK looked through our luggage (which contains all of our stage costumes and props) and wondered what the hell these six freaks that allegedly are here on holiday are doing with fur bikinis, whips, fake rats, fencing foils, masks etc. Work permits? With our useless Manager? Forgeddaboudid! Sean and I get in a yellow cab at 2AM. The driver turned round saying: "You guys are English right?", and through the grill hands us our first Yankee-style spliff. We get so stoned that we have no idea where we are going. It's a Scorsese kind of moment; his red eyes keep checking us out in the mirror.

Strange conflicts, both personal and creative are beginning to simmer in the group. Barbie has to settle for Carole's company in spare moments as Sean and I are off, like unleashed puppies, exploring what ever comes our way. I feel bad deep down but for some reason she and I don't talk about it. Or I don't want to listen. The sensible side of resentment and recrimination is somewhere we don't reach. Yesterday, two Coneheads hailed a cab outside a theatrical costumiers somewhere along Broadway and no one took any notice. A girl with bright blue hair stares from the window of room 2510 and wonders how the cleaning staff are coping with the Crazy Colour dye-stains on the hotel towels, sheets and pillows. Carole spends her free time scouring vast and expensive beauty-product emporia in the unending quest for more effective hair conditioners. Robert and L.A. are loose on the streets, somewhere, wearing their chosen outfits of Cowboy/girl romance.

We went on stage at three in the morning. Everything is like a scene from a movie, vivid, brash, recognisable and fast moving. I feel like my brain is taking Polaroids, little fuzzy-focused snapshots that try to capture it all. I have had my hair totally coloured fire-red with black at the edges and that, combined with Barbie's aquatic follicular hue, makes our daily bathroom look like someone has slaughtered a mermaid in the tub.

NEW YORK POST, SATURDAY, MARCH 21, 1981

Rock shockin'

By ED NAHA

SHOCK is one of the few acts around that looks exactly like you'd expect them to.

A three male, three female aggregation, Shock is a British musical mutation that is one part dance, one part mime and one part bump and grind.

Performing at the Ritz through tomorrow, the sextet presents imaginative physical tableaus set to bizarre snatches of pop music. Everyone and every thing is used in their musical backdrop from the synthesized strains of Gary Numan to the soul shoutin' of James Brown to such original Shockers as *Angel Face* and *R.E.R.B.*.

As the music blares, the group goes through the motions . . . and what motions they are. Frankenstein's monster takes a soulful sax solo while mini-dressed go-go girls gyrate. Faceless aliens swim through Earth's thick gravity with reptillian ease. Sadomasochistic couples, all dressed up with no one to beat but themselves, taunt and savage each other on stage under the stammering stare of strobe lights.

The sum effect of this collection of strange sights and sounds is quite unsettling. Humor and pathos collide head on. Inspired coreography and peep show titilation mix in exaggerated sexual stand-offs. It's *Alphaville* meets *The Rocky Horror Picture Show*, but live and in person.

The current scourge of the British musical scene, Shock may find it difficult to make an impression in this country; attempting to evoke dream-like imagery for rock audiences whose dreamy state often arises from bottles of both the liquor and pharmaceutical variety.

EAST 11TH ST. BETWEEN 3RD + 4TH AVE.

SHOCK

DIRECT FROM THE UNITED KINGDOM!
ONLY AND EXCLUSIVELY APPEARING AT THE RITZ
MARCH 13,14,15,16,17,18,19,20,21,22.

A FUTURIST, ROCK'N'ROLL, THEATRICAL, ELECTRONIC MIME GROUP!
A ROCK'N'ROLL THEATRICAL SHOCK! THE RITZ

★ MAR.16 ($1), MAR.18 (PEOPLE'S PALACE NIGHT-$2), MAR 19 (FUTURIST NIGHT-$2)
★ ALL 3 SHOWS STARRING SHOCK.

Sean and I go back to the shop on Broadway and Somewhere in Wales is a man whose memory contains a bizarre little moment from over twenty years ago. Shock had done their stuff at a club called The Stables in Rhyl and, against good advice from locals, decided to drive back to London that night. It had snowed thickly for hours during the evening and the roads were treacherous, especially when we started to climb up into mountainous regions. Suddenly the van slid to an unexpected halt by the roadside and the engine spluttered pitifully then died. Yep, out of petrol and stranded miles from the nearest town. After chastising our road manager and informing him that he would very shortly be leaving the employ of the group, we sat in the already cooling van and wondered what the fuck we were going to do. The six of us were ludicrously clad in our New Romantic fashions that suddenly looked utterly alien and completely impractical. All we could think of as a plan was sitting out the night in the Transit until hopefully came by in the morning. Christ it was cold! For the first and only time we all cluster up together like sardines to share each other's fading body-warmth. Somewhere later in this dark night's soul we hear the sound of an approaching car. The driver, in between wipes of the windscreen blades, sees a white van parked at an odd angle on the slope. Suddenly the side door slides back and a young woman with exaggerated make-up, wearing fishnets, black vinyl, and the brightest blue hair leaps out into the snow and hops up and down, gesticulating wildly. Her mouth opens and unheard words are shouted, her gestures assuming increasingly desperate velocity. "What the fuck?" He accelerates away into the silent white void, just glimpsing six pale open-mouthed faces peering at him from the vehicle's interior as he roars off.

Barbie screams with fury, sobs with frustration and stamps her immaculate pointy-booted feet in the snow. She gets back in, the door slams shut and, in the frigid darkness, I huddle up and wonder which of us will be eaten first by the others. In the first light of the next day some kind person did stop and let us siphon enough petrol from their tank to enable us to reach the nearest town. Sean volunteered to suck this guy's gas, as he was by far the most practical of us all. Robert and I would have swallowed the lot. We passed the guy about five miles down the road. He'd run out of petrol! We waved to him as we cruised past on our way home. Whoever you are I'd like to thank you on behalf of us all and to apologise.

Three days off to sleep, do laundry etc. then we go to Holland for a twelve-day tour. Tensions start to manifest increasingly now, with Robert and L.A. versus the four of us. Promoters used Sean's picture as the poster to announce our gigs all over every town we went to, which was kind of peeving. But, he was very pretty though. We were based in some kind of motel affair in a hamlet that sounded like 'Spunkenberg' and which was very central in the geography of 'The Lowlands' which meant we could rove out to each gig, perform and drive back easily. One night Sean and I in our new Conehead masks (that covered our entire skulls and gave us an ominous and pointy aspect) and Robert, clad in a black whole-head Executioner disguise, went to a local tavern in the town for some beer, that was located on the edge of a sinister looking dyke (plenty of those in Amsterdam too). We could drink with straws through the mouth holes of our masks and the three of us sat there minding our own business, whilst pretending not to notice the ascending murmurs of confused and threatened locals. As things started to approach confrontational meltdown we decided to leave the place and go back to the Bates motel.

Suddenly, out in the sobering, moistly dark and deserted street, we were surrounded by a group of about half a dozen youths who'd followed us out from the bar. They started to persistently chant: "We want to see your faces! Take off the masks!" I prayed that Pereno would do nothing to aggravate our situation, luckily he didn't. I mean, really! What were we thinking of? At the Melkweg in Amsterdam we came out on stage to start our act through a haze of dope-smoke from the seated audience so thick that it rendered our dry-ice machine redundant. We were all stoned by default. Then we blew all the fuses! They stared up at us, we stared down at them, and vice versa for quite a long time. They must have thought it was the weirdest most inactive mime show they'd ever seen. Sean decided to break the hideous inertia by blowing fire for the first time ever in his life. He did it with aplomb, twice. He'd obviously got the taste for petrol after our snowy Welsh calamity. If I'd tried it The God Of Clumsiness would have decreed that I flame all the hair off my head, and if Pereno had tried it? God knows. He would have more than likely immolated the whole building.

SHOCK!!

SHOCK — the futurist dance group proved a great success when they livened up the disco for two fantastic nights — more please.

At the Coconut Grove

Gary Numan, Bunny Liz and one of 'SHOCK'

Chapter 14 - The Big Gig

In late April we got 'The Big Gig'. Gary Numan had caught our act at the Embassy club, a streak of red in his hair and a can of Coca-Cola in his hand, and he generously offered us the support slot at his three nights of 'farewell' shows at Wembley Arena. He said: "I think you guys are fucking great!". This was not unconnected to his having the hots for Carole if truth be known. I'd seen Bowie's 1976 *Station To Station* tour at this venue, so to be playing it myself five years later was yet another 'Golden Moment'. How many people did it hold? In the vicinity of 8,000, and Gary had sold it out for all three performances on the back of three consecutive No.1 albums. We rehearsed for lighting and sound on the largest stage at Shepperton film studios for a few days, but our show was already tight and high voltage from all the relentless work we'd been doing over the last four months. This really was Shock at their peak, before and after were not comparable in terms of content and energy.

Thank God Gary had a crew to film our act as it would have vanished into hazy memories, dreams and reflections by now. For those of you who need to know these minutae, this was our set at Wembley in April 1981:

Intro - the chorale from the *2001* soundtrack. Dry ice, ultra-violet light. Tik and Tok as faceless, white-clad, slowly undulating aliens. Robert, with spotlight hand-held under his face, mouths the words to:

I Dream Of Wires - Robert Palmer and Gary Numan. Robert leaves, allowing Tik & Tok to glide around the stage as the dry-ice clouds bloom and the music shifts into:

The Wheel - Georgio Moroder from *Midnight Express*. Sean and I move out to the edges of the stage as the three girls enter, each clutching sci-fi hand telephones. They have on white lab-coats and look like Kubrick nurses. Reading across their backs in black ink are the letters: 'E = MC2'. They mouth the lyrics and we all do some choreography to: *Einstein A Go-Go* by Landscape. This segues into:

Land of a Thousand Dances by Wilson Pickett. Over the intro and into bright stage lights, Robert appears wearing a huge plastic mask of a grinning Negro face and a glittering outfit. He's joined by Barbie and L.A, in black and white satin mini-dresses, doing a kind of mutated go-go dance. Pereno whips of the big face to reveal that his head is actually that of Frankenstein's monster. He mimes playing a toy silver saxophone. Carole, clad in a skin-tight, red Lycra cat suit with studded belts, struts out as the music changes to:

The Steps by Visage. It's just L.A and Carole on stage now and the two of them engage in a high-kicking catfight. A defeated Carole slouches off as L.A. goes into her dancing stick routine and is then joined by Robert. He eventually gets his own magic-wand weaving at great speed around his entire torso. You can't see the fishing-line under the stage lights and it looks pretty surreal. They skip off as the backing cross-fades into:

Breathing - Kate Bush. It's Barbie solo at the start, she mimes the exquisitely yearning song beautifully, wearing a sequined green crepe ballgown. She's joined by yours truly clad in a red and white diamond-patterned harlequin costume. I do a puppet mime movement as she manipulates my imaginary strings. As we exit the lights fade-out and we hear the intro to: *Seconds To Late* by Cabaret Voltaire. This is Sean's robot solo. It's just him moving across the stage for the duration of the track with precise mechanical majesty. His wearing the metallic plastic robo suit by Mezz re-vamped with lights covering it. He dies in slo-mo at the end and the lights come up lurid red for the intro to:

Dynamo Beat by Shock. The three girls, wearing Kahn and Bell Flamenco dresses and clutching fake roses, surround our prone android-like widows in a Lorca play. I come out, move to the mic and announce the song. I sing the vocals live over the backing but, unfortunately, at the end so does Robert. His voice is flat and completely emotionless. I really don't like this track at all, and I wish I were singing something else. Sean is revived by the attentions of the girls just in time to mime the violin solo in the outro on a plastic and metal space-fiddle. I've left them all to it so *I can change costume for:*

Claire De Lune (Debussy) as performed by Tomita. Green light comes up revealing me wearing a black, sleeveless body suit and a bright green mask of a frog's head! I mime punting, fishing and swimming until I'm joined by Barbie. Her hair is in bunches and she's dressed like a little girl. We have an enchanting froggy courtship to:

Stranger In Paradise by Vic Damone and Ann Blythe. As the song fades my attention is diverted by L.A flouncing on wearing a leather biker's hat, fishnets, black vinyl thigh-boots and a massive cape with a green and white tulle dress underneath. She mimes to *I Wanna Be Loved By You* by Marilyn Monroe. I leave when she spurns me and takes up with Robert, who has entered wearing the executioner mask that the Dutch boys liked so much, a striped poncho and cowboy boots. They start to dance to the track: *Coitus Interuptus* by Fad Gadget. They do a routine that is part rehearsed, part improvised. In which Robert mimes cunnilingus as L.A. does the splits whilst doing a handstand. Yep, I've watched that particular moment many times! They get even more frenzied as we now go into:

I Zimbra by Talking Heads. The maskless Pereno is revealed, as is a pair of trousers with a red devil's face applied on a flap covering his crotch, and a black fishnet top. He is manic, pale and sweaty as he screams into the mike: "This is Wembley Sex Dance!". His face leers and snarls when not hurling L.A round himself by her wrists and ankles. We fade lights and sound, and the ominous intro starts of:

Doll's House by Landscape. This is basically Sean and I (after an early appearance by Carole as a tu-tu wearing pirouetting ballerina) dressed as cavemen with face-masks of white skulls topped with wild black wigs. We're clutching large white plastic bones. We do some primal mime that is quite terrifying when coupled with this dark piece of horror music. Strobe lights stammer the action when we segue into:

Frequency 7 by Visage. We're herded off stage eventually by Robert who is clutching, for some reason, a life-size prosthetic leg. Now Pereno The Beast asserts himself in the most gigantic way both physically and verbally as the music cuts into:

R.E.R.B by Egan and Burgess (B-side of the single). Over the backing and into the mic he spits and shouts his own improvised lyrics. Which mainly consist of "Burn!", "Shock!", "Dance Ritual!", "Wembley Ritual!" Which are then repeated, in no particular order, at random intervals to the beat. The dribble flays from Robert's mouth and his eyes are black and savage. Barbie, clutching flourescent green light-stick things, does a pagan dance whilst avoiding his battering arms. L.A's out towards the end of the track, in her white fur bikini. She throws her hair and her body around the other two. Now it's the last song: *Angel Face* by Shock. We're all on stage now for the first time since *Einstein A Go Go*. Sean and I flank the others as per the promo video, but this time we're sword-wielding Arabian Nights guardians. The onstage energy is awesome. We give it absolutely everything. White back-light fans out from ground level behind us and we look like we're dancing through the smoke-lit fingers of a giant. Every spotlight on stage flashes to the pagan rhythm of the track. We look like an unstoppable well-oiled machine at maximum power. The music judders to a climax. We all bow and then we're off into the wings. The audience cheer us wildly (and generously, considering we were only the support act).

Gary's show was breathtaking. A Sci-Fi extravaganza of epic proportion, visually and musically. I've still never seen a show to beat it.

Looking at the Wembley video 21 years later what comes across to me is that Robert is absolutely borderline psychotic. Carole is bemused, abused, but functioning well in her role as foil for Robert and L.A, and she moves with lithe assertive fluidity. Barbie, especially during *Angel Face*, *R.E.R.B* and to an extent in *Breathing*, is venting like mad and enjoying a true outpouring of repressed emotion. L.A. is every man's wet dream. She knows it and revels in it but is still at the dangerous mercy of Pereno's uncontrolled genius. Sean is succinct, beautiful, and very powerful. And me? Well I'm a gangly, nervous and insecure gargoyle. Safe only when hidden behind a mask and doing what I do best. And that really says it all, doesn't it? We were destined to shine greatly and to then self-destruct. It was inevitable and it makes perfect sense. Malcolm McLaren should have been our manager, he would have delighted in our fiery finite flounderings and would have sold us to the world as an accident waiting for you to happen. Fate decreed that it would be all down hill from now on.

After the Numan shows, which in terms of spectacle, power and audience numbers, were the most beneficial we ever did, we imploded. At a gig the next day in Newport, South Wales, Robert caused L.A. to break her wrist onstage during their dance routine to I Zimbra. We huddle pale-faced and vulnerable in the Emergency waiting room as she gets plastered-up. Is Robert chastened? Not on the surface anyway. To him it's like inadvertently stepping on one of the props from the act. Nothing more, nothing less. The rest of us look at each other and question how it got to be so careless, so unthinking.

Rusty by now has fallen out with Richard Burgess, and the six of us are split. Rusty's fearless experimentation is mirrored by Robert (and by default L.A.); Richard's methodical, pedantic but chart-worthy perfectionism is reflected by Barbie and myself. She and Richard have formed a liaison that I seemed oblivious to at the time that didn't actually revolve around creating music. My fault I guess. If I hadn't have been so wrapped-up in, and exhilarated by, the newfound bond and activities of Sean and I, I would have seen her pain and unhappiness and perhaps delayed the inevitable. Most bands have a five-year career that yields great success then acrimony; we managed to fit ours in to an eighteen-month period. But we blazed our little moment brightly enough and well enough to still be remembered and loved. That's all we could have hoped for.

At our first headlining gig, at the Lyceum on June 21st, 1981. Robert chose to announce that he and L.A. were leaving the group. He conveyed this to the audience halfway through our set, so it came as utter disbelief and secret relief all at once. There goes the Magic... Just like that. Gone now, swept away in the tide of a confused man's ego. We were left stranded, none of us wanting to admit out loud that the very essence of the group was no longer with us - Robert, a fantastic ball of energy; L.A., a great singer and dancer. Now what do we do? To be honest it didn't bruise me like it did Barbie (and to a lesser extent Carole) because Sean and I already had other plans. But stupidly we stuck it out as a four-piece for another six months. Four gigs were arranged for Shock Mk II and some press too. The unsatisfactory *Dynamo Beat* was released by RCA in October and pretty much suffered the fate of its predecessor. We shot the promo ourselves at night in Brompton cemetery. It wasn't shown anywhere. *Dream Games*, the B-side was good though. Slinky, funky, with a sly lyrical dig at TV culture. Co-written by Richard, John L. Walters, Barbie and myself, it got a lot of play in the New Romantic clubs and I felt pretty proud of it. We enlisted a girl named Leslie, who, with no clothes on and covered in gold grease-paint, fondled a seven-foot Python named John on stage. We also used a body-builder, Steve Ausden, to augment our paucity but we all knew it was all over. Better to have burned brightly for a short while than to have never shone at all. Thank you Mr. Pereno. We all owe you respect and gratitude at the very least.

Mott The Hoople (in all their post-Bowie, glammed-up ineptitude) had a song that contained the lines: "Well it's a mighty long way / Down Rock 'n' Roll, / From the Liverpool docks To the Hollywood Bowl." And that seems to sum-up this 'small', in the scheme of things, but 'unmissable at the time', venture named Shock. I don't recall actually sleeping throughout the whole period. Sometimes, in insomniac torment, my mind is like a lunatic running amok in a Library. Ceaselessly opening one book after another, reading one page only and then discarding it for the next. Thoughts randomly connected ad nauseum and I seem to be powerless to stop the activity. An infinite spiral of interlinked and useless information holds me captive in it's centre. I feel like a rabbit trapped in my own headlights. It would be fascinating and amusing if I weren't trying so hard to reach sleep. I twist and contort myself into endless repetitions of body shape like a crab with bedsores, but no position lasts for more than a few minutes. I mean there's really only four configurations for attempting the longed for state of slumber, left or right side embryonic, face down with feet protruding into the swarming, chilly darkness and on your back with fingers drumming silently on clammy chest. If I was being filmed by a night-vision camera from above and the footage subsequently speeded-up I'd look like a naked man doing a perverse horizontal dance routine that would make Whirling Dervishes and bulging-crotched male members of Modern Dance groups viridian with envy. There is of course the magnificent embarrassment of actually falling asleep on a train or plane, only to wake an hour later vivid with cramp in one leg and a drool of previously unsummoned spittle connecting your slack and gaping mouth to the headrest. For full humiliation this intimate moment should be accompanied by some frozen four year-old staring at you with inquisitive horror whilst whispering: "Mummy, Mummy, look at this funny man! He's dribbling!".

Chapter 15 – Return of the Jedi

In January '82, Sean and I got a call from Desmond Jones our old mime tutor, asking us to come to his school and audition for roles in the third *Star Wars* movie. He'd been approached by the producers to find half a dozen mime artistes to play aliens in the film that was, at that time, still entitled *Revenge Of The Jedi*.

About twenty-five of us turned up at a rather chilly church hall in Shepherd's Bush. Desmond was there, and Robert Watts, the co-producer of the movie. We changed into our rehearsal gear and were asked to do 'alien acting'. Mimes are very good at getting into a costume and making that costume real. We can pretend we are very heavy or very fast or very weird.

Sean and I got the job and we're soon off to Elstree studios for three weeks to perform in a major Hollywood Film. We play members of the entourage of Jabba The Hutt, a monstrously fat slug-like creature operated from within and below the costume by a team of puppeteers. Our roles seem to consist largely of lolling around in Mr. The Pizza Hutt's palace watching the action taking place in front of us. Our costumes are enormous and heavy and take about three assistants to get us into them. After every take we have to have our creature heads removed so that cold air can be blown at us, because we're in danger of hyperventilating under the heat from the lights and the weight of the suits. Sean resides inside a towering camel-like head and mine resembles that of a multi-tusked mammoth. *Star Wars* fans know far more details of our characters' names and genealogies than we ever did. For us it was the best fun we could imagine just being there.

We liked Mark Hamill (Luke Skywalker) a lot; he was friendly and down to earth, with that kind of gung-ho American enthusiasm that is very infectious. We pointed Mark in the direction of a few clubs around town that he might enjoy visiting. He did. Harrison Ford seemed to be permanently preoccupied and more than a little surly, so we didn't approach him very often. "This is not High Art or some Method Acting venture, Mr. Ford, so lighten up a bit, OK?" I didn't say that, of course, I just thought it. Carrie Fisher looked great wearing that bikini-like costume as she was writhing around chained-up to the Jabba, and we all longed to swap places with him. In my mind I asked her for shag but she refused (I should have removed my costume head first maybe?).

What amazed and delighted us about the filming was the constant attention to minute detail and the absolute realism of the set. It had walls, floor and ceiling and felt completely real. You'd come in the next day and one wall had been removed so that they could shoot the same scene from a completely different perspective. It really was cinematic magic in every way.

We also got to appear on Jabba's desert sail-barge and play Mon Calamari Officers in scenes involving Admiral Ackbar and the crew of his rebel spacecraft battling against Darth Vader and the Evil Empire. In these we had to flap around a lot in a panicky, squid-like fashion, which came easily to us after the bulky and cumbersome lethargy of being mere toppings in Jabba the Hutt's 'extra-pepperoni' palace.

Tim Dry as a Mon Calamari officer in *Return of the Jedi*
© Lucasfilm Ltd.& TM. All rights reserved

Chapter 16 – Unconcerned Androids

We were still doing Robots at Coconut Grove every Friday and Saturday, if we were available, and we met a lot of interesting people through doing that. One was a sixteen-year old named Georgia, a gorgeous sexy schoolgirl, in Vivienne Westwood clothes, who liked to hang out there with her friends. We chatted after we'd done our act one Saturday, and the two of us went off to a club to snog the night away. We ended up going out together for four or five months and for a while it was a real turn-on. I've never had as much sex in my life with one person. She would visit me in my flat several night every week and on other days we embarked on the task of fucking in every room in her Mum and Dad's large house in Loughton, culminating in a memorable and lengthy 69 on her parents' bed one languid, summer afternoon. Say what you will, but for a thirty year-old man to be able to revel in young uninhibited sensuality and flesh is a dream to which most males aspire. It couldn't last of course as, after the first few glorious months, the grim realities of the age-gap become increasingly apparent. No, I do not want to go ice-skating or hang out with your dull immature friends! Yes, I do want to stay in and try and create some new music for Tik and Tok and then go to that new club that's just opened, etc. Bless her sweet, open nature and the pirate dress she floated in on. I hope she made the good life she deserved for herself, and I sometimes wonder what she does now.

Another lady I met at Coconut Grove was Barbara Machin, a TV producer for Granada. She was intrigued enough by Tik and Tok's act to craft an entire play for television around us, and managed to convince the powers-that-be up in Manchester that it was a viable idea. It was called *Lover Come Back To Me* and was a tale of two parallel couples. One pair was Tik and Tok playing mannequins in a window in a shopping arcade, who get bored, decide to escape from their glassy cage and go off exploring. The other couple are two bitchy actors having a relationship crisis whilst filming a Hollywood musical set in the 1930's. But here's the twist, I play the arrogant gigolo-like male lead with manifest insecurities and jealousies (Type-cast? Moi?) and Sean plays the female lead! I must say that with the make-up and dark Louise Brooks-style wig, he looked very fetching indeed. The only problem was that he'd neglected to shave his legs. To cover up his hirsuteness they gave him three pairs of tights to wear! Under the lights the conflicting moiré patterns produced by the layers of nylon made his legs look like varnished wood and it was very difficult for us to keep straight faces, especially when we were required to dance together. Barbara and her director, Nicholas 'Bad time to give up cigarettes' Ferguson (who directed Bowie's *Heroes* video), came out with the notion that in order to add to the dislocation we should mime to our own pre-recorded dialogue. I'm amazed it even got made let alone broadcast, but viewers seemed to like it. We also got to record our own backing music in a proper recording studio for the mannequin sections. It still sounds pretty good in a lo-fi, electro way.

I'd wanted to record a cover version of The Lovin' Spoonful's *Summer in the City* when we were still signed to RCA as Shock, but they were determined that we do our own stuff (which they failed to market and promote) so I put it on hold until Sean and I were free from our contract with them. In this we were helped by Adam Ant,

"Lover come back to me" Granada T.V. June '82

whom we'd supported and who was having a fling with Carol. Adam put us in touch with his lawyer, Alexis. Incidentally, RCA own the copyright on the word 'radio'! Which in theory means that every time someone uses that word in public in a professional context they should be paid a royalty? Anyway, Alexis freed us from RCA and, come mid-summer '82, we're ready to go. I've got the studio booked; Rrussell Bell, a very talented guy from Gary Numan's band. I do the lead vocals, Sean and Peter Godwin do back-ups, and Peter is producing (he co-wrote *Criminal World* which Bowie covered on *Let's Dance*). It sounds good. We've kept the structure and feel of the '60's original but given it a clubland 1980's groove. Peter creates an insistent New Romantic drum riff at the prerequisite 125 BPM. Rrussell plays funky guitar and synth brass parts and we're done and dusted. We also craft a big fuck-off 12" that kicks some serious frilly-shirted butt and now we have to sell it.

Enter Mr. Don Mousseau, a mustachioed, fearless chancer from the US of A who is part Mic-Mac Indian and part Hunter S. Thompson (but with more drugs inside him). Don appears to be Peter's representative here on Earth as well as having business dealings with Georg Kajanus from the then defunct Sailor (Is that my future I see winking at me from a distance?) and has managed to insert his digits in most of the pies in the music biz. I don't give a flying syn-drum who does what and how; I just want this single out, and as soon as possible (Summer is upon us and you can't release a song called *Summer in the City* in the Autumn!). We do a deal with Essex Music for my publishing (whoops, bad contract alert!) and the main man there, Frank Richmond, gets us a singles deal with some small Indie label called Survival Records, who say they can put it out in two weeks if we sign a deal for five-singles and an album. We sign. And the rest is history.

I nearly forgot - I did actually meet Kate Bush! Summer '82 and Tik and Tok are doing their stuff at an EMI convention in a stately home in the Sussex countryside. The company's flushed with anticipation because they've just signed and groomed for stardom five goons who've christened themselves Kajagoogoo, and this is where they have to showcase their act to the big-wigs to prove that they may actually be worthy of 15 minutes of fame and a lot of EMI money. I think Nick Rhodes from Duran Duran produced them as an added incentive. We weren't overly impressed to be honest, one hooky song and a lot of fillers, too much make-up and this month's haircuts. Hey! That's exactly what the press would be saying about Tik and Tok in a year or so!

Anyway, after our spot and before theirs, I'm standing in my red tailcoat and full make-up with a glass of warm champagne when I notice a girl next to me with long dark brown hair and a green velvet dress. I look. I look again... It's her! She sees this android apparition giving her the wide eye and she smiles at me. I flush (difficult under all that white pancake) and smile back. I say hello, she says hello. A thousand questions, praises, 'do you remember the two sad fans who were apprehended breaking into your gig at the Palladium' etc. swarm into and then ruefully vanish mutely out of my brain in about ten seconds, and the moment has gone. For a transient instant we were just two artistes occupying the same space, wondering what the hell we were both doing there at that convention of corporate misguidedness. I sighed for years to come.

Sean and I bought ourselves a 4-track Portastudio, a digital delay unit, a Drumatix drum machine and two analogue synths with our earnings from *Return of the Jedi*, and we started creating little bits of music for ourselves at home. We did a silly little throwaway track we called *Crisis*, and Survival Records wanted it as the B-side to *Summer In The City* (actually it was all we'd got at that time).

I also splashed out on a Casio keyboard, one of the white plastic kind that have a selection of about a dozen really cheesy pre-sets and we used that for the long intro to our first home-grown track. One of our two synths was a Sequential Circuits 'Pro One', and it had a hundred-note sequencer built in, which we discovered we could trigger from the drum machine to create robotic-sounding rhythms. Wow! This was all terribly exciting for us, being able to get stoned and fool around in our inimitable fun-loving way.

At this time Sean was still living in his parents' house in Knightsbridge, but as his Dad was a Colonel in the army, Mr. & Mrs. Crawford were away overseas a lot, so we took over the ground floor for our little musical and social adventures. One night we scored some fearsomely potent grass, got the instruments talking to each other and embarked on creating a long and very spacy piece of what could pass for music on another planet. About an hour in to the wild and chaotic, dubby whirlpool of sound I kept hearing a distant knocking noise, I removed my headphones, gasped at the seething external silence and glanced at the window to my right, a huge fly with human torso and limbs was tapping insistently on the glass. Don't you just hate that? I nearly Biryani'd my pants in terror! How long Sean had been out there I had no idea, but after he climbed back in through the window we collapsed into helplessly out-there convulsions of laughter. Little bastard, he was always doing things like that. I think it helped to keep us sane?

One night in Dublin, after successfully doing our act in a newly opened nightclub, we were having several drinks with the promoter and a few hangers-on. I said to our man (who'd organised our visit in a style we appreciated greatly, a pink Cadillac to meet us at the airport? No problem boys!) that I needed a woman. Whether I was being serious or merely flirty didn't seem to matter. He gets up, disappears for a few minutes, and comes back with a young blonde girl clad in fake leopard skin and lycra (it's only 1982 remember, and we are in Ireland). She doesn't say much when she sits down next to me but she puts her hand on my thigh, so after about ten minutes I cut to the chase and take her back to our shared room. Which now has a large, hand-written sign in felt-tip stuck with chewing gum on the door that says: "Tikky is Gay!" Inside is Tokky apparently sprawled asleep on his bed, oblivious to the frantic coupling that the young lady and I indulge in. Or was he? About five or six years later, when we're out together again on a rare occasion, he says with a mischevious chuckle and apropos of nothing: "You thought I was asleep back in that hotel room in Ireland didn't you!".

One day, we're walking down a London street in our finery and we pass a white Transit van parked by the side of the road (the type that usually has Clean Me!' fingered into the dust and grime of the back doors). The nearside window winds down, semi-evolved knuckles are revealed bearing the tattoo'd epithet H.A.T.E and a gruff cockney voice bellows at us: "OI! I'm glad I didn't see you come out of my house!'". We were baffled at first until we realised shortly afterwards that what had actually been directed at us was: "OI! I'm glad I didn't see you come out of my arse!" Oscar Wilde-Boy thought he was being most profound, and we thanked him profusely for his eloquent contribution to the Oxford Book Of Verbal Abuse and laughed and skipped our carefree way down the pavement. Another favourite was: "Faaack me! You look faackin' weird!". To which we'd jovially riposte, "Yeah, but we get paid for it!". Residing permanently at No.1 in our Top Ten of responses to shouted calls of "POOFS!" or "WANKERS!" from chimps high up on scaffolding was, "You keep laying bricks, and we'll keep laying chicks!"

What really pissed us off more than anything was if journalists (or anybody in fact) spelt our names wrongly. 'Tic and Toc'? Uh uh. 'Tick and Tock'? NO! Some chose to hedge their bets and call us 'Tick and Toc'. That used to frenzy us out completely, and led to Jane Kahn making us arm-bands with our respective names embroidered upon them, so there could be no more ambiguity. In publicity photos I'd always stand to the left of Sean in the frame to further help people out. We started to live out these characters for real in our day-to-day lives, as a safeguard against the slings and arrows of dubious reality. We only referred to each other as Tikky and Tokky in public and to the press, and we refused to tell anyone what our real names were. Of course, the unknown, hideously suburban, truth was that both of us had been parentally cursed with the same middle name, Nigel. The very word still sends a chill spinewards and is eternally synonymous with knee-length grey shorts, Airfix kits, glasses held together at the bridge with Elastoplast, scones for tea, and all things polite and mundane. There, it's out. My soul is cleansed at last and I can finally stride forward into a golden future, unhindered by my shameful secret. Tim and Sean largely disappeared under our new identities. Tik and Tok provided us with the perfect alibi for our extravagantly anti-Nigel behaviour.

We'd got our hands on a demo copy of a beautiful song called *Vile Bodies* written by a sadly unknown composer named Marek Rymaszewski (mind you, with a surname like that it's not too surprising he's not a household name) and we wanted it to be the second Tik and Tok single. Somehow we'd made contact with the producer and musician Thomas Dolby, whom we admired a lot. We had a meeting at Sean's place with the talented Mr. Surround Sound to talk about the possibility of him producing the track for us. He was up for it but his manager (as usual) was wary and then Survival said, in their finite wisdom, that they didn't think it would be suitable for a single. How wrong and short-sighted they were, as was born out a while later when it became the high point of our stage act, and the audience would go berserk every time we performed it.

The two people who ran Survival (whose names I can't bring myself to mention without resorting to grotesque insult and the re-kindling of ancient anger) demanded that we make a single out of the instrumental piece that we used for our Robot stage routine. I'd heard black guys on the street in my 'manor' saying: "Cool Runnings, Mon!" as a greeting to each other as they'd embark on those curious and intriguingly complex Rasta handshakes, and I thought *Cool Running* would be a good title for a song. I banged out some simplistic lyrics about alienation, city life, and unrequited love. We recorded it and *Vile Bodies* (for the B side) at the Essex music studios in

Poland Street, Soho, in a three-day session. On *Vile Bodies*, we used Rrussell Bell again to play most of the instruments and it turned out really well, if slightly dry in terms of the mix. I sang it as well as I could back then.

Cool Running was pretty much me playing everything, with the two of us singing together. It was supposed to sound like Yello and Bo Diddley crossed with Kraftwerk but due to my inexperience as a producer, and a strange lack of conviction from the two of us, it didn't really cut it. I think we were pissed off we had to do it as a single against our will. We even did an eleven-minute version for a 12" in a moment of stoned madness. In retrospect it's interesting to see just how far up one's own arse one could go!

We knew Ronny, the androgynous and elegant female singer with a penchant for Weimar-esque imagery, from when she and Shock were on the same bill at the People's Palace Ball at the Rainbow in February '81. We decided to combine our talents and put on a live show at 'Heaven' in Charing Cross in April 1983. She was a good friend of Vangelis and, after a meeting with Sean and myself, he kindly let the three of us use his large recording studio 'Nemo' to rehearse our show. We watched this big-hearted bear of a man, a huge talent, creating the score for a movie called *Antarctica* surrounded by a selection of keyboards that mere mortals can only dream about. A monitor in front of him played the scene from the film he was working on, and he'd play one synth with his left hand and another with his right, then swivel round and coax unearthly beautiful strings or choirs from yet another keyboard. It was all done live with no programming and everything was recorded straight onto multi-track tape. I've never seen anything like it. The music flowed straight from his soul down through his chubby fingers like a celestial symphony.

'Heaven' was London's largest gay nightclub. We reasoned that between us we could pull a large crowd of Persons Of A Non-Heterosexual Persuasion and a proportion of our loyal Tik and Tok fans. We were right. Ronny, wearing her Anthony Price man's suit, started off the proceedings with a couple of her own songs, then we came out and did our Robot routine followed by *Summer in the City* and an uncertain new piece called *Dangerous And Unafraid*. She came back on at the end of our first spot in a slinky and glamorous gold lame cocktail dress to sing a song written by Ryuichi Sakamoto. Then it was us again doing *Vile Bodies* in our ultra-violet mutant outfits and, after a hasty change into our Biker Boy plastic pervo kit, we slunk through a very camp version of *Screen Me, I'm Yours*, complete with two leather-clad whip-wielding blonde babes named Angie and Dena. Ronny then joined us for a ramshackle finale of Bowie's *Rebel Rebel*. It was a chic and vaguely decadent evening's entertainment in a futuristic Cabaret kind of style, but not unfortunately in anyway comparable to the berserk and energetic creativity of Shock Mark 1.

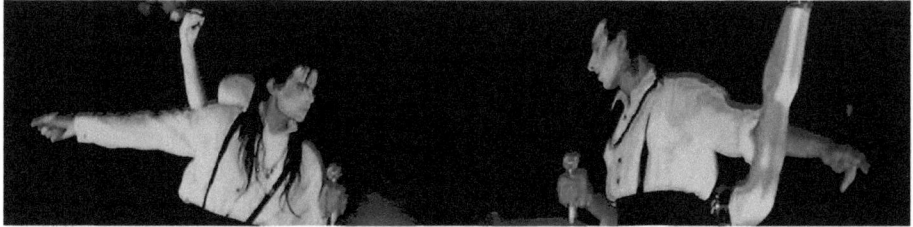

Chapter 17 - Japan

A 1950's black London taxicab, in perfect condition but with the decadent addition of gold leather upholstery, cruises through downtown Ginza in Tokyo. It's October 1982. The driver is a big Japanese man named Kenichi Segawa and he is clad from head to toe in Jane Kahn's Kabuki/Samurai influenced New Romantic clothing. He looks magnificent, so wonderfully out of place amidst the hordes of businessmen in black suits. Sitting in the back of the cab are Tik and Tok, wide-eyed behind their green-mirrored shades and excitable like children at being in this extraordinary city. Unlike our sojourn in New York, where every street or building seemed familiar from all the movies we know so well, everything here is alien. We have no reference for anything we see and it's breathtaking to be in the midst of it all. Sean and I had been obsessed with Sci-Fi, Japan, and mediaeval Japanese culture for quite a while, plus some of the music reaching England from this island like Sakamoto, YMO and Sandii and The Sunsetz, we liked a lot. It's the home of technology, musical equipment, cameras, computers, digital watches - you name it - and we wanted it all. But we didn't have the money to partake of that much of it. We did buy a set of Samurai swords each, a Roland SH-101 synth (the one you could wankily wear round your neck if you were Howard Jones or someone of that ilk), scarves, *Transformer* robots (of course), bottles of Sake and other bits and pieces.

Kenichi was an affluent antique dealer who'd come to London a few times each year to purchase items and have them shipped back to his shops in Tokyo (including his beloved and immensely cool taxi). He'd found the Kahn and Bell stall in The Great Gear Market, fallen in love with the clothes and bought masses of them to parade around in back home. That's pretty bizarre if you think about it, a youngish Japanese man buying London fashions that are directly influenced by his own country's history. Most of his contemporaries thought he was unsettlingly eccentric (not a Nipponese character trait in any shape or form back then).

One night, Kenichi and his wife took us to the oldest and most exquisitely traditional restaurant in Tokyo. Named Kejoen, it had many rooms in which diners sat shoeless and cross-legged at low wooden tables. Geisha waitresses, in full costume and make-up, bowed to you and served each dish with absolute serenity and grace. Paper screen walls could be opened to reveal a garden of unearthly beauty and tranquility, with musical notes sounded by water flowing over strategically placed stones underneath cherry trees like every Hokusai print you've ever seen. There were long gaps inbetween each course of delicately flavoured and immaculately arranged food, in which you'd sip tea and drink small cups of warm heady Sake. So utterly civilized, so timeless, and absolutely unlike anywhere I've been to since.

What the hell were Tik and Tok doing in Tokyo anyway? Sadly nothing to do with music (although *Summer In The City* had recently been released there on a small label to a minuscule amount of acclaim and press). No, we were there for the Rizzo brothers' salon 'Sanrizz, choreographing and performing in a Hair event where all the leading stylists or 'Cranial Artistes' competed for the coveted prize of Salon Of The Year or some such. It was a massive two day event, costing thousands and thousands of pounds, with literally hundreds of models sashaying around the stage in grotesquely un-hip outfits, and people snipping away at unsuspecting victims of ever more outlandish styles of Barnet-modification that no-one in their right mind would contemplate being seen with on the street. Our job was to make Sanrizz the most memorably OTT act of the lot, and we achieved that goal remarkably painlessly after only two days of rehearsal. Slight difficulties were had with conveying our odd choreographic vision to thirty models who spoke little or no English, but we got by with the magic of mime and a couple of interpreters. Naturally we did our Robot routine as the climax of the presentation and the audience response to it was heart-warming and spontaneous. Of course! Living Robots! The Japanese LOVE all that stuff! Another perk was our being adopted by two girls named Carole and Jackie (both Oriental but not Japanese) who not only took us out shopping and sightseeing but also got us delightfully laid in the splendour of our room in the New Takanawa Prince hotel. The only drawback to the two of us sharing a room was a moment like this, it was the first time both of us were with girls and getting down to some serious action in proximity to one another. You had to somehow stay focused on your own activity and close your ears and eyes to your friend's. One pair on the floor on the far side of one bed and the other couple on top of the second bed. After the first time you lose any sense of embarrassment or competition, and it becomes more natural. After all, Sean and I were together nearly every day for three years. Through thick and thin, good and bad. We had no secrets from each other, no inhibitions or guilt and no sense of anything outside of our own 'Here and Now'. It was us in a hermetic little bubble, protecting each other from the outside world. I owe him so much and I am very, very pleased we had our time together.

We always used to enjoy a spliff or two in hotel rooms when we were off adventuring, so I took a modest lump of Moroccan hash out to Tokyo with me, and decided not to let Sean know as our combined nerves might well give the game away. I ruminated for hours on where I could safely stash it. I'd thought at first of concealing it behind a tape inside my Walkman, then rejected that notion and decided to place it deep inside a bottle of viscous liquid foundation make-up. Whatever happened to Helena Rubinstein? Max Factor! First thing I see on our arrival at Narita airport are large signs everywhere informing passengers that drug smuggling into Japan is not only obviously illegal, but is also punishable by an immediate ritualistic disembowelling in front of everyone in the airport. Or you might, if the authorities were feeling lenient, get off with merely life imprisonment on a mosquito-infested island for you and every member of your family.

On seeing the warnings, Sean turns to me and says: "Fuck Tikky, thank Christ we don't have any dope with us!" I grin nervously and agree with him. Of course the first place the customs officials (who now closely resemble sadistic guards from *The Bridge On The River Kwai*) look is inside my Walkman after they remove the cassette. Once ensconced in the apparent safety of the hotel room I break the bad news to my innocent friend. "You utter, utter BASTARD!" was his justifiably intense response if I remember correctly. He came round pretty quickly considering the shock he'd just undergone, but now we had to try and buy some cigarette papers. We took a questing stroll around the nearest shopping area but in every tobacconist we visited, the reaction was the same: a blank, inscrutable face of suspicion at the sight of these oddly-dressed Gaijin attempting to mime rolling a cigarette, which was followed by lots of furtive looks left and right and 'I can't and won't help you' shoulder-shrugging. We gave up eventually and made our puzzled way back hotelwards to start removing the tobacco and filters from our legitimate fags, and then glueing the papers together with spirit gum to furnish some kind of spliff. We even put damp towels against the bottom of the door to the corridor to prevent any fumes escaping. It became apparent later, when talking to our two female companions about our dilemma, that walking into a tobacconist's in Japan and asking (either verbally or mimetically) for rolling papers is akin to parading around wearing attention-grabbing t-shirts emblazoned with: "Hello! We are foreign drug users who are shamelessly flaunting our habit in your faces. Please have us arrested at your earliest convenience".

One day there was an Earthquake. (I thought I'd just nonchalantly slip that in about here). It wasn't a full-on Richter scale job of the cinematic type that induces crumbling buildings, fleeing terror-stricken inhabitants, cars disappearing into vast and gaping chasms, and angry and vengeful prehistoric lizards released from captivity in the bowels of the earth. It was simply a disquietingly subtle shift in the surface of the city, a bit like that moment when you first step onto a moving escalator. A weird, understated dislocation of normality that left you feeling slightly sickened. Apart from us no one seemed to take any notice of it, but it looked good when we excitedly wrote about it on postcards that we sent home that afternoon.

Every morning of our nine-day tarriance in Tokyo, Sean and I would order the traditional Japanese breakfast on room service. We'd get a tray each, stacked with small round wicker baskets full of seaweed-wrapped Sushi of every variety: fish, prawn, crab, vegetable etc. And a tiny mound of a lurid green mustardy additive whose name I can never remember. On the first excited morning we both ingested a chopstick-laden mouthful of it. Of course you're not meant to do that. The burning that ensued rendered us virtually speechless, copiously sweaty and orally punished, for hours. The hotel bathroom (a designer-symphony in chrome and white marble) had the kind of toilet with a shelf inside it that enabled you to gaze in scatological curiousity at your bowels' recent escapees. After breakfast one day, late into our visit, I glanced down into the bowl after smoothly relieving myself and saw a foot-long, black eel with a pointed head looking up at me, it was coiled and sinister and it frightened the life out of me. Just before I was about to beat it to death with the toilet brush, I realised it was simply a turd of awesome proportion and eerie hue, the extrusional result of starting each day with a diet of raw fish and a huge quantity of seaweed.

The downside of our Tokyo jaunt (apart from inadvertently eating sea-slug in a restaurant) was the journey back. For reasons I can't recall we had to fly to Hong Kong, stay over for two days and then get a flight back to London. Somebody had arranged that we do a couple of club P.A.'s to promote *Summer in the City*. The first night we had to sleep on the floor of an office that was something to do with either the local record company or a pop magazine. We were rudely awakened at 6 a.m. by a frightened security guard who naturally spoke no English, had no prior knowledge of our presence, and who proceeded to throw us out into the street! We'd stashed our cases and Samurai swords at left luggage at the airport, so we were fairly light in terms of baggage, but with no money and no knowledge of where in the name of Ho Li Fook we were. It was a trying few hours to say the least. Eventually someone turned up to rescue us and then took us for lunch in what looked to be a very grubby working-man's café, full of weathered, black-eyed, old Chinese men scarfing down bowls of unrecognizable and frightening-looking ethnic food.

The part of Hong Kong we'd landed in was squalid, noisy, dirty and ill mannered after Tokyo and we hated every second we spent there. It was so much like *Blade Runner* it was almost exciting. Huge opulent skyscrapers with garish signs advertising Hi-Tech products loomed over the sordid stalls of street-vendors selling noodles and decapitating live chickens in front of your aghast Western eyes. Vast electronic billboards with moving images towered above sidewalks teeming with hunched peasant bodies under bamboo hats staring at us as we'd daze past like extraterrestrial visitors, thousands of rickshaws, bicycles and the buzzing of flies and neon. There was even a fine drizzle of rain to add to the Ridley Scott-esque cityscape. The club we did a P.A. in to rapturous indifference was in the moneyed part of the city, overlooking the harbour with its pleasure cruisers and yachts, all presumably owned by gangsters, drug-dealers, bankers and relatives of Bruce Lee. It was like the sort of club we'd outgrown in London two years ago and was called Mingles Disco. To compound our gloom and dissatisfaction, the only place we could stay in on Night Two was in the YWCA. Not the YMCA, oh no! Sean and I end up trying to get some sleep on cots in the Young Women's Christian Association! That rounded off our visit with perfect irony.

In full Samurai regalia, we played malevolent Samurai guards in a pop video for an artist named Nazia Hassan. Her song was called *Dum Dum Dee Dee*. The director was David G. Rose. David Bailey took photographs of us in our Jane Kahn Japanese clothing in '82 for a fashion spread in *Ritz* magazine. What a cool geezer and well handy with a camera, too. He was down to earth and not remotely condescending or patronising to us. We just took everything in our stride, as it came our way, but years later when I was working myself as a professional photographer I thought back to Bailey and wished I'd asked all those questions you store up in later years.

The legendary artist Felix Topolski painted our portraits too, after meeting us at the book launch for Simon Napier-Bell's dubious memoirs, *You Don't Have To Say You Love Me* at what used to be the old '60's Pop Star haunt, The Scotch of St. James. Another venerable giant of British Art, he too was gracious and generous and worked from an enormously cluttered studio under the arches on the South Bank. A kind old gentleman with a history to die for.

Chapter 18 - Pop Stars

Duran Duran are onstage at Birmingham Odeon, in late November 1982, and they're halfway through *Planet Earth* when, from the high reaches of the theatre, Tik and Tok slowly descend on nearly invisible wires. We hang suspended above the band and their 3,000 strong audience of (predominately female) screaming fans, rotating slowly like satellites from *2001*. The harness that enables us to achieve this stellar entrance cuts into my genitals in a most disquieting way. I look across at Tokky on the other side of the stage and he's managed to achieve an upside down position with his hair curtaining southwards on either side of his head. The kids go

berserk when they notice us and most of the band are quite surprised and impressed too. Simon Le Bon slyly suggested that we attempt our acrobatic entrance after he'd shared a couple of lines of so-so coke with us in our dressing room on the second night of the two shows in their home town. Mr Charlie (in his inimitable and irresistible way) gave us the faux courage to actually do the outrageous and possibly dangerous act without fear of failure.

Unfortunately Mr C. also gave me an uncontrollably streaming nose for the next two days. It was like I'd been infected with some kind of alien allergy, and nothing of paper or chemical origin could stem the incessant flow of clear, watery mucus from my proud proboscis. I was forced to resort to explaining that I was somehow the recipient of some inexplicable flu virus. We knew the Duran boys because Simon The Good had once had a liaison with Jane Kahn, who was now Sean's paramour and the designer and provider of all of our street and stage wear. They asked if we'd like to be the only other act on their two Birmingham gigs. We didn't um and we didn't ah, we just said yes. The Gift Horse will only open it's fabled mouth once in a while and we weren't going to let this equine moment slip by. On the same night of our descent from the gods we'd also done the second of our two support slots. I'd stood a little too close to the lip of the stage during our last number and clammy, over-excited, teeny hands pulled me into their midst. I lost my stage glasses and gloves in their feeding-frenzy to be close to anyone proximal to their panty-moistening idols, but you know what? I loved it! Seeing The Fabs back in '64 had left me with the previously unobtainable desire to experience fan-mania on a personal level and, lo and be-fucking-hold, here I was! It's a musky shark-pool of pubescent energy, all-powerful, sexual and primal and it will not be denied. Of course they weren't The Beatles (no-one will ever be, absolutely cannot ever be) but they were as close as you could get in '82, and these girls were going for it like predators after plankton.

Tony Mitchell, who wrote for *Sounds*, and who was pretty much our journalistic ray of light in the indifferent darkness of the pop press, gave us a two-page Tik and Tok spread called 'Time Waits For No Mutant'. On the smudgy pages, we laid out our ambitions to transcend from being just two weirdly dressed guys who did robotic mime with spikes stuck to our heads. We had big plans for music, films and stage shows. Already I was formulating blueprints and schemes for our first album, a concept venture that would be very futuristic in theme and would be called *Intolerance* (it was about attitudes to people who are different). Five month later Tony, who was now an ally and a friend, graciously pointed us in the direction of the opening night of a new club called Skin Two. Which was the very first Fetish Club in London. It was run by the entrepreneurial David Claridge in a disco called Stallions just off Charing Cross Road. We told him that we were looking for two girls to supplement our stage show, and he introduced us to a pair of well-built female strippers who could possibly assist us in our quest. Ingrid and Melody were a blonde and brunette double act who worked at a club named Sunset Strip in Dean Street. We met, we chatted and, one memorable night, just the two of them came over to my flat in Bayswater to talk about their possible involvement in our live act. About an hour later they took off their clothes at my request and things turned frisky. They kissed and caressed each other whilst I watched, wishing, wishing, and wishing that I had film in my Polaroid camera. Now Ingrid (the blonde) was on all fours demanding that I whip her with my riding-crop. Which I did, but not violently enough for her taste apparently. She was the first girl I'd met who enjoyed receiving pain, and it caused a momentary dichotomy within me. Which resolved itself when Melody slid to her knees and began to suck me. They egged each other on whilst making sure I was involved and happy.

We didn't end up using Ingrid and Melody in our act, but it was a joy to have auditioned them (or maybe they were auditioning me for their act?). It wasn't the first or the last threesome I enjoyed back then either. I discovered to my delight that girls who like to hang out with bands after gigs usually travel in pairs, and if you desired one of them the other had to be there too. For example, after one of our shows, two teenies came up to me in the scrum of people waiting outside the stage door and asked: "Are you going home with anyone tonight?"

"No. No, I'm not"

"Well, can we come back with you?"

"Let's go!". My major regret about the early 1980's is that no one had yet invented compact lightweight and affordable video cameras. Just think of the fun we could have had with a couple of those about our persons! Domestic VHS machines were clunky noisy artifacts the size of suitcases. Sean and I didn't have grown-up cameras at that time and it took us until 1984 to buy recordable cassette players like those used by reporters. I had a rudimentary Polaroid camera but, as the packs of film were prohibitively expensive, I didn't use it as much as I'd have liked. All our little Tik and Tok debaucheries and adventures were recorded straight into our internal memory banks, a somewhat less than reliable method of storing information, especially when played back twenty years later. Sometimes scenes are fuzzy round the edges and lacking detail, others are clear and focused. What we needed were Sensurround cameras plugged directly into the cerebral cortex and able to record sound as well as vision.

When, in 1982, Tik and Tok decided to shave the front part of their heads and glue little metal spikes and coloured jewels to their scalps we got a lot of attention from the press. A journalist named Robin Smith, who used to write for *Record Mirror*, gave us a full page in colour and spent most of the article inventively imagining how we'd had the spikes implanted by a Japanese company specialising in technology, and that we could actually pick up TV signals from around the globe. We loved that. It showed that if you gave these jaded hacks something a little different, a little bit more intriguing and tongue-in-chic they'd run with it. The spikes were a great hook visually, especially when combined with our hair, make-up during the day and Jane Kahn's extravagant clothing. Almost overnight we became the darlings of gossip columns everywhere, and we took it to the max when and wherever we could. I said in one interview that you had to learn to sleep in a different way in order to avoid shredding the bedding; in another Sean said that we were going to be moving into body-modification next. We lied outrageously to grab their attention, we told everyone with column space that we were working on a stage-show that would utilise props and SFX from the makers of Dr. Who; we planned to have two real female robots on stage with us called The Trans Sisters; we told one guy from *Smash Hits* that we were like *Mad Max 2* on ice!" *No.1 Magazine* got the info that we were teaching our cats Robotics! *Record Mirror* (again) were informed of our desire to have 'special medical calipers made for our necks'. And so on and on. All we did was just warp the truth enough to whet their appetites, and naturally they came running because it sells papers and makes readers sit up and take notice for a short while. Let's face it, in 1982 to early '84 there wasn't really that much happening to give you a jolt visually or musically, so we filled a little gap until Frankie Goes To Hollywood came along. The fact that our records were almost universally panned in the press wasn't too disturbing either really. We knew that we were well loved by our fans and in many ways that was enough. Although deep down I harboured an unreasonable and continuing desire to try and write the ultimate pop song. This was to our detriment really, as I should have just gone with the flow and let our music be as free form and inventive as our image and stage show were.

My two favourite single reviews are: "Could you take men with blue lips seriously?" (The single line review of the re-issued *Summer in the City* in *Melody Maker*, 1983) and "Effortlessly horrendous. That's all I can say." - Morrissey reviewing *Screen Me, I'm Yours* in some forgotten music paper in February 1984. The press were almost outraged by our desire to make music, how dare these two clowns soil our perceptions? Once they see that you have more ambition and creativity than they previously credited you with, they turn petulant and vindictive and it really is predictable. They do it to this day, they nurture someone and build them up, then when everybody starts to sit up and take notice, they feel that their power is threatened, so they try and denigrate the person. Even on our little plateau of fame it was apparent what goes on, imagine what it must be like to be hugely popular and successful and go through all that spiteful negativity.

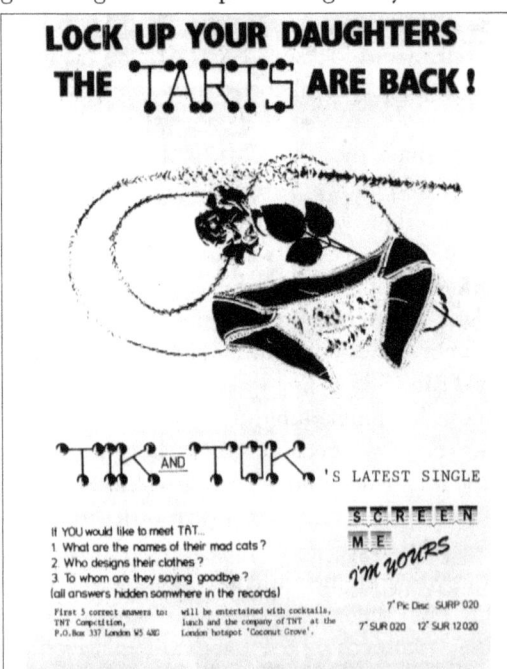

Chapter 19 – Warriors

> *"A huge bang ripped through the hotel. I ran down the corridor as Tik and Tok came out of their room, slightly dishevelled but laughing their heads off. Somehow they had blown up their toilet!"* Gary Numan *(Praying to the Aliens)*

Stoke-on-Trent, October 1983. Girls are throwing bras, panties and garter belts at us on stage! Sadly we realised quite early on that they weren't ripping the items off their excited moist bodies from the midst of the audience, but had brought along spares to fling at us. Fake roses are big gifts for us too, and our dressing rooms are like a fetish florists. The girls smear on heavy lipstick in virulent colours and kiss their signatures onto notes and letters. We've also noticed that an impressive number of girls in each town are wearing some items of clothing like our own: a leather cap with jewels and studs, a Jane Kahn frilled shirt, lots of crucifixes and bracelets, vast amounts of hair spray and big eye make-up. We also are given large quantities of cuddly toys, like monkeys in little jumpers with our names badly embroidered on the front. Other offerings include stuffed cats, dogs, frogs and a whole load of Pierrot dolls with slightly sinister painted faces. We are signing autographs everywhere we go. This is a first for us and it's making us feel like little stars for a while. Sometimes, with tongue in cheek, we sign as The Duke of Desire and The Prince of Pleasure and other times just as Tikky and Tokky. It's all wonderfully sweet and loving in a strange kind of way. There's also an undercurrent of teen sexuality that we seem to have tapped into. We get letters signed 'whippingly yours', 'spank me, I'm yours' or 'love and lust' and no, they are NOT from the boys. They are much more concerned with details of recordings, what instruments we use, "You got any T-Shirts?" and what did we mean when we said "blah, blah" in such and such magazine. I appear to be seen as the slightly more dangerous one and Tokky as the pretty one who needs mothering. Between the two of us, all tastes are catered for and we're certainly putting it to the test in as many hotel rooms as possible!

The sheer exhilaration and adrenaline rush of that moment just before we make our entrance onto the smoke-filled stage is unlike anything I've ever known. The audience are excited and noisy with anticipation as our intro music starts: a low bass drone with sound effects panning left and right across the P.A. The heart starts to pump, we have our ritual glass of brandy and quaintly shake each other's white-gloved hands before Sean makes his way round to the other side of the stage. We're wearing our red Kahn and Bell tail coats, white dress shirts, black bow ties and black jodhpurs tucked into black studded boots. We have white made-up faces, blood red lips, dark vampire eyes and our hair is long and dyed blue-black. It's a very powerful image. We have our round green mirrored ski shades on and, as we take our positions on the stage in the black out, we can survey the barely discernible crowd without eye contact. The red floor lights fade up through the haze from the smoke machines, the intro shifts into our robotic dance music (God, that's nice and loud), and we are revealed utterly motionless, frozen and awaiting animation.

On the first snare crash of bar five we start to move. In our perfect practised android motion, we glide across the stage and the audience goes bananas. It's an

extraordinary feeling. We really do feel exactly like machines! It's hard to convey the sexy power of this kind of movement, especially when you add it to strict mechanical beats and dramatic lighting. Towards the end of this four minute 'Robo Intro', we align with each other centre-stage and, when the backing track breaks for two bars with a very odd-sounding tearing noise, we turn our backs, raise our tail coat flaps and reveal two sets of preposterously proportioned plastic arses! Oh, how we laughed! It really was the most perfectly inappropriate finale to our Robot section. I wish I'd kept my pair of tie-on bum cheeks. They would have been a real conversation starter if they were mounted on my living room wall, like some kind of modern day stag's head, or possibly Aunty Mable's stuffed but no longer extant tabby Brian in his little plastic tank.

We segue into the drum intro of *Summer in the City* and take off our bow ties and tail coats. Sean always manages a suggestive little tease and wiggle as he removes his kit. Being more ungainly and impatient, I do a kind of rip and hurl action and hope the bits will be retrievable afterwards. We move to the microphones and say hello to the audience. It's a great moment as it shows Tik and Tok as real people up there, and reveals all the characters in the crowd to the two of us. We sing live over the taped backing track, moving around like newly freed prisoners of RoboWorld. We scamper off stage and do the first of several very quick costume changes. Number one is our post-nuclear, gas-masked assassin piece. It probably looks good from out front but to us we never quite capture what we think we should be doing in it. If nothing else, it gives us a chance to be abstract and vaguely unsettling for a bit. Plus we get to wield these brilliant thermo-rifles that our friend, model-maker, Rod Vass, gave us. However hard I try, and the harder I try the clumsier I get, Sean is ALWAYS ready before me.

After *The Gasmen*, we hobble out as our mutoid puppets in white skin-tight outfits with painted-on veins in fluorescent green. This section is lit only by ultra-violet light. We really do glow like fallout victims from space. This is a good one for us to show off another example of our Mime technique. The music is a kind of mutated dub Japanese Koto warped through a cheap transistor radio. We segue very neatly into *Vile Bodies* (without a doubt the best thing we ever did on stage or on record. It's a moving plea for tolerance in an uncaring world (it still gives me a shiver when I play it). Every time we perform it we know that the audience have been emotionally triggered by it. That is a truly splendid and special feeling.

To lighten the mood, we reappear as leather-capped, long rain-coated, fetish boys for *Screen Me, I'm Yours*. The song has an infectious quality and rhythm to it that enables us to tart around onstage and whip the girls' excitement up a bit. Somewhere during this number (I vaguely recall it being in Manchester at The Apollo), as on the Duran gig, I got just a little too close to the front row and to my delight I was pulled into the audience again. This was like being a proper Pop Star! I had all those damp little hands pawing at me and, for about fifteen seconds, I knew how Iggy Pop or Bono must feel every performance. Then some over-excited bastard stole the hat off my head! Oh well. I clamber back on stage and finish the song, high but chastened. (Hey! Story of my life!).

The finale to the set is our current single: *Cool Running*, released the day the tour started and on it's way up into the Top 70. We dash around a lot, throw out our Walkerprint promo cards, say our thanks and bye-byes and scurry off into the wings, heady with the thrill of it all. God what a rush! It was probably the best seven weeks of my life. I'm writing this thirty years later and I can still mentally recapture that sexy powerful energy. To this day, I get e-mails from people who were in their mid-teens back then, saying that experiencing our act was the most exciting thing they've ever seen. We were, quite simply, unique. That's why people remember us so vividly. I don't think that's an arrogant or boastful statement, it is an honest fact. We were undoubtedly very confident but we were never vain or condescending. I wish that there was some video recording of us at our live peak, but sadly there isn't. Lots of fan photos but no moving footage. I wish I could have seen us!

The two of us on that tour knew that it was a definite peak and we grabbed it with both claws. For the first time in my life, girls would approach ME, wanting to sleep with me, to share a moment in my company. It's what every hetero man dreams of and in those pre-Aids days it seemed perfectly natural, honest and somehow liberated. No one got hurt, no hearts were broken or trusts destroyed. I was young and single, and I went for it totally.

How did we get there? Gary Numan had undertaken a seven-week tour of Britain to showcase his album called *Warriors* and he had invited us along to open every show for him, starting at Glasgow Apollo on September 20th (Sean and I missed the tour bus and had to make our own way there!), taking in many major venues, including four nights at the Hammersmith Odeon (Hammersmith Odeon! The Beatles in '64! Bowie's retirement show in '73! and now in 1983 me! me!! me!!! me!!!!) and ending at The Dominion Theatre, London, on November 6th.

Numan's stage set is a colossal evocation of a blasted apocalyptic city, with various band members playing in shattered tenement block windows. Warriors of The Wasteland indeed. The lights create a blood red sick-looking sky as a backdrop. It looks utterly brilliant from the audience - like a real movie set.

Gary is stage centre in his ripped leather and metal outfit. His bleached hair glows under the lights. He moves well, punctuating beats and breaks with a thrust or a hand gesture, and his unique voice is much stronger than you'd believe it to be. He's flanked by the ever-amiable Rrussell Bell on lead guitar, and Joe Hubbard on slap bass. Joe was a sphincter of the first order! What made it worse was that he actually was a blindingly good bass player, but boy did he know it. The sound of the band is awesomely rich and powerful and loud like metal thunder.

Every night when *Cars* kicks in, after its famous wobbly synth intro, the whole place is up and going ape-shit, and we are too. Seeing 3,000 plus kids in every city, dancing and singing along to the encores from Gary's viewpoint must be the ultimate hard-on for the head.

After the show at Victoria Hall in Hanley, Stoke-on-Trent, Sean and I are changed and make-up less in our dressing room, entertaining visitors. A young male fan gives us a plastic baggie full of dried magic mushrooms as a gift (well, it beats being offered yet another embroidered simian). He says: "Don't take more than thirty, you might get a bit paranoid." Gary and the band, his Mum and Dad, perhaps some of the crew, and the two of us are staying in one of those grand provincial Victorian hotels. Normally home to weary travelling salesmen with body odour and bad posture, they are woefully inadequate when catering for a rock band on the road - the bar WILL shut at ten-thirty and you may just be able to persuade somebody to rustle up a cheese and pickle sandwich if you're very polite and very fortunate. I'm sure things are different now, but back in the early '80's it was still Tony Hancock land. The lounges in these places always seemed to be occupied by out of date copies of *The Radio Times* and at least one grumpy, moustachioed, ex-army Major who'd hide, seething and blushed with outrage, behind his newspaper as we checked in at the desk. We console ourselves with the thought that his granddaughter may quite possibly have lobbed a pair of her panties onto the stage about two hours earlier this evening.

Sean and I eventually find our room somewhere down a labyrinthine corridor and begin to create 'Tik and Tok World' as suits our needs. This usually involves re-arranging the furniture, removing bedding, setting up our small ghetto blaster and selection of cassettes, and emptying suitcases. However, this time we add a new diversion. We open up the bag of evil-looking little brown fungi and pour a carelessly huge amount into the metal teapot supplied as part of our room's 'refreshment facilities' (no mini bars in 1983). We add boiling water, stir and leave to stew for about ten minutes. We drink the brackish infusion as quickly as possible to avoid tasting the stuff, leave and lock the room and go down to the bar. It's luckily empty of travelling salesmen and carmine-hued ex-Servicemen and is now populated only by the two of us, Gary, most of the band, and a few partying crew members. We sit and do our charmingly eccentric social double act. Luckily, as it turned out, we'd decided not to wear our Cone Head masks that evening. In some other hotel in some other town, we had indeed gone to the post-gig party wearing these wonderful disguises. Whereas everyone else saw our little masked act as harmless and fun, Joe 'Neanderthal' Hubbard decided to take offence. He got mightily miffed about us sitting there as Ronnie and Reggie Dome (As we'd christened these eccentric characters), rose to his corpulent height of five foot six plus a six-foot ego and demanded violently that we take them off. He was trying very hard to impress some new girlfriend and assumed that we were in some way deliberately overshadowing his trumpet-blowing moment. Stick to playing the bass, you turd!

About fifteen minutes in, I feel a stirring in my blood stream and a quickening heartbeat. I look across at Sean and his dark eyes look like black holes in his mischievous face. The answer to my unasked question is obviously "Yes!". We are now in that 'us and them' alienation moment and we're having fun with it. We've been out-there together many times before and we trust each other. Somewhere at the edge of our hearing we become conscious of an insistent but gentle tapping noise. It seems that only we are aware of it. It stops. It starts again.

"What IS that?" None of the others have picked up on it. Then, to our amazement, a pair of hands appears, clutching at the sill of the outside window directly opposite us. A head comes into view, male teenoid, and peers into the room. Sean and I are transfixed, but still the rest of the cast are oblivious. The head tilts down, the hands disappear. Next moment the guy's whole upper torso comes into frame, obviously now standing on someone else's shoulders. He's holding up a felt-tipped placard that says, "TIK 'n' TOK - WE LOVE YOU!".

This event triggers us into the onset of helpless giggles and we decide to quit the party before it gets too frisky. We stand up to leave and say our goodnights. Blood surges upward and we lurch our way to the door. As we leave, we sense a kind of 'what's up with them?' vibe but it's not unfriendly. We seem to now be walking through warm, sticky mud and the perspectives of the lobby begin to undulate. We find the lift and hurry in with relief. Just at the moment of the grill closing, two teenage female fans squeeze through, breathless and giggly with nerves. They say, "Hi! How are you? Where are you going? Can we come with you?"

Fuck! Where did they come from? On a normal night we'd all enjoy ourselves up in our room, but things are changing uncontrollably quickly and we HAVE to be safely on our own RIGHT NOW! So we reluctantly ease them back out of the elevator with apologies and rise up to what we hope is our floor. Walking through mud has now become walking over the surface of a vast corridor-shaped bouncy castle. The floral patterned carpet is writhing underfoot and its tendrils are growing at an alarming rate. What the FUCK is our room number? Suddenly I find myself crawling along the jungle floor and laughing uncontrollably. This is so much like a scene from *The Shining* that it's now becoming scary. YES! There's that snake-like fire hose uncoiling from its wall mount. I see Sean far, far away, down the wrong end of a telescope. He's waving at me and I feel like crying. I hear his reverb'd-voice from a long distance, saying that he's found our room! I struggle upright like early New Romantic Man and weave to join him. We stagger in; lock the door and fall onto our twin beds and surrender. Every cell in my body, and indeed of everything else in the room, is visible and moving, like vast floaters in front of my opened eyes. I hear a big dog breathing urgently right next to my ear and I realise that it's me. My balls and cock feel odd and I want to hold them just for a while. I try closing my eyes but the view inside is so intense that I force them open and try concentrating on the tiny holes in the Styrofoam ceiling-tiles. The inside of my head feels like lizard skin, and it will NOT keep still for a moment. How do we get down?

Did I say that out loud? Is my every thought now being spoken? I can't stop staring at the skin of my palms, every painting that I've ever loved is there in my hand. The skin seems transparent, like a window into a chaos-theory universe. How do we get down? Do we get down? Can we get down down down? I shiver, feel sick and cradle my groin. Then we seem to plateau out and a frisson of 'normality' returns. Hey, this isn't so bad, is it! Sean and I are dazed and panting. I open the teapot, start counting and see that we must have taken at least sixty of the mushrooms.

Oh, Fuck! ... er ... what? "Don't take more than thirty, or you might get a little paranoid." Whoops! Suddenly we're gone again, thrust brutally back into this surging experience. It's like being forced back onto a painted carousel that keeps taking off. I look down and see us laughing. The dog is back, too. I wish I knew what his name is. We need music. I melt over to the tape deck and hit 'play' on whatever is in the machine. THANK YOU LORD! Donna Summers' majestic *I Feel Love* has been chosen for us. This really is a monster. Uncoiling, sexy and hypnotic. We play it continuously for several centuries. We lie on our beds fixed like astronauts leaving the Earth. The music pulses like God's heartbeat inside and outside us. It feels SO good - we can't stop laughing. WE ARE THE LIZARD!!! The Mushroom Journey is operating in 15- minute cycles, it's official. And now that we know that we're starting to get acclimatised. I glance over at Sean and see that he is kneeling on his bed, drawing with felt-tip pens all over the white sheet. An amazingly complex and extensive cosmic doodle. I find my own party piece. This involves turning the light in the bathroom on and off very rapidly whilst staring at my face in the mirror. In the jump cut, strobe moments, I see everybody I've been and who I'm going to be. I see myself in a bathroom in a house in 1976, 1972 and just for a second in a bathroom in a house in 2002. My face is a slide-show of interchanging personalities, some I know and recognise, others I'd rather not.

I remember the little stash of fireworks that Sean and I had accumulated in the run up to Guy Fawkes' Day. We've got baby rockets, squibs, wheels and serious bangers. I place one of the rockets in the holes in the sink socket and light it. It shoots upwards, burns right through the polystyrene ceiling and vanishes from view. Bloody Hell! We can hear it thrashing around up inside the gap space like a very angry hornet. Unbelievably it suddenly re-enters the room a few feet away and dies hissing on the lino floor. Not knowing or caring when to stop, we then get one of those big bangers with the pointy red end, light it, throw it into the toilet bowl and close the lid. It goes off a second or so later with a truly deafening explosion that flings back the plastic cover and showers the entire bathroom with water. Like trainee Keith Moons we escape out into the corridor, laughing madly, to be confronted by bemused Numan and musician faces. (The red-faced, ex-Army Major, being used to loud and unexpected explosions, slept on peacefully in his bed. He is dreaming of a lass named Lucy that he knew in his youth who in that weird dreamtime logic is now wearing a studded leather cap, fishnets and far too much make-up. She proffers him a synthetic red rose as he peels back the bed sheets.)

Still spaced out, we're back on the tour bus at 8 a.m. the same morning to drive down to the West Country for the next leg of the tour. On the journey, I doze fitfully when not watching *Mad Max 2* The-Only-Video-On-The-Coach for the umpteenth time and muse on how I got back to Earth with my brain still intact. I did, didn't I?

Towards the end of our tour with Gary we were contacted by the organizers of The Royal Variety Performance. This year's show was to be themed around dance and movement, so they'd decided that Tik and Tok would be the ideal act to open the second half. The irony was, that over the preceding months we'd done a huge amount of press interviews, and in every single one we stated that we were going to drop the Robots for good in order to be able to concentrate on music and other types of mime movement. But we saw this live TV appearance in front of HRH as a very good way to bow out whilst on top; especially as approximately 14 million people would be watching it. It's almost impossible to comprehend that figure, FOURTEEN MILLION watching little ol' me from Buttfudge, Illinois (sounds better than Redhill, Surrey don't you think?), and my pal, doin' our thang.

The night of the performance was also the last night of the Numan tour. A Limo whisked us to the Theatre Royal in Drury Lane. We had very little time to rehearse, but we didn't really need it as we'd been doing the robot stuff for three years and it

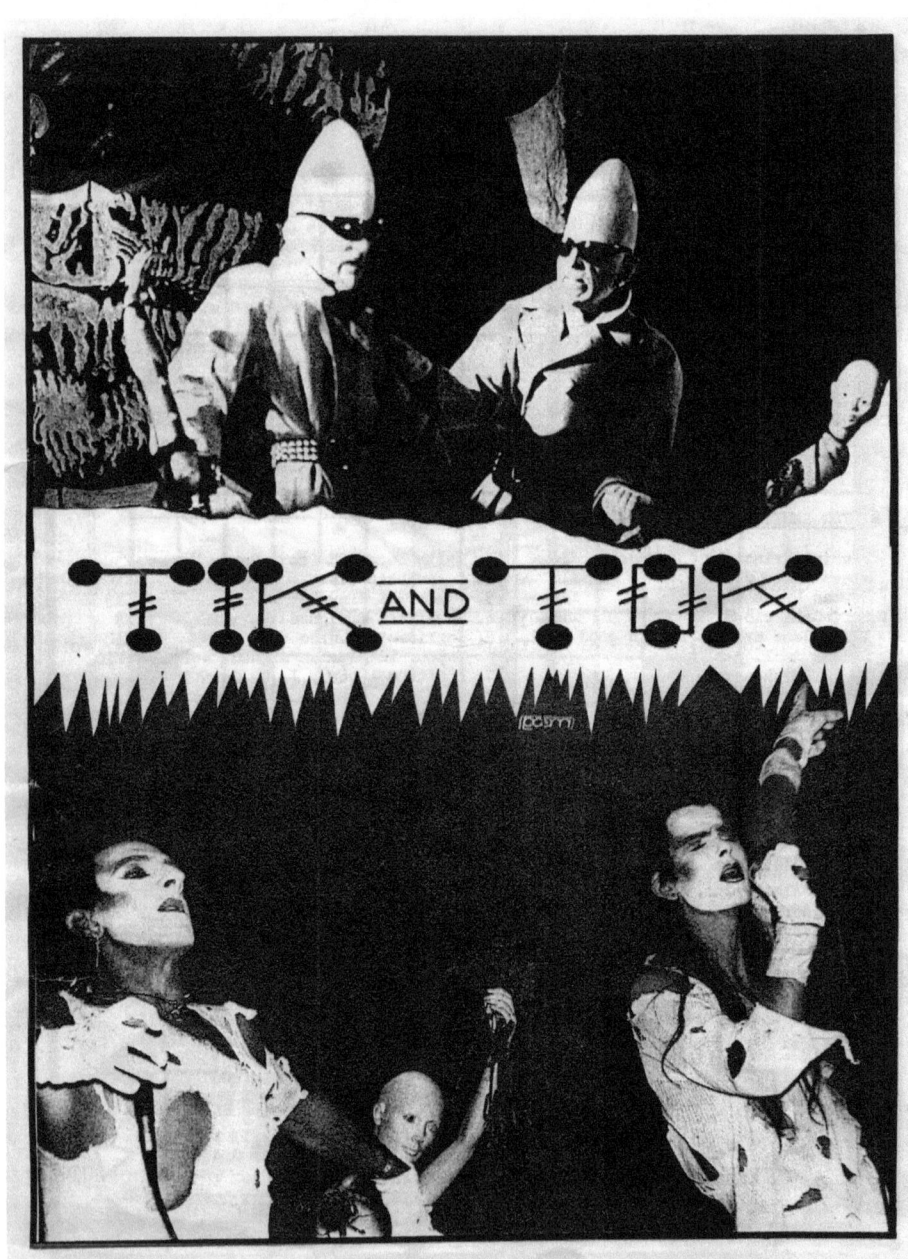

The Park fanzine (1983)

was second nature to us by now. They gave us a tape of the 58 seconds (!) of music we'd be moving to (a session man's facsimile of electro-funk), we played it through a few times and we were ready to go. Looking at the footage now is very amusing. You've sat through all manner of lycra wearing horrors, dancing schoolkids and tacky tap artistes, then this insistently rhythmic music starts and the compere announces: "And now, opening the second half of the Royal Variety Performance 1983, here are Tik and Tok!" The curtain rises up to reveal black knee-length boots, black jodphurs then the rest of us. HRH must have thought she was watching an enactment of some pre-war Fascist ritual. At the finale of our brief but glorious routine we had to incorporate a robotic bow to our bemused Sovereign and her consort, before we glid off into the wings. I was immensely relieved that the God Of Clumsiness didn't cause me to fall on my arse in front of the viewing millions.

The after show line-up was entertaining too, as poor, long-suffering Liz had to greet and inanely chat to the assembled participants who are, one by one, furiously bowing like mad as their turn comes round. We were at the back of the throng and because Her Maj is somewhat lacking in the stature department we only caught a glimpse of the top of her regal head. Phillip probably would have called us a pair of poofs, clipped us round the ears and told us to join the Navy if we'd been in his vicinity. We were heavily into our studded-leather, fur, jewels and crucifix look at this time and our entrance to the post-show party was a pleasing jaw-dropper-squeals of delight from camp male dancers and stern glances of disapproval from the more orthodox balletomanes. Lord Laurence Olivier was there too and professed an admiration for our act and our image (he may possibly have been lying through his theatrical teeth, who knows?)

The void of inactivity opened up after the hectic hedonism of the last few months of '83, and we were at a bit of a loss as to what to do. So we reluctantly accepted an offer to support The Flying Pickets (Remember them? Why?) at the Dominion Theatre on the 17th November '83, where only less than two weeks ago we'd done what was probably the best show of the whole Warriors expedition. On this unenchanted evening the audience appeared to hate us and manifested that emotion in the most vociferous way. As they largely consisted of retro-loving Doo Wop fans with drooping thinning quiffs, their inbred kids running amok in the aisles, and a sprinkling of indecisively 'Right On' lefties it wasn't a great surprise. Where were our girly fans with sexy gifts? Where were the screams and shouts of love and appreciation? Not there that's for sure. After a modest hail of insults and scrumpled-up paper consistently came at us over the footlights we were so pissed-off by the end of our Robot section that we ripped off our plastic bums and lobbed them into the audience. Hah! That'll show them! As soon as we left the stage at the end of our act we slunk rapidly from the theatre and caught a cab to Prince's Gate, Kensington where the mighty Vangelis was holding a party. Our bruised egos were bathed and soothed luxuriantly enough for us to breathe deep and think about what on earth we were going to explore next?

Chapter 20 - The Robot Finale

Tony Pony was the answer. A lanky streak of charismatic piss from Manchester with more front than Selfridges and a style of clothing and hair that latter day sociologists would fight over to work out. Who put the 'Anal' in analyse? Or indeed the 'Turd' in Saturday? I can tell you that it was Kevin 'Tony Pony' Gould. That boy could sell you anything, and do it with such charm and style that you were powerless to resist. He was working as a waitress in a cocktail bar when we met him. No he wasn't, that's just a cheap quote from The Human League, but he was working as a travelling salesman for a company that sold plastic bags of every size, shape and purpose. To his credit Kevin had come up with a tag line for a prospective kids' nappies manufacturer: "We're Number One for your Number Two's!" and that endeared him to us greatly. If anyone could sell Tik and Tok to the masses it must surely be this boy. He'd previously been managing the bass player Joe Hubbard, whom Mr. Numan had so graciously put up with on the Warriors tour, but he had inevitably grown tired of that onanistic string-slapper and had subsequently become obsessed with the idea of representing the two of us.

We kept him dangling for a month or so in a Bee Gee fashion to see how deep was his love, and in January '84 we finally agreed to a union that would hopefully benefit us all. Kevin could also provide a buffer between us and the two clowns who ran Survival Records, whose every action seemed to send us further back down the food chain. *Cool Running* had got to number 69 in the charts and was poised to climb higher but they blew it by spending no money on radio promotion and advertising. It was Sean and I who worked our plastic arses off to take that record into the Top 75, all they did was provide some Walkerprint give-away photos and a few TNT T-shirts that no one could buy. We were tied to those tosspots for five singles and an album; I loathed myself for signing to them almost as much as I loathed the two of them. Tik and Tok just seemed to be a wank-hobby for those upper middle-class toilet-eels, and now I'm recalling it I realise that I'm still full of spleen at the throwing away of our recording career. We were the best thing their crappy set up had and they were too cheap to do us justice.

But I have to say right here that even in the serpentine pit that constituted Survival we somehow found a great friend and ally in the beautiful persona of a young man with a talent for visual and creative ingenuity. Step forward Mr. Paul Edgley. His graphic design skills, and the innumerable evocative photographs he took of us are still cool and definitive today, and we loved and appreciated them very much. We made a verbal agreement with the talented Mr. Gould and he became our manager sometime in January 1984 and we ventured out onto a little sea of adventure. Now there were three of us in our bubble and we'd cruise the length and breadth of our tiny kingdom in Kevin's white Saab Turbo convertible. We persuaded him to lose the moustache, modify the hair, dump the 'Tony Pony' schtick and get a tad more audacious in his sartorial schmutter. He's got a good and generous soul that boy and he will flourish in whatever venture he turns his hand to.

I had a nice treat on my birthday that winter month, when two of our inner-circle female fans came round to my flat, knocked on my bedroom door, came in and flashed open their leather jackets to reveal two pairs of pert and naked teenage breasts for my present. We romped for a while and I realised that being thirty-two wasn't going to be as bad as I'd thought (I must admit that I had to my shame shaved three years off my age for press purposes, so they thought they were dallying with a mere youth of twenty-nine). I immediately went out and had 'Old Enough To Know Better But Young Enough Not To Care!' tattooed in Gothic script across my upper back. Or did I? Sean did in reality have a tattoo of a Geisha girl done on one of his bum cheeks, which I thought was terribly daring, and that did prompt me a while later to have two tattoos of my own done by an ink artist named Lal Hardy.

I met the seductive ex-punk singer Beki Bondage in July and we embarked on a relationship. I had a big penchant for bleached blonde, red-lipped girls in fishnet and leather and she was the Queen of them all. I fell in lust with her image and in love with her heart and her talent and invited her to come and live with me. It was good for a while and we wrote songs together, smoked a lot of dope, fucked and had fun, but in retrospect we really shouldn't have co-habited. It took away the spice and danger. But what can you do? You go where your heart or your sexuality leads you, and there's little point in regret or recrimination. I'd probably do the same thing again tomorrow if it came my way.

Nick Rhodes from Duran Duran told us to contact their A&R man at EMI to see if he'd be interested in signing Tik and Tok to the label. We met the oddly distracted man in question, Dave Ambrose, and told him of our plans for our future - films! TV! Video! Albums! Spectacular stage shows! He seemed to be attentive and impressed and said he would dispatch someone to see the next gig we did, and he'd like to hear more songs. Kakapoopoo had hitherto hit the transient heights with *Too Shy* and he was obviously keen to snare an act to follow them up the charts. It could be us! We were so excited; this could be the break we'd been looking for!

He even said that if it came to it, EMI would quite possibly buy out Survival for our recordings and release everything on their hallowed label. The next day I rushed to the Portastudio and started writing a song I hoped he'd like. It sounded suspiciously like Duran Duran (to my ears anyway) and was called *I Know That You Know*.

The momentum with EMI kept on building over the next few months, with deals and possibilities being dangled in front of us on a weekly basis. We did a blinding headline gig at The Venue in June - we literally filled the place with fans from all over the country, plus star guests here and there, and performed our best stage show to date. And WE DIDN'T DO THE ROBOTS! A few weeks later we did the same in a large club in Basildon, Essex and another excitable rep from the A&R department was there. He loved it and waxed long and hard about our golden future with EMI, and how good we were all going to be for each other. We believed it, totally and prematurely. The next day, Kevin sent a bunch of red roses to the secretary of every A&R man at the company saying: 'Congratulations on your imminent signing of Tik and Tok!'. It was a motivated and romantic gesture on his part which unfortunately fell on stony ground, as most of the Head Honchos at EMI had no knowledge of Tik and Tok at all, let alone the fact that they were going to sign us. Dave Ambrose then had to cover his tracks with his bosses and say that it was only an idea that he'd been toying with, and of course he wasn't going to sign these RoBozos to the label. To further secure his tenuous position in the company he basically told Kevin (and by default us) to piss off. We slunk back into the arms of Survival records and gritted our teeth. Where do we go now then?

We were so fucked-off with everything that we embarked on an extended, consoling relationship with cocaine and resigned ourselves to gamely trying to struggle on. We recorded and released the *Intolerance* album which included, *A Child with a Ghost*, a new song given to us by Gary Numan and he sang backing vocals and played keyboards on another track. I remember he walked into the studio with a couple of synthesizers under his arm; plugged them in, played them beautifully, and nailed it in one take. Tessa Niles sang backing vocals on the album. The following year she sang with Bowie on Live Aid. The album sold fairly well and actually got good reviews but it didn't bring us the joy we craved.

The rest of the year was filled with gigs, PA's, press interviews and dear Kevin trying hard to keep us buoyant, high and optimistic. Bless him, but that wasn't enough either. Nothing was ever going to be enough now. We were doing lines of coke before any movement we made. Need a piss? Have a line first. Had a piss? Well, let's have another line to celebrate. We'd talk all night, every swollen-tongued night, about what we could do, where we could go. No one else knew all this of course, it was just the three of us in the bubble, and we took care to keep up appearances in order to maintain what business we had. Even that started to crumble and we'd find ourselves hoovering-up seconds before we did a radio interview and then seconds afterwards.

We were booked to perform at Peter Stringfellow's club The Hippodrome on October the 11th, and decided it would be our last show as Tik and Tok. For me it was one of the saddest choices of my life. How could it have come to this so soon? What had we done wrong? Why didn't it work out? Was it my fault? If not, whom do we blame? Should we have just stayed 'Loveable Robots' forever? No, that would have been even more frustrating and unproductive. I don't actually think we did anything wrong, we may have made some erroneous choices here and there, but all in all we did what our hearts told us to. Ironically, this final show was the most spectacular we'd ever managed to produce. Visually and aurally it was adrenalin-filled and brilliantly theatrical. We got paid more money for it than we had ever received before, but we actually received less than we had for years. We had a lighting and stage crew to finance, plus our manager's percentage, but the truth of it was that the balance had already gone up our noses just so we could get through our farewell. I've got a video of our last gig and it's a sobering but yet, at the same time, intriguing chronicle of that moment. Except from our vociferous fans down in front of the stage, the audience are by and large indifferent to our performance. This, plus veins pumped full of powdered artifice, makes me angry and charmless and at one point I sneer at them all and shout: "What is this? The Night of the Living Dead or what?" I wanted, demanded a response, not from the loyal ones dancing in front of us, but from the mass of plebian and bored spectators who filled the rest of the club. It felt like we were giving ourselves to an arena full of jaded Roman aristos, bereft of taste and enchantment. Anywhere else would have been more suitable for our concluding offering, some sticky-floored dive out in the sticks, or a dark Gothic cave in Soho. But no, I guess we were ultimately the victims of our own indecision about EXACTLY where we wanted to be, and so it was almost inevitable that we'd bow out in the very type of place that we despised. On the video, right at the end, you can hear me say: "This is the last show we're doing by the way".

And that was it. Gone but not forgotten. The Internet hums and seeks out our name and our story. See Youtube weep and smile as it shows forth our performance on a Cliff Richard TV Special; dancing with Hot Gossip and Sid Snot on *The Kenny Everett Video Show*; hiding within cone-heads as Leo Sayer and a blue-haired Gary Numan perform Gary's song *This is New Love*. See us fall upwards from the low of a Larry Grayson Generation Game to the rock and roll high of Channel 4's *The Tube*, where we shared the bill with Iggy Pop and Lemmy. And see what we've been up to since. In some parallel universe, where time is non-linear and fluid, we are still out there. Just as we always were. We're only a mouse-click away.

Chapter 21 - Click

1989. I am having my photograph taken in a studio in North West London. Robin Chaphekar is a contrary but attractive mix of consummate artist and incipient alcoholic. He has very generously over the preceding years taken several portraits of me in different guises for free. Today we're doing "I'm An Actor, Daarling!" kind of publicity shots, much to our mutual boredom. I was not a conventional actor and dear Robin was not a conventional photographer. After an hour or so we capture whatever it was that I thought I needed at the time. We take time out to relax and be friends, not subject and hunter, and we drink lots of beer and whisky. I notice with envious glee that in one corner stands proudly (in an historical kind of "Eric used one of me back in '67" way) an original vintage Gibson SG, solid-bodied electric guitar. Robin (with a largess that I wouldn't even countenance outside surgical gloves) hands me this Rosewood baby to caress. And play!

He has a small but revealingly loud little Fender amp that he guides Mademoiselle Gibson through. I play some cringey sub-Clapton-esque clichés, then sit back and wistfully dream about "If Only's." Robin, to my joy and later Jungian recognition, picks up Her Fretfulness and proceeds to play, note for note, the entire guitar solo from the middle section of Steely Dan's *Reelin' In The Years*! How joyous that little moment! A connection made between then and now by some simple, well-placed notes of music. To this day I really admire Robin's ability to have sat himself down and painstakingly learned that part note by note. And he was primarily a photographer! Not a Failed Suburban Guitarist Wannabee, just a stoner with a lens who thought Why Not?

Chapter 22 - Mr. Sod and the Travelling Salesman

And the Lord said, "Let there be TV Commercials!" And lo! It was good. (And if not good, then at least very, very expensive). In 1982, Godley and Creme, internationally known for directing Duran Duran videos, hired Barbie, Sean and me for a wonderful surreal Wrangler Jeans advert. Barbie and I played a pair of Tango-ing robots and I drop her on her arse. I became 'normal', and, in February 1987, I signed up with Crawfords, the agency that still represents me. One of the first ads I did was filmed in Paris on some hideous factory estate, way beyond the boundaries of the Golden City. No shops or restaurants, no Boulevards and NO elegant beautiful women. I was playing a youngish, nerdy-type desperately trying to impress a girl behind the desk of a sports shop. (I think it was an in-house credit card sort of struggle.) I'm wearing a rather fine Prince of Wales check suit and brand new shoes, the soles of which were so smoothly unworn that each step anywhere was like heading onto the ice of a skating rink. After an eternity of waiting and growing boredom, I thought "Fuckkit" and went walkabout. I reasoned 'There's always a bar SOMEWHERE in France' and, sure enough, I find the most unattractive one in the most unattractive part of this wasteland beyond The Peripherique. I slide in on my skate shoes and come to rest only because someone had thoughtfully placed the zinc counter straight in front of me. I stand nonchalant from the waist up clutching the edge of the bar and ask in passable Francais for a cognac and a hard-boiled egg (don't ask). My guilty, slippery reverie is all too brief.

For after a mere few minutes of nearly consistently vertical relaxation, in bursts one of the crew, puffed and pissed-off, demanding my immediate presence back on set. I down the remains of the brandy in one gulp and, whilst gliding gracefully out of the door, brush tiny bits of eggshell off my suit. Am I chastised upon my return? Mais, OUI! The last scene of this 'not quite up there with Truffaut or Godard' oeuvre inexplicably involved me having a dirt-filled plastic flowerpot dropped on my head. It was small but HEAVY. The sadistic bastard insisted on filming at least twenty takes of this increasingly painful event. I ended up having to wear a kind of Yiddish skull-cap (black to match the dyed-hair I used to sport back then) to soften the blow. Finally, after his ego was satisfied, I was driven to the airport at about 150 miles an hour by some gleeful young runner on the crew. He had either just snorted a terrifyingly effective amphetamine, was wearing my shoes from wardrobe, or had never in fact been behind the wheel of a full-sized car. We got there, to his disgruntlement and, sweating like a drug smuggler, I tore up the plane steps as the engines started to kick in. I made it to my seat. Then realised I was still wearing the skullcap and had dirt coating me from crown to chest. Oi Vey, c'est une vie etrange!

The food chain that holds the whole thing together looks like this: THE CLIENT, with their PRODUCT to sell, contact an ADVERTISING AGENCY CREATIVE TEAM who, after heavy Groucho Club or Electric House sessions and a few token hours in front of the latest laptop, come up with an IDEA. Apprehensive Client receives or rejects said idea. If the Client says: "YES!" then the idea is developed further until it becomes an entity that will chew up a budget like a piranha coming off a two week no-meat diet.

I once participated in a commercial to promote the invigorating properties of tea. It was filmed over five days at Pinewood Studios, with complex and futuristic sets built on two sound stages and a company of seven actors. It cost a vast amount of money and, after presentation to the Client who rather churlishly declined to either like it or accept it, the whole thing was dumped quicker than a Mexican bean casserole. It is probably still languishing on a dusty shelf somewhere, alongside other scrapped masterpieces such as the mooted Sinclair C-5 Campaign: "Hey, Sir Clive, sure we can make it sexy. No problemo." Or the stylish and excruciating pilot commercial for a haemorrhoid ointment named 'Chalfont' that shamelessly parodies *The Grapes of Wrath*? (Incidentally directed by a certain Sebastian Scott, the younger and now unfortunately institutionalised sibling of Ridley and Tony). Commercials owe a huge, and in the main acknowledged, debt to the films and TV shows of yesteryear. Homage becomes pastiche, and it seems that no masterpiece is exempt from plagiarism. "*Citizen Kane?* Yeah, cool. Very fuckin' cool! We'll nick the whole lot for the new baked beans campaign." I look forward to the day when some Soho House 'Creative' decides to steal Polanski's *Repulsion* for a tampon ad. Everything goes into the blender: fave films, comic icons, music, fashion, technology, art and last, but certainly not least, sex. There is really no division between any of these media anymore.

"Life is just a series of Final Cut Pro jump-cuts, man. Find, and negotiate for, a cool song or piece of music, mash it up with some edgy, trippy visuals and we're in business!" Often, to kick-start an idea into gear, someone will decide to employ the use of look-alikes. You can rest assured that every well-known personality on the planet, living or dead, has a double who can be called in to replicate our screen dreams for advertising purposes. I know for a fact that Marlon Brando, circa *The Godfather*, lives in a small terraced house in Chiswick and rides a bicycle to auditions, and Jean Harlow (or is it vintage Madonna?) shares a flat with a colonic irrigationist in Clissold Park. Why not have a Brad Pitt clone, teeth whitely semaphoring health and cleanliness, clutching New Improved Whatever-It-Is for a thirty-second tease? It's certainly a lot more fun to watch than some scrofular, over-loud DJ or comedian down on his luck doing the same.

Back to our ever-growing food chain. The Agency must be titled only by the initials of its movers and shakers. This is mainly because their long-suffering receptionists invariably burn themselves out at an early age by having to chant continuously (in that weird sing-song manner adopted for some reason by all people who answer phones for a living) "Good morning. Bingle, Bargle, Cratchitt, Crackel, Boggs and Dingle. Can I help yew?" Four weeks of that and our Sharon will wake up screaming in the middle of the night. There may well be private clinics in the Essex countryside, populated solely by gently rocking, ex-Ad Agency receptionists, softly crooning, "Good morning! Bardle, Fardle, Bodle, Wodle, Biggs and Friggitt. Can I help yew? Can I help yew?" She will become mad-eyed with an immovable helpful smile plastered across a cracked Baby Jane face. Perhaps the doctors give these poor girls small plastic toy telephones to cradle lovingly in their pearly-nailed fingers?

The Ad Agency now has to find a PRODUCTION COMPANY. These people will find a team: Director, Assistant Directors, Wardrobe, Make-up and Hair, Crew, Runners, Caterers and (last but probably least) Actors! Then the Production Company approaches a CASTING DIRECTOR. These people are very powerful. They can decide whether to send or not to send an actor along for an audition. If they get on with you, and especially if you are lucky enough to get the job in question, they have a sense that you are capable and wanted. Therefore, they will keep you in the front of their minds the next time they are casting something. There must be a collective noun for Casting Directors, but I have yet to find a suitable one. In the meantime, we can posit and ponder on a 'snide' of actors, a 'bend' of hairdressers and a 'wank' of directors.

We do all know that none of this business should be taken too seriously, don't we? Otherwise, you really would end up barking mad. We also fathom that you could work at the National or the Royal Court for years, clutching your spear and posing for cheerful and unthreatening *Spotlight* photographs, and no one will know you from a hole in the ground. However, star in one commercial for a beer or a bank and every time you step outside your front door, some bum cleavage-displaying workman will grunt: "Ere, it's that geezer in the advert, innit?" Or bank clerks with pimples and Next suits will say in their strangulated City Speak voices, "Eeoh, gosh, saw you in that advert last night. You know, the one with the cactus and the gal in the bikini. Marvellous! Must be great fun to do, yah?"

"Er, yes it was. Now about my overdraft?"

No one gives a monkey's gust whether it's Joe Soap or Sir Johnny Big Job advertising their favourite deodorant. We don't care, we're not proud. We're not Sir Larry, saying in that resonant, thin-lipped, Old Vic voice that we'll never do Commercials, and then buggering off to America at the first opportunity to advertise Polaroid Cameras. Everyone is clamouring to take part.

"What's my motivation, love?"

"Do me a favour! Last week you played a nonce in The Bill. This week you're driving a Nissan around Stage Three at Shepperton in a poncey suit and hair-cut, extolling the incomprehensible virtues of yet another ozone-destroying vehicle. What's your motivation??? THE MONEY, LOVE, THE MONEY!"

They've all done it: Terence Stamp, Richard E. Grant, Joan Collins, John Cleese, the late Nigel Hawthrone, Uncle Tom Conti and all. You don't have to believe it to sell it. They know that Mr. Bank Balance is burping contentedly, tie loosened and relaxed, while Mr. Artistic Integrity can still go out and strut his stuff. Actors should get plastic Oscars for their contributions to Advertising. Why not?

Actors have AGENTS, a necessary evil. And actors always want to change their agents - this is a constant. Yet, secretly they know that they're lucky to have anybody who cares about them, let alone indulges and nurtures them. The Agent is asked by the Casting Director to suggest suitable Actors that they represent for various roles in the commercial, be it a 'fat, bald man with no teeth', or a 'blonde, sexy teenage girl', or even a '6'2", shaven-headed, big-nosed, character actor who moves well'. (Yes, that's my category, reading millions.) You dutifully go to a Casting Studio, usually in Soho or Covent Garden, and sit in a room with half a dozen others who fit into your category. You exchange 'Actor Small Talk', such as: "Hi, how are you doing? Been busy?" (desperately hoping that they've been as bereft of work as you have.) "Yeah. Just been in Scotland working with Mel on *Braveheart*.".

"Oh, really, that's great. Well done!" (Subtext: "You tosser! You couldn't act your way out of a paper bag!") In reality, of course, "Working with Mel Gibson" really means you were 'Angry Peasant Brandishing Weapon In Background', and not actually exchanging bon mots, drinks, drugs, and life stories with the Mega Mug. However, like all insecure and easily threatened people, they use what they can to gain a foothold on that slippery slope to stardom. At some point, a pretty but vacant assistant to the Casting Director will hand you a script or storyboard. "If you'd just like to take a look at this, Tim." Included on the clipboard are one or two forms that you're obliged to fill out, stating what recent work you've done (HA! HA!), your measurements, who or what your Agent is, and how you will cheerfully agree to the commercial getting shown all over the planet for no enlargement of your fee whatsoever. There is a sentence on these forms that implores you to state 'Any Current Commitments'. As this means absolutely bugger all, I invariably insert the words: A LARGE OVERDRAFT. This is in the vague hope that, if anybody actually reads these accumulated forms with their attendant supremely ugly Polaroids, they will receive a frisson of amusement at my cynical but charming honesty.

You're then ushered solo into another room where a harassed-looking Director awaits your presence. Also occupying the room is a long-haired Camera Operator who would much rather be filming a Rammstein gig, but "It's a job, innit?" who grins inanely at your nervous witticisms as you ingratiate yourself on tape. The Director says, "OK, Tim, we're just going to have a little chat, so give us your name and agent to camera and then tell us about what you've been doing, all right?"

With mini-interview complete, you endeavour to interpret the Creative's idea as a reality. Nothing we are called upon to do in these featureless rooms is too embarrassing or too undignified. After all, we're desperate for some easy money, aren't we? The most amusing scripts you are given are usually those originating from Europe. One in particular sticks like a skid mark in my mind. It was a German commercial for toilet air freshener (Is that whole nation obsessed with arses, body organs and shit?). Anyway, I was told to pretend that I had just delivered a particularly noxious bowel result in some closet-sized domestic lavatory.

In order to cover up the imaginary venomous whiff, I had to emerge sheepishly, frantically waving my newspaper, whilst shrugging in an embarrassed manner at my concerned spouse: "Aaach, if only we had a floral bouquet spray, my kleine duckling, all vould be clean und fresh!" Performing my little pantomime in a bare room to two bored people is bad enough, but the Director made me go through it at least half a dozen times to achieve the correct degree of finesse and degradation. Needless to say, I didn't get the job.

I have seen a giggling group of gorgeous girls reduced one by one to stripping down to their underwear for some perverse creative idea, captured on the Thrash Metal One's videotape. I have seen fat persons humiliated; ugly persons made to feel uglier; small persons reduced further. Can you imagine the miles and miles of footage the-powers-that-be must have stored somewhere that could reduce our already fragile egos to next to nothing? Do they run off footage of these horrendous humiliations to show at parties? "Hey, have a look at this!"

"Blimey, isn't that the geezer from *The Bill?*" After your Casting Session, you go home, visit your therapist, tear up pieces of old newspaper or whatever else you do in post-audition moments and try to forget all about it. Friends or loved ones say, "How did it go?" You mumble some perfunctory responses and resume your delicate modelling of the Starship Enterprise in used matchsticks that just might be presentable at the end of the decade. Then, maybe a day or so later, the phone rings. It's your agent, "You got the 'Golden Moments' job!" You break the good

news to all and sundry. Mum is benignly proud, actor friends are jealous (unless they are at the National), partners discreetly hint at holidays and new clothes, pets lick their lips and the Credit Card Family flex and clear their throats to attract your attention. Just for an all-too-brief moment, it all seems worthwhile and you've been bought a little bit of freedom. It's a good feeling. You muse briefly on what it must be like to receive regular money for your work and to be able to keep all the balls in the air at once.

I met my She-Devil of an ex-wife as she strode towards me from the fiery pit of Hell. No, this is not the vindictive and over-dramatic outpourings of a now bachelor. It is in fact a depiction of how I really did meet One Of The Few Great Loves Of My Life. December 1988. In a dingy, black-painted basement in Soho I went for a Casting as a Devil for a German commercial for the new Ford Fiesta. Geezer Graham, the Director, tells me: "Awright, Tim. What it is, yeah? You're like the head-Devil right? You've got this bunch of other Devils, yeah? And you are rilly, rilly pissed-off at God! So, just give me some anger, yeah? And tell that big fucker what you fink of him, awright? In your own time." Sure.

"OI! - GOD!! WHY DON'T YOU GET YOUR BIG ARSE DOWN HERE AND HAVE A LOOK AT MY FAAACKIN' MOTOR!?"

"Fuck me! That's brilliant!"

"You want me to do something else? Lower key maybe? More? Less?"

"Nah, That's triffic!" I get the job. Pinewood Film Studios. Early a.m. (Horribly early AM, in fact.) I'm in make-up having prosthetic horns, ears, nails and hairpiece glued to me by ever-cheerful, ever sympathetic, make-up ladies. I LOVE these girls! Whatever time of day or night they're always soothing, sympathetic and tolerant. If only I could have one for every day comforts. All the Devils (and there are nine of us, including Ross Kemp, as well as nine Angels) are wearing a very Germanic take on demonic fashion: lots of black leather, hi-tech accoutrements, tails and big biker boots. (Sean and I, in Tik and Tok glory days, somehow ended up in a club in Wiesbaden where everyone looked like this.) I feel good in this disguise, powerful and nicely wicked. I long to keep it after the shoot and thence STRIDE into Barclays, pushing aside awe-struck Devil-fearing customers and DEMAND TO SEE THE MANAGER! HA! HA! HA! HOOHAHAHAA! I'm actually the Head Devil and I've been told by God to create, with my acolytes, the ultimate motorcar. Unbeknownst to me the Big Guy has also charged a team of Angels with the same task. Oh, do hedge your bets! In the chair next to me is an (even at 7 a.m.) irresistibly sexy and attractive female Devil also undergoing The Glue (The glue incidentally is called ProsAid and was developed to attach missing bits of bodies to victims of explosions, war, and Saturday night fights in Stockport. It is fearsomely strong and the recipient will later spend many happy hours picking out bogey-coloured remnants from every orifice). It transpires that her name is 'Rosie' and she is warm, vulnerable, funny and very beautiful. We small talk and smoke fags during the long breaks to set up the next shot. We even swapped leather trousers before scene one because hers were too small, so I gave her mine. Aah!

By the end of day three of the shoot, I'm smitten. Like Barbara eleven years earlier, this is a girl I need in my heart and in my life. Rosie and I went to the studio bar at lunchtime in full costume.

"Oi! Look at ol' Bill Zee Bub - 'e's got the orn!!! Ha, ha, gurgle, gurgle."

"'Ello Darlin' - you look horny! Hur, hur, blurgghh." (The Niven inside me says, "I say, do you chaps mind! We're ACTORS don't you know? and these are our bally costumes!") "YOU WOT? YOU WOT? YOU WOTTTT???"

"Honestly, Darling - Directors in the bar - always the same!"

We had a few drinks and talked about life, the universe and everything (well, some of it at least). I felt I'd known her all my life. After consulting my personal make-up lady at the end of day three, who said, "Yes! Go on!" I plucked up courage, picked out glue-snot and asked Rosie if she would like to go out one evening. She said, "yes" so quickly that I thought she might have misheard. We were married eighteen months later. But more of that further along ... The actual commercial itself turned out so well that it was promptly banned in all the Catholic countries in Europe. Which titillated the cast, the Director and The Germans, but made Mr. Ford Fiesta himself rather pissed off. Well, what did you expect!

In 1992, I went to Prague, Czechoslovakia as it was then, to make a commercial for a French cheese named Chatelain. I'm met at the airport by two young Czech Dudes who I just have to call Bill and Ted. Trust me, if you were eighteen, ripped to the gills on what must pass for dope in Check 'O' Land, you'd be exactly like these two. I think. "This is cool, any minute now we'll turn into yet another factory estate and I'll meet, greet, and try on my frock for the job." Wrong. Two hours later we're still on the motorway, with Prague a mere stain on the far, far horizon.

Unfortunately before I left to do this job, I had watched the original version of *The Vanishing*. This is a bit like viewing *Coma* the night before you go into hospital to have a transplant. Bill and Ted have now forsaken talking to me about life in The West and movies and music, etc. In fact they've stopped talking altogether. Bill stares sullenly out of the window at the endless flashing-by dullness of the countryside and Ted drives hunched forward like Janet Leigh on the run in *Psycho*. And yes it IS raining. My foetid imagination whispers "Have I been abducted?" Bonhomie and cheerfulness at having another mini-adventure have been replaced by a creeping sense of utter isolation and, in all probability, imminent premature burial. Finally, just as I've definitely decided upon having *Bohemian Rhapsody* as the only music to be played at my funeral (if they ever recover my body) we turn off the German built Autobahn (keep those tanks a rollin') and head up a majestic avenue towards the most Hammer Horror Gothic-looking castle I've ever seen. Both Bill and Ted are now sparky and chatty. They tell me that this Schloss is where we're going to be filming and that it was the Headquarters of the local SS during The War. Apparently I'm playing Baron Frankenstein.

I'm not actually staying at The Castle. I am billeted in a bunker-like hotel in the nearest town. The hotel has armed guards in the foyer, the most hysterical décor this side of the early '60's, and a tiny black and white TV in the room that you can just about watch and still retain your tenuous grip on reality. Of course there is absolutely NO Pay Per View channel. Instead there are a humble three channels seemingly consisting of baffling Czech sitcoms and game shows, and intermittent sinister propaganda documentaries. I take several badly exposed piccies with my camera on the self-timer of me surrounded by a ziggurat made of my Per Diems (a huge selection of local currency that I can neither spell or pronounce, that in Sterling would amount to £30 tops) in a vain attempt to amuse myself. I do however have a nice cossie for my character, and an Igor-like sidekick whose real name is 'Bobo' (who allegedly is the bodyguard of someone powerful in Prague). I'm wearing a wig and a moustache that make me look like the guitarist in a West Coast Psychedelic band from 1968. It may be just my nostalgic and perverse sense of humour, but I've sometimes wondered over the years what I would look like as Ray Dorset, the singer of early '70's band Mungo Jerry. You know, *In The Summertime*? Anyway, sometime in 1998, I got my wish. I'm in Capetown advertising a lemon-flavoured soft drink for the Germans. Why Sarth Ifrica? Because it's a cheap place to hire crew, locations are totally unreal, and normally the weather is reliably consistent. Unfortunately the day I hit town the climate changed from tropical to Skegness.

"Mein Gott, alles is scheisse!" Yo, Fritz! You may have your technical problems but HAVE YOU SEEN WHAT I HAVE TO WEAR? OK, I'm adorned with Mr. Dorset's improbable Afro (yes, very inappropriate) and sideburns too, BUT I have to wear a pastel, lilac, track suit-jogging kind of kit, with horror-beyond-adequate-description fawn leather slip-ons!!! How much more suffering can 'My Art' take? Compounding my sartorial cheesiness is the fact that I have to spend an entire day running up to and smacking my head into, a seven foot high dummy bottle that is wrapped in bright blue fabric.

"It's for ze 'Blue Screen' Tim, you know?" Yes, I do know. Thank you.

We're filming on a grassy knoll (I checked earlier for hidden snipers) in front of the turbulent grey power of the Atlantic Ocean. It looks like Tellytubby land and a large crowd of bemused locals is standing directly in my eye-line watching my repeated activity. It's about as surreal as you can get, and apart from a throbbing head from repetitive bottle-bashing, I realised that however absurd this work may appear for a grown man to be doing, I love every second of it. The previous evening I'd dined on prawns the size of a baby's arm, followed by Ostrich steak in a beautiful colonial-style restaurant on Long Street (very much like old-town New Orleans). I'd pleasureably swigged down a bottle of local red wine, savoured a huge brandy and lurched back to the guesthouse hoping that I didn't look affluent enough to be seen as a target. When not avoiding eye-contact with shadowy individuals lurking under trees I passed the duration of the walk counting the vast amount of ARMED RESPONSE! signs attached to the doors and fences of virtually every home or shop. One major source of embarrassment and amusement occurred during the filming of a commercial for a detergent in Milan. I'm playing a burglar trying to jemmy his way into a padlocked shop door late at night. I've been kitted out in T-shirt, grey hooded sweatshirt, black plastic coat, trainers and severely shabby looking jeans with holes in the knees. I was ordered not to shave for five days before I flew out and, with the manky costume and stubbled-up face, I'm looking 'well dodgy'. I look like Eminem's father after a massive night of debauchery in Milan's red-light district (is there one? I've never found it).

The film crew have taken over most of a side street in a quiet part of the city, and it's full of the paraphernalia of Italian film-making: a Winnebago with interior bulb-lit mirrors and a malfunctioning chemical toilet; endless supplies of tiny plastic cups of neat Espresso coffee; crew members in black and quilted all-weather gear; snaky cables writhing all over the pavement and road; a sad and bored looking guy whose only function appears to be squirting evil-smelling fake smoke from some kind of Zyklonesque canister before every take of every set-up; Director and DP crouched in front of the playback monitor and, most amazingly, a huge sphere of light encased in a balloon-like edifice tethered high above us that illuminates the whole of the deserted street. It hangs like an omniscient artificial moon over the entire location, and I've never seen anything like it before on any other job. There's another recruit whose sole purpose is to spray the pavements and any adjacent object with a fine mist of water before every turn of the camera, and that includes myself.

I was called on set at 8pm and, after a chilling cab journey to watch the final takes of the interior set-up, was told that we'd all be now going for dinner. The Production Company had appropriated a restaurant in an adjacent street for this very purpose and we hurried in like vultures who've been granted an expense account. I take a place next to the Director of the 'Meisterwerk' and his DP at the end of one of two long tables. We have fresh bread, pasta and risotto, as a starter, veal, potatoes and lamb as a main course and, in a gesture unknown and uncountenanced in good-old-anal Blighty, we're served copious amounts of red and white wine to enhance our pre-shoot respite. The Director and his Director of Photography are both Swedish, and they tell me with glee that, whilst filming some unmentionable earlier commercial in Budapest, they'd stumbled upon a restaurant serving as one of the main courses a dish with the glorious name of 'Shite Burger'.

They smirked but did not partake. I laughed and told them that, according to my Norwegian friend, Georg, in his wintery homeland they have a dish that is pronounced 'Shit Kakke'. Upon being asked by the Producer if I could speak any Italian I proceeded to tell them the two phrases (apart from 'yes', 'no', 'please', 'thank you' and 'how much?') that I had recently mastered with the aid of my quatrolingual last girlfriend: "Fuck Off!" and "Shit-Dick!" The silence was deafening. My foot has my own name written upon it, and therefore has an unerring ability to enter my own mouth.

It's now 11.30 PM, and it's time for me to spend the next seven hours doing what I'm here for. I pretend to be an Actor and make my way in front of the cameras to simulate a desperate and twitchy burglar crouched in a doorway with active crowbar. We do several takes of variations of my furtive motions and afterwards drink yet more coffee and smoke more cigarettes until the assistant tells me that they're ready for my big moment. This will involve me running full pelt along this lunar-lit street in an attempt to evade the searchlight beam that has mercilessly pinned me. I stand behind the crew and Director and wait for the universal chimp-call of "Action!" It comes and I launch-off down the street as fast as I can go. Unfortunately my arse has other plans. And it chooses this very moment to unleash an unexpected fart of such fearsomely reverberant power that I doubt my own humanity. I wisely decide that the best thing to do is just to keep on running and hope that they're not recording sound at the same time. About 100 yards further down the street I hear a distant Director-voice yelling, "Cut!" I stop and search for breath, and in that "Oh, God, I really did blow-off like a bean-fed trouper" instant, my knee-ripped and far-too-wide-around-the-waist jeans choose to drop slowly but inevitably and degradingly to my ankles as I stand panting on this once-proud and elegant

Milanese street. My ego was swallowed like a Panto-Whore's jizz and I shuffled my way back to the starting position for several more takes. Nothing was said about my Bottular Expulsion, but you can bet your life that if there's an Italian Dennis Norden then he will be replaying my glorious 'flatulente' in surround sound for your prospective Euro TV pleasure.

Early autumn, 1994. It's late morning on a dull weekday in one of those vast Orwellian shopping centres that you now find on the outskirts of every large city in any segment of the world. It could be Milton Keynes, Paris, Dallas or maybe Hell. This one in particular is out near the airport in Hamburg in Germany. The sky that lowers above this chosen wasteland is dark grey and thunderous like a cinematic bruise, heavy with imminent rain. The featureless monochrome area seems to be devoid of people. Cars and coaches slick in and out as if in a hurry to be away fast. In the epicentre of this temple of Mammon that compels yet repels, squats a neon-lit hamburger restaurant with its familiar red and yellow colours glowing invitingly in the gloom. Panning through the metal and glass doors you will spy inside blonde families with noisy excitable children who squeal, climb and want to eat everything they see, whilst the somnolent parental eyes slide dully down the plastic menus. Sporadically placed are older German couples who, suddenly estranged from their methodical and comfortable tourist guidelines, are now bemused by the vivid and futuristic atmosphere with its noisy American-style flashiness: "It's not food as we know it, Willi. What are we doing here? We should be having our normal beer and sausages. But because we thought we were only just passing through, and are now suddenly feeling slightly lost and peckish, here we are."

A gaggle of teenagers huddle at a couple of tables, loud with the braggadocio of youth. They are invariably clad in T-shirts logo'd with the names of Death Metal bands or Rap artists blazoned in red and white on black. The boys, sporting bum fluff moustaches, bad hair and cracked voices, feel powerful with newborn machismo. They feel spurtful and thrusty like Colin Farrell or Snoop Dogg in some cable TV movie. The girls are pert-breasted, smooth skinned and wear their hair teased to musky virgin perfection. They chew gum and practice their pouts. Efficient staff, wearing cheery smiles like Stepford Wives, and clad in neat uniforms but sadly burdened with the additional horror of very bad skin, endeavour to serve everybody as quickly as they can. There's a slight hesitancy when ordering from the older patrons. These American names and phrases sound new and un-comfortable, like the jargon of a world that no longer contains them. They crane their weary heads upwards and try to dimly focus on the photographs of available food displayed above the counter. Yet in some way it all fits together. It's fast food for faster lives, the old and the new.

Suddenly, without warning, the doors of the Burger Bar burst open and in lurches a 6' 6" gleaming silver Robot, obviously in trouble as he is weaving and staggering in an alarming way. One brutal arm is thrust out at a wild angle, while the other spasms uselessly and randomly at his side. His head, helmeted like some fearsome ancient warrior, swivels uncontrollably as if desperately searching for something or someone. Scattering once happy eaters like skittles, he continues his berserk motion through the restaurant. Huge and heavy booted feet stamp their progress on the patterned tiled floor. Thighs like galactic metal tugboats churn with dwindling power. He not only has the gift of speech but he also appears to have learned German, for as startled Woppa munchers dodge his mighty Titanium torso, he says: "Entschuldigung ... Entschuldigung" (Excuse me).

Mouths gape, milk shakes shake, French-fries fly and silence descends like Mime Show muzak. Hands with ketchup-smeared digits freeze-frame in mid-motion. Now the staffs' smiles really are stuck on their pimpled faces, as if caught in some alien wind. Slowed down drastically as if walking through a sea of peanut butter, the Robot valiantly carries on until he reaches the back of the restaurant, near the counter. His voice, once feared throughout Empires, is now reduced to a sound similar to a midget whispering in a bucket. With one final, immense, grinding shudder he stops dead, arm still extended, standing on one leg in mid-step. Unearthly hissing and buzzing drifts from his visored visage.

Nobody moves, nobody speaks. The air regroups itself around his stillness. A brave little girl with blonde cliché pigtails like Gretel timorously walks toward our Heavy Hero. With a charming innocent smile, she reaches up and hangs her bright plastic school bag on his rigid, out-stretched arm.

"AND ... CUT!" says the English Director in his cosmopolitan cockney voice. The entire restaurant clientele of extras and film crew burst into spontaneous and genuine applause. And I smiled grimly to myself. For inside the Robot's metallic suit, sweat drenched and aching, was yours truly. One of my two wardrobe assistants swiftly removed my helmet so I could breathe properly while I enjoyed a brief respite before the camera turned again. My head was flushed and pink. I was playing a character I shall discreetly call 'Robo Burger' in four commercials, shot one a day in Hamburg (very appropriate), to promote a free newspaper named Kino News in all branches of a particular Global Hamburger Conspiracy. How did it all come together?

At a Casting Session I'd showed the Director and the Clients a bit of mime-based robotic movement, luckily impressing them enough to land the job. Then a few days later I was summoned to the depths of south-west London to the workshops of a large and successful company who specialise in making props and special effects for TV shows and films. It was there that I had an appointment to have my first fitting for 'The Suit'. After a quick tour of the vast building and its contents, room after room of monsters, spaceships, severed heads and hands, mutilations, futuristic cars, bits of torsos, and weapons of every description, I was ushered into the Plaster Room. If a severed hand for a certain scene in a horror film is called for, then someone like myself has the relevant limb encased in a bucket of Alginate, a hybrid concoction of various sea-weeds that is pink in colour and smells vaguely minty. It was originally developed for orthodontists to use for the casting of patient's teeth and gums quickly and easily in order to make dentures. It dries amazingly fast, forming a hard but very flexible compound from which a plaster master is made, which can then be modelled into a hand or limb.

Having dunked your digits in the Alginate and been left to dry, your hand is then eased out, it feels like taking off a very thick and tight-fitting rubber glove, leaving your skin feeling clean and refreshed. I personally swear by the stuff, and never leave home without at least a ten-pound bag of it somewhere about my person. You never know when that tired old skin might need a bit of a pick-me-up, do you? I can hear an annoyingly twee little jingle composing itself somewhere in my head even as I write. I see gently waving field of summer flowers and a inanely grinning post-nuclear family gambolling playfully, coated from head to perfectly formed toe in bright pink shiny seaweed compound. "Oh, no! Little Johnny's fallen over!" "Don't worry, Mom, he'll just bounce right back into shape!" STAY CLEAN AND FRESH, THE ALGINATE WAY!

I'm back in the Plaster Room about to have my whole body cast. They need to get my exact shape replicated so they can model and carve the plated armour in which I shall be interred. After stripping down to my black M&S undies (no Calvins for this boy), I had to stand stock still with my arms slightly outstretched while three not unattractive young women smothered my torso in Vaseline. This is the sort of thing that most men have fantasized about at some time or another (I know I have, although the situation would really have to be a tad more exotic and playful for my taste) but any frisson of sexual thrill rapidly evaporated once I was glistening and slippery and saw the girls stirring vast quantities of plaster into plastic buckets of lukewarm water. Then they started wrapping the front half of my shininess in four-inch long strips of plaster-soaked gauze bandage. Very quickly I was coated from toe to neck. It gets pretty hot under there. Making a seam down the entire length of my body, they then covered my back half in the bandages and five minutes later I was immovable and rigid, only able to rotate my head.

So far in my life, I have managed to avoid being buried up to my neck in wet sand, but if I am ever unlucky enough to have it inflicted upon me at least I'll know exactly what it feels like. Now the girls, who had transformed in my imagination into Macbeth's three witches, eased a bathing cap onto my skull and were covering my face and the rest of my cranium in plaster, having Vaselined that, too. Front and back were also done in two halves.

So there I was, like some ancient Golem, frozen in plaster, unable to see and barely able to wriggle my toes, hearing one of these sadistic sisters say in my ear, or where she hoped my ear was, "OK Tim, we're going for lunch now, we'll be back in an hour or so." Oh, ha! ha! That's most amusing! But now the most bizarre feeling oozed through me. I started to feel as if I was falling slowly and inevitably backwards. Luckily, all three girls were actually holding me up and proceeded to tell me so. Edgar Allen Poe, eat your telltale heart out. I know how it feels to be buried alive. Then, a thought popped into my head like an insect eating its way towards my brain, "I CAN'T BREATHE! I'M GOING TO HYPERVENTILATE! HELP ME!" This was genuinely frightening and I could feel myself in the early grip of real panic. Intuitively the girls yanked off the plaster head coffin and suddenly I was back, feeling like I'd finally reached the surface after a deep-sea dive. One last moment of torture to go: having the front half of my carapace removed. However carefully I'd been greased, there inevitably were stray pubes embedded in the rock hard plaster. They were rapidly removed from my body with a feeling that those girls who wax their bikini line will know oh so well. I suffered for my Art, believe me, Dahling!

A week later and the wardrobe masters, Chris and Colin, had laboured long and hard to create the suit I would wear as 'Robo Burger'. I felt positively Medieval once I'd been strapped, squeezed and Velcro'ed into the armour. What I hadn't realised was that because of it being manufactured in fibreglass, my jointed and angled magnificence was not only incredibly heavy, but also very uncomfortable in a chaffing, pressure point kind of way. After a long day on location, coupled with my inability to sit down unaided, this caused a virtual rainbow of bruises on my thin but oh-so-muscular body. However, one must always recall my personal Rule Number One In The Making of TV Commercials: ALWAYS REMEMBER HOW MUCH YOU ARE GETTING PAID FOR HOW LITTLE YOU ARE ACTUALLY DOING.

All the work the two good-natured wide boys had done was pretty mind-blowing. Once the gloves, huge boots, wires, LED's, strange markings and insignia had been added it all looked bloody amazing. I knew I would scare the scheisse out of innocent citizens in Germany. I had a remarkably well-defined codpiece to cover my groin, but having a piss would inevitably involve removal of my mid-section. A certain amount of planning ahead would prove to be necessary, along with a reduced caffeine intake. Chris and Colin had never been to Hamburg before, and being the sexually charged whippets that they were, I took them out on the town. First we stopped at a busy, lively, new restaurant and then we moved on down to the red-light district, the infamous Reeperbahn. A seedy, dangerous, exciting place to visit, with its Fuck Clubs, sex shops, dingy bars, neon signs and hookers perched in windows along Herbertstrasse. It makes you think of how thrilling it must have been for the young speed-fuelled Beatles to play and stay there for months at a time in the very early 60's. You can buy guns, flick knives, throwing stars and any manner of dispatch items in the tourist shops along the Reeperbahn.

Bizarrely, these are on full view mixed in with souvenir snowstorms, hateful china statuettes and assorted Hamburgian mementoes. I wonder how many visitors have brought back home mementoes of a very different kind from the Reeperbahn whores? It makes you pray that you're never down there on a weekend when the sailors have hit town and the bars have just closed. Chris and Colin's lusty bravado was dimmed somewhat by our discovery on open display in one particular sex shop of various coprophiliac magazines. 'Po Po' was one that remains in the memory. Suffice it to say that seeing women and men as recipients of someone's barely digested; squeezed-out food is not what they or I got off on. Shock-horror turned rapidly to amusement as similarities to various brand name chocolate bars were spotted and this diffused the disgust to some extent.

For these commercials I was required to deliver my dialogue in German, and one particular section of dialogue in the last ad caused a little bit of a problem. Robo had to march menacingly into an ornate and grand hotel lobby, straight up to where a harmless and mild-mannered businessman sat reading his *Kino News*. Robo says, "Hi". The man, startled and nervous, says "Hi" back. Robo then points up to the ceiling and says, "Schauen sie mal die hubschen vögel da oben?" (Can you see those pretty birds up there?). Mr. Startled follows Robo's gesturing, diversionary arm, which then snatches the Kino News out of the executive's limp hands. Robo strides triumphantly off, yet again scattering gob-smacked bystanders. Unfortunately, what actually emerged from my mouth during take three was: "Schauen sie mal die herbly gerbly turdy burglies?" Which caused not only Herr Robo but all the cast, crew, clients and the director to crack up completely. This was helplessly repeated in every subsequent take. Once your mind has made that awful leap to speaking the wrong bit of dialogue, it is almost impossible to correct it. However, the client was particularly impressed by my improvisational flair. He asked me to record my extemporaneous phrase into his DAT recorder for God only knows what unholy use. Po Po News, maybe? Thankfully, Robo strutted his stuff quite magnificently in all four ads and people were quite genuinely scared of him. Yes, I did play up to that. It was great fun really and the money I earned kept me afloat for months. The bruises faded eventually, too.

Chapter 23 – Carpe Diem

"Mea Culpa... / Is it love / Or is it lust / That makes us do those foolish things?
Is it God / In whom we trust / Who will tell us what tomorrow brings?
Bye, bye darling Don't cry... / What we do / And what we share,
Must lead to something or so they say. Is it right / Or is it fair
How we give and then we take away? / I'll smoke another cigarette,
Pour myself some wine... Bye, bye darling / Don't cry..."
Darling by Noir ©1996

I never thought I would end up being married. It seemed an event and a state of being that others sought and achieved, others who were less fearful of long-term commitment and maybe more grown up than myself. Being an ex-hippie, and still carrying a fair amount of impractical bullshit leftovers from that distant incarnation, marriage seemed somehow old-fashioned, the sort of institution that previous generations had rushed into for breeding and security. Oh, and for love of course. "It won't happen to me," I told myself over the years and, as the early to mid 1980's gave many opportunities for casual sex and short-lived romances, I was glad that it hadn't. But then out of the blue in the summer of '86, my friend, Tony, announced he was actually going to do it - take the plunge, tie the knot, get hitched to a girl he'd been with for three or four years, and that came as a bit of a surprise. He'd always presented himself as a perennial bachelor, a rake loose on the streets of European cities, discarding maidens left, right and centre and laughing with devil-may-care abandon as he leapt onto his horse from yet another balcony and left town pursued by vengeful fathers or older brothers. So his decision cast some odd shadows. Not only about his true needs, so well concealed all those years, but also about a possible shortcoming in myself. The cynic in me questioned his staying power, and all that declaration stuff in the sight of God, and the twee quality of traditional wedding ceremonies, with their floral-crowned bridesmaids and proudly flushed relatives, left me a little unnerved. It felt like that inaudible siren-like call actually does lure every one of us to an altar. Paradoxically, I also envied him. He'd found someone that made it all work, that gratified him and his ego, that somehow balanced him. A partner. And there was one point in the church service, when he and his bride were

exchanging their "I do's", that touched me deeply. It was the look of happiness on his face as he turned to her. It re-kindled a deep longing that smoldered subliminally deep down inside me. I was there with my ex-partner, and my now best female friend, Barbie, and I know the moment touched her in the same way. We both held back tears and gave each other's hands a little squeeze, as it wasn't that many years earlier that she and I could have taken those same matrimonial steps. But, for reasons that would become clear in the not too distant future, we hadn't.

B and I were still clinging to our mid '80's personae and images so we were dressed all in black with coloured hair and lots of jewelry; sorely standing-out like septic thumbs in a sea of white. Everything was white: dresses, suits, clouds, flowers, cakes, teeth and veils. If Billy Idol had been invited he would have run home screaming, tearing at his peroxide roots, and been compelled to bang-out a crude demo of *White Wedding*. It was surreal, amply illustrated by the fact that neither of us featured in any of the wedding photos. We could almost see the thought bubble above the bored wedding photographer's head: "Jeez, how do I move the two spooks out of frame?" Maybe when they clustered around the contact sheets, Tony and his wife would discern, through the magnifying loop, two silhouettes manifesting on each image like a scene from *The Omen*?

Anyway, the momentary pangs of longing receded shortly after attending the event and I settled back into bachelorhood. I continued to dally and frolic with abandon until all of a sudden the spectre of "The Big Disease With The Little Name" (as Prince succinctly described it) began to loom over our hedonistic lifestyles in the hetero world. Had Tony got out just in time? Was I now the boy on the burning deck? I was certainly fiddling a lot, and if Rome was indeed on fire I couldn't see it from my flat. Peter Godwin was out on the prowl much like myself in those days but, being a good-looking bastard, his Lothario charm reaped considerably more rewards than my own endeavors. We used to hang out together in bars in South Kensington and in innumerable smoke-filled cellars we'd talk about girls, chicks, babes, dames, broads whilst hurling back Martinis and listening to Bird and Basie albums on original vinyl. We'd stand up, brush down our Deco-patterned ties as yet another weasel-faced gangster with unsightly bulge under his jacket and blonde on his arm was introduced to us, "Hey Charlie! How you doin'?".

Sometimes Peter would sit at the old battered piano, up on the red-lit stage, and smooch out a couple of Cole Porter numbers to the admiring movers and shakers in the audience. After a few more cocktails and insistent urging from the admiring crowd I'd modestly shrug my way up to join him and together we'd lurch through a few Rat Pack boozer songs that had all the made-guys and their molls swaying along. Gee! Those were the days! Invariably the actual end result of an evening out would find the two of us back in grey realism on a pavement outside his flat in Earls Court, talking about how does one meet a partner? Is it in a club or in a bar? In a doctor's waiting room or aisle 3 at the huge new Sainsburys? All I knew is that for some reason I had a feeling I would meet someone through work, and that's what I told Peter. He seemed less than convinced and implied I was being possibly shortsighted and should get out more. But I was actually working a lot at that time, enjoying the fruits of my new-found success in TV commercials and subsequently not only feeling very confident but also optimistic and unburdened from poverty by suddenly having brass in every pocket. Two weeks after our last chilly conversation on the street I got the job as head Devil in the Ford Fiesta Ad and met the love of my new life.

Flash forward to New Year's Eve 1989. Just before midnight. Rosie and I are sitting on a sofa in someone's house in Tunbridge Wells, suffering some interminable celebration of another year about to arrive. Tony and his pregnant wife, Jenny, are present along with a few others. R and I are bored and would much rather be anywhere except here. It's the home of someone else I was at art school with and its manicured and character-less interior design shrieks of politeness. It represents not only the nadir of pursuing the dream of being a Graphic Designer, but it's also exactly why I dropped out of that very course. Out of the blue, Rosie turns to me and says: "Why don't you ask me to marry you?" An incredible array of thoughts and emotions surge through me and I take her hands and say: "Will you marry me?"

"Yes!" And in the instant of her immediate and positive response I felt like every happy man who has ever lived. For one absolute 'Golden Moment', a door opened in my heart as I looked upon this beautiful woman, and a feeling so rare, so special and so needed flooded me and drowned every cynical negative cell of doubt. And I knew exactly why we do it. Why we stand before a God that may or may not exist, in front of people who love us, facing the universe and every breathing soul and say, "Yes". We announced our decision to our hosts and we all drank the New Year in with excess and optimism. We set a date for our wedding: Midsummer's Day, 1990.

I was engaged! I felt unlike I ever had before - joyful, proud and yes, just a bit more grown up. Because Rosie had been married before, and only recently divorced, we had to go for a Registry Office service, sadly a somewhat less than sublime event. Our closest friends, parents and relatives all attended, but it was oddly efficient and disconcertingly business-like. We were signed, sealed but undelivered. It didn't feel real at all; even the posed and professional photographs outside seemed somehow stagey. However, what we'd decided to do to compensate for the above, and to consequently celebrate our snake-like union, was to have a blessing of our marriage in a mediaeval church in a tiny hamlet named Swinbrook in Oxfordshire. We found the place one afternoon while cruising around the county looking for the right sort of church in the only car I've ever owned (well, co-owned): a 1971 Volvo Amazon: retro looks, white body-work and red leather upholstery. It was a big solid saloon car that was built to last in a way that vehicles these days sadly are not, and the interior smelt like a 'proper car' (Dad would have been pleased). Image-wise, Victor The Volvo suited us perfectly as we were a glamorous stylish couple that looked as if we'd stepped out of a '40's cinematic romance.

As we turned off the A40 and drove down the single-track lane to Swinbrook, a rainbow appeared in the sky ahead of us. I don't normally go for or experience portents or signs but this was far too beautiful to dismiss - our location had been chosen for us. The village hall was ours to rent for the reception at the grand sum of £20 for two days, the local priest was cool and open-minded. We'd organized caterers, live music by the Oxford ensemble The Folk Orchestra, and bought in a massive amount of wine, and a couple of barrels of ale for the butch members of the party. For probably the only time in my life, every facet of my past, present and future was there to celebrate, in one place at the same time. How cool and cinematic it was to look down from our head table and see friends from every different era of our lives gathered there to join with us and eat, drink and get exceedingly merry. Needless to say I had to release the inappropriate but truthful clown within me by declaring to all and sundry in my little speech that I felt like a dog with two dicks! To his undying shame, Tony H., with spouse and first-born, man- aged to blow his 'best man' speech in the most spectacularly self-embarrassing manner. Rosie's best friend, Emma, saved the day with her humorous words as 'maid of honour'.

Our parents (sadly not Dad as he was dead by this time) smiled benignly at relatives that no one had seen for years. Barbie was present with her new and permanent paramour, Georg; Peter G. with a well-built but vacant ex-stripper (so very Peter); Ken Cranham and Peter Firth with their partners; Sean with his future wife, Melanie, and a video camera; Steve Cook with his omnipresent stills cameras and a Thai wife; R's disastrously misbehaved brother; many home town and London friends and Uncle (and Aunty) Tom Cobblers and all. Sean did a great dub version of a wedding video, the sort of thing that somehow captures how you felt in your heart and how you were seen in that moment. But that video had to be burned in a self-cleansing cathartic mini-bonfire on my patio, along with almost every other remnant of our time together, some years after the day in November 1994 that Rosie walked out of my life. That evening, she had returned from Bromley where she was performing in a short-lived stage production of *Star Trek, The Lost Voyage* and dropped the bombshell that temporarily shattered my life. One brief, baffling and one-sided conversation later, which didn't in any way clarify or explain her decision, and then she was gone. She stayed at a friend's flat with a packed bag containing her immediate necessities while she found the inner-space she said she needed. For weeks afterwards the flat was like The Mary Celeste with everything just as she'd left it: underwear on radiators, slippers on the floor, toiletries in the bathroom and her essence everywhere. Ironically she'd chosen to leave the night before the day I'd arranged to start to write songs with Georg Kajanus. Georg and Barbie were an absolute pillar of strength and love throughout and beyond in all the following painful weeks. It must have been so sad for them to watch as everything within me fell apart. Although I tried to go literally overnight from husband to friend I just couldn't do it. I don't think anyone can reasonably be expected to. We were together for six years. Sharing, exploring, arguing violently sometimes, being silly and lovingly childish at others, having spontaneous and rude sex in unusual places, travelling, enjoying our home, being creative and socially active. It was the best of times. Mind you, there were moments when I almost glimpsed that, just possibly, we weren't ultimately right for each other. But then that little spark of doubt was extinguished by more adventures and distractions. If we'd been able to talk about things in an honest way when sober, without recrimination and resentment, we might have transcended our emotional paraphernalia and really aimed for the stars as a committed, loving couple. But, for reasons that I hope one day will be clarified and shared, we didn't.

The burning followed a final angry phone call in 1997 when it struck me violently, around the head and the heart, that Rosie would never see or speak to me again.

That was when the part of me that felt so pleased, so happy, so faithful, so optimistic, died. I know now that it's never just one half of a relationship that makes all the mistakes and fractures it, that both parties are culpable for whatever reasons. But for a long time after she left, I convinced myself that it was all my fault. That I had in some subconscious self-destructive way punished myself by hurting her. There is definitely a degree of confusing truth in this realization, but Rosie had her own demons that contributed to this ending, a constantly restless need for commitment in a long-term relationship but a fear of it at the same time. When the going gets tough, the weak get going, hoping that their next partner will give them what they need. But of course they never will, because whatever blame you apportion to someone else. it's always you that is running from yourself. The saddest thing is that I can never get 'closure', because when a loved one dies they're gone forever physically. You will come to terms with their absence, but as she is still out there, and it seems that we'll never be able to make peace, it's not over. For the two of us to meet and to be able to say, with the wisdom of distance and time, that we both fucked up, would somehow make a kind of sense of it all.

Chapter 24 – The F-Stops Here

"Please allow me to introduce myself - I'm a man of wealth and taste."
Sympathy For The Devil © Jagger / Richards 1968.

A middle-aged man, with legs that look too short for his lithe torso, and seemingly wearing a wig of dubious profusion, is escorted onto the set with a minder on each side. He's dressed in a black leather jacket adorned with buckles here and there, a singlet, tight black trousers and soft ebony suede boots. He holds one hand in the other in a camp limp way and he looks frail and effete. When he takes his position in front of the camera, the lined and weathered face is instantly, unavoidably, recognizable from countless bits of concert footage and a billion photographs from four decades of hedonism and debauchery. And, of course, sonically and socially potent music (pretty much everything from '64 right through to the mid '70's, with a few later flashes of energetic rekindling of dwindled fire.) Although I knew it was Mick Jagger, and was expecting his imminent arrival, it was still a shock to see him there, just a few feet away in front of me. A living icon, a man whose music and image helped to shape my teenage years. It's Jumpin'Jack Flash in the ashen flesh! The Rock 'n' Roll Satyr stepped down to earth, right here, right now, and I am about to take a great many publicity photographs of him for his record company.

His face looks like it's been carved from the bark of an ancient tree that grows only in the shade. It's almost a caricature by its very familiarity, like seeing the real man replaced by his Spitting Image puppet. He's achieved that rare blend of ugly and beautiful that only those with a lengthy accumulation of success, sensuality and experience, map for themselves. The fabled mouth that fueled hot and moist teen fantasies back then has now grown almost too big for his face. Actually, his visage is more heroic than you'd expect, and thinking about it now, he resembles a stone sculpture from the Mount Rushmore of Rock or the Easter Island of Excess. It isn't

a wig (the make-up girl confirmed it during a break a bit later on). He's follicularly intact and wears the same style he's favoured for nearly thirty years. It's reassuring in a way. We don't want our Olympian heroes resorting to hairpieces, weaves or The Swoop, and if he had actually done that apocryphal deal with Mephistopheles sometime around 1968, it was obviously not without its physical compensations.

I wiped the sweat from my palm and shook his hand. Not a strong or firm grip but rather that of a man who no longer needs to try and impress anyone. I prayed that I wouldn't babble at him about seeing The Stones in Richmond in '64 and '65; the Hyde Park concert; Mars Bars; Marianne Faithfull; drugs; Altamont; Keith; *Performance* and I didn't. After I'd taken some shots of him against a graffitti'd wall with his arms outstretched in a crucifix- ion pose (he seemed to enjoy the irony of that) I just said that I was the stills man for this video promo shoot and told him to subsequently ignore me.

In mid-1993, my friend, the gloriously and appropriately surnamed Janice Crotch (no, really!) was working as Mick's PA. Janice knew of my ambitions, and burgeoning photographic skills, and asked if I'd like to take photographs during the making of the promo for Mick's solo single *Out Of Focus*. I huffed and bluffed and said I'd try and squeeze Mick into my hectic trajectory of 'I'm A Photographer Now' activity. Instead of spending the prior evening checking and rechecking cameras, film stock, lenses and flashguns, like a true professional, I agonised over what to wear. Should I go casual and scruffy like Smudgers are wont to do? Should I opt for a tad more elegance, and thereby possibly impress Ol' Rubber Lips with my innate sense of style? What if it rains? Maybe it'll be hot and I'll be overdressed and less than spontaneous? Oh, God, the pressure! In the end, I'll always be inept in a sartorially practical way. I'm just not an all-weather kind of guy, unlike the gaffers and geezers on location film crews who, if the sun breaks through for a short while, are instantly strutting and rigging in T-shirt and shorts. If it inexplicably snows or hails five minutes later, these same geezers are scurrying around in puffer jackets, fleeces and those nylon trousers that make a noise like a huge mouse rubbing its back legs together when you walk. Only I could end up clad in white linen trousers, deck shoes and a black shirt whilst scampering after the next set up in a very dusty and rusty disused warehouse down in the far reaches of the East End Docklands.

What I did witness during the early stages of the shoot was Star Metamorphosis. We've read about Norma Jean being able to turn 'Marilyn' on and off at will; how she could divert attention in public if she didn't want to be recognized or photographed. And when on a whim she did, she could project her alter ego out to attract people. Well, it happened on the count-in to the backing track on take one of the first shot. The portable Bose monitors pump out an impressively frisky level of sound and the instant the song starts to play, the frail and oddly postured ageing man is hurled out of the way and in his place is MICK JAGGER! Right before our eyes! It is like a form of possession. This charismatic demon, so well known, so redolent, has usurped the boundaries of ageing and is bestriding the music like one of the Four Horsemen. It is incredibly exciting to witness. It's all there, the lascivious mouth that pouts like a pair of fully aroused labia, the hair shaken in ecstatic abandonment, the oh-so-slim hips gyrating and grinding out the libidinous rhythm.

The once flaccid hands curl like snakes around the song's lyrics. It's riveting, and you get a sense of how exhausting it must be to consistently and willingly assume this mighty persona to order for so long, but oh how sexy and powerful it must surely feel. Mick has the unique facility and desire to be able to stretch out a two syllable word like 'Focus' into something aurally resembling a lizard's tongue intent on a cunnilingual foray. That's why he's still doing this, he relishes this moment. His timing is unique and impeccable; he's still having fun with it.

The primordial power of music as sex: Prince had the same ability, David Lee Roth and Kate Bush had it too. Michael Jackson got fairly close but there's something disturbingly asexual about his groin fixation let alone his Frankenstein face. Who else? Early Lennon at the mike with his Rickenbacker played like a Liverpool whore on a Saturday night, his cynical teasing of all those screaming girls who fear but at the same time long for the realization that The Fabs weren't just out to 'Hold Your Hand' after all. Elvis, of course, in all his sneering gyrating pre-army magnificence: "That ain't tactics Honey. It's just the beast in me!"

How unsurpassable, how perfect that even hetero men would metaphorically give their arse to The King in his prime! Bowie had 'It' in spades in the early '70's, but his version was knowing, sly and exquisitely choreographed. It made you long to fuck a lithe female alien under a changeable sky with a taste in your mouth like aluminium and lace, to the crooning icy soundtrack of *Drive In Saturday* or *Lady Stardust*. Robert Plant, that sinuous Medusa of power chords and mysticism at Zeppelin's apogee, took girls in their teeming heads to a mythic Celtic mountainside, where they would be ravished and the mysteries of Glastonbury explained to them as they lay panting and post-coital with grass adhering to their cooling backs. Anyone else? Jim Morrison, the Baudelaire in black leather, had the gift. A hoped-for transformation of his audience through Shamanistic structures of his own poetic aspirations and excesses. Even the young Sinatra had it (not the be-wigged and corpulent lover of The Mob, horses' heads, and Vegas in later years). Look at him in the '40's and early '50's, whippet-thin with cheekbones you could grate parmigiano on, and great clothes, enticing those pony-tailed Bobbysoxers to dampen their seats and dream of one rough crooning night in a neon-bathed hotel in downtown Staten Island.

And what are we left with here in the 2000's? The sad turds left floating in the deep pan of Pop Idol? And look at all the other interchangeable, choreographed nonentities who think that ululating twenty notes when you could actually sing five good ones means you could pass for a Superstar? A Diva? C'mon! Pop is now the new Soft Porn, gleaming, moist and streamlined straight from conveyor belts into your I-Pod. In our depleting desire to embrace even one truly dangerous and innovative icon we seem to have lost our discretion and sensibilities. I don't buy it. Do you? Is it really now just all about marketing and cynical replication? Hasn't Rock 'n' Pop always been about pushing the envelope, transgressing boundaries, carving your niche in the Wailing Wall of wide-legged anticipation of sex to come, with a blood-rich backbeat mirroring your heart and pheromones? The inherent need to defy people's small-minded expectations of the soundtrack to their formative years? We demand revelation through stimulation. Whoah! I nearly forgot JIMI! The undeniable voodoo child of the electric guitar, the tumescent sorcerer of sound. What bubble was that genius straining to rend? "I'm black, I have a big dick and I play guitar like a fallen angel! I'm humble, magnetic and my soul is barely restrained within six strings. I want you to surpass me but nobody seems to be able to. I scream in frustration "I HAVE SHOWN YOU THE DOOR!" Come on! Don't just follow the safe patterns laid down before, flow with me. No? You're just content to simulate and emulate? Fuck it! I'm outta here!" That's why it was an honour to photograph Mick. I could briefly snuffle my nose and lenses in the trough of true stardom and legend. It doesn't happen very often, if at all, but I was there, just briefly, to catch a glimpse of, and to try and capture, the fleeting presence of a genuine star on 35mm monochrome film.

I think in some way I've always seen the world of my imagination in black-and-white. That's more than likely why I was drawn to study Mime in the first place. I needed to explore that silent and evocative art of illusion, with its protagonists in stark light, white pancake and black clothes (well that's how it was back in 1976 anyway). Onstage you'd proffer a brief sporadic smear of a red-tinted mouth splashed against a painted face, with hands disembodied like pale puppets. Nothing extraneous, nothing visible that isn't meant to be seen.

Being the age I am, and thus growing up in the '50's, most of my childhood memories are contained on small square photographs with crinkly edges like those that border postage stamps. Dad used to take his negatives to be processed at Boots the Chemist in Reigate High Street, and he'd get them back a few days later in a paper wallet that had pastel coloured stripes printed on the outside. Neither he nor Mum had ever really addressed the concept of actually framing a picture, most of the time they'd just point, shoot, and hope. For years I thought that none of my relatives possessed heads. In some shots they had huge blurred thumbs manifesting like some ectoplasmic entity all down one side of the image and obscuring most of their decapitated torsos. I remember being fascinated but somehow disturbed by looking at the negatives; they had a strange smell and texture that unnerved me. They seemed to be little portals into a world where everything was reversed and people were dark-skinned with white mouths, hair and eyes and spoke backwards like the dwarf in *Twin Peaks*. Television was black-and-white too, as were most of the films we saw at the cinema (discounting the occasional Hollywood epic and lurid musicals full of impossibly healthy people inexplicably bursting into song). Our first set was housed in a tall wood- veneer cabinet that was the same height as me when I was four. The screen occupied the top quarter of the unit and was about the same size as a convex-surfaced hardback book. A night's viewing invariably involved Dad intermittently cursing, rising up from the sanctuary of his chair and glass of whisky, furiously twiddling huge Bakelite knobs the size and shape of cup-cakes or striking the side of the set with the flat of his hand. The image would judder through variegated horizontal lines of wavy interference for a few seconds, then dissolve into a snow- storm of hissing static and finally stabilize into the programme again. It all seemed terribly hard work just to watch some fresh faced and harmless TV Gorm doing the act he used to do on the Music Hall stage. But the irresistible virus was being nurtured in our safe suburban homes even then. A cancerous cell starting a DNA trail that leads us right up *Celebrity Big Brother* and all the other mindless horrors which pass for entertainment in a dumbed-down world. Like Topsy, it just kept on growin'. But there was one artist in the '70's who had noticed the erosion:

"I am gross and perverted, / I'm obsessed and deranged. / I have existed for years But very little has changed. / I'm the tool of the Government / And industry too, / For I am destined to rule / And regulate you. / You will obey me while I lead you, / Eat the garbage that I feed you, Until the day that we don't need you. ... Your mind is totally controlled - / It has been stuffed into my mould / And you will do as you are told / Until the rights to you are sold. / Have you guessed me yet? / I'm the best you can get I'm the slime / Oozing out / From your... TV set!"
I'm The Slime © Frank Zappa, 1973

Some years later, when I was twelve or so, Dad came home from his job as Sales Manager at the Caterham Motor Company with a camera that some negligent potential customer had left in a car in which he'd been taken for a demonstrational spin. It was of German manufacture (a Voigtländer in fact), had a silver body, and came with it's own brown leather case that had the same contours as the camera and was attached by a press-stud. It was just a simple 35mm fixed lens model that could perform the basics adequately and didn't cause decapitations or manifestations from beyond the veil. Eventually it was given to me to play around with.

I opted for throwing things like twigs or model aeroplanes into the air and simultaneously snapping their motion against the sky. All I ever ended up with was a series of blurred whatevers just visible at the edge of the frame. Maybe it was a latent desire to try and replicate the enigmatic object I'd seen hovering in the air above me from Chapter 2? Becoming bored by my failures to simulate UFO activity, and discovering a pull towards drawing and painting, I pretty much left the world of photography alone until 1990. In that year, an impulse engendered by finally having cash to spend, and an inquisitive creative urge, led me to buy my first 'grown up camera'. Because of the addictive side of my personality (it's never enough until it becomes too much) I didn't stop at just buying a good manual camera and learning how to use it properly. Oh no, that would be far too boring and practical. I went out a few days later and bought two more lenses, a box of filters, flash-guns, tripods, how- to books and a huge padded case for it all that could serve as luggage on a six-month trip abroad. I turned my spare bedroom into a Darkroom and discovered the solitary, and evil-smelling, enchantment of spending hours in a pitch-black airless room with your hands in trays of toxic chemicals.

To my delight I realized that I was actually quite good at all this. Photography enabled me to transcend my frustrating limitations of imagination and technique as a painter and illustrator. All the tricky stuff like perspective, form, light and shade were taken care of through the lens, all I had to do was to find the subjects or objects of choice and press the shutter. What excited me was the ability to manipulate the world into how I saw it, through the use of toning, different papers, pushing exposure and development in the Darkroom and, above all, montage. Suddenly I was getting press in all the photographic magazines: "Actor becomes artistic photographer!" and I could always give them a good story. Especially now that my portfolio included

Jagger, Joan Collins and Steven Berkoff. *Hot Shoe* was one of the most prestigious journals at the time and I was given a front cover, a self-portrait of me as a horned Devil. I bleached-out and sandpapered the background all around the image of me that I'd printed onto textured photographic paper. Then, on one of those unexpected artistic whims, I applied layers of coloured inks and crackle-glaze varnish to create a suitably distressed and ancient-looking picture of myself as Dark Tim. I was very gratified with the effect of this technique and subsequently used it to create a series of 'Angel' portraits of my friend Kathy, who modelled nude for me in various poses of heavenly dissaray. I montaged-in her wings, put a twinkle in her eyes, and got a new satisfaction from the finished results. For once I'd discovered a style of expression that was all my own. Inevitably it's usage was non-commercial and short-lived, as seems to be the way of a lot of my good ideas, but I'm proud of those pictures and they're ageing well somewhere in a dusty portfolio.

Rosie, my wife, was a willing and very photogenic subject for several experimental ideas. Being an actress, she was well-versed in the art of sitting for a photographer, even if he happened to be her wildly un-thought-out husband. One session in our basement living room involved her nude body covered in white make-up, her hair (caked in the same) slicked back, and a strange Japanese mask held up to her face. In my excitement, I'd neglected to lower the venetian blinds behind her, and so passers by and neighbours, from their street level perspective, saw only her tungsten-lit pallid nakedness seated on a stool in front of the window, masked-up and strangely postured (I was too far back behind the camera and tripod to be visible). Whatever could they have thought? "Eoh, it's that gal from '66' exhibiting herself again! How wonderfully eccentric! How very... Bayswater, Darling!".

A later un-witnessed indignity saw Rosie nude once more, but this time in the privacy of our patio, being sprayed from head to waist with a can of theatrical fake cobwebs. I thought this would look great in a decaying Gothy sort of way, especially with the addition of some plastic ivy that had been similarly treated. Neither of us had foreseen that this stuff is in no way meant for contact with human skin, and therefore would itch and burn like a syphilitic alien's ejaculate. Poor girl, through her gritted fiery eyelids she could make out my hopping form oscillating between concerned husband and creative photographer.

I got myself a photographic agent in the form of the long- suffering, but beautiful and creative, Natasha, and together we set about marketing myself as a worthy and employable artist. It worked pretty well; myself and my 'book' were being called for consistently by Advertising companies and magazines. But, deep down in the unpredictable bloodstream of true visual exploration, we both always somehow wanted more. Baffling isn't it? A great many photographers would give their left 'fish eye' to exhibit at the National Portrait Gallery, The Royal Photographic Society (twice), and the Association of Photographers Gallery, but I was an ugly duckling and water just slid off my back. Maybe because of my previous and concurrent successes in the Wonderful World of Showbiz it all seemed a little flat and un-glamorous? That's the insidious nature of so-called fame, it makes you feel that the real world is quite often tawdry and somehow less than desirable or interesting once you've savoured the aroma of it's poisoned yet so alluring breath.

Natasha did manage to pull a good one out of the hat in March 1997. She'd somehow managed to blag an exhibition in the British Embassy in Hamburg for myself and four of her other clients. A strange choice of venue for this eclectic bunch of creatives, but the Embassy officials seemed keen to extend their hospitality. We'd obtained cheap flights but this meant flying out on the Wednesday and killing time until the exhibition on Saturday. Six crazed artists on the loose in Hamburg for three days and nights? Uh oh! Let's just wait and see what happens shall we?

I'd painstakingly and very clumsily fashioned two six-foot screens faced with red velvet from my old living room curtains, and several lengths of wooden battens, upon which I would hang eight framed pictures. If you didn't look too closely or breathe out too hard in their vicinity they might just pass muster and stay upright for the duration. The problem was there was no way to take them onboard an aeroplane. So Natasha and I strapped them to the roof-rack of her car and she drove to Southampton or somewhere to have them shipped out. As she proceeded away from me, along my street, they started flapping wildly and it looked like she was about to be the first woman to fly over the Channel in a maroon velvet Wright Brothers prototype.

Denis was a talented, pale and quietly intense, young photographer whose speciality at that time was creating large transparencies in very vivid colours of close-ups of liquids. So close-up in fact they looked like snapshots from another galaxy. His idea was to have twelve of them displayed on a six-foot long light box with a black matte over the top cut out to reveal his creations. Brilliant idea, as the result looked like a cosmic stained glass window. But imagine taking that onto the plane. It took four people and a trolley to get it to the check-in desk. "Just the one item of hand luggage, Sir?" Well, somehow he managed it and the massive glass and metal edifice made it to the Embassy in one piece. Also with us were two brothers, Martin and Colin, who worked in the strange and little known area of Kerlian photography. Basically, a method of capturing the electro-magnetic aura that invisibly surrounds any organic item, be it a human hand or a leaf. You can see an example of the technique in the opening credits of *The X-Files* and in the concert programme for Bowie's *Station to Station* tour. Don't ask me to explain or even understand how it works but the results are spectacular and unearthly. A bit like Martin's character as I came to realize on our jaunt. Ten minutes after take off he'd managed to charm one of the Hostesses into giving him two mini bottles of Smirnoff, which he'd sunk before the seatbelt sign went off. I looked across at him and thought: "Hmm, another Wild Boy. I think we're in for a bumpy ride!" The sixth member of our assault group was a gifted portrait photographer named Anthony, who pretty much kept himself to himself for the duration. Wise choice as it turned out.

The Embassy had arranged a Hotel for us in Steindamm around the back of the Hauptbahnhof. Knowing how straight most officials are who work for the Government, I was expecting to be in some bland identikit chain establishment, of the kind in which I've been incarcerated so many times. But to my delight we'd been accommodated in an ex-Brothel! The Hotel Village (oh, I do so hope it's still there) was a small five-floor establishment that used to cater for the needs of Embassy employees amongst others. Every room was themed in red and slightly decayed looking, with mismatched and shabby furniture. But the jewel in the tarnished crown of each of our rooms was a four-poster bed (ideal for tying clients to) made of dark wood with a canopied roof with a large mirror behind the bed, and when you lay on it and looked up you saw that the entire ceiling of the canopy was mirrored too. Oh God, I need this back at home! I then discovered a little switch by the side of the bed, that when you pushed it, caused the mirror to rise and fall. So you could zoom in and out on the action. As long as you or your willing adventurer managed to keep one hand free, that is. There were some intriguing scratch marks on the bedposts, so I guess that possibly some German shepherd and his 'best friend' might have occupied the room at some dark point in the Hotel's chequered past. I checked for dog hairs and hidden cameras and made my way downstairs to the bar to join the others.

Naturally enough I led us down to the Reeperbahn for a drink or three. Turning right onto the Grosse Freiheit, we found nothing suitable for our needs, so we turned into another street that was even seedier than the main drag. We went down some worn and dank steps and entered the sort of bar that I thought only existed in my imagination. It was dark and hazed with evil-smelling cigarette smoke. Slowly, through the gloom, you could discern shapes slouched at tables, with distorted faces straight out of a George Grosz painting, silently staring at us from the sunken eyes of history. The walls were the colour of cancerous lungs, and adorned in places with faded pictures that looked like someone had smeared 40-year-old chip fat over them. Even the barman was perfect. He had one normal eye, albeit blank and bloodshot, but its twin was milky with an advanced cataract. With a smouldering untipped cigarette stuck to his lower lip, he inclined his head upwards in the kind of greeting you'd normally reserve for something stuck to the sole of your shoe. We ordered beers and stood at the bar whilst they were poured. An inch of ash dropped from his cigarette onto the paper circlet at the bottom of the stem of a glass and he glared at us in a manner that dared us to make comment. We didn't. There were drunken sailors here and there at the tables, some in pairs with heads like nodding dogs, and others with beefy tattooed arms clasped round the slack shoulders of women that made Rosa Klebb look like Anita Ekberg.

Denis and I were excited by this Weimar-esque spectacle and then suddenly realized that we were the only ones talking above a whisper. It would be about now that some stubbled behemoth with 'I eat Englishmen' inked across his mountainous chest would inevitably rise unsteadily to his feet, lurch to our party and, with fearsome ease, pluck each of our heads off one by one and drop kick them through the door and out into the night. Time to go? Yes please. Especially as I had a dreadful fear that Martin would give them all a Nazi salute at any moment. We drank up and left, only to find ourselves a few minutes later in another bar in another side street equally as bad. This one however was adorned with Union Jacks and English football teams memorabilia and was, in the main, populated by the sort of loud, drunk, and xenophobic Brit that you have to avoid at all costs, especially in another country. We should have sent them off to meet the sailors in the Grosz bar and let them all bloodily re-enact past grievances.

Finding a quieter corner we sat with beers and Schnapps chasers and got drunk (in an artistic and peaceful way of course). After an hour or so, two of our party decided it would enhance our evening enormously if we pooled together and scored some cocaine. Oh, why not? It's been thirteen years since my last indulgence. After asking the friendly bunch of students seated to our left if they could help, the duo bravely disappeared with one of them into the murky corridor containing the toilets, emerging ten minutes later with smug and excited faces and some loud sniffs. Back in the hotel we opened bottles of Aquavit and fell upon those evil paper wraps with the dreadful and needy glee I remembered so well from before, and proceeded to spend most of the night with nostrils like racehorses, laughing hysterically as we lay on someone's bed watching our rippling reflections zooming in and out of focus.

Naturally we did the same the next night too.

The hottest Alternative Comedian in Germany at the time was Hans Werner Olm, a guy roughly my own age, a sweet and funny artist that I got to know through a mutual female acquaintance, 'B'. He invited Natasha and I to see his show at the St. Pauli Theatre on the Reeperbahn, in exchange for entrance to our show at the Embassy the following night. Luckily for us, that although Hans's dialogue is totally Deutsch, he is very visual and uses a lot of music and props in his act. It's the sort of choice that perhaps I should have pursued earlier in my life, wherein you mix mime, comedy and music together to create a show that transcends the limitations of language and nationality. Oh, I've already done that haven't I! Anyway, I enjoyed his act immensely and, after seeing Natasha safely into a waiting taxi, went back to his hotel with him, 'B' and his beefy and bearded road manager, to drink a fearsome amount and do some serious bonding. You know that late night, slurred, arms around each other "I love this guy!" sort of thing? After an hour or two of that, 'B' and I repaired to her room to let Hans get some sleep.

We opened up her mini bar and inexplicably found ourselves on the sofa, entwined semi-naked, with tongues like writhing snakes. She was a well-stacked girl and I wasted no time in freeing those beauties from the cruel confines of her brassiere and devoured them with my hands and mouth. I pulled off the rest of her clothes, pushed her warm thighs back towards her chest and, kneeling on the floor, lapped at her like a drowning man. She was pink, sweet to taste and very wet. I bit the inside of both her thighs with my sharp teeth, leaving red indentations that made her squeal. I brought her to orgasm and then I stood. She pulled down my opened trousers along with my underwear, took me in her mouth whilst holding her breasts up towards me, and sucked me like a Valkyrie.

I got back to the Hotel Village at 6.30 in the morning. Lay down for an hour then cursingly got up, had a shower, managed to somehow pull the glass shower door off its hinges and staggered downstairs to join the others for breakfast. I thought it expedient to keep my shades on even though it was only 8.am. In charge of the breakfast was a strange-looking Hausfrau, dressed in black, with hair coiffed into something that resembled nothing I'd ever seen before. She glanced at this Orbison-like apparition swaying in front of her and asked: "Do you vant to have some EXX?"

"Excuse me?"

"Vould you like EXX?" The word 'eggs' seemed especially important to her judging by the unnatural stress that she placed upon it. This, of course, reduced me, and then the others, to barely-hidden giggles, especially when we remembered that classic Benny Hill sketch set in a German grocers' shop in which all the dialogue is spoken in capital letters: "F.U.N E X?"/ "S,V.F.X!" / "M.N.O.X." "O.S.A.R!" "F.U.N.E.M?" / "S.V.F.M!" And so on. Go on, read it out loud!

The show itself was pretty successful (I sold three pictures to galleries) but really for me it was all about the adventures we had. There's more of course, but I haven't signed the Official Secrets Act and I don't want to get anyone into trouble...

Cosmopolitan was the one major magazine that employed me on several occasions. One idea the Editors came out with in 1996 was a spread of portraits of famous and rich men without their clothes on. Not exactly my cup of tea, but at least I wouldn't be harbouring lustful and distracting thoughts during the shoot. I was given the task of photographing a young man called Carl Crompton, who had won £9,000,000 on the National Lottery. For some naïve reason he'd neglected to tick the 'No Publicity' box on his winning entry and was now the unwilling recipient of a lot of media attention. "Oh suffer!" We shouted with weighty sarcasm. The only visual idea that came to mind was to have him kit-less, lighting a fat cigar with a wad of burning £50 notes and standing in front of a flat circular plinth strung on a fishing line with six different-coloured balls. Our truculent Carl sneered at my jesting pile of photocopied '50's, saying: "It's awright, I can use my own real ones!" He was s a good-looking boy, fit and well-formed, but he seemed strangely at a loss as to how to deal with his new fortune and seismic life-shift. In those days I used to employ a female assistant. Zodie was blonde, well-curved top and bottom, technically proficient and charming. Unfortunately, at the moment that Carl relented and removed his bath-towel, Zodie chose to bend over and adjust something to do with the lighting. Almost instantaneously, rearing and sniffing the air, was a proud stiffy worth millions. Indeed it was The Horn of Plenty. In profile, Carl looked like one of those priapic fake-bronzes you buy for a laugh at Athens airport. I don't know who was more flushed, me, the dick or it's owner. I banished the bemused Zodie to a spare room, waited for the organ's graceful descending arc and finally got the shot. Luckily not The Money Shot. How wonderful God's perverted sense of humour is, when on a whim of granting certain mortals their wishes, he flaunts a young, handsome millionaire with a big cock at your impoverished lens.

I was fortunate enough to photograph a considerable number of young, beautiful and talented women. And what amazes me is that, despite the few remaining social and relationship ineptitudes I am still prone to, I have a strange facility to put girls at their ease in a photographic situation. It's my interesting combination of charm, honesty, humour and guile. Oh, and copious amounts of wine will often help too if required. The secret is that once a model is relaxed and doesn't see you as a threat or a perv, they will become trusting and turned on by the experience and give themselves (or a fantasy version of themselves) to your camera. That excites me too. I mean, let's face it, in the dull grey real world what are your chances of asking a girl you barely know but find sexy to disrobe and disport? Slim for most of us, unless you're rich, famous, good-looking or very powerful. You know that it's only one or two vertebrae that prevent men from being able to blow their own trumpet?

An inspiring commission came in from Katharine Blake, a real photographic muse, a voluptuous and sybaritic young lady, party girl par excellence, who leads an all girl group named Mediaeval Baebes. There were nine of them at the last count and they sing mostly acapella versions of traditional ballads from our dark, magical and mysterious past. They are foxy and evocative, winsome and lustful, and they've sold a healthy amount of albums in the UK and America. They needed photographs for their tour programme. I obliged. Thanks Baebes.

Chapter 25 – Feast!

Without warning, just as the camera is about to turn over for another take, a male African of terrifying proportions, clad in a bulging tight fitting black dinner suit, with eyes too big and yellow for a man of even temper, emerges from a club doorway in front of us and bellows in a resonant and deeply malevolent voice: "I WILL DESTROY YOUR EQUIPMENT!" He really looked and sounded like he was about to pick up the two of us in each vast inhuman hand and render us both splatteringly asunder. *Predator? Alien?* Forget those ugly galactic wimps, this guy was widescreen and very angry. What in the name of Satan's Fiery Codpiece is happening? Where am I? Who am I with?

Georg Kajanus and I, as the duo Noir, are standing in our inky suits, shades and correspondent shoes on The Reeperbahn in Hamburg at midnight, smeared by the soiled and lurid neon lights of the street's Fuck Clubs, dangerous bars and sex shops. We're filming a link for the Channel 4 Food and Drink series, *Feast!* in the summer of 1997. Entschuldigung? How the Nigella did that happen? It goes like this: November 1994. Georg has been with Barbie (my ex-lover) for a few years now. She and I are like sister and brother in the best ways possible, and Georg has subsequently become a very good friend. We haven't met Jules et Jim yet, but to a few of our close friends it seems likely that we will. We're that tight. Eighteen years earlier I'd seen Georg, the Norwegian composer, songwriter supreme and son of a Russian Prince, fronting his eclectic band, Sailor, on TV and thought he'd be an interesting person to know. I was right. Georg is one of the most focused, artistic, talented, perverse and generous people I've ever met. He is Beethoven in a black suit with a perfect smile and charm to die for.

In the fall of '94, I'd finally coerced him into the notion that he and I should attempt to write a song for The Eurovision Song Contest. Oh, Mecca of all cheesiness! Wogan Be Thy Name! You either get the camp and delicious irony of this yearly Trash Fest or you don't. If, like the three of us you unashamedly do, then you'll revel in the magnificent and tawdry possibility of having a song of your own performed and packaged in front of millions of TV glued national stereotypes from every country in Europe. It's the Grand Prix of Shameless Promotion; the Cup Final of Indignity and Joy; the Nuremburg Rally of Retro Style and Taste. The two of us sat down at the table in Georg's kitchen, overlooking the sinister oily waters of the Grand Union Canal in West London, and we wrote a song called *Talking*. It was good enough for us to realise that we had the sperm of a musical idea fighting its way towards the egg of a creative partnership. After recording it in his computerised home studio, we crafted another song a few days later from the bare digital bones of a notion that Georg had birthed sometime in the preceding weeks. This one we titled *Walking*. It had a lyric about the lost, lonely and lustful searching for sensual fulfilment in a mythical and romantic Paris. In turn, we speak the lines of the verses, and jointly sing the choruses astride a ZZ Top meets Techno backing. It is poetry in motion! The last section of the song shifts into kicking musical arse cheeks in a most relentless, zestful and sexy way, and it is everything I've ever wanted from making music. Here's a lyrical sample:

> "Hungrily searching through the city's rainy streets,
> Don't look up because the sky is grey
> And the buildings threaten you with their size.
> I saw a face in a window
> Maybe she was lonely
> Or waiting for her lover...
> A car does a three-point turn
> And roars into the distance.
> Sailors meeting angels in bars
> To drink and fuck their lives away.
> There's a red room in the heart of town
> Where you can be
> The object of a strange desire
> To see Salome dance
> In Time's dusty mirror
> While the music swarms inside your skull.
> Waitresses in black
> With aprons and red lips,
> Sexy little things
> That you want to take home for the night.
> Streetlights mirrored in puddles,
> Stray dogs with matted coats
> Trot towards the dustbins
> That spew their rubbish in the road.
> A couple arm in arm
> Hurry to their party
> As a Gendarme smiles at their innocent love.
> A coffee and a cognac
> Will help you tell your stories
> To your best friend."

Walking by Noir. Words & Music © 1996 Tim Dry and Georg Kajanus

God, how I'd wanted this moment! Ever since Beatles, John and Paul, created the new Bible of collaborative song writing, I'd dreamed of what it might be like to bounce, reject, share and amplify ideas on a musical level with a partner. It's joyous and good, and it gets better when the combined energy stimulates motivation, movement and meetings.

Ten years after the demise of Tik and Tok, I was back in the running with another compadre. After abandoning the name 'Louche' for being just a bit too obscure and difficult to pronounce for sad old Johnny English, Georg and I christened ourselves 'Noir'. As we both always wore black and shared a love of the seedy underbelly of Europe, especially France and also the Film Noir genre of the '40's and '50's, it seemed apposite and easy to remember. Coincidentally, the two of us were also owners of those wonderfully evocative black-and-white brogue shoes as worn by sneering gangsters with Tommy Guns and a bad Widmark attitude. This clinched the fact that we were meant to give the venture a shot. The image arrived with perfect and organic grace: black hair, black suits and shirts, black shades, a silver ring, set with a dark stone, worn on the same finger of our right hands, and the lustrous correspondent shoes. We looked like a new millennium Gilbert and George in negative, especially when we discovered we could walk in step with each other at 135 bpm whilst miming to our lyrics.

In mid '96, Noir found a manager in the form of the eccentric and alluring Falcon Stuart ("Our Falcon, whose art is in Heaven, hello'd be thy name") Son of a famous sculptor, he'd been around the music biz for years. In fact, I'd first met him back in the very early 1980's when he managed a band called Classix Nouveaux and Shock shared a tour with them. Although somewhat lacking in business acumen (to put it discreetly), he had a non-linear approach to life and art that seemed to suit us. He had a face like a mischievous Pan, wore sandals with socks all year round and rode a bicycle everywhere. Sadly he died unexpectedly in 2002. His passing saddened us and all who knew him. St. Peter probably said: "Sorry son, you're not coming in here with that bicycle. The sandals are OK though." Anyway, blurring past precise and pedantic details of how, when and why, Noir ended up with *Walking* released as a single on a German record label called Koch (pronounced as in sucker) we got the promo video for it shown on Top of the Pops 2.

David Pritchard, a renowned director of food and drink programmes, was putting together plans for a somewhat different gastro show, when he found himself watching the clip of us striding around Munich in syncopated elegance on his TV. He loved the song and in the mirror saw that thought bubble of ingenuity rise above his head. He called us up and told us of his idea. As a segment in four programmes of the six week series provisionally titled *Let's Eat*, Noir would be paid to be filmed walking around Euro cities of our choice, to the soundtrack of *Walking* reworked with relevant foodie lyrics, and eating and drinking in as many restaurants as our stomachs and their budget could handle! There really is such a thing as a 'Free Lunch'! So, ha, ha! (As the Austrians declaim in moments of extreme levity) to all you cynics out there who deny the existence of this fabled creature.

Paris, *bien sur*, was our first choice. We Eurostar'd our way there in April '97 with David, a four-person crew, and Barbie too in a hastily made-up role as our wardrobe and make-up artiste. She could have 'her boys' on each side, mother us, help us and scold us, and justifiably share the perks of a gig like this.

Disregarding the functional ugliness of the Ibis hotel where we were staying, Paris was a blur of unchanged beauty as we strode cinematically around its sunlit streets. In April, the city is feminine and newborn, it feels like a languid virgin on silken sheets opening her warm thighs for a painter's eyes. In Montmartre we gorged on Cous Cous Royale in a tiny Moroccan café in the Place du Charles Dullin, ate oysters fresh and spunky from the beds of Northern France, with a glass of chilled Chablis in a pavement bar. From huge earthenware bowls we slowly spooned fresh onion soup, laden with melted Gruyere cheese, to our waiting mouths in a small Brasserie full of black-and-white photographs of Paris in previous decades. Ever since the legendary Brassaï and his holy lens scoured the mean streets of Montmartre in the '30's to capture street life and decadent liaisons, the Mother of Romance has whispered that she is best captured in timeless monochrome. At the wondrous restaurant 'Chartier' in Faubourg-Montmartre, we ate escargots juicy with fresh garlic and butter and washed them down with cheap but sexy Bourgogne Pinot Noir, followed by steak au poivre or brochette de poisson. As a dessert, I always opt for their *Crème de Marron avec Chantilly*. God, I love that so much - my ideal woman is the one who suggests, in a husky candlelit whisper, that I may care to spread this puree of chestnuts, cream and vanilla all over her lower belly and use my tongue to devour each sticky mouthful ...

Sorry, just had to break off for a quick date with one of the palm sisters for a few minutes there. Where was I? I've been coming to Chartier since 1977 and no sojourn in Paris is complete without a meal in its bohemian, turn of the century, faded ambience. It's always full of students, artists, writers and unashamed nostalgicists desiring a glimpse of Belle Époque elegance. After you've finished your final cup of Expresso, the surly but charmingly Gallic waiters (who all look like Jean Reno or a young Serge Gainsbourg) appear at your remnant-strewn table in their long black aprons, and add up your bill on the paper tablecloth. Then, after you've paid, they telepathically usher you quickly from your seat and out into the teeming streets. It epitomises what cheap and pleasurable eating in a capital city can be like when a country and its people rejoice in culinary sensuality. I have pinched one of their Deco-styled menus as a souvenir on every visit. I have kept them all with pride and it is still the most inexpensive place I've ever found in which to eat and people-watch.

The irony of doing the on-screen eating in one of these 'foodie' programmes is that, by the end of meal two, on any day, your internals are well on the way to achieving Hindenbergesque dimensions. You fear for your straining trouser zip and sphincter and fret that the local plumbing may not be able to withstand the imminent onslaught. But surprisingly, after a few more Techno-Tempo Walkings on DigiCam in different locations: down by the Seine, in front of Sacre Coeur, the Eiffel Tower, etc., you're beginning to feel just a tad peckish, much to David Pritchard's glee and his directorial 'what shall we do next that'll look great on camera?' thought processes. We do a series of shots in the biggest open-air food market in the city one morning, at the Rue D'Aligre. Apart from the two of us walking in slo-mo through hordes of baffled shoppers, this involved us sampling the wares from a man whose huge indoor display contained approximately 1,000 varieties of cheese from all over the nation.

To urge into action our somewhat flagging taste buds and acting skills, David takes us to one side and motivates us. In a conspiratorial whisper with cognac-scented, lunchtime breath, he says: "This man lives for cheese, he eats, sleeps and breathes cheese. He IS cheese. He Cheesy!" With renewed vigour we attack the task of nibbling at least twenty small titbits of different variations of admittedly very palate-pleasing milk product. The owner of Le Monde Incroyable de Fromage (not in fact the real name of his establishment) smiles benignly down at us from behind his magnificent moustache as these two black-clad oddities mime near orgasmic delight at every offering. It's so wonderfully European, isn't it? Here's a man who has found his vocation and a joi de vivre that revolves solely and simply around the purveyance of taste-bud-titillating dairy comestibles, fresh from farm to market. In England you can't buy anything from the same genetic family that isn't sealed in hard and impenetrable plastic, or that doesn't taste like a fell-walker's socks. As Georg so succinctly defined it, people like us are "Continental At Heart". Sounds like a song title? Well yes, it was another Noir track actually.

After filming in the market, the three of us have time to ourselves. We wander into the shabby back streets behind the Place de Clichy and end up in a small local bar of dodginess par excellence. There's a mangy and ferocious Alsatian dog with a collar made of thick rope acting as a bouncer on the door: "No jeans, no trainers. Oh, you three look weird and edgy, so come on in!". The once passably impressive marble floor is strewn with thousands of cigarette butts, peanut shells, expelled sputum and innumerable canine-cleansed finger bones. We sit at a grubby Formica table, sweep off the disturbing detritus, order three glasses of Ricard and suddenly feel strangely at home. The dog and his mute, and quite possibly one-eyed owner, have accepted us for the visiting extraterrestrials that we feel and look like and leave us to ourselves. After round three of the soothing aperitif, Georg starts to convulse with laughter, tears are streaming down his still made-up face as he curves forward in his seat. Barbie and I crane towards our Scandinavian hero in bafflement. What! What is it? With chortles catching in his throat like the phlegm of a berserk clown he manages to stutter: "HE CHEESY!" as some kind of explanation.

Somewhere in his mysterious Norwegian psyche these words have looped and triggered the onset of helpless and infectious giggles. One goes - we all go. Barbie, Georg and myself are moist-cheeked and literally holding our sides. The sparse selection of other patrons in the bar shrug and turn back to the football match playing in grainy vision on the small TV high up on the mottled wall above the counter. The barman raises his eyebrow in the cryptic way that people who have seen everything inevitably do, and resumes polishing the glasses and flicking gobbets of flesh of dubious origin to his canine chum who sprawls nonchalant but ever vigilant by the sticky glass doors.

In the *Walking* promo, for a few bars of the song, we're seen playing electric guitars when the chorus get more rocky, and we came up with an inspired visual gag to Mr. Pritchard's delight. At the same point in the song we'd be filmed miming the guitar parts clutching large long fresh baguettes! You can imagine the bemused faces of onlookers as we filmed the routine in the Place des Abbesses in Montmartre, behind Guimard's exquisitely designed Art Nouveau Metro entrance. Laugh? I nearly joined the Foreign Legion!

At some point during our four-day Parisian jaunt, David starts to entertain the notion that maybe Noir should present and do links in each programme as well as our four *Walking* slots. We do a screen-test in the empty hotel bar, which he shows to the producers when we get back to England. I like the idea because of my mime and acting history but Georg, quite understandably, has some reservations. After all, English is his third language. I can't imagine having the faculty of thinking and speaking fluently in one foreign tongue, let alone two. But to his credit he rises to the challenge with his customary attention to detail and creative imagination. Our image as a duo and the combination of our different personalities plus our musical skills means we get the job. This is really exciting, a 'Golden Moment' to be sure. They asked which three other cities we'd like to go and film in and we quickly chose Amsterdam, Barcelona and Hamburg (we wanted Berlin but they said it was too far, the cheapskates) and we went off to Holland a couple of months later. The gap in the shooting schedule gave us time to write a short piece of music for a possible theme tune just for the hell of it. We came up with a tag line of inspired simplicity and humour: "If food be the music of love - let's eat!".

Falcon came with us to Amsterdam, quite possibly just so that he could look at the swarms of teenage girls riding bicycles. Did he used to sneak off on his own sometimes and caress and sniff still-warm saddles? Who knows? Never trust a man wearing socks with his sandals that's what I say, and certainly never, ever have any dealings with men who have those awful beards cultivated only on the chin and jawline, with nothing above their mouth. They're all serial killers believe me. Have you seen the original version of *The Vanishing*? The proof is in that film. Bizarrely a lot of Dutch men of a certain age have opted for the facial folly of the murderer's beard, which must mean something. Maybe these men are part of a secret brotherhood of assassins whose mission is to systematically erase the chefs in every traditional Dutch restaurant in the capital? Because to be honest the food that is prepared in them is not exactly on anyone's list of 'must sample and enjoy' is it? We had to feign pleasure and satisfaction in one of these establishments and it was a textbook acting job. I mean what else can you do but lie outrageously with your body language when confronted with the house specialty which is a large bowl of pea soup with little bits of pink sausage floating in it? And pancakes the size of a spare tyre with queasy combinations of toppings? We found to our horror that we were becoming increasingly reliant on that facial expression that wine tasters consistently use to denote an almost sexual joy at what's swilling around in their mouth. And for added indication of enjoyment we'd combine the look with those hand gestures where you fold your digits into a point and swirl them around in front of your unshapely and mobile cheeks.

The best meal we were filmed imbibing was naturally enough in an ethnic restaurant, one of the myriad Indonesian establishments that proliferate in Amsterdam. One reason there's so many is because of the blandness, girth and density of Dutch cuisine. Another reason is because most of the people in Amsterdam are so stoned from partaking of legal hashish in coffee shops that their taste buds are screaming for: Flavour! Delicacy! Style! Variety! And lots of really ... kind of ... like interesting shapes and colours, yeah? I nearly blew a gasket on camera when I carelessly swallowed The Chilli Monster in our sumptuous Asian restaurant. After one mouthful, my face looked like a malignant make-up artist wielding a can of fire-red paint had sprayed me. If I'd been stoned I may have seen it as an instant internal sauna. But I wasn't and I didn't. It was the only time that my on- camera reactions to what I was eating were real. Georg had his turn when our new director, Simon, thought it would be an amusing shot if one of us was seen partaking at one of those curious canal-side establishments that offer you a glass of neat Dutch gin and a paper plate with a dead Herring on it. I mean, really! Who in their right mind desires fast food of that nature? Is it possible that ingesting these dubious morsels on a regular basis causes your facial hair to stop growing above your mouth and also instigates a chemical shift in your brain that whispers constantly in a watery voice: "Go out and kill"?

I refused to undergo this action, as a few years before I'd done some creatively berserk German TV commercial where I had to have a raw fish in my mouth as I rotated my head from side to side repeatedly. It looked wonderfully surreal when they sped up the footage but, after Take 3, I could feel the sweaty fish's head starting to become detached from its body. Not at all a pleasant feeling. It made me wonder briefly (very, very briefly) what it must be like giving a man a blowjob. Poor Georg, being a Scanda and therefore well used to scoffing dead marine animals, got the short end of the scaly straw. It wasn't pickled! It was just a dead apologetic-looking fishy on a dishy that he had to slide into his mouth and pretend to consume repeatedly. That's why you have the gin as a supplement, I guess, to wash away the vile taste that must resemble the ghastly result of a cod liver oil capsule bursting before you swallow it.

To me, the Dutch language sounds like people conversing with a mouthful of unexpellable mucus and a decayed selection of very loose teeth. I'm sorry, but it's not an attractive sound is it? Ironic really, as Amsterdam is a very pretty and unique city populated in the main by preposterously good-looking and blonde young people. Along with the furtively active, badly bearded, serial killers, too, of course. Nearly everyone we meet is open, uninhibited and friendly in the way that hippies were in Glastonbury back in 1971. I'm pretty sure that the proliferation of coffee shops with their displays of every type of hash and weed found on the planet must add to their natural bonhomie. We did our miming to the guitars of *Walking* down by a canal but this time we strummed on long bouquets of plastic daffodills. Laugh? I nearly opened a restaurant!

So, onto Barcelona a week or so later. The three of us had spent a New Year's Eve there eighteen months before and we'd found some perfectly filmic restaurants and locations. The show was now to be called *Feast!* which sort of left our punning piece of theme music somewhat unconnected, but they ended up using it anyway after we substituted the word *Feast!* for the previous 'Eat!'. Barcelona definitely sits just behind Paris in my lexicon of sexy cities. It is imbued with passion, energy, heat, history, lust and the towering presence of Antonio Gaudi's insanely beautiful buildings. The mad genius of Catalunya and his work are un-matched by any other architect or designer ever. Have you seen or been to the Sagrada Familia cathedral that he was vainly trying to get completed before his death? It's a work of astonishing schizophrenic organic audacity and ingenuity. Nothing in any other city anywhere compares to it in scale, vision or fluid imagination. His work deserves a chapter in a book all of it's own (but maybe that's part of another project of mine?).

And let's not forget the libidinous and questing life and works of another local boy, Pablo Picasso, who lived in Barcelona for nine years when he was a young man. It's a great life isn't it? You not only create some of the most challenging and unique art ever, you also get to shag a phenomenal amount of beautiful women, father kids willy-nilly in whatever country you currently reside, wear a succession of blue and white striped fisherman's jumpers and end up on film being portrayed by Anthony Hopkins. I often imagine dear grumpy old Pablo sitting around pissed with a few chums in a bar somewhere: "You know what amigos? I'm bored. I've done Traditional, gone through my Blue Period, my short-lived Pink Period, invented Cubism one Sunday lunchtime and turned art on its head. I even knocked out Neo-classicism for five years after that. What can I invent next? Ho hum, another day, another genre. What do you reckon on this stripy shirt? Does my legend look big in this?" Pablo stands up and weaves his way through the adoring throng to the Caballeros, hunches over the galvanised steel of the urinal making a sound like a cat spasming up a furball, and unleashes all over its surface the copious and acidic splatter that always results from far too much Catalunyan wine and cognac, "GUERNICAAAAAAAAA!".

On day two of our stay we did our usual slo-mo walking through crowds. This time parading down the dusty, tree-lined, and energetic length of La Rambla in hot sunlight and in perfect synch with each other. By now I'd worked on correcting my wayward timing (I'm always slightly behind the beat) so at least we could walk and gesture in harmony. But right at that moment I needed the entire coat of a large dog to revive my punished and pulsating internals. Either that or I was going to throw up somewhere in the vicinity of the large indoor food emporium we had just finished using as a location for food-tasting shots. I really didn't want to be confronted with the sights and smells of a gaping-mouthed five-foot long tuna fish staring at me with flat dead eyes, or writhing piles of pink and glistening squid, whose every sucker looked like a pulpy dank asshole. In the throbbingly bright light of the morning it seemed unfortunate that the night before we'd all been out to what, in my mind, is the best bar on the planet, and certainly I had drunk far too much Absinthe for my own good. It doesn't make the heart grow fonder, trust me. This is the booze that has been unobtainable almost everywhere else in Europe for decades. It assisted both Lautrec and Van Gogh and many other artists to achieve vivid creative madness. It's the crack cocaine of alcohol and is deceptively benign in its aniseed meets liquorice taste, but when the fresh air hits you as you weave to where you hope your hotel still is, you are GONE!

I managed to avoid lopping off an ear when I eventually made it to my room, but I did have fantasies about capturing and torturing the inhabitants of the floor-level air-conditioning unit in my humid numbered refuge. That small band of tiny but vociferous, elderly Spanish peasants with severe asthma malignantly laughing at me from the corner of my room are driving me insane! And their incessant gossip about Hollywood Stars and their bowel infringements and afflictions! Please, shut up! I need to lie down. I need to - bluuuuuurghhh! What time is it? Who am I?

The Bar Marseilles is in the red-light end of the Carrer de Sant Pau in the Barri Xines, down the street beyond the magnificent faded grandeur of the Hotel Espana, past winos, unhealthy-looking hookers and junkies clustered on some derelict waste ground, and it's on a corner to your left. You wouldn't know it was a bar from the outside. It doesn't shout its presence in a "Hello tourist! Please enter and make an arse of yourself!" way. But when you walk in, the vibe comes up to you and sticks its musky Catalan tongue straight down your throat. It's just one very large room full of wooden tables, benches and chairs, a long bar with boozers draped across its marble counter, huge flyspecked mirrors everywhere, dusty bookcases strewn with old bottles, books, etc. and the absolute romance of whirring old propeller blade fans keeping the moist air at some kind of distance. Miraculously we find a table that can accommodate us, and our slimmed-down crew, and we hastily order bottles of San Miguel beer and Absinthes all round. Music of every conceivable type plays from speakers on the walls and the crowd is a perfect mix of the young and lithe, the older but intense, and the venerable beret-wearing patrons who were probably around when the place first opened in the 1920's. I pan across to look at the inhabitants of the bar and notice a young male and female couple repeatedly staring at our party and then looking to each other and talking excitedly, presumably about us. With the bravado of alcohol and potentially imminent TV celebrity I gesture them over to join us. The man is very camp and, when he discovers that Georg used to be the main man in Sailor, he squeals "Oh, my Gard!" and coos with delight at being able to bask in the proximity of one of his icons.

The girl sits next to me and asks who we are and what we're doing in Barcelona. I tell her. She's brunette, most definitely straight, has a perfect tan and had been poured into a skin-tight black mini dress for the evening. It transpires that she actually originates from Warrington or somewhere equally grim, but has been out here for a couple of years now. Her job is providing the sound effects for local porno movies. "Do tell me more!" I fume over her dusky bare shoulders.

She proceeds to demonstrate her gift using the middle of one hand and her mouth to audibly replicate the action of someone giving fellatio in a most liquid and energetic manner. Her talent was very realistic in its simulation. In my excitement, I unzipped the back of her dress and clutched at her pert upper bum cheeks, she responded by nonchalantly opening my fly and resting her warm hand on my crotch. We indulged in some tongue wrestling and things were looking promising for a later liaison, but 'he who must be obeyed' decided to remain curled and unresponsive to her subtle administrations. Oh how I sometimes hate that willfully perverse organ that lives between my thighs! What a perfectly debauched evening we could have had if only Senor Absinthe hadn't conspired with my manhood to trash my ego. Well, it's always amusing to speculate on what might have been. I wonder what noises she herself makes when she's having sex?

Late in the evening, after Georg and I had been filmed eating tender suckling pig, crema catalana, and downing bottles of a rich ruby red wine called Raimat Abadir, in the bustling fiery restaurant, Los Caracoles, in the side streets above the medieval Barri Gotic, the two of us and Barbie sat in the Placa Reial while the crew wandered off to get into mischief somewhere else in town. The large 19th Century square, which you find through an archway off La Rambla, is a focal point for nighttime Barcelona. It has cafés along its edges, is fringed with tall palm trees that hide colonial style apartments, and has a fountain with statues of the Three Graces in its centre. All round the square are black Art Nouveau lampposts designed by Gaudi when he was an art student in his teens. Fire-eaters, jugglers, acrobats, shoe-shiners, musicians, North Africans selling trinkets on blankets, beggars and drug dealers all ply their trade here, and we sat in the warm, scented midnight air with large glasses of the sweet Spanish brandy, Fundador, and watched it like a three-dimensional movie playing all around us. It was one of the most pleasant ways to unwind after a hard day's work of walking, eating, walking, drinking and eating. "Oh suffer!" I hear you sarcastically sneer. Justified perhaps, but we were in no way complacent about this miracle of a job we'd landed. We knew it would be short-lived so we soaked up as much of everything as we could. On day three, the Noir trio and our crew are sitting having a relaxing aperitif at a bar near the bottom end of La Rambla. The sun is hot and it's nice to just sit and observe the parade in front of us. Not just because we all want to, but also because of the fact that somehow the Digicam they've been using to film us with is inexplicably malfunctioning. They have to get another sent out from England. We don't mind the delay naturally, as we're happy just to be here and indulge in the sensory sights and perfume of the city.

I have to say it, I'm convinced that if it wasn't for Sean and me in our robotic Tik and Tok disguise, the streets of almost every major European city would not be filled with Living Statues. Those immaculately costumed and made-up renegades from mime or dance schools who busk so marvelously on piazza and pavement? Well, all I know is that before Tik and Tok there was nobody else doing that stuff as a way to get some cash out on the street. Anyway, the three of us are at a table, outside on the pavement, basking in that sleepy dislocation you achieve when you've tortured the candle at both ends. The crew have muttered their way back to the hotel to make pleading phone calls to their boss at the Production Company and remonstrate with each other about faulty RAM chips, Flash cards or some other techno-bafflement. About twenty minutes later, after their trainer-clad feet have receded into the distance, we hear vague, shouty kind of sounds in our adjacency but think little of them. Then all of a sudden Barbie sits bolt upright, swivels her head down and to her left and exclaims: "Oh my God!" She hurls herself vertical and disappears at speed around the corner into the adjacent street. What? Before I even have a chance to make eye contact, Georg is off too in the same direction.

"Hello? Hola?" My slack mouth opens and closes like that of a bewildered cod and I feel like I have dramatically entered an episode of *The Outer Limits*. They were here. Now they're (gulp) gone! I glance to my left and see, in the portico of some hitherto un-glimpsed governmental building, a uniformed soldier gesticulating with his rifle and shouting something at me. I stand up and shrug, using the instinctive body gestures of the linguistically impotent and turn the corner to quite possibly confront a shimmering gateway into another dimension through which my partners have inexplicably vanished. No such luck. (I don't mean because I'd have liked to have witnessed my best friends' departure into somewhere David Lynchian and strange but because I'd have loved to have seen the paranormal portal for myself and perhaps stepped over its threshold to see what happens on the other side).

Back in Normal World, the reality was that some klepto-fuck had spotted Barbie's bag, perhaps cogniscent of its contents of stills camera and camcorder, and lifted it from under our dozing noses and made off with it. Insurance claims were made, tawny policeman spat chewing tobacco phlegm into spittoons, sweating men in crumpled, once-white suits sat beneath rotating fans, forms were filled in and filed and everything was resolved very much later. Georg and I replicated our mimed guitar passages in *Walking* for the Spanish segment of *Feast!*, but this time we used long lengths of garlic cloves bound in netting. Laugh? I nearly joined the Basque Separatists!

Hamburg. A few weeks later. On the Grosse Freiheit, a time-traveling Japanese tourist approaches some longhair, wearing a dingy white suit with round glasses and a full beard, and bows. He asks: "Excuse me, prease. Do you know where young Beatles are praying? Where is famous Star Crub?". John Lennon (for it is he, briefly revisiting Earth for some Karmic shopping) says in that so-familiar, deep Scouse accent: "You wha'? How the fook do I know? I'm fookin' dead aren't I!"

That astral vignette came to me courtesy of a restless night or three spent in the Hafen Hotel down by the Elbe docks in this exciting city that must be psychically twinned with Liverpool. In spite of all the great gifts that Germany has bestowed upon the world, its art, poetry, music, film, and writing, the nation's traditional food is unavoidably dull and overtly carnivorous. It's basically all animal body parts, the ones that you don't really need detailed descriptions of, fried or boiled or grilled and mixed with potatoes, cabbage of some sort and eggs. What is it with the Germans and offal? Our accepted mission as Die Schwarze Mensch was to not only sample the traditional cuisine, but also to seek out and explore the contemporary and unknown. So it was that we were drawn on the first evening to a hectic, expensive and very trendy, restaurant in the arty part of town where we could be filmed genuinely savouring some real Neue Kuisine. It was all black polo necks and leather a go-go. So very us, liebling! The next morning we went down to the docks with our digi-crew and ate fresh prawns on paper plates and small light pancakes with a dusting of sugar and lemon juice. Our booze of choice for our visits to the more plebeian type of restaurant was a livener of Schnapps followed by massive tankards of Pilsener or Weis Bier. We had a deep-fried selection of every fish that ever shivered beneath the cold waters of the Nordsee in a family restaurant called Fischerhaus further down the banks of the Elbe and, on another day, we were confronted with every possible permutation of cooked meat in the setting of the dark wooden paneling of 'Der Alte Piersendorfe Bierstuben'. It's the sort of place where, if I hadn't have been restrained by both Georg and a fretful Barbie, I could have easily launched into a spectacularly inappropriate and retribution worthy rendition of *Tomorrow Belongs To Me* from *Cabaret*.

We did, of course, find a moment to do our customary shot of us miming to our guitar parts in *Walking*. This time we're in front of the town hall, in a very public square, using large fat and phallically expressive sausages as our instruments. Laugh? I nearly formed my own party!

Our Director thinks it a good visual gag to film the two of us on the Reeperbahn streets late at night miming to the choruses of our song. As Georg said before we turned over on take two: "It's like we've got a target painted on our foreheads". Sure enough, a short while later a man whose job description decrees that he has to be vigilant and intimidating at all times in his capacity as doorman, takes it just a bit too far and, to bring this chapter full-circle, sees us and our crew as a baffling and unwanted addition to his nightly duties. If I were a Casting Director I'd be on the first flight out to Hamburg to get him into movies, quick. God knows what illegal activities were taking place in the club behind him, but he obviously found the presence of a camera and lights and two guys in black suits wearing sunglasses at night a little too reminiscent of undesirable confrontations. We moved on up the street away from him before he had time to make good his threat.

The series was broadcast on Channel 4 in the autumn of 1997. A big press launch and a blush of acclaim. We were hot! The BBC wanted us to do *Walking* art programmes, Georg and I walking around Florence talking about art and architecture. "YES PLEASE!" But the offer disappeared into the woodwork when the audiences for *Feast!* declined week by week.

We wrote but did not release ten songs called Talking, Biking, Dreaming, Darling, Travelling, Believing, etc... (echoes of the lyrics to *Screen me, I'm Yours*) before retiring the project with dignity, after two last hurrahs! The Irish and then the London walking forums took up the original song, persuaded us to write new lyrics and filmed us on locations all across London.

In April 1999, I purchased my first Apple Mac. Yes, I was a late developer in that sense, as all of my creative friends it seemed had been using these wondrous devices for several years. For example, a fairly large proportion of the time I'd spent crafting music with Georg Kajanus was spent looking over his immaculately clad shoulder as he worked on our songs using a fairly primitive precursor to Logic called Notator, on a black and white monitor, in a once white but now nicotine coloured housing. I was fascinated watching him move notes and Midi information around exactly where he wanted them just by a click of a mouse. It was a very far cry from the clumsy analogue recording process back in the '80s, with its racks of kit, vulnerable and easily damaged magnetic tape, huge keyboards, moving mechanical parts in machines prone to malfunction, stoned or partially deaf engineers, exorbitant costs, stale and windowless rooms still ripe with the farts of vegetarian producers.

I finally succumbed to the Siren song and (with a penurious loan from a bank with a blue logo) got myself a G3 desktop Mac, an Epson flatbed scanner, a 28" monitor (that weighed a ton) and an A3 Epson printer. That's when my life changed irrevocably and I realized exactly what I'd been missing out on for a considerable amount of time. The last kid on the block to get geared up for the New Millennium! I fell in love with all that technology instantly and it blew my mind that contained within that well-designed and futuristic casing was everything I needed to create in any medium. That welcoming chime as I booted up the Mac each morning reassured me and excited me. It seemed to declaim: "Hi Tim! How are you today? Ready to create some FABULOUS new work? You are? Well then, let's go!"

Unfortunately, at pretty much the exact same time I took delivery of all those wondrous tools and toys, my girlfriend of the time chose to move in with me. Oh dear, now I am utterly torn in two directions! And after a few months of my day-to-day obsession with this new and digital aspect to my life, she quite rightly stood to one side of the monitor and hesitantly said: "You know what sweetie? I think it's probably best if I try and find my own place somewhere?"

"Um what? Sorry! Oh, hang on honey - ah, just got to save this. Phew, made it! Anyway, what did you say? Hello? HELLO? Oh shit!"

Chapter 26 - The Tenth Kingdom

In September 1999 I got a part in a 10-episode mini-series called *The Tenth Kingdom*. It's twelve days filming at Pinewood Studios! The cast includes Ann-Margret, Rutger Hauer and Diane Wiest! It's lavish and expensive!

I'm wearing a flesh-coloured thong and nothing else! Sorry? Mr. Sod (the accursed inventor of that famous law) couldn't let me have a part with gravitas and dignity, could he? Oh no, he decrees that I have to parade 99 percent naked in front of a full cast and crew for the duration of my scenes. I grit my teeth and remind myself of my own Rule No.1 when filming anything: the money was good! Naturally I wasn't called for a Wardrobe fitting! "OK, Mr. Scriptwriter - pitch me the idea. Make it short because I'm doing lunch in fifteen minutes with Spielberg."

"The series is a new take on fairy stories of the Brothers Grimm variety but, this time round, it's 200 years after Snow White, etc. strutted their mythical stuff. A girl from present day New York City finds a magic mirror in Central Park that sends her, plus her dog and her dad, through the dimensions of time and space into a land of mystery and castles, elves and goblins, witches and Queens. They have a whole load of exciting adventures, meet lots of famous story-book characters, and the girl, get this, falls in love with a handsome young man who is part wolf, part dashing romantic hero!"

My role is that of The Naked Emperor's Grandson. Who has inherited the odd family gene that says 'No clothes, ever'. They've given me a gold crown and the sort of wild silver wig usually sported by actors playing mad professors in sci-fi movies, so at least now I'm down to 90 percent nudity. The thin band of the thong immediately scurries into the deepest recesses of my arse the moment I don it and, for the duration of the shoot, I resolve not to have a 'download' after I eat breakfast or lunch. Flossing my bum is something I've managed to resist all my life so far.

With Ann-Margret

I have a very sexy, jewelry-draped Earth Mother lady whose job is to cover my whole body in skin-coloured make-up every morning at 8 a.m. Believe me, it took a great deal of teeth (and buttock) clenching to avoid getting a hard-on as her hands blended the liquid foundation into my most dangerous areas. I innocently sat in the make-up room on day one having my body administered to, when I glanced down and saw to my embarrassment that testicle 2 was peeping-out from the right side of the thong. I really shouldn't have felt-tipped a smiley face on it before I left home.

I'm given a lightweight dressing gown to wear before and after takes, so at least I can get there and back from the set without turning blue. I also have two male servants in red livery who clutch huge ostrich feather plumes at waist height to further give the impression that I am totally nude. Unfortunately the one who is stationed behind me has taken a bit of a shine to my rear and for the next twelve days he will endlessly repeat "Ooh! Suits YOU Sir! Ooh!" every single time the gown comes off before a take. The first time we prepare for action, and the robe is removed, I feel the eyes of 200 extras plus the other supporting actors checking-out every inch of my torso. I'm glad I'd spent the previous week working out, but I wish I'd had the foresight to stuff a cucumber and two onions down the front of my g-string,

Ann-Margret's first scene involves her swooping regally down a magnificent staircase and acknowledging the applause and cheers of her loyal subjects, who form two ranks on either side of the ballroom. Her character is meant to be 200 years old, which probably accounts for the rictus-like immobility of her face. Doesn't it? Or has her plastic surgeon given her some Method acting tips? Anyway, it's Take One and down she comes, graciously bowing her head as she moves past us all. I wave, gyrate lasciviously behind my feathers, and grin wildly at her. She sees me, stops, exclaims "Oh my Gahd!" and puts her hands up to her horrified face. "CUT!" Of course, she had no idea that I wasn't totally naked, and certainly wasn't expecting to be confronted by a leering lunatic wearing only a crown. She wiggled her finger at me and said "You are SO naughdy!" I wanted to reply, "That's as maybe, Ann-Margret, but what we all want to know is: What was it like to shag Elvis?" (I didn't of course).

Our redheaded Leading Lady had the habit of annointing herself before each roll of the camera with a short spray of some aromatherapy unguent. As she'd chosen a different flavour to mist over herself each time, by the end of the day an invisible miasma of whiff had settled around her, which was nearly toxic in its density. Another little quirk of hers was to make little barking noises under her breath before a scene that involved dialogue. We wondered whether she had a little yapping dog of Chinese breed stashed away under the voluminous folds of her gown and I fantasized at length in my dressing room about the notion of having a Peke up her skirt.

Most of us retain memories and images of Rutger Hauer as the blond, Aryan Replicant, Roy Batty in *Blade Runner*. So I was surprised to wander on set between scene-changes on the day we knew Rutger was going to be in, and find that the only new person there was a forlorn-looking overweight gent, with a pony-tail, sitting on a chair and staring into space. He wore a sleeveless brown leather jerkin, and grubby suede trousers tucked under a protruding belly. If he hadn't been cradling a crossbow I would have sworn he was the drummer of a heavy rock band from the 1970's, somehow adrift in time and waiting for the other members to join him. But no! A breathless female extra informed me that this was indeed the legendary Rutger (incidentally, it's pronounced 'Rootger'. He gets very tetchy if you say it wrongly and may well smash your head through a wall or snap your finger-bones if he chooses to manifest his displeasure).

"Blimey! What happened to you then?" I said with a laugh in my voice. Before I could add: "Hauer you doing?" he picked me up by my thong and threw me down the length of the ballroom. I landed with my wig askew and my bum in the air, to hear the echoing gasps of "Ooh! Suits YOU, Sir! Ooh!" from the crowd watching from a safe distance.

In fact, I said nothing to him at all. He turned his head and those cinematically cold and blue eyes swept over me, all they saw was a naked man in a pale blue dressing gown with wildly dishevelled white hair. I think he was more alarmed by my appearance than I was by his. Rooooootger is here to play The Hunter, whose sole purpose is to pursue The Girl, Her Dad and The Dog throughout the dimensions and kill them. I would have joined him on his quest, as the trio ooze a Disneyesque tweeness that cries out for them to be annihilated with maximum prejudice. He seems monumentally bored and indifferent to all around him (except some of the more fetching females in the cast). After one take he resumed his seat next to a very large potted plant. One of the frond-like leaves kept brushing his face and instead of moving the chair a little further away, he starts to repeatedly nibble on the plant, with curious snappy motions of his head and a strange dog-like vocal sound. I tried to imagine him and Ann-Margret in the sack together, but all I could see in my mind were two canines yapping and growling under a duvet, with frequent breaks for aroma spraying.

The American actor playing the 'Handsome Hero Who Is Half- Wolf' is named Scott Something or other. His hair is immaculate and he really should be hanging out at Trader Vic's with The Werewolf of London. He exudes confidence and pseudo-Yank charm and tries to ingratiate himself with us to not much joy. We're English don't you know? And we find his D-List charisma a bit too cheesy for our taste. Of course, we envy his positive qualities and wish we had the front that he has. It illustrates the gulf between them and us quite perfectly, we suffer for our art and drudge around the place bitching about everyone and everything in sight, and he (as a representative of American actors) has an open, positive-minded will to succeed. I'm sure that underneath it all he may well be just as insecure as we are, but he doesn't manifest it in the way that we do. One of the other Brit actors in the film on the same level of importance as me, a few lines here and there, a named part, own dressing-room, car to and from the studios, employment for twelve days, blah, blah says: "Well, at least the money's good anyway!"

"How much are you getting?"

"Oh, about four and a half"

"Is that all?"

"What! Er, how much are you getting?"

"About six I think."

"What?" With pale face he leaps up, rushes to phone his agent.

In truth I'm getting the same as he is but the beast in me (hi Elvis!) just wanted to see what his reaction would be.

The word 'Werewolf' back there triggers a recollection that just screams: 'Worst Job! Bad memories! Alert!'. Before I joined the agency, I was floating around not sure if I was an ex-mime artist or a would-be actor. I did some Extra (or Background Artiste as it's now called in that faux PC newspeak) work here and there. For example, if you go the Al Pacino movie, *Revolution*, frame-by-frame, you can see yours truly grimacing away amongst hundreds of others as 'Angry Villager' or, if you are of a masochistic nature, you could do the same and spot me in *Death Wish 3* as a punky gang member. A small agency called Dancers got me a job for a promotional company that wanted to plug a new board game (a board game? that shows how long ago this was) called Werewolves of London. I met the people in charge and they told me they had a unit at a three-day Games Fair at the Olympia exhibition hall in West London. It was £150 a day for me to dress up as a Werewolf and scare people walking past their display. I said, "OK!" Then they said I'd have to provide my own costume and make-up AND make my own way to the centre. To myself I said, "Uh oh!".

First off, I went to the local Oxfam shop and bought the cheapest cotton shirt and pair of hideous trousers that I could, took them home and tore holes in them. Then I went to Theatre Zoo and bought a large coil of fake hair and a lot of spirit gum (theatrical glue), some false nails and a set of those plastic vampire teeth that fit over your own. So far so good.

I arose fearsomely early on day one and started applying the hair that I'd previously chopped up into huge piles of short tufts. Two hours later I've just about finished gluing a massive amount of it to my face and neck. The floor of my living room looks like that of a barbershop for gorillas. I have to be at Olympia for a ten o'clock start and it's now 9.15. I furiously adhere more clumps of the scratchy artificial hair to the bits of my chest that are visible through the rips in my shirt and to my hands and forearms. I have a big problem with the teeth, not only do I start to gag as soon as I insert them, they also pop out and fly across the room if I open my mouth wider than a vole's bum hole. Fuggit! I'll put them in when I get there. I tug on some big boots that could suggest that a pair of Lycanthropic and clawed-feet are barely restrained within, and phone for a mini-cab. Naturally I've left it too late and they're booked up for the next hour or so. "But I'm a Werewolf!" I sob into the receiver. "Yes, I'm sure you are sir, but I can't do nuffink until at least 11 o'clock". I tear out of the flat to try and find a black cab going west. You can picture what I look like can't you? Luckily I'm too stressed-out to be self-conscious as I pant along the street up to Notting Hill Gate. Innocent pedestrians and walkers of incontinent and expensive dogs cower away from my snarling hirsute aspect, concerned mothers cover the eyes of their excited offspring just as they spot my speeding form. I hurl myself into the first taxi that stops. Inevitably the sliding window is opened with a sound like the doors in *Star Trek* and the Cro-Magnon behind the wheel says: "Fuck me! You 'ad a rough night or wot, mate?"

At Olympia I elbow through the crowds of anorak-wearing Games fans, showing my laminated pass to all and sundry, and find the stand for Werewolves of London.

"Ah, there you are Tim! It is Tim isn't it? We were starting to get a little concerned." I stick on the false nails that I'd distressed the night before (they now resemble those of someone who digs graves with their bare hands for a living) and take my place outside the display stand. Someone's coming! Quick pop in the teeth! I do so and then leap out at the hapless, pimply young gent who appears to be vaguely interested in this fab new game for those lonely, retentive and solitary evenings. "GRRR-RRR!" I snarl. "OUCH!" he exclaims as a pair of saliva-shiny plastic teeth strikes his left eye. As he fumbles away to seek medical help, I realise that my own, grimly discoloured, smoker's fangs will have to suffice for subsequent visitors. There is absolutely nowhere for me to sit down for a break due to the thoughtless design of the display and, after two hours of half-hearted leaping and growling, I need a fag and a piss desperately. Upon my return I'm told I really shouldn't just wander off like that without telling anybody. I pounce upon the officious little shit in his cheap and shiny suit and bite out his tongue, decorating all and sundry with an arterial-spray of his sluggish blood. Kneeling on his heaving chest I commence to savagely tear at the skin of his throat whilst howling in a manner that dogs of wolverine descent could hear from miles away. The longest seven hours of my life snail past and at five P.M. I walk home through Holland Park ignoring the stares and jibes of all in my way. It took me as long to depilate myself, as it had to hair-up all those hours ago.

The next day the whole sorry saga was repeated again and was even more unbearable, so on the morning of day three I phoned Dancers and told them that I had overnight fallen victim to a rare skin-disease previously only known to afflict Alsatians and Irish Wolfhounds and that I would sadly be unable to leave the quarantine of my home for at least another week. They had little choice but to comply. Even today, whenever the moon is full, I feel a familiar but disquieting stirring in my blood that makes me crouch on all-fours in my lunar-lit patio and howl for my distant brothers and sisters.

I've done my token two or three lines in TV programmes like *The Bill*, *Eastenders*, *Casualty*, etc. Everybody's done the same shows and only the truly sad or desperate would add them to their C.V. Having said that you'd be amazed at how many Thespabees actually do this. You'll go along to some play in the West End, sit there in pre-curtain up inquisitiveness looking at the over-priced programme and sure enough, nearly every single one of the supporting actors will say in their brief resume: 'TV appearances include: *The Bill*, *Eastenders* and *Casualty*'. Ho-hum.

Some of the best work I did as an actor never made it to the Magic Rectangle (as Victor Lewis-Smith wonderfully defines it) because they were performances in student films by aspiring directors at The Royal College of Art or somesuch. We do them in the hope that, if these potential Roegs, Ritchies or Jonzes ever make it through to moneyed first-feature success, they'll remember those of us who 'gave so much for so little' and return the favour by bestowing upon us massively rewarding major roles in their Hollywood debut. Do they fuck!

My personal fave in my pantheon of the above is called *Terence Walker on the Moon* in which I play a pervy character named Dr. Whippss. For one of the few times in my career I achieved absolute minimum in terms of body language and facial expression, and therefore my character had a realism and humanity so consistently lacking in most of my filmic follies, e.g. I had the part of a Tube station ticket man in a TV film called *Dead*, directed by the gifted Sandy Johnston of *The Comic Strip* repute.

Our hero (Robert Bathurst) returns to London after a fell walking vacation and attempts to buy a Tube ticket at King's Cross station with a no-longer extant credit card, only to be confronted by moi as a singularly unhelpful and odd employee. We rehearse the script as is and then shoot a couple of takes. Sandy takes me aside and slyly suggests that this time I do the whole scene in slow motion. Like a zombie or as a member of the cast of *Neighbours*. Maybe as someone who has only just recently smoked a massive spliff of the most physically debilitating kind? We turn over and up comes Robert expecting me to repeat the performance of takes one and two. Not happening. What he gets now is a Stepford Husband who's working in a vacuum of his own making. Mr. Bathurst's reaction is real and very amusing. They'll keep this one for sure! Then Sneaky Sandy suggests that I play the whole scene without looking at Robert at all, he doesn't exist in my periphery in any real sense whatsoever. I do it and it's another natural, exasperated, and confused response from our innocent leading-man. I could hear Robert's professional soul crying: "What the FUCK is this guy up to? How dreadfully unprofessional!".

Our impish Director now instructs me to do it as written, which I do and poor Mr. Bathurst's response is even more lifelike and true. You clever bugger! That's why he's a very well respected and eminently employable director of TV comedy. In the wake of 'September 11th', the programme was re-titled *Goodbye, Mr. Steadman* and is unfortunately why most of us involved in its making actually missed it when it was broadcast on TV in October 2001.

Chapter 27 – Observations Whilst Not Being At Home (Beetle Mania, Alien Vomit & The Skin Of My Teeth)

Spetses, Greece. May 2001. Sitting in an open air restaurant by the harbour, I ordered taramasalata as part of my starter. Whereas on previous visits it had been cream-coloured and chunky with fresh garlic, this version resembled the result of an alien throwing up onto a plate. It was a huge crudely-ladled dollop of livid pink goo, with a desultory, embarrassed-looking, black olive crouching in its centre. The colour, I realised with horrified amazement, was exactly that of a vile American stomach medicine named Pepto Bismol. Perhaps the Chef had decided to cut out the middleman and make the mixture part of the meal? Sitting behind me, a couple, probably both in their late sixties, were having their evening meal. The man had a vocal quality akin to that of an elk undergoing prostate massage. It was stentorian in the extreme and, in my proximity to it, deafeningly loud. He sounded vaguely Scottish and had obviously had been employed as a human foghorn on some grim windswept northern isle.

People were craning from windows in the far distance, fearing an earthquake, as their crockery trembled on shelves, and household pets cowered with paws over their ears. Jock McRichter (for that shall be his name) was not only bellowing indecipherably, but also gesturing wildly with an upheld empty fork. His poor wife, barely allowed to utter more than a couple of sentences had, in comparison, a voice so quiet that she made Marcel Marceau seem rambunctious. Suddenly there was a monumental crash and the sickening sound of breaking glass. Jock had stood up to shout and wave his crazed arms at some innocuous Greek family unfortunately seated at a nearby table and had managed to knock over his chair, on the back of which hung a carrier bag which had, up until this moment, contained two bottles of wine. So there I am, one minute wondering whether to measure my taramasalata with a Geiger counter, the next sitting amidst streams of piss-coloured spilt Retsina, which puddled around my sunburnt feet. Far from being contrite or embarrassed, Jock continued to bellow and gesticulate, as his long suffering wife attempted to mime being trapped within a glass box.

There are flying beetles in Spetses that dive-bomb across your path as you walk around. They have fat armoured bodies the size and colour of pine kernels. If they had human faces they'd be leering in a power-drunk way, like heroic fighter pilots in the comics of my youth. With tiny, beetle-sized flying goggles pulled down, they zoom in on the target, "This is Red Leader. I'm going in. Good luck chaps! See you back in Blighty for tea." The sound these un-fab insects make is identical to that emitted by the grubby little mopeds that everyone here seems to ride in an awesomely carefree way, scattering black clad moustachioed old ladies and scowling red-hued Englishmen with equal disregard. For me, handling a mountain bike is as brave as it gets. Although the torture my bum and thighs are getting would happily allow me to confess to any crime that I may or may not have committed.

In my mind we cut to a bare Greek prison cell. Swarthy uniformed guards turn the table lamp at my chargrilled visage, and say to me in comedic Hellenic voices: "So Meeestair Dryee, you don't like our taramasalata, eh? You Engleeesh pig-dogs think you're too good for our traditional dishes? By the Holy Brush of Domestos! You will pay for this, oh - how you will pay!"

They dissolve into fearsome manic laughter, as men in tight brown hipster trousers and short-sleeved nylon shirts bring into the cell a succession of plates, each piled high with livid pink alien vomit. The sound of a million Bazouki-playing, goggled beetles swarms ever louder in my ears.

Hot news just in on the voices front! This very evening, as I was attempting to devour the world's largest tuna fish salad in an otherwise deserted restaurant, my gently humming reverie was interrupted by the arrival of another grotesquely un-balanced English couple. These two were the exact polar opposites of Jock and Marcel. This time the woman was the vociferous one and the man rarely spoke at all. When he did, his voice resembled the strangulated, tight-sphinctered, tones of John Major, delivered in a hoarse whisper as if he had a kamikaze beetle lodged in his throat. The female had the most unusual vocal habit of speaking sentences with RANDOM words suddenly SPOKEN extremely LOUDLY for no APPARENT reaSON. All this was happening behind me, so I could happily grin to myself, as if I'd just read some particularly amusing chapter in my slim book Pop Music And Fashion From Greece. In turns, they made their way to the toilets and to my virtually uncontrollable mirth, I saw that they were both the proud possessors of matching hair-do's, of the type most commonly worn by village idiots in Hammer Horror movies of the '50's and '60's. I fully expected them to turn to me at some point, whilst crossing themselves in a loopy, gap-toothed way, and say: "You doan wanna be goan up to the Old Mill. A lot o' strange things be 'appenin' up there."

Well, excuse me, but 'a lot o' strange things' seem to be 'appenin' before my very eyes right here. As the male of the two passed by my table on yet another visit to the lavatory, I caught a good glimpse of him. Underneath the 'Prince Valiant having a bad hair day' cranial covering was a face that resembled that of a Squid Man from *Star Wars*. He had bulging fish-like eyes and a chin that started underneath his nose and sloped backwards at a forty-five degree angle to join his neck. His head swayed from side to side as he walked, as if searching for air-born plankton and his shoulders hunched forward like those of a camel. I really hoped that he would burst into excited Kalamari speak about destroying Lord Vader's Death Star, but sadly he didn't. Upon his return, his mate CONTINUED to speak AT him IN her UNIQUE and disquieting WAY and I thought that the pair were genuinely barking mad. So barking in fact, that I fully expected them both to be wearing identical round bronze neck tags, engraved with 'If lost, please return us to the Sunnydale Home for Village Idiots'.

Back at my hotel I posited a ghastly and unholy union between the RANDOM woman and Jock McRichter, until I fell into a sun-burnt slumber and dreamed of sad Kalamari Men being attacked by swarms of vivid pink-coloured flying fridge magnets that only inhabit the environs of: Gatwick Airport, June 2002 - pre-flight, 11AM. I love the smell of jet-fuel in the morning. A large Jack Daniels (no ice) and a Kronenbourg chaser as a little livener. In a distant corner of my imagination I hear the hideously catchy chorus of *Y Viva Espana* immediately followed by gunfire, laughter, then silence. World Cup mania is raging like a simian disease all around me. Far too tight and revealing sportswear in retina-abusing colours proliferates. Señor Snob is on his way to Spain. I am utterly indifferent to the hysteria and passion for football.

I learnt quite a long time ago that for me it greatly facilitates movement through airports if I am dressed well. All those lost years as a hippie, or Goth-lite ersatz Rock 'n' Roller made life difficult and pedantic when going through Customs. These days they call me "Sir" and usher me through with politeness. I think, and hope, that I must resemble the person I am becoming: elegant, confident and well off. Having just written that, I proceed to empty the entire contents of the ashtray all over my trousers and the veneer table, as Mr. Clumsy exerts his evil and inescapable hold over my character. As much as I love, need and cherish the company of a female partner when travelling, there is a part of me that really gets off on being the solitary visitor to other countries. If you can ignore the yawning hand aching void of no sex in the foreseeable future, there is an observational thrill to be had.

Looking on whilst in the midst of teeming humanity is like those scenes in a film or a TV commercial, where the central figure is motion-less and the swarming crowd around him or her is blurred and fast moving. The romantic part of me conjures up images of Hemingway in Harry's Bar in Paris or Isherwood in Berlin, sitting at aged scarred tables, writing and watching. Sipping at leisure from glass or cup, with no need or desire to be anywhere else. I love being a spectator. I'm a kind of non-sexually motivated voyeur. To observe the way that people walk and talk, their sense of themselves, body language and dress, fascinates me. I recently spent a joyous two hours with my best friends in a Café in St. Sulpice in Paris, drinking, watching and making vociferous and guilt-free comments on people's hair, clothes and style. The potential stories behind their waitings, pacings and promenades. Oh, to be invisible! A two-way mirror kind of guy!

French women are so gloriously elegant and confident. Italian and Spanish girls are vibrant, musky and sexy. German women are sterner, but still cool and classy and would quite possibly enjoy punishing me in ways that only the great Onan himself could speculate upon. Scandinavian girls combine the qualities of all the above, plus the added charm of birch twigs and natural blonde sauna-loving open-mindedness. Why do the Germans have such a penchant for black leather? Why do young German and Dutch men still favour the justifiably abused 'mullet' hairstyle?

Malaga - midnight. A week later. A vast, echoing empty space. *Metropolis* mixed with Grand Central Station. Only three check-in desks open. People scattered here and there on unforgiving plastic chairs: waiting, waiting. "Senor Godot? Paging Senor Godot?" Silence. Sleeping. I go to the desk populated by a barely awake attendant. "Good morning Sir. One piece of baggage to check? Did you pack the item yourself?" (Imagined response.) "Well, no actually. I enlisted the assistance of a swarthy and sinister-looking stranger. He joyfully added to my suitcase his own items of death or drug-abuse."

"Gate C. Boarding will be announced later." I am able to buy booze after the witching hour! Two-quarter bottles of Sangre de Toro. A pack of Camel cigarettes, pen, paper and a suntan. This is all I need at this moment. It's civilised. Try asking for even a coffee at Gatwick at this hour and you'd be lucky to get a smile. Even the plastic glasses you get with your 'Bulls' Blood' look good and wine-shaped. The pre-announcement jingle over the PA sounds like the opening bars of *Lucy in the Sky With Diamonds*. It triggers bemused recognition. An acid-soaked Lennon flashes forward thirty years into pre-flight waiting room purgatory. Next decade's tips for airport muzac have to be Radiohead, Black Sabbath, Marilyn Manson and Eminem, "Get on the fucking plane, miserable, depressed, paranoid Mother Fucker!"

More wine, tan fading, eye-bags growing, ashtray overflowing. My flight on The Web's Favourite Airline (oh yeah?) is now delayed a further hour and a half. Over and out. No one looks good at this unearthly hour. The ghastly overhead lighting makes us all look like extras from *Evil Dead IV*. A robot voice has just informed us that smoking is forbidden by "Royal Command". Excuse me? Explain, "por favor", why every table in this Formica covered circle of Hell has an ashtray cynically placed in its centre? Voices swirl like a dub mix of nationality. Hispanic teen girls with impossibly tight and low-slung hipster jeans and skin kissing tops, sashay back and forth, berating their polo-shirted boyfriends who sprawl engrossed in mobile phone soccer updates. An over-tired and bored toddler repeatedly hurls himself to the floor unnoticed. A huddle of Belgians at a nearby table discuss the astonishing demise from the pop charts of Plastic Bertrand. A French couple talk and gesture, no doubt discussing Sartre, the joys of incest and the enormous coolness of not giving a flying fuck about any- one beyond their own borders of elegance and style. Jealous? Moi? Two late middle-aged American men talk about business in voices so low and resonant that they make that guy who does EVERY voice-over for movie trailers sound like a whispering Castrati. They also happen to be wearing those virulent, pastel coloured, chequered golfing trousers that even circus clowns long ago dismissed as being just a trifle OTT. Their teeth are so white in their walnut-tanned faces that I have to shield my eyes and avert my gaze instead to the spectacle of an arguing Italian pair of angry travellers. The speed and vehemence of their dispute is staggering and ably demonstrates the negative aspects of intense and sustained caffeine abuse. Just as I'm about to offer them some pure crack cocaine as a soothing sedative, it's all over. Scowls are now smiles and they're a-huggin' and a-kissin'. Aw, shucks! If I were the man I'd drag her into the nearest toilet and pump her full of apologies. We'd adjust our clothing and snort a couple of massive spoonfuls of neat Espresso off the top of the cistern.

At the end of the "Please do not leave baggage unattended" intrudivox, there was a subtle but noticeable intake of breath, as if the announcer intended to say more, but was cruelly curtailed by his overseer in the smoked glass booth. What did we miss? Possibly a lonely and despairing dissertation on the basic futility of the unending human struggle to achieve fulfilment and bliss? Or maybe ... "Look, I know it's late and you're all tired and borderline psychotic about your delayed flight, but I have feelings too, you know? You just hear me as this disembodied voice and I DO understand that, but hey! I have needs as well. My wife has just run off with the sixth most famous person in Belgium and I am really, really in need of some serious sympathy right now, OK?".

Oh dear. I'm so sorry, I had no idea. Jesus! That girl's nipples look like doorstops, I'd give my ... ALERT!!! Engrossed in fantasy, I'd completely forgotten to check my mythical flight departure. Horror and double horror! Nowhere on any screen, anywhere, was it mentioned. Panic oozes and sweat manifests. Blank screens and uncomprehending shrugs from the burly, under arm sweat-stained passport controller, who Surprise, Surprise suddenly speaks NO EENNGLISH in the moment of my crisis. Once elegant lightweight suit becomes the recipient of a perspiring Denholm Elliot-a-like. What the Eminem do I do now? I secrete charm at Spanish securios and through the magic of Mime manage to convey my dilemma. They allow me through the x-ray machine again (which luckily fails to register the small plastic bag of Italian coffee lodged halfway up my rectal passage) and I emerge into an utterly bereft-of-anyone-who-could possibly-help-me concourse. I churn thoughts and contingencies: my flight has left, I have no credit card or money and the battery indicator of my mobile is winking at me in a feeble, apologetic manner. The next flight to somewhere that I really don't want to go to is in three hours. Who can I phone? My brother is at this moment driving between here and a home two hours away. The airport is now a Sahara of paranoia and sudden un-being.

No longer the suave Englishman abroad, I am reduced to gibbering Euro-Speak. I feel like Anthony Perkins in Orson Welles's film of Kafka's *The Trial*. The central hall is massively empty of officials and comforting signs. Even the bench-ridden sleepers seem to have gone back to their holes. If I could only muster more than a mouse-testicled squeak, my voice would echo - echo - echo in a reverse zoom moment. Just at the very moment of "OH, FUCK!" I see a tiny, tiny monitor announcing that my flight is NOW BOARDING! I stride in that shrugging, 'silly me' kind of way back past the amused customs hombres to Gate C50, where other baffled and relieved refugees from Kafkaville pant and queue. If my teeth had skin, I would have made it by them.

Amazingly, even at this greasy time of the morning, the plane is packed with tattooed golfing lobsters and their over-bleached and frizzed wives, who spent seven days either chargrilling them- selves on a beach full of clones, or peering, empty-bowelled and despondent, from the window of their fudge-coloured, tiled, en-suite bathroom, regretting eating the local paella. For they have just spent a short vacation in ... The Toilet Zone (you know the theme music). It's like a scene from *The Sweeney* on these flights: bent nosed geezers who'll "Give you a slap, my son" if you inadvertently glance at their 'birds' or their golf clubs. Presumably they've been out to visit Ferocious Frank, Malicious Mike or Antisocial 'Arry who, whilst avoiding being banged up in The Scrubs, wait out their exile in pool side reminiscences about the glory days of The Twins and dodgy dealings in Dalston. Thankfully, I'm pissed enough in a moderate kind of way to not even give a monkey's. I'm in my seat and that's all I currently care about. The fact that a medieval ducking stool would be the height of luxury by comparison, is by the by.

But wait! A 'Spanglais' announcement intrudes into my reverie about twenty minutes after take-off (and this is verbatim): "This is a non-smoking flight. Anyone caught smoking will be taken to the back of the cabin and asked to leave."

We are 30,000 feet up in the air for fuck's sake, in an orange logo'd cigar tube. How in the name of Zeus do you ask someone to leave? We've all seen *Goldfinger* sucked like toothpaste through a shattered plane window. Forty a day and I can see that my punishment for this sin is to be squeezed out over the central Spanish landscape. Oh well, I always like to leave an impression on the countries that I visit.

A very good way to observe the English at their most parochial and least attractive is to travel as a foot-passenger on the Dover to Calais cross-channel ferry. I willingly suffered this violation recently as a cheap alternative to the glorious Eurostar. On the boat it's like a Desmond Morris master class in surround-sound and vision, a living catalogue of bad clothing, worse posture and grotesque mannerisms. A human zoo of the semi- evolved.

Am I a snob? Well, if it means I think its important to present oneself in a dignified and cultured way then, yes, I stand accused. Coming back from La Belle France (which of course they all hate with a vengeance that is matched only by their jingoistic jealousies) these drones stagger under the weight of thousands of cigarettes, beer cans by the bootful and, for the brave and possibly more refined, some local cheeses and wine (but only of the most basic and plebeian kind). I find the only un-occupied seat in a lower-deck bar that reminds me of the Cantina in *Star Wars*, and attempt to enjoy my usual livener (a large Jack Daniel's without ice and a beer of some exotic origin). If you and I ever meet, dear reader, that is undoubtedly what I shall desire when you propose to buy me a drink, unless book sales have exceeded all known records, then I shall ask for, nay demand, only the finest vintage champagne).

As the ferry oozes slowly out of the harbour at Calais, and I think of a gruesome re-make of *The Poseidon Adventure* set in the English Channel, the place next to me is taken by a slightly un- steady gent of roughly sixty years or so, with breath like a Belgian brewery. His face is that of Harry Dean Stanton's identical twin brother who, having been separated from his sibling at a very early age, was raised in the East End of London by foster-parents who worked in Billingsgate fish market and consistently force-fed him a diet of jellied eels and pie and mash. His clothing comes direct from a mail-order catalogue that fell out of one of the Sunday supplements and the lace on his left shoe is undone and therefore could pose a hazard when he attempts to leave the ship. Hey, who says I don't care for my fellow travelers? After about five minutes, he's joined by a friend who weaves his way to meet him, clutching an opened bottle of wine and two glasses. He moves like a man on an invisible tightrope and really cannot blame the motion of the boat for his peculiar gait. He anoints the immediate furniture with a generous splash of Chardonnay and lurches into the following conversation. He is Geezer 2 and his 'mucker' is Geezer 1:

2."Wot you doin' 'ere then?"
1."Wot?"
2."I said, wot you doin' ere then?"
1."Wot you mean?"
2. "Wot you mean - wot do I mean?"
1. "Wot?"
2. "I said I'd meet you upstairs."
1. "Wot's wrong with this place?"
2. "Wot?"
1. " Well, 'ere's awright. I doan wanna be upstairs."
2. "Yeah, but we said we'd meet upstairs!"
1. "Oh. But I'm dahn 'ere. It's awright."
2. "Upstairs is better."
1. "Better than wot?"
2. "Beein' dahn 'ere."
1. "Wot? I'm 'appy beein' dahn 'ere."
2. "Yeah, but we said we'd meet upstairs."
1. "I like it dahn 'ere!"
2. "Wot?"
1. " Oh faackin' 'ell!"

Geezer 2 launches himself upright as if he were a marionette manipulated by a sadistic puppeteer and negotiates the Niagara of the bar like a somnambulant Houdini'. With glee, I scrabble into my rucksack and extract my notebook and pen and start to scrawl down their Abbott and Costello-esque exchange. With immense irony Geezer 1 now turns to me and asks me what I'm writing: "Sorry to interrupt you, but ... er ... seein' you there writin' away I 'ad to ask wot you woz up to." I tell him I'm writing my autobiography, and that "I really enjoy little journeys like this as a means to make notes and to try and achieve an objective overview on my life so far in a way that is sometimes not facilitated by remaining in my home environment."

"Wot?"

In reality, and to my horror, I find myself replying to his sociable inquiry in a vocal accent born somewhere between Surrey and 'Sarf Lundin'. Why do I do that? It's a chameleon-like attempt to blend in that I find quite unnerving, but at the same time fairly satisfying in an 'I used to be an Actor!' kind of way. As it turns out, Harry Dean's name is actually Ken and he lives in Ashford, Kent (since the advent of it becoming a stop on the Eurostar journey it is now known as 'The Gateway To Europe'). Ken was born within the sound of Bow Bells (and thus qualifies as a true Cockney), served in the RAF, been happily married to 'Her Indoors' for over thirty years and believes (quite rightly) that life is short and we shouldn't waste our time on regrets or unfulfilled desires. He's traveled all over the world, (but never visited Paris, Texas) is unpretentious and is a man happy in his eel-nurtured skin. He wishes he could give up smoking but he just can't seem to faackin' manage it. I empathize with the latter and feel chastened by my previous judgment of him. In a way, I enjoy our conversation. I point out that his errant shoelace could be a stumbling block and he seems grateful. He gives my shoulder a chummy hetero squeeze and says with exhalation redolent of an empty wine bottle with two dead fags floating in it: "You're awright and doan you forget it. Good luck wiv everyfink you do." I'd take his honest affirmation and encouragement over that of some woolly-thoughted, pony-tailed, smugly benign, lentil- merchant any day of the week. He graciously spends some time in a lace-adjusting loop so I can continue to write. I don't tell him that I'm describing where I am at this moment because it's too 'flies-open' for comfort.

Geezer 2 magnificently announces his re-emergence by hailing his friend with a Thames Estuary bellow, tripping over a chair leg, whilst managing to brandish aloft another opened bottle of white wine, and immediately bouncing back upright with a sickly grin stuck somewhere in the vicinity of his perspiring face. It takes years of practice onboard cross-channel ferries to perfect this all-in-one motion and it's breathtaking to behold. Somewhere during his journey down from 'upstairs' No.2 has apparently had his face glazed and his limbs replaced with those of an inebriated puppet. He sways his head in a vain attempt to focus on No.1 and says:

"Wot you doin' 'ere then?"

"Faackin' 'ell! Wot?"

This is Samuel Beckett in the flesh! Godot reality TV! I can't write quickly enough or take the smile off my face. Unfortunately No.1 now decides to venture off and hurl himself into the peaceful ocean of the duty-free shop. I am left with Geezer 2 who, with the inexorable head-swing of a basking lizard, asks me what I'm writing. I tell him that I'm writing my autobiography, and that 'I really enjoy little journeys like this as a means to make notes…'.

"Wot?"

"Welcome to *Deja Vu!* The new Game Show that sends contestants out into limbo armed with nothing more than pen and paper!" No.2 proceeds to inform me (in the sloping fashion perfected by those who have been boozing consistently since 9 a.m. and are now on their way back home on a cross-channel ferry in the late p.m.) that he himself was once a barman on the P&O line before he went off to The Falklands. I have a sneaking feeling that, instead of serving in the armed forces, he may well have simply and stupidly undertaken an adventure holiday on those islands or even better, been exiled there like a naughty Napoleonic dipso forced in solitude to confront his addiction. His eyes by now have achieved the '1,000 yard stare' look, much favoured by Vietnam Vets, and I'm finding it difficult to follow his roving alcohol-seeking gaze. Eventually our faces momentarily come into mutual focus and we have a kind of slurry, in and out, type of chat. When a male dog listens to humans talking at him all they hear is: "blah blah blah blah blah blah REX! Blah blah blah blah blah blah REX?". It was a bit like that with my unwanted companion until the words 'Bill Bryson' leaped into 'the fumes between us'. (Hey, song title?). I was amazed and then enthralled by the knowledge that even this fuzzy, incoherent froth-blower had read and enjoyed our Continent-spanning preceptor. Again, I was humbled by the awareness of my hideous and as yet inescapable tendency to pre-judge people. Until that is, the moment that my conversational confidant chose to keel, like a sinking once-proud battleship, into the floral waves of the carpet in the downstairs bar of a ferry from Calais to Dover.

Chapter 28 - You are a Chad!

She sits opposite me in an impersonal room full of medical paraphernalia. Her arms folded into her lap. Her expression is blank but somehow inviting. Not smiling, just waiting. In fact the room is an adjunct of my GP's surgery and I'm here voluntarily undergoing a season of counselling to try and remove the swirling dervishes of confusion, angst and fear that are plaguing me. It's now the year 2001 and although I should theoretically still be flushed with anticipation about the new Millennium, Kubrick's visions of space shuttles, monoliths and all that they may promise. In fact I feel more adrift, bereft and more dislocated than I've ever felt before in my life. What the hell happened? "So, what do you want to talk about this week?"

"How long have you got?"

"It's OK Tim, in your own time. Whenever you're ready".

I exhale deeply in the manner that those about to release some ghastly truth are prone to and commence to try to reach the origins of the things that are currently disturbing me. Just last week I was at a dinner party and a female friend asked me how I was. Never being one to shirk from honesty if I trust the person who's asking, I replied: "Well, my Mum's got breast cancer; I've had to have my darling female cat terminated; there's no current lover in my life; I haven't had a job for months and to cap it all my landlord is taking me to court to try and get me evicted. Apart from that I'm fine. Honestly."

The flinch was manifest and it was at that very moment I knew I was in trouble. No recourse to anti-depressants was going to work this time. I had tried them before in times of pain and all they did was to numb me a little. Numbing down was not the answer. Especially when, one night, I stupidly drank a large amount of fearsomely potent Polish vodka in conjunction with those 'Mother's Little Helpers'. I woke up five hours later lying on my back in my living room covered in blood. How? Because somehow I'd slipped, fallen and cracked my sad head on the parquet floor as a result of some dangerous self-abuse. A few years after that, when the cycle of depression reared its ugly head once more, I moved into the well-publicized and overrated arms of Prozac to try and achieve some stability. Oh you evil fucker! You may well allegedly alleviate the symptoms of depression after a few weeks, but the sting in your tail is that I will consequently suffer jarring ocular displacements at random times of the day, headaches and most disturbing of all; impotence. You insinuate yourself within my bloodstream, giving with one hand and taking with the other. But guess what? I've suddenly met a beautiful and willing sexual partner who turns me on in everyway but now I can't get it up! Thank you so much. I am kneeling on my bloodstained floor praising you.

I realised that these chemicals were in fact Satan's way of leering at Earth's population. Oh, didn't I tell you? I have now become a born again Christian, and I realise that my role here on Earth is to somehow enlighten you, and then persuade you to join me in my belief system based upon a two thousand year old credo of Chinese whispers, lies and gossip. No? You're not buying it? Good! I came to the conclusion that the only way for me to achieve peace with my self was to willingly undergo a course of Therapy. Or Counselling. Call it what thou wilt. It is something that I'd previously and naively been dismissive of. I, the self-defined 'Cynical Romantic', can tell you that it really does help. It works. It's not a manipulative system, a process of capitulation or an admittance of failure or whatever. It's just about talking one to one with a person who is not there to judge you, that doesn't know you or have any agenda. They will listen to you objectively and try to guide you through the maze of your past actions and emotions to reach a clearer understanding of where you are right now and how and why you got there.

So, here I am. In a room next to my Doctor's surgery, surrounded by latex gloves in boxes, tubes of unguents and all the other disquieting trappings of physical healing, expounding my secrets and fears to a benign but comforting middle-aged lady who seems pre-occupied with the incessant movements of my hands as I speak. And so I commence to vent. The major problem for me at my Secondary Modern School was that there were only two Grammar streams but four streams of bruised-knuckled retards regressing further back down the food chain, an unhealthy number of whom saw me as a target. If I'd carried a huge placard saying: 'I am infinitely superior to you in every definable way. Your manifest mental and social inadequacies are risible, and you are all inevitably headed for life's scrap heap.' I could have perhaps understood their resentment of me. One particularly sad individual named Terry Nicholson (oh yes, his name is deeply-etched into my Pillar of Revenge, along with 'Skit' Squires, Mick Tanner, Jock McLaine and all the rest) used to run by me on his way to the 'How To Fail Dismally In Life And Father Five Kids Class' and punch me hard and swiftly in the stomach whilst sneering: "Get your 'air cut!". It's 1967. I'm fifteen and this malevolent little polyp is only thirteen. Hardly cause for concern on paper is it? But I was weedy, arty and strange to anyone that didn't know and like me, and he was already bursting with testosterone, pimples and brute unchanelled physical force. And because of some misjudged verbal comment of mine after being pestered by some of his less-developed minions, he chose me as the target of his hormonal aggression. 1967 was most definitely not the

Summer of Love for yours truly, trapped in the leafy confines of Oxted in Surrey with a sociopath in the making on my back and in my face.

The daily stomach punches continued but now I had other, smaller kids sidling up to me between classes and gleefully saying: "Nicholson's gonna get you!" I wondered when and how this was going to happen. I felt like Ralph in *Lord of the Flies*, powerless to delay or evade my fate. Why was this happening? I was scared and confused, without anyone to turn to for help. I assumed he'd jump me after school, on the long walk to the bus stop. So I made sure I had the accompaniment of two or three friends for protection. No, our Terry had a much grander form of pain and humiliation in store and this manifested itself one lunchtime. I'd been told repeatedly by his little acolytes all morning that: "He's gonna get you today!" Can you conceive of what this felt like? It really was as if I was stuck inside a waking William Golding dream full of persecution and fear. I imagined that one of the bolder ones would tell me that he's "Sharpened a stick at both ends". I went to the empty library and sat at a desk hoping that the hour would pass and I'd emerge unscathed. I looked up as a Prefect entered and made his way to where I am sitting.

"Come on Dry. It's time."

"But why? Why can't you stop this?"

"You have to go now."

I followed him out of the room and down into the playground. My heart pounding and my head swarming with unanswerable questions. Surely a Prefect's job is to assert discipline and order when needed? Why weren't they doing that? To my horror as I stepped out into the sunlight I saw what looked like the whole school gathered together waiting for my arrival, with Nicholson standing in front of them with arms bunched into fists at his side. This is absurd! This is exactly like being led out into the Gladiatorial arena to face a fearsome adversary without a weapon. I'm not a fighter, never have been and I'm certainly not Russell Crowe. We faced each other with the crowd at my back. Another boy with a flushed face (we were just boys after all) approached us and said in Referee terms: "Make it a fair fight. No kicking." What?

He stepped back and the two of us faced off. I looked at the crowd, willing them to make it stop. But all I could see on most of their blurred faces was a palpable blood lust. Those that I knew either turned their heads away or left the throng altogether. Luckily, I couldn't see R my girlfriend anywhere. What must she have been thinking? I squinted in the glare of the sun. Now I really was Ralph on that dreadful island, with the mob gathered to witness and clamour for his destruction. Nicholson comes up close and I swing a wild punch at him, which of course he nimbly avoids and returns by hitting me in the side of the head with a right hook with the whole weight of his body behind it. I staggered back, my head reeling as if I'd been smacked by a bag of wet sand.

I sensed the crowd moving closer. He hit me again, under the left eye and pushed me down onto my back. He straddled me with his right arm drawn back and his thighs pinioning me to the ground. I screamed at him: "Please! Please don't". His face was a contorted mask of ugly power and I knew that I was going to be very badly damaged. I started to cry because of my utter helplessness and my own weakness.

How can you prepare yourself for a beating? How much is it going to hurt? How long was it going to last before he'd had enough?

Just before he made his move, he was hauled off me by a Master and two Prefects, who led him away after asking me if I was all right. No I wasn't. I was very far from being all right. The boys in the crowd shuffled away, their disappointment at being cheated of their spectacle audible even from where I stood. My gratitude to the Maths Master who rescued me was unbounded, especially when I heard that Nicholson had received six strokes of the cane and a severe reprimand. To add to my grotesque humiliation I had to sit out the rest of the afternoon in classes with the realisation that at some point during my ordeal I had literally shat in my pants. Not a bowling ball sized knicker load, but enough to make itself felt. When I got home I had time to clean myself and ditch the soiled garment before Mum and Dad returned from work. Dad said: "I hope you gave the other chap what for!".

I lied and said that I'd given him bruised ribs. This seemed to satisfy his antiquated notion of 'Men being Men' and his want for his second son to be a butch pugilist who always gives The Cad a damned good whacking. Not so in my case. I've never punched anyone in my life, and the fact that I didn't have the capacity to land a single blow on my tormentor's body moiled me up inside for months and months to come. Now of course I was subsequently being informed by the members of his tribe that Nicholson was still going to 'get me' and that he's going to do it after school one day very soon. Christ! What was it with this guy? He was like a juvenile *Terminator*: "It can't be bargained with. It can't be reasoned with. It doesn't feel pity or remorse or fear. And it absolutely will not stop, ever. Until you are dead." Did James Cameron go to the same school as me?

"Fuck it" I thought and played truant everyday for the next week, hoping that his ardour would diminish by my lack of visibility. It did incrementally. But I can tell you that this incident scarred me greatly and very deeply. And it was most definitely a large factor in creating problems that I've been tormented by at times as an adult. Just talking about it to her after all those years and all that life still made me palpitate. And I've had to inject a modicum of humour into the writing of this in order to lessen it just a little. And there are three little vindications that went some way to helping me deal with this trauma:

One: Because I was exceedingly adept at throwing it I became Surrey's Intermediate Javelin Champion (must be the Roman nose on me) and I took part in one particular Inter-County contest that had on our team Master Nicholson in the flesh. He was probably representing Surrey by hurling barrels of cement over vast distances or something. I saw him in the changing room. My heart leapt again with dread but on his semi-evolved face this time was a look of grudging respect, as if I'd somehow measured up in his book. I doubt that our Terence has ever opened a book in his life that didn't consist solely of pictures of Gladiators, World War 2 Commandos with leering faces and lunging bayoneted rifles or preposterously proportioned women in disarray.

Two: Quite a few years later when I was post Art School, I was out with my friend, Tony, walking in the countryside that surrounds Oxted. We were still sporting long hair and unusual clothing and our pleasure came from dropping a tab of acid and wandering off into the pastoral pleasures of England's timeless glory. It was approaching dusk, one speckled sky summer, and we were standing at the side of a road that somewhere down its span contained a factory where the sad and ambitionless ended up. Just laughing and chatting, being there in that Lysergic come-down freefall, when I spot a distant figure approaching us. As he drew closer to us I realised who it was. Yep, it's Terry the Term drudging his way back home after another exciting and fulfilling day stamping holes in little bits of metal (or whatever it was that people like him were chosen to contribute to life). Now this poses an interesting dilemma. There's two of us and only one of him. No audience. No comeback. Tony made it clear that he'd be more than willing to assist me in exacting some Droog-like Ultraviolence on the kid who ruined my life back then. I was torn. It would have been so easy. But you know what? As he walked up to and then past us I just stared at him and smiled. He knew who I was all right and, in that moment, I realised that revenge is the poor man's option. It's too easy to reduce yourself to their level. Power comes from the knowledge that you could have battered him into apology but you chose not to.

Three: In the 80's when I became well-known and highly visible through my work as half of Tik and Tok, and later on when I was doing all those commercials, I took great pleasure in knowing that it was precisely those malignant fuckwits who had persecuted me then that now made up the audience for my many TV appearances. Who's the Daddy? Tell that one to your brood of distorted children: "Hey Wayne, Shane, Duane, Elaine and Lorraine come 'ere. Look at the telly! It's that weird looking geezer I used to duff up at school!"

"Wow Dad, I hope we all grow up just like you!" Don't fret kids, you will.

She lets me finish and then allows an almost motherly look to cross her face. "Thank you Tim. I understand how painful it must have been for you. Unfortunately we're out of time now. But perhaps next session we could explore why you think this happened to you?". Hmm. Plain old bad luck? Perhaps I was born with a bull's-eye birth-marked on my face that is visible only to the intellectually challenged?

In Redhill in the early Seventies there used to be a hot-dog stand parked outside the Co-Op on a Friday and Saturday night. Like an ice cream van but with the intoxicating yet repellent smell of fried onions and grease fanning outwards from it like a beacon of cholesterol and carnivorous desire. You have to imagine that back then there were no McDonalds or Burger Kings or indeed any fast food outlet in town, apart from a rather grubby Wimpy Bar that sold the only items that could pass as a hamburger and closed at about 10pm. So, post Pub piss up and peckish for some ventricle-threatening sustenance, the local wide boys would congregate at the van and consume small, flat and pretty much taste- less, bits of hammered mince wedged into chilly buns and feel exotic and American. God, times have changed haven't they! For those of us in the Hippie tribe this was most definitely a place to be avoided at all costs, especially when trying to look and feel 'normal' after an evening of smoking a vast quantity of Red Leb and imbibing the new Steely Dan album.

One night, obviously a bit worse for wear after *Reelin' In The Years* and all that that entails, I forget my customary practice of crossing the main road and thus slinking home shrouded in dark anonymity and find myself walking past the Dog van. As

I draw near a sharp looking geezer in a dark Mod suit steps away from the hatch holding a slightly steaming something that resembles a small cow pat in a bap and approaches my black-pupiled self. He says: "You – are a chad!"

"Hm? What?"

"I said, you are a chad!"

"I'm sorry, what's a chad?"

"It's an arsehole, you cunt!"

"Oh. Thanks. Thanks very much."

I zone homewards and then sporadically spend the next forty years pondering upon that strange little word that has no meaning or history. But maybe, through his pilled-up eyes and his Sarf Lundun tones he managed to succinctly convey exactly how us Heads were perceived back then. But then again it wasn't me that was 'Destined pretty damn quick for a short violent youth followed by a life sentence of mortgage, kids and pensions'.

Chapter 29 – The Emerald City

May 2003. I woke up with the recognition that I had been a London resident for twenty-six years, that's half of my life in the same city, and I'm still (metaphorically) wearing the same pants since the day I followed the Redhill road to the city paved with Dick Whittington's gold. My gob is suddenly smacked by the shivery rush of memory and reflection. Whole civilizations have risen and fallen in this time-span, entire species of insects and reptiles have vanished, governments have toppled, two of The Fabs are dead, Mick Jagger is now a 'Sir' and Pop Stars are created in laboratories. It's like I've emerged from a spell in The Dead Zone: "Anyone seen my hair? I know I had it when I moved in. What are these eye-bags and lines doing on my face? I didn't order them." My body has decreed that several parts of it are goin' south, and may be gone for some time, unless I really apply myself to physical maintenance.

Things are the same in many ways but paradoxically different, as if we really are slaves to *The Matrix*. Sometimes it appears that the swarming 'everyones and everythings' are mundane and unreal, like I've been inexplicably and without warning cast as an extra in a film directed by someone with a different vision to your self. Or as if I have now become the indulgent protagonist of Sartre's *Nausea*, fascinated and verbose enough to spend two or three pages describing the texture and the connotations of my hand clasping a doorknob. I find myself suddenly mesmerised by the invariable downward motion of the ridged silver panels of a moving escalator, at other times I'm distracted by observing my distorted reflection in a tube train window when I move my head slowly in different directions. I shudder at the disconcerting random stutter of fluorescent tubes, and at the urban legend that says there are now three times more rats than the human population of London, breeding and plotting in the Stygian depths of the Underground network.

People's body language is an infinite source of bemusement, admiration and concern for their mental state. Hands and heads, the maps of character, demand my discreet, fascinated attention. On occasion, just the sheer volume of noise, the dense mass of faces and voices is like an assault on your sensibilities, as if something in the air is stripping away layers of immunity and bringing your nerve endings perilously close to the surface. When the hub-bub becomes overwhelming, and in order to balance myself, I mentally compile a list, ever changing and lengthening, of all the things that make me go "Grrrrr!" For, unfortunately, as much as I love and cherish being in London, there are times when I venture out from my domestic cocoon onto the teeming pavements of this metropolis when I want to verbally and sometimes physically abuse fifty percent of the people I encounter.

It features at No.1: the sad Pimply in a cheap suit engrossed in his mobile-phone conversation, who seems to have lost spatial awareness and any concept of there actually being someone else apart from him and his self-importance on the pavement. Followed by the cunning little shabs who sit so cleverly right by cash-points and try to engage me in pointless and ingratiating conversation as I stand next to their grubby, blue sleeping-bagged presence and hope that the machine will let me snatch another £50. Dumb idea really on their part, as people don't extract loose change from ATMs. There used to be a nice guy up at Notting Hill Gate tube station who sold *The Big Issue* (or as he announced it – "Gissue!... Gissue!") with bonhomie. Every time I bought a copy he'd give me a thumbs up and tell me that I was a "Diamond Geezer!" Another source of tension are the swaggering shifty young dudes in impossibly white trainers, hoodies and excessive quantities of gold jewellery who brutally push open swing-doors of large shops, obliviously letting them slam back into whoever is unlucky enough to be behind them. You are most definitely featured in today's Top 5 at No.3.

And, residing permanently in the high echelons of my Chart of Angst, is having to endure the incessant dry crunch produced by gormless gluttons in cinemas wolfing down an entire two-foot high jumbo tub of popcorn throughout the duration of a movie. That stuff smells like old mens' farts and has the taste and texture of those white Styrofoam globules that are used to protect newly purchased items from Hi-fi shops. The constant motion of hand noisily scrabbling into box and cramming into flaccid mouth drives me absolutely barmy and induces a helpless, clenching anger. Add to that the people who loudly explain the plot to their companions in an ethnic and excitable language, the seat kickers and bag rustlers and you have a recipe straight from Satan's malignant kitchen. Ruling these denizens of the underworld is the monstrously selfish moron who not only hasn't turned off his mobile phone, but if it rings, actually has a conversation on it! What happens now is that I spend far too much precious and expensive viewing time churning with imagined acts of retribution and extreme violence that would far outweigh anything showing up there on the screen.

OK, I'm obviously looped-in to some cathartic venting here, so let's get it all out ... A malaise has subtly overtaken this beautiful city in the last two decades. People seem to have become so self-obsessed, and in so much of a hurry, that important things like courtesy and respect for others are disappearing fast and I find it deeply upsetting. There's an increasing amount of anger and indifference manifest in peoples' conduct, faces and attitude now that is new and frightening.

Up until fairly recently there were always some eccentrics roaming the London pavements and parks, proclaiming their peculiar worldviews to all and sundry. The most consistently visible, and therefore the most famous, was the sweet little sixty-something year old man wearing a cap, gloves, shirt and tie and a short raincoat, who would parade up and down the length of Oxford Street holding a placard on a stick. His sign carried the words: 'Less passion from less protein: Less fish meat bird cheese egg peas beans, nuts and sitting', written in white block letters on a battered piece of black card. His punctuation and syntax were enough to raise a smile on their own, but it was the addition of 'sitting' at the end that got me every time I saw him. A tiny little extra sign hung from one bottom corner that said almost plaintively: 'Ask for a booklet, 10p.' People would tidally swarm indifferent and incurious around him on his endless promenade and I never saw anyone purchase a booklet or even ask him a question. Sad in a way, but you have to admire his dedication to his dietary message whatever it may have meant.

Someone who had no written or verbal information to impart was the ageing black man in a long grubby fawn Macintosh who would trudge the west London streets with a very large white-painted crucifix over his shoulder. I tried to imagine his laden journey by public transport to his daily starting-off point, but couldn't. One day on a closer inspection, I saw that the crucifix was very cleverly hinged and therefore could be folded up and carried under his arm.

Another elderly Negro used to inhabit a shop front on Westbourne Grove. He was about six-foot-five with filthy matted dreadlocks and a stained greatcoat. Everything about him was dark grey. He looked as if he'd been dipped into a vat of river mud and hung up to dry. He would stand absolutely motionless in his doorway and thereby become almost merged into the background, like the alien in *Predator*. Occasionally, he'd emit a subsonic groan or two and then resume his silent vigil. Deeply unnerving if you happened to be strolling by at night.

Unnerving too was a rather unpleasant character whom you'd have the misfortune to meet sometimes in supermarkets in Westbourne Grove. He dressed like a city gent in bowler hat and suit and carried a rolled umbrella every day of the year. He wore a manky pair of long Edwardian-style sideburns and a permanent scowl. He'd produce a dog-eared copy of the Bible and harangue the bemused Muslim shopkeepers with quotations bellowed in a voice that made Ian Paisley in full flight sound gentle-voiced and discreet. Bowler Head was aggressive and completely lacking in charm, and to the relief of us locals he disappeared a few years ago. Unfortunately, he returned a while back in a new guise: he is now Sherlock Holmes Man! Yep, the full outfit of chequered-tweed deerstalker hat and cape (but no pipe or magnifying glass) and the same in your face biblical bullshit. His temporary retreat did nothing to restrain his anger or rudeness. What is it about certain born-again Christians out on the street that makes them so vocally aggressive? I was staying in a flat in Victoria during the so-called renovation of my own property, and one afternoon I kept hearing a distant screeching coming from the vicinity of the station, not someone in pain or a drunk abusing the world at large, but more like a one person mob. I just had to go down and have a look. Near the bus terminus is a small island in the middle of three intersecting roads, with an ornate little clock tower where some people arrange to meet each other and others beg for spare change. Striding back and forth and screaming at the top of his voice was a red-faced man whose demeanour made Basil Fawlty or Hitler at their most manic seem soporific and sedated. I saw the Bible clutched in his hand. He was well dressed, like a youngish country squire, in a tweed jacket, cord trousers and huge shiny brogues the colour and sheen of freshly dropped conkers. He looked like an out-take from the famous scene in Cronenberg's *Scanners* of a man's head about to graphically explode, and he was ranting profusely about Jesus. Well, I'm sorry but if he represents the sort of people that The Lord has got on his spiritual payroll it's no wonder that Christianity is going down the toilet. You don't get Buddhists haranguing people at the tops of their voices do you? Or Krishna devotees? They just swirl past you in a haze of saffron, chanting and hitting things, which is almost uplifting if you're not in their flight path. London has always tolerated its eccentrics with good grace but these Born-Agains are starting to piss most people off.

To round off my rants and recollections here are a few of my favourite contemporary London things: Tate Modern. The view from the replacement Hungerford bridge along the Thames at sunset. The new architectural delights in the City, that shouldn't juxtapose with the old buildings but somehow do. Boarding Eurostar and travelling from the heart of London in King's Cross into the bosom of Paris, Lille or Brussels. The magnificent comfort of the newly renovated Electric Cinema in Portobello Road and the downstairs cinema in the Sanctum Soho hotel. Enjoying icy Żubrówka vodka before a hearty meal in Daquise, the renovated Polish restaurant in South Kensington and the same in Ognisko in Prince's Gate. The Bar Americain below the Brasserie Zedel in a side street off Regent Street, the continuing vibrancy of Brick Lane. The journey by catamaran from Embankment pier down to Greenwich on a spring morning. The secretive glint of reflections on the river watched from an Embankment bench at midnight. The IMAX cinema at Waterloo.

The Jubilee Line extension out to Canary Wharf and the photogenic design of the new tube stations. The continuing existence in Notting Hill of The Gate cinema and The Coronet (which has now reverted back to being a theatre). The interior of Leighton House. Still playing The Kinks' *Waterloo Sunset* in my head everytime I cross over the river. A concert in the Union Chapel, Islington. The Italian Fountains, the Orangery and the Round Pond in Kensington Gardens. Selfridges. Every old baroque theatre in the West End. Visiting the few remaining Dickensian pubs mid morning or mid afternoon before the gelled-haired City Boys in their ill-fitting suits and long pointed shoes take over. Viewing all the wonderful exhibitions at Gallery 286 in Earl's Court Road. Uncountable Ghosts. An infinite choice of multi-cultural food everywhere. The Deco splendour of the upstairs room in The Lansdowne Club in Mayfair. The decor of The Grill Room at the Cafe Royal. Simpsons' in The Strand. Everything about the I.C.A. The romantic sprawl of Kensal Green, Brompton and Highgate cemeteries on a clear autumn morning. Cheyne Walk. Portobello (just about), the architecture of the MI6 building. Strolling the towpaths of Putney and Richmond in summer. The smell of freshly-ground coffee in Soho at ten a.m. as it struggles into wakefulness. The Millennium Bridge. The creative vibration of every artist who ever lived and worked here. Chelsea and Albert bridges at night. The Japanese Peace Gardens in Regent's Park and Holland Park. The golden Buddhas of the Peace Pavillion in Battersea Park. The beautiful girl I saw on a tube last week. All of the South Bank. A smile from a stranger walking their dog in park or upon pavement. Every historic architectural gem that hasn't yet been destroyed by corporate greed. The energy and the all-pervasive history.

In the Blind Beggar Pub in Whitechapel two ageing and resplendent Pearly Kings relax with lukewarm pints after a hard day's work on a float as part of a 'Cockernee' theme day for Japanese tourists: "Ere Dave!"

"Wot?"

"You'll never Adam and Eve it, but my Trouble and Strife has just 'ad 'er Hampsteads done!"

"Well, I bet 'er Boat Race looks well tasty now 'er North and South is sorted ... how's your 'Aris?"

"I still got the Chalfonts, but havin' a Pony aint as bad as wot it was."

"Wot abaht your Gregory?"

"That's Kosher, but my Cilla ain't 'alf playin' up!"

"Well then my son, this'll cheer you up a bit: Knock, knock ..."

"Who's there?"

"M.A.B - it's a big horse . . ."

"M.A.B it's a big 'orse who?" (They sing and sway in unison):

"M.A.B - it's a big horse I'm a Londoner, that Iluuuv Lundun Tahn!"

These days I don't really do clubs or gigs in the way that I did earlier in my life, but every so often I get invited to something that makes me think 'why not?' Here are some examples that illustrate how London has changed in the first 25 years that I've been here, and how in some ways it hasn't changed that much at all. This city is living proof of the archaeological fact that cultures and civilizations simply rebuild on the remnants of their predecessors.

Two friends of mine are one half of a band named The Sepia. They play full-on industrial, techno music that utilises the full arsenal of digital technology, but still sounds funky and punky at the same time. Kate, who subtitles herself The Wicked Witch of the Web, works with Marc Almond and helped me to create the first version of my web site. Jules Seifert, her creative partner in the band, re-mastered all of the original analogue Tik and Tok music into the digital domain in order for me to put it onto saleable CD, and is a gent to whom I am greatly indebted. They played at a place called Inferno or Vom or Purgatory or whatever, in Kentish Town one Sunday night. I walked in knowing that I'm sorted for guest list entrance, get my hand stamped in that smudgy blue 'hint of concentration camp' way, push open the door into the downstairs gig area and am instantly and excitingly bludgeoned by the combination of hot bodies, stale beer and gut-wrenchingly loud, bass-heavy, dark music that I remember so well. The whole club is black - walls, floor, ceiling, clothes, hair and eyes. This place makes The Monolith from *2001* look like a cheerful and inviting beacon of welcome. It could be 'none more black' in fact. I go to the long, ultraviolet-illuminated bar, order a beer from an inky Goth babe with a tremulous, unignorable cleavage and the sort of eyes and lips that could suck your very essence dry under pale and mysterious moonlight, and survey the Stygian gloom.

It's exactly where I was in 1984 - 6! For that reason I find it endearing and sexy. These people are almost my bastard offspring from the '80's. The children Tik and Tok wanted so desperately to have but were sadly unable to. It's like one generation has been replicated by a younger version wearing the same clothes and getting off on the same music, and it makes me feel curiously at home in a detached kind of way. There's probably only about fifty or sixty people in the club and a mere shadowy handful pay any attention to the support band starting up. And for apparent good reason. The band were a veritable smorgasbord of cack in every way. They were so dreadful that I almost liked them, but their ineptitude and charmless anger got on my tits, and what they tried so hard to present wasn't in any way some kind of ironic post modernist statement or some other bullshit journo-term, it just sadly stank. The singer, a lanky, ludicrously cocky and disjointed pinhead with vinyl trousers and shoulder-length greasy black hair, clutched the mike stand in the familiar manner of one who spends too much time in front of his bedroom mirror, and, as the chorus of their first number, screamed out in a sub Rotten style: "I hate you. I hate you... I hope you die in a road accident. Fuck ... YOU! FUCK YOU!" At the end of their mercifully brief but utterly nihilistic set the female bass-player, who looked like a sulky Yorkshire pit pony in drag, threw her guitar down onto the grubby stage floor and stomped off in a welter of piercing feedback. Even the two Gothed-up and pierced girls from Liverpool next to me at the bar said that the band were "Fookin' Shite" and, as they'd travelled all the way down to London on a coach to partake of some cutting-edge Metro gloom and excitement, they were justifiably pissed-off.

A lady of perhaps my own age nuzzled against me as I sat in bemusement on my bar stool and struck up a conversation. I felt odd because she looked like a parent trying to recapture her youth and I prayed to myself that I don't come across like that. She was sweet and open, and perhaps just a little bit the worse for wear drink or drug-wise, and I identified with her and the Scouser Babes all at the same time. She asked me what I thought of the support band and I told her. Then she told me that her niece was the bass-playing hooved tantrum queen, but agreed with my honest appraisal of their humourless and ugly music.

The Sepia played a blindingly powerful and very loud set. The programmed bass drum felt like a vengeful mallet-wielding dwarf attacking your gut at 145 bpm. With Jules and Jim (no, seriously) playing their wearable keyboards like splayed-legged Rock guitarists everyone was soon fired up with adrenaline, and getting jiggy in a 'we are nonchalantly cool, dark and enigmatic' way. All except, of course, the singer of the support band. He just staggered around on his spindly legs knocking into the rest of us, flicking his greasy locks into people's faces, spilling their drinks and cursing loudly. This poor hopeless boy obviously suffers from the delusion that Keith Richards or Iggy Pop in their most zombied-out, smack-head, Rock 'n' Roll outlaw phase were emulatable figures.

One of my ex's from the '80's, Beki Bondage, had reformed her Punk band called Vice Squad and was out there again energetically gigging in her fishnet stockings, blonde mane and thigh boots like she'd never been away. Groups and artists that we'd long since consigned to the 'where are they now?' columns are back and re-strutting their stuff before your very eyes. New bands sound like old bands. I saw The Osric Tentacles playing in 2000 and it seemed as if the last thirty years had stood still. Not the hair, the clothes, the smell and the vibe of the audience or the sound of the band. It could have been Gong playing their Pot Head Pixie music in Virgin Records in Brighton in 1972. A short while back I watched a musician named Mee perform her dubbed-out, metal violin meets drum'n' bass, soundscapes at a converted warehouse called Cargo in the revitalised East End, and the venue epitomises the changes that had swept through London. It and all the others like it are designed for people to either watch live music, chill out and talk seated in comfortable chairs or just hang out and look at some wonderful art on the walls.

I went to see the reformed Soft Cell on stage at the new live music location called Ocean in Hackney (they played the opening night in 2001). They were perfect. The audience lapped up every sleazy electro second of their short set. Marc is now a mischievous, multi-tattooed, blond Puck crossed with Piaf and Jacques Brel. It's a very, very long way from being the cloakroom attendant at Leeds Warehouse back in 1981. Bless him. Naturally their set climaxed with *Tainted Love / Where Did Our Love Go* and every person in the place was dancing and singing along. Again it was like the last twenty years hadn't happened, and this is what I find so intriguing and stimulating about the times we live in, the city I live in, and the age that I am. It seems that all media are now available to everyone of any age, without the limitations and discriminations that I suffered when I was a youth. A lot of my friends, who are the same age as me, have offspring who are in their early to mid-twenties, and these kids are far hipper and more open-minded than previous generations aspired to be. They listen to Led Zep, Trip Hop, Lounge, The Fabs, R & B, Death Metal, whatever and just hear it all as music without limitations, preconceptions or categorizations. The same goes for movies, different cultures, books and clothes, too. They're like the generation that we thought we were going to be, and maybe what our lot did was to chop down the undergrowth of the past so that these new adventurers could boldly come through.

If there's one journey for me that encapsulates London in the 2000s, it's the one that takes me from a friend's home back to my own. Steven Cook is a designer and 'Time-Travel Photographer who lives in a converted church in the lower East End at Bromley-By-Bow. Until a few short years ago, this area was the no-man's land of London. You would never find yourself there unless you'd badly miscalculated your directions to the Blackwall tunnel. It was bombed to bits during WW2 due to its proximity to the Docks on the Thames, and then in the '60s and '70s it started to be rebuilt with lots of low-level housing blocks and estates amidst whatever Victorian warehouses and factories were still standing. Suddenly, in the 1980s, the whole Docklands stretch became highly sought after and conversions were taking place all down the river from Bermondsey to the Isle of Dogs. Canary Wharf loomed onto the London skyline seemingly overnight, along with its attendant futuristic office blocks and a light railway, and the tired but almost indefatigable city became reborn yet again. Steve saw a window of opportunity and bought his flat in the huge old church at exactly the right moment. We like to relax inside his strangely structured but beautiful little home and drink a lot of Spanish red wine, smoke a fair amount of spliff, talk about life and the universe as we see it, and listen to selections from his vast and ever-growing music collection. It's like being in a cozy and safe oasis of civility, with the walls and shelves filled with Steve's and other artist's pictures and hundreds of books, cds, DVDs, magazines and artifacts from all over the known galaxy.

By about midnight I'm too far-gone to seriously contemplate braving the horrors of the outside world, let alone getting onto the much-too-brightly-lit, sluggish and possibly dangerous entity that is The Last Tube, so we call a minicab. I've always enjoyed being chauffeured around whilst in an altered state ever since I was successful in the early '80's, and this is as near as I can get at this present time to recreating those moments. The gum-chewing drivers with a repetitive sniff (uh-huh) are far more intent on replicating *The French Connection* car chase to even attempt to engage me in conversation, which suits me and my brain just fine. We start from the Bow wasteland, twist and turn through empty and grimy side streets and emerge at the long stretch of Whitechapel High Street with all its Kray and Ripper connotations. You still get glimpses of a real and darkly remembered East End of legend and history as you speed along in the shelter of the car. It's like having a movie projected all around you, or hurtling across a vast deserted film set. In my mutated state it feels as if I'm going through a terrestrial urban version of the Stargate in *2001*, with the neon of shop signs and the sodium of street lamps stretched and streaking by on either side. The drivers invariably have the car radio tuned to some late night beamed-in pirate station that plays an exotic melange of styles and ethnicity and this provides a perfectly apt soundtrack to the journey.

At the end of Whitechapel, past mosques, bagel shops, bars and grim old pubs, looms the steel and glass horizon of the new City of London - the gleaming hi-tech Emerald City of corporate power silhouetted against the orange night sky. This is where London now is so very different to how it was twenty-five years ago. H. G. Wells would love it, as it resembles his prescient vision of a metropolitan future in *The Shape of Things to Come*. Like a speeded-up film scene we skirt round the futuristic space station of twenty-first century commerce, steam up the dull length of City Road and surge down to King's Cross. The area glows with the seedy light of porn shops, massage parlours and greasy fast food joints for boozers, pimps and junkies. Sunken faces atop slumped bodies outside metal-grilled shops; a fight next to a slippery kebab take-away; two winos shouting over their beer cans in the station entrance; dirty money-changing hands in the furtive shadows. A lone shivering hooker waits under cold streetlight with hollow eyes, plastic miniskirt, and bare white legs, remembering sirens and the flickering blue of police lights. We blur past the red stone bulk of the new British Library that squats inscrutably amongst the sleaze, challenge the traffic lights along Marylebone Road, flash past Madame Tussaud's and the Planetarium; nostalgically swivel by the registry office where I signed up with my ex-wife; and ooze over the mini-Middle East of Edgware Road into Paddington. We finally cruise down the comforting home stretch of Westbourne Grove, and I lurch forward to tell the driver (who invariably starts with surprise as he remembers that he's actually got a passenger) to let me out here. He will then do a preposterous and probably illegal turn in the middle of the street and roar off back eastwards with his jaws working furiously and his radio cranked to the max.

Newton, British Library © Tim Dry

I came back from Steve's late one night, sat down at the Mac and, with the wondrous facility of Logic Audio Platinum, wrote, played and digitally recorded an eclectic piece of techno music that satisfyingly represented the cinematic homeward journey. Naturally I called it *The Emerald City*.

Chapter 30 – Return of Return of the Jedi

Chicago, September 2004. My kinda town! I'm sitting with Sean and a blonde lady named Christine (who was in the first *Star Wars* movie) in a bar on the highest floor of the Hancock Tower in The Windy City. Why do they call it that? Well, if you daily ingest as much pure cholesterol on a plate the size of a coffee table that most Americans do in this city, you'd be providing your own transport, believe me. If you look down from the heights of this building all you can see (and hear) are thousands of people farting constantly and self-propelling themselves through the airways above the city. It's like *The Fifth Element* with a whiffy twist. Until recently, this edifice was the tallest building in the States. An elevator shoots you up 63 floors in mere seconds, and when you emerge at the apex - Jesus! The view is absolutely mind-blowing. The bar, which occupies the whole of the top floor, is walled from floor to ceiling in double-glazed glass., which affords a panoramic vista of the sky-scrapers and blocks of central and downtown Chicago, and the endless flat grid of the rest of the city, and Lake Michigan stretching away on the other three sides. With its sandy shore, Mediterranean blue water and hazy horizon, it looks like a mythical, endless ocean; an expanse that makes the word 'vast' seem inadequate. I'm fascinated to see that a brave but quite possibly geographically-challenged spider has somehow manoevered itself between the two panes of glass and built a small web. Now that is a serious fucking climb, boy!

"How's your Margarita Sir?"

"It's good, thank you. But maybe just a little too – sweet?"

"Oh Sir, I'm sorry. Would you like me to change it for you?"

"No, no. It's fine (reads waitress' lapel laminate) Wendy."

"Say, are you guys from Ingerland?"

"Why yes, we are."

"I knew it! Wow! That is just SO cool!"

"Aah! thanks. Can we have three more of these please? But maybe more Tequila, less Cointreau?"

"Comin' right up!"

Skyscrapers – what a wonderfully evocative description. For Brits in the USA a turn of any corner in any city reveals a scene or a location so familiar from every movie or TV series we've ever watched. It's Disneyworld as it ought to be. We don't want mice in human clothing with helium voices or six-foot ducks in sailor suits escorting and exhorting us to visit the Goddam castle. We want hard-bitten cynical cops who smoke furiously, wear great suits with perfect hair, and roar in big cars through the Crime-filled streets, one heroic hand clutched to the wheel as the other places the flashing red dome on the roof. You know those dark blue all-weather jackets that the good guys and girls wear at crime scenes in all our fave US TV series? The ones that say in big white letters on the back: 'FBI' or 'CSI'? I want one that says: 'ARTIST' so that I can shoulder my way through the watching throng as I exclaim: "Let me through. I'm an Actor!" The overweight, firm in manner but still somehow comforting, Chief of Police will hold up the yellow Crime Scene tape so that I can duck underneath it and approach the site of yet another heinous murder. I make my approach. And what I see lying face down on the sidewalk is the corpse of a man in his late forties dressed in the costume of a furry alien from the Cantina scene in the first *Star Wars* movie. I tut and shake my head sadly as I look up at the Chief and say: "There's no doubt about it. This is the work of the Jedi Killer."

At that very moment, I hear a commotion in the crowd and turn to see two of Chicago's finest restraining a middle-aged man who is gesticulating and screaming, his face red and veined out to the max: "It shoulda been me. ME! I coulda done that damn Convention TOO. All they had to do was ASK me! Why DIDN'T they?"

He sounds like Kirk Douglas with painful piles trapped in his own sound bite. I rise wearily to my feet and say: "Ok Chief, take him down." As he's cuffed and led away for interrogation our Perp fixes me in slow-motion with his too-pale blue eyes and snarls through magnificently gritted teeth, "Why I oughta –"

"Save it Bud. Hey Chief, get him outta here!"

Sirens wail through windy canyons in the distant below, drifting up to the 63rd floor. That spider has moved incrementally since I last looked. What's he gonna tell the kids when Momma drops them off for the weekend? "Hey guys, I got us a really good apartment on the top floor. You hungry? You want a take out? With extra flies, yeah?"

Like a wheel within a wheel, the circle turns and turns. I'm in my room on the third floor of the Ramada Inn out by O'Hare airport in Chicago. 'Inn'? Wow, that really does suggest some kind of Olde English resting place for weary travellers doesn't it? There's the comforting crackling fireplace with sleeping hound, here's the serving wench with brimming cleavage and tankards of ale. And just possibly a duel is taking place behind you between two young blades who look remarkably like Colin Firth and Hugh Grant. Yep! Make that a double room with a Kingsize for three nights. I am comforted yet repelled by the knowledge that every room in every Ramada Inn in any country in the world looks and smells exactly like this one. Except that most of them don't have me pacing back and forth, smoking like a chimney and flipping through 97 channels of brain-sucking pap on the TV. It's appalling! It's shallow and gross! And I can't take my fucking eyes off it. It's like the eye of Medusa. Try as hard as you can you cannot look away and inevitably you will be turned to stone. "That's right Folks, don't touch that dial!"

Too late! I'm watching an eerily coloured documentary about the Swinging Sixties and I can feel myself becoming Noel Harrison (son of Rex not of George) rewriting his one and only hit *The Windmills of Your Mind*. What a ghastly title for a song even for the sixties. Wasn't this the young man who sat on a stool on *Top of the Pops*, wearing a polo neck and looking fey and wistful whilst miming those horrendous lyrics? I'm straight! I'm an actor! What am I doing here with all these over-mascara'd dewy-eyed Hippie chicks gazing up at me with adoration? I should be striding the boards or gracing the silver screen like dear old Dr. Dolittle Dad. Then on comes Peter Sarsted, sporting the worst moustache in living memory (apart the face fungus sported by dear old Englebert), to sing *Where Do You Go To (My Lovely)* and find that he's become some kind of Summer of Love icon along with his Yank counterpoint Scott 'where am I now?' McKenzie: "If you're going to San Francisco be sure to wear some flowers in your hair." Try pulling that one on the No.48 from Stoke Newington in the UK back in '67. What was it with men and moustaches in the Golden Years? Who really ever looked good with one apart from Hitler, Stalin and David Niven? I mean, you've got fag and pussy juice lodged in there, remnants of last night's supper, and God knows what small but determined insects inhabiting therein. At some point in the future all men will be bald from crown to neck and will be super-intelligent. They will hopefully solve the mysteries of Deep Space and how to instigate the female orgasm with laughable ease whilst wearing shiny, synthetic-fabric boiler suits.

So, ruminating on the Cyclic Nature of Time, I see how apt that line from Noel's dreadful ditty actually is. Twenty-two years after Sean and I played our parts in George Lucas' third masterpiece, *Return Of The Jedi*, we're suddenly thrust back into some alien limelight as guests at *Star Wars* conventions all over the world. Out of the blue, some guy emailed Sean and asked: "Would you like to make some money signing pictures of yourselves in *Star Wars*?" In the interim we'd grown, evolved, succeeded, failed, risen, been married, been divorced, got on with other things, put on weight, lost hair, put on hair, lost weight, pursued different dreams etc, etc. But through the chance connections of the Inter- net and its inherent possibilities we've been plugged in to a completely new world. Whilst the two of us got on with new and different lives after the demise of Tik and Tok, we had no knowledge that the global *Star Wars* obsession, franchise and fascination was actually growing year by year and not receding back into a galaxy far, far away. For us it was a film that we participated in back in the day. And it was enormous and exciting fun to be involved with. But now it's suddenly a whole new career and income.

In 2003, we did a couple of signing shows in Basildon in Essex with some other *Star Wars* people. Now promoters actually pay us to fly to different counties to sell our autographed pictures to thousands of people who are totally fixated by these movies! We stay in an hotel for a night or more, get fed and watered then we turn up at a large conference room somewhere, armed with our wads of pictures of us as Furry Aliens and Squid Men and then people gleefully hand over cash clutched in sweaty fist.

There are usually about a dozen or so of us *Star Wars* ex-pats, gathered together from each episode of the now complete saga at these events. Some of them are utterly self-obsessed arseholes, who have really done nothing else since if truth be known and who are subsequently quite content to wallow in the shallows of that big ocean. Others have real lives and charm and see this moment in time's baffling and continuous flux as being one to enjoy and have fun with. We're in that one. It's good. In post convention, daily free-time (when not drowning ourselves in Southern Comfort or being mothered by elderly waitresses who thought we were too thin, ha!), Sean and I would head for the Ramada's outdoor pool. There we'd bask in the hot Chicago late afternoon sunlight, lying on our backs in the water like Hockney-esque sharks and watch the planes overhead landing or taking off from O'Hare. In my room, I'd slide wide the windows and film the traffic passing by on the Freeways on my mini-cam and hear Phillip Glass music looping through my head. If I'd been doing a lot of coke I'd have felt exactly like Bowie did back in the year of the *Diamond Dogs*. Even without it I felt exhilarated and oblique, like I was in some bizarre travelogue.

We were picked up at the airport by a female chauffeur in a white stretch Limo. Oh yes! Six of us in the corridor-like interior, black leather seats and smoked glass windows. There's a veneered wooden cocktail cabinet built into one of the side panels. Who's gonna open it up? Who's gonna pour a huge amount of Jack Daniels from a cut-glass decanter into a tumbler and drain it at leisure whilst soaring down the Freeway? Yep, ol' furry face from Jedi. This is every American movie I've ever seen and now I'm in it! Grab it. Savour it. Swallow it. Don't be some prissy English wuss who takes it all so fucking seriously and is currently flashing me disapproving looks. Hey man, don't worry. I'll be there tomorrow, same time and place as you, doing this new job in the same professional way. Get over yourself! Your Pay TV bill is going to be so much larger than my room service bill.

I've known Sean now for thirty and more years and I have never seen him get angry. Not even with me. And God knows I must have warranted it at times during the Tik and Tok years. But this one 'actor' (whose only claim to fame outside of *Return Of The Jedi* was appearing in a series of UK commercials for a household cleaning product), one night during dinner, decides to have a go at Sean. "Oh Sean, you just don't take all this seriously enough" was the gist of his misjudged harangue. Baffled, Sean replies that yes, he does in fact actually take it seriously enough to do the job that he's here to do and to do it well. Does 'Mr Muscle' accept the answer and leave it? He starts up again with this bullshit about how he really does devote himself to these Conventions and services his fans and therefore so should Sean. Basically, the guy is an arse-licking crawler who is desperate to sell himself anywhere, anyhow and anyway. And he's also a queen who's still hiding in the closet. That's the nub maybe? An exasperated Sean says, "Look. The day before yesterday I was putting the kids in nappies and then re-wiring our home. That I do take seriously. Today I'm signing photos of myself dressed as a giant Yak. What do you think is more important?".

Does our clean queen let it lie? Nope, she's got a bee in her bonnet. Quite rightly, placid and charming Sean is now getting fairly indignant. He leans across the table with a face that I've never seen before and reiterates through gritted teeth exactly what he said just now. And so it goes on and on. I rise to my feet and slur, "Okay girls. I'm going to bed now. Hope you sort this out."

In my room I thrill to the idea that maybe by this time 'Dark Sean' has been summoned and that an irate 'Yak Face' now pinions Mr. Squeaky to the carpeted floor of the restaurant in this Ramada Inn. Straddling the chest of this foolish and misguided Perp and drooling noxious and alien saliva down onto his cheap nylon shirt. What was once Sean's head has now grown massive and fearsome and is slowly waving from side to side before the imminent killer strike. "TAKE THIS

SERIOUSLY MOTHERFUCKER!" Wow, with that amount of arterial spray you really could get your kitchen looking clean and sparkling fresh!

Luckily for us the Chicagoland Entertainment Collector's Expo (catchy title!) is being held within the Ramada, so we can nip up to our rooms or out to the bar if necessary. It's taking place in the usual huge conference room with piercingly cold air-conditioning. The room is always lined and aisled with hundreds of tables, each piled high with all the merchants' wares. You can buy autographed posters and photos of the famous and the furry, toys, cards, comics, t-shirts DVDs, books and anything else that pertains to the movies. Scattered amongst the stalls you'll see, each with their own stacks of glossy pics and an array of waterproof marker pens, a few *Star Wars* aliens or baddies, some *Star Trek* vets and, at this particular Convention, a collection of strange-looking actors from long lost American Soaps. Their skin is orange and has been pulled so tightly across their faces that you fear that their skin is going to rip open if they grin too much. Of course the teeth are un-naturally white and perfect too, and the voices are deep and resonant. And that's just the women. It's fun to observe some of these people up close and personal, especially the ones who ran into alcohol and pharmaceutical problems after the first flush of fame. They haven't worn that well (look at the necks!) and carry that kind of post rehab and therapy shaky flakiness about them, as if they stared just a little too long into the abyss and are somewhat baffled by how they came back.

The first thing you set eyes on, once the doors are opened and you are seated behind your neatly ordered table, is an approaching belly. Several minutes later the rest of the body waddles into view. How do these people achieve this state of corpulence? Endless TV Dinners, too much time alone in a basement room devoted to *Star Wars* memorabilia, and absolutely no exercise, may well explain this. They hover like the barrage balloons tethered above London during the War, shadowing over your seated form and asking you odd but repetitive questions. They are The Orcas. A quiet species that are seldom seen in daylight. But every so often they emerge from their gloomy subterranean domains to merge with other members of their tribe at gatherings such as these. We smile and answer cheerfully (trying not to imagine just how an Orca couple actually fuck with comfort) and sign their chosen portraits of us disguised as aliens and then we charmingly usher them away so that we can meet and greet the next supplicants. The questions we get asked are invariably the same, regardless of which country is hosting our appearance: "Is that you in the costume?" / "Was it hot inside the costume?" "Did you meet George Lucas / Harrison Ford / Carrie Fisher?" "Was it fun to make the movie?" The answer to all is "Yes".

By the middle of the afternoon we're in need of a livener or two. I go the hotel bar first. It's empty apart from two guys in baseball caps and plaid shirts watching American Gladiators on the widescreen television suspended from the ceiling. Fuck, that is a weird show! It's one step away from *Rollerball* or *The Running Man*. These men are the opposite of The Orcas. They're thin and weathered-looking and probably drive Pick Ups with a shotgun and a banjo mounted above the windscreen. "Squeal! Squeal!" Don't look at their eyes! Instead I turn and order two large Southern Comforts and two pints of beer from a charming and polite black man dressed in bow tie, white shirt and waistcoat. He probably had trousers on too but I didn't dare check. Each glass is placed delicately on a circular paper napkin, and the shots in their tumblers look like every drink placed in front of every lonely barfly in every film I've watched. I love it. In my head I pretend I'm Steve Buscemi. It all just seems so – civilised. The service is good everywhere we've been in Chicago and it makes such a change from the dour retards who deign to serve you in English pubs. There you're lucky to get a bored "Yes?" as you stand stuck to the floor with your fingers drumming on the counter. I leave a two-dollar tip and retreat back into the hall.

Here comes BarBara Luna! This lady has history and a body to die for. She was in the original series of *Star Trek* as some voluptuous and enigmatic female alien and, before that, she was on Broadway singing and dancing. She started her movie career in the early '60s playing alongside Sinatra, Spencer Tracy, James Stewart et al. and ended up in TV Soaps as a succession of *Bad Girls*. How do I know all this? Because we bonded and chatted in a very gratifying way; during the day, at dinner and at breakfast. I think she saw me as some kind of cute English gentleman, which is a first for me! Once upon a time she was married to Doug McClure (*The Virginian*) so I guess she's pretty nimble in the saddle. She's no spring chicken that's for sure but she looks amazing for her age. It's fairly obvious that she's had some work done to maintain her looks but who hasn't and who cares? She was real, open and honest and I respond well to that. She did a little dance for me in front of my mini-cam and her face was alight with memories as she shed the years and went through some of her old 'Showgirl' moves.

A while later, a loud voice suddenly rips through the air behind us exclaiming: "HEY JOHNNY DONUTS! HOW YOU DOIN'?" We swivel round and see a very tall, very Scorsese-esque, guy in a black suit with slicked-back dark hair holding out his arms in greeting in that familiar De Niro fashion. "I'm doin' good. Howsa bout yous?" Believe it or not this guy actually does sell the finest donuts in Chicago. And God knows what else too. Couldn't tell if he was packing a piece or not but he should have been. He turns to us: "Hey, you guys are English right? You gotta try some of these!"

We take one each from the proffered box and yep, they were good. It was an offer that we couldn't refuse. Thank Christ his name wasn't 'Johnny Horses Heads!' The next day, come lunchtime, one of the organisers of the event says: "Hey guys. You're in Chicago right? Have you had pizza yet?" We hadn't. "Well, you just gotta!" He makes a fast and furious call on his mobile and about thirty minutes later another young guy approaches our table dwarfed by the four pizza boxes he's struggling to carry. They're opened up and we gape and marvel at the size. Forget loaves and fishes JC, you could have fed the whole of Judea with those monsters. We could only manage two slices each. Any more and we'd start to morph into baby Orcas. Way back in the early '60s, my only reference for pizza came from *Mad magazine* or movies. You couldn't get pizza anywhere in my part of England and I was intrigued by those triangular wedges and was desperate to try one. My parents, my brother and I went to Paris for a short holiday and we sat for lunch in a brasserie somewhere on the Left Bank. To my joy, there on the menu in tiny letters, was the magic word 'Pizza'. My brother ordered it for me in his passable French and I waited, moist lipped with anticipation. Ten minutes later the waiter swirls towards us, distributes plates to my family and then plonks down in front of me a dish of bright green peas. David says, "What's this?" And the waiter shrugs and says, "It's peas, uh?". God, I was gutted!

Bowie once sang 'I'm Afraid of Americans'. Well, I'm afraid of Americans too if you're talking about Fundamentalist Christians who hold their fingers above the Armageddon Button, Presidents with eyes too close together, McDonalds and everything else on that vast and terrifying list. But at the same time I love America for it's Gung Ho optimism, it's belief that anyone can become the leader of the nation, be they a successful comedian or a famous serial killer, rock 'n' roll star, assassin or actor. What touched me most was that on the 11th of September, half-way through the day, a voice through a microphone announced that there would now be a two-minute memorial silence for all those who perished during the attacks on the World Trade Centre. I found this profoundly moving and as I stood with eyes closed and thoughts a teeming like everybody else, I felt and shared the true sense of outrage, horror and grieving, that most Americans do when they remember the bewildering and inexplicable indignity of being violated right in the ventricles of their breathing heart. Then I thought about the Blitz on London in the '4os...

Meanwhile, back in the unreal world, all this Convention stuff is great fun believe me. It's global now. It's an absurd way to make money by some peoples standards, but I don't care. It just seems so wonderfully me. We've now done three Memorabilia autograph shows at the NEC in Birmingham and it struck me how weird it all is in the UK. You're in a featureless hall the size of an aircraft hangar, which is completely full of every possible item on sale that relates to entertainment and sport. And I mean really full. Looking down from its ceiling the venue must look like a vast maze, which might explain the dazed and confused look on some of the punters faces. Each section of Star Guests is partitioned off from the next. I mean you can't have them rubbing shoulders can you? Nope, the Sportsmen are over there, conveniently right opposite the Bar and everyone else is scattered throughout the building at oblique angles to everything else. You turn a corner expecting to find yourself back where you started, but no. You've somehow strayed into the stall of the people who make statues of movie characters as turds! It's true! I must admit that a small number of the celebs that I've met at these Conventions actually do deserve to be immortalised as excremental sculptures.

As you're sitting at your table awaiting the next customer who's going to pay you £10 to sign a photograph of yourself as an Alien, your ears suddenly zone-in to the sound of the place. From your left repeatedly at loud volume comes John Williams' theme tune from *Star Wars*, to your right is the Radiophonic soundtrack from *Doctor Who* and, inexplicably, somewhere in front of you is the *Eastenders* music (huh?). If you add to that the incessant cacophony from several arcade sized Playstations (it's all Light Sabres a go-go and deafening Galactic explosions) you are in the midst of a spacy dub mix of awesome sonic proportion. Your arse is numbed by sitting on a hard plastic chair all day; your face is contorted from the continual cheerful grinning and your signing hand is going to need some serious physiotherapy when you get back to London.

Here's an eclectic mélange for you. At the last show you could choose from *Star Wars* guests like Dave Prowse (Darth Vader) and Anthony Daniels (C3PO) at the top and those like us at the bottom; David Carradine (then a celeb again thanks to *Kill Bill*); assorted well preserved Bond Girls from the '60s and '70s such as Caroline Munro, Martine Beswick and Shirley Eaton; a surly Paul Gascoigne (at least he wasn't in floods of tears throughout the weekend); a curiously lipped but still popular Britt Ekland; Frank Bruno, three different Doctor Whos; some guys who were zombies in *Dawn of the Dead*; a blonde girl who apparently was in *Buffy* and *Angel*; and the Hammer Horror babe, Ingrid Pitt. Plus you also had Jack Charlton; Freddie Truman (the English cricketer and very friendly Yorkshireman with a grip of steel); Eric Bristow the darts player (Hey, I've just sold 180!); the actor Richard Todd from *The Dam Busters*, and the very funny and wicked Danny John-Jules from *Red Dwarf*. All of us are staying in the same hotel in Solihull. Yep, it's another Ramada. Virtually identical in layout and decor to its US or European counterparts, but somehow lacking the same efficiency and amenities.

Imagine the scene in the hotel bar at about 8.30 at the end of day one. There's Carradine sat drinking at a corner table with a few people, dressed from head to toe in black and chain smoking. I walk in dressed head to toe in black and smoking like a chimney, he looks up at me with those mystic, stoner eyes, points at my suit and husks: "Hey man. Cool!" I nod and smile at him and do my usual thing of not asking the great many questions that I'd like to. Sean, myself and two other *Jedi* actors find a table, settle in to the first of several glasses of Southern Comfort, and overhear Dave Prowse telling Vader stories in his soft West Country burr to a couple of fans that have somehow snuck their way in. It's sad that these days Mr. Prowse is now reliant upon a crutch for his mobility but even when he's Off Duty he always takes the time to speak to his audience. He's just self-published his two volume autobiography. He's called it *Straight From The Force's Mouth* Love it! Up at the bar the Bond Girls are standing with their drinks, dressed to kill and ready to hit the highspots of Solihull's nightlife. Don't hold your breath girls! Britt is nowhere to be seen and neither are the three Doctors. Maybe they've collectively whisked her off inside the Tardis to meet her younger self at play in the 1960s? The assorted sportsmen are not present either luckily. A six-foot-seven Cherokee Indian named Lightning Bear has now joined our table. We opt for calling him 'Ning' for short. He's a Stuntman with an impressive CV. Ning has the longest hair of any male I've ever seen and a voice as deep as Lake Huron. A very droll and funny man who tells us at some point that he's now only got half of each lung left but still smokes a pack or two of 'Luckies' a day. Now, for me, that really would be The Great Spirit's way of saying: "It's time to quit don't you think?"

Somehow in the midst of this starry and strange gathering has appeared some pissed up local dude by mistake. He's very far-gone and is wearing shades indoors, which is a bad sign at the best of times. He's clad in shabby black leather and has a face the texture and colour of a Docker's glove. He's shouting a selection of incomprehensibles at anybody within earshot. Somewhere in his blurred vision he clocks yours truly all in black and weaves to his feet exclaiming: "What are you, the fuggin' SS? Sieg Heil!" He flashes me a Nazi salute before he's escorted from the room by a couple of brave hotel staff. Half an hour later, as we leave the Ramada to find somewhere to eat, we spy Carradine in the hotel restaurant seating at the piano with fag between his lips, doodling away like a true barfly and completely oblivious to all and sundry. Now that is cool!

A disquieting aspect to the shows we do in England is the large amount of disabled people who attend. It's not their proximity or their deformity that is disturbing, it is the realization that, in spite of the vast quantity of shit that genetics has thrown at them, they have overcome it and found a very necessary solace in myth and escapism. Why is that disturbing? Because it makes you realize how glib and banal are the day-to-day worries of those of us that are physically able. How we take all this health and mobility for granted and fall into a trough of self-indulgent despair the instant we have a headache, can't pay that bill, or inadvertently erase the harddrive on our computer. *Star Wars* can be seen as an allegory for how we can live our lives and surmount adversity. The late Joseph Campbell recognized this. In his book *The Power of Myth*, he says: "*Star Wars* has a valid mythological perspective. That movie communicates. It is in a language that talks to young people... It asks, are you going to be a person of heart and humanity – because that's where the life is, from the heart – or are you going to do whatever seems to be required of you by what might be called 'intentional power'? When Ben Kenobi says, "May the Force be with you," he's speaking of the power and energy of life, not of programmed political intentions." Even though circumstance has taken away a lot of activities for people with a handicap, this movie saga and the ethos behind it gives them the strength to cope. It enables them to see that in spite of it all there is still more to life than the hideous enormity of being trapped within a body that does not work properly. It's about choice. I have the utmost love and respect for them and if, in some tiny but maybe significant way, we can help them through the web of their lives then that can only be good.

I do secretly admire anyone that actually has a hobby or a need to collect. Call them 'Anal Wan Kenobi's' if it makes you feel better but it's not these people that are bored and vindictive with a need to lash out at the innocent. They're not baying like rabid and vengeful dogs at the fact that some retard wearing a number has just kicked a round piece of leather into the wrong goal at a football match. They aren't the ones hanging out on the street in E14 kicking the shit out of someone who innocently walks past them. And they certainly aren't the pissed up morons throwing up over a stranger's shoes outside a bar in Soho at 2am. No, they're at home counting the infinite array of Hasbro toys of *Star Wars* figures that they've collected over the years, or watching every scene from the movies and lip synching the dialogue or spending weeks knocking up a Vader costume to wear at an event where they feel at one with others. It's harmless and gentle and provides a buffer against the grim realities of the Matrix.

Wendy brings us round three of our liquid relaxation in the vertiginous bar of the Hancock Tower. I tongue the Margarita salt from off my lips and look across at Sean. We're back in The Zone, Tik and Tok world. After all this time. We're still the same boys but now let loose in a different toyshop. One day not so long ago, out of the murky blue and after many years of trying to re-instigate our magic and for good reasons being denied, Sean suddenly calls me after our first few *Star Wars* conventions and says: "Do you want to do something new? As Tik and Tok?"

The little brown spider in the window glass looks up at us with his many eyes and says: " I knew it. What did I tell you? You guys! Y'know, you got something special. People love you; you know whad I'm sayin'? Just go for it! Got any donuts?"

Chapter 31 - Parisian Spirits

I re-read Charles Baudelaire's collection of poetry called *Les Fleurs du Mal (Flowers of Evil)* at a friend's house in France a few years ago, having originally enjoyed its evocation of the soul's underbelly when I was a young hippie in the early '70's. It wasn't until I picked it up again all those years later that his work really began to resonate with me. This was possibly connected to the fact that I read a new translation. The one I had back in 1972 was translated in the '30's and '40's and suffered from that oh-so-English, dry and academic rendering that basically makes things hard for me to get my teeth and spirit into. The new translation was spunky, dangerous with clarity. It was exhilarating. But the main reason Baudelaire got to me this time, and seeped in through the pores of my imagination, is because I'd done a lot of living in the interim.

After many years of practice, I had mastered the art of self-indulgence and immoderation. I'd been in love and I'd been hurt and, sadly, I had hurt others. I had travelled a lot, slept around with abandon, dressed with style and taste. I had suffered, and had relished the slings and arrows of a measure of fame. I'd earned and spent far too much money. Inevitably I'd also taken a substantial amount of most drugs known to man (except heroin, which is one to avoid at all costs if you have an addictive personality like mine). I started to think more and more about his life and my life. All my actions listed above were ones that Charles had luxuriated in a century earlier but without any restraint whatsoever. Of course his legendary self-loathing and guilt outweighed any similar notions that I have entertained over the last few years. One of his most relevant and abrasive poems has a magnificently unwieldy title: *L'Héautontimorouménos* (The Self-Punisher) but contains a very revealing line about the man's true feelings: "I am my own heart's vampire." God, I wish I'd written that! Well, there's still time isn't there?

Anyway, all of his newly rediscovered literary gems got me motivated to set a number of his poems to my own music. Armed with the recently acquired joys of a piece of computer software called Logic Audio Platinum, plus the EXS 84 sampler, a Les Paul guitar and my trusty Apple Mac G4 (how's that for product placement!) I set about doing it. All of a sudden I have a 24-track digital recording set-up my desktop, complete with more EQ and FX than you can shake your cock at. Believe me, after enduring years of airless recording studios, partially deaf engineers and banks of cumbersome analogue recording equipment in the '80's, you tend to shake your cock around quite a lot in the face of this glorious technology. I roped in a few friends to perform vocals that I wasn't able to do myself; most notably Katharine Blake, Gena Dry, Francis McGee and Nikki McKevitt, and a girl named Mee played metal

violin. And after a year of recording, mixing, indecision, re-recording and editing I'd finished. A large part of it I really liked and still do, but having completed what I naively thought might be my Grand Oeuvre I decided I couldn't face the horrors and frustrations of trying to sell it. I felt that bad memories from my past failures in this grim arena might slide all too easily to the surface and insinuate their soiled worms of regret into the ME that is here NOW. Shit! What do I do?

Internal voice says: "OK Tim, keep the music on ice (because you never know when you might find a way through with it) and try writing a fictional biography of Baudelaire instead." It's funny how life sends you down unexpected side roads, isn't it? All of a sudden, at what you could say is an obscenely late stage in your physical and spiritual development, you discover a creative facility that you'd never previously contemplated. And somehow, the ceremony begins and things start to flow from your brain and out through your nicotine-stained fingers that jab furiously at the keyboard. I'm focussed, willing and ready. I write a first chapter. Perversely, I've decided that the book shall start with Baudelaire's death in his mother's arms at the age of forty-six.

After finishing chapter one, I start to entertain doubts about being able to sustain writing the story of a 19th Century man's life. Something wasn't happening. I knew I could get inside this poet's head and speak his thoughts, fears, and obsessions but retaining myself within the environs of a long gone world didn't excite me as much as I'd hoped it would. I wanted my Baudelaire wearing an i-Pod, earphones and a head full of downloaded MP3s with which to abuse himself. But I wasn't brave enough then to make it so... until the moment I realized that the dead are in fact all around us, every moment of every day, and that with just a mere nudge of our consciousness we can observe them at play. And so I chose to do exactly that. I would go to Paris, stay for a few days in a hotel and, under the influence of alcohol, hashish and opium, tune into the debauched brain of my literary hero. Bingo! A thousand light bulbs suddenly illuminate and cinematically flicker inside my head. So how did I make this happen? Here's how but it is painful:

"Let me tell you about heartache and the loss of God." Jim Morrison (1969).

My Mother died from cancer of the brain in December 2003. Watching her slip away from me in that ghastly hospital ward, connected by tubes to her life support system, is an image that I will never ever be able to remove from my head. But at least I was able to say goodbye to her. I cradled her in my arms, indifferent to the stares of other patients and ward staff, with tears coursing down my face as I stroked her thin, white hair and told her how I loved her with all my heart. She stared up at me, and although she could no longer speak or even move her frail skeletal form, I believe that somewhere inside her she did know who I was and what I was saying to her. I asked her to let go, just go to sleep now. Everything will be all right. I called her "Mummy" for the first time since I was a young boy and in some way our roles were now completely reversed. She was my ailing child and my love for her was completely unconditional. Writing this now I am barely able to see the screen and keyboard through my tears. When I got back to London I howled and sobbed in my flat with a gut-wrenching anguish so deep and primal that I hope to God that

I shall never, ever feel that amount of indescribable loss and pain again. It was a scream out into the void from my very soul. Every shred of maternal love, comfort and security was now stripped away from me. No more safety net. No more joy at her indomitable spirit and humour. No more comfort and sympathetic ears for my honest outpourings of emotions and events. She never judged me; always encouraged me, and I shall justify her pride in me whatever it takes. Bless you, my darling.

After the private (and sometimes public) grief, organizing the funeral and wake, probate, solicitors' dealings, I found myself the vendor of her flat in Reigate. It sold five months later and I was the recipient of a large amount of cash (by my standards anyway) and I used a fair proportion of it to finance my creating this idea for a new book. I spent two months preparing and planning, and decided to embark upon this crazed but necessary experiment in July. Why? Because Baudelaire entered into terminal decline in July of 1867. That's good enough for me. Plus the fact that Paris is even more beautiful in the summer.

My strange joy at being able to stay in the immediate vicinity of his creativity and self-destructiveness was unconfined. For me it was as a way of getting 'close'. Is that any weirder than going on a pilgrimage to the Holy Land or wearing an effigy of an agonized man nailed to a crucifix around your neck? I'd also love to rent an apartment in the Dakota building, take a leak and a peek in the toilet at Graceland, and spend a night in the same room in which Marilyn pilled her life away.

For my three days in Paris I booked a double room on the third floor of the Hotel du Quai Voltaire on the Left Bank, because that's where Baudelaire rented lodgings for two years or more and wrote *Les Fleurs Du Mal*. It seemed to be the perfect place from which to start my internal journey. I knew it was going to be fairly expensive for me to do this the right way but I believed that for my creativity it would all be worth it. I packed two medium-sized suitcases, one chocka with clothes, personals and toiletries; the other brim-full with books, pens, lap-top, props, my digital camera, and every intoxicant I thought I'd need. Namely: two bottles of Remy Martin V.S.O.P and two bottles of now legal Absinthe bought from that wonderful cluttered booze shop at the Wardour Street end of Old Compton Street, Soho. I also smuggled out half an ounce of soft and heady Afghan black hashish. How? Let's just say that where I stashed the dope on the outward journey slightly modified the way I walked and sat. As those metallic, potato-loving aliens from a distant TV Ad might have cackled: "For smash-get hash!"

I wanted opium really, because that was very much an ingredient of Baudelaire's internal explorations but, these days, it's not only impossible to get your hands on it's also labelled as a 'Class A' drug. It nestles high up on that inventory of self-abuse just below heroin, cocaine, methedrine and crack. Unfair in many ways, as this dream-inducing poppy paste only sends you somewhere peaceful and physically parallel, and doesn't motivate you to drape yourself in a soiled sleeping-bag and lurk next to cashpoints in big cities, mug people or wave guns from the passenger window of stolen fast cars in South London. I tried it once or twice back in the early '70's, in one of those reckless adventures: "Hey guys, let's be Thomas de Quincey for an evening!" We smoked the soft black pellet in a pipe and shortly afterwards I became Tim de Queasy, whose body decreed that any vertical movement might provoke a large amount of spontaneous technicolour vomiting. I had no option but to lie down, surrender and experience an hour or two of pleasurably sensual hallucinations. I was now prepared and able to go way out in appropriate style in the same locations and with the same substances as my protagonist. I felt that I had to experience some of his highs and lows in order to truly do him justice. It's a personalised and potentially dangerous literary equivalent of Method Acting, what you could call the 'Fear And Loathing In Las Vegas' factor. I wouldn't condone it or encourage it in others, but it certainly worked for me. So what I hopefully end up with is a new book created within the mind of another mind that dreams of yet another mind. Are you with me? Get on board the train of thought, crank-up the volume, and let's go!

I caught the 9.23 am Eurostar from Waterloo to Paris on a bright and clear early July morning. After struggling on board with my bulging suitcases and an arse stuffed with a cling film- wrapped illegal substance, I settled back into my plush First Class seat and thought on the strange adventure that I was about to undertake. Somewhere in the midst of the train's interminable crawl through the outer suburbs of London I swayed my way through two carriages to the buffet car and got myself a large Cognac and a double Espresso. Well, might as well kick off in style, I reasoned. I tried out a winning grin on a gaggle of virulently-clad American tourists, mulling over the choice of snacks printed on a laminated menu: "Gee, what's this 'Ham and Cheese Melt' thing?" I could have answered that it's a microwaved sandwich layered with lukewarm French cheese and ham whose taste resembles that of a polystyrene bag, but I didn't. One of the men, whom I've named 'Ed', sported a sandy-hued toupee of the type favoured by Charlton Heston (that always look a bit obvious around the back of the neck) flashed me a disapproving glance as he spotted my own journey refreshments.

'Gun-loving Xenophobe', I laughed inside my head. 'Drug-needing Limey Fag', he silently muttered. Mentally cocking an invisible trigger as I paused inside the crosshairs of his imagination. Back in the safety of my seat, I savoured the fiery burn of the brandy as it slid down my throat, and planned out a rough itinerary for the next three days. The Hotel overlooks the Seine just down from the Musée D'Orsay. Back in 1856, I imagine the building was fairly decrepit, an affordable stopover for doomed poets down on their luck. Now it's a modest, tastefully furnished two Star hotel with great views of the river and the Louvre sprawled along the opposite bank. During the long night of Day One I shall follow Baudelaire's documented instructions for the taking of hashish and see where it leads me, and on Day Two I shall do the same again.

Just after 2 p.m, following a white-knuckle taxi ride from the Gare du Nord across the blisteringly hot heart of Paris, courtesy of a sneeringly misanthropic driver with a bald head shaped like a thumb, I entered the hotel with my almost adequate French on full display and an hopefully unthreatening and sincere smile plastered across my face. I staggered across the lobby under the weight of my nefarious cases to the check-in. I was wearing a lightweight black suit, a grey short-sleeved shirt, and a pair of Paul Smith white suede brogues. This type of outfit always gives me the look and essence of being 'somebody', and not just another scruffy tourist or gauche Brit who, inelegantly clad and socially unwieldy, still believes the world owes him a tug of the forlock. Barring social activity, dealing with the fallout from Mum's death, and rare pieces of work from the remnants of my previous incarnations as an actor and photographer, this project had become my sole focus.

It's all in the details, do you see? For example, I chose an eau de toilette for Charles from the very charming and elegant 'Diptyque' Parfumerie on Westbourne Grove. It's the sort of emporium that, should Peter Süskind wander in by chance whilst writing the sequel to *Perfume*, he would have to indulge in a masturbatory scene of olfactory frenzy only glimpsed at in his moist dreams. What I purchased eventually was a musky, almost Frankincensual, aroma called *Trois*. Which makes one 'Redolent of a wild-eyed hedonist at 4 a.m. staggering homeward wreathed in the exotic fumes of recent debauchery and decadent intoxication'. Well, that's what it says on the front of the box in my imagination anyway. I went to Selfridges to purchase the sort of dressing gown in which I presumed one could recline intoxicated à la Baudelaire without mirror-based embarrassment. There's not a lot of choice these days for the needy aesthete craving a garment within which to nocturnally enjoy himself. It's paisley time! MC Hammer probably still sports extravagant and regrettable pantaloons in this over used pattern. Ponder, if you will, upon a man doomed to strut and sweat his hours within the dingy storeroom of Hell's outtakes in unforgiveable trousers. It's OK, Mr. Hammer, we don't want to touch that! I ended up with a satisfactorily elegant, full-length, maroon silk robe with a black velveteen collar and cuffs. From Liberty's I bought four large silk scarves in sympathetic colours and designs that I thought might fulfill their imagined purpose further down the 'Rue le Day' (I wouldn't be wearing them), and subsequently packed them along with half a dozen small church candles, a set of six metal drink coasters, with felt on the underside, two packets of different flavoured incense, and two flat wooden holders designed for burn- ing the fragrant sticks. And, before I left home, I burned a CD of eight of my own Baudelaire Set to Music tracks, naturally entitled *Dark Flowers*. The compilation would be useful for getting me into the essence of the poet's work and therefore facilitate my own writing.

I decided to keep my venture pretty much to myself as I didn't want intrusions or even possible dissuasions to enter my conviction. I did, however, tell my two friends who live in northern France exactly what I was going to be doing, and gave them the phone number of the place where I was staying. As far as everyone else was concerned I was just going to be spending a few days in Paris in order to chill out and research a mooted idea for a book. I thought it wise to take out some comprehensive travel insurance, so I'd have a safety net in case things went wrong.

My hotel room is inherently cheerful and light. The beckoning demon of the mini bar is crouched and imploring beside the TV, to whom I gibe, "Not this time, pal. Ha!". Carpet-length floral curtains in hues of Autumn frame the paired French windows; two fake antique and therefore arse-unfriendly chairs, upholstered in powder blue, are positioned either side of a repro Louis XIVth writing desk; and two shaded bedside lights on swivelling arms protrude from either side of the bed. The cover on the Kingsize is soft red quilted and looks vaguely opulent. It's time to re-arrange. Time to get wise. Opening up the lids of my two black Samsonite suitcases,

I desport their bizarre contents upon the innocent surface of the bed. After clothes are hung, toiletries placed, and accoutrements gathered, I hesitantly start to garner my needs for the inducive night. Removal of the stashed hash in the bathroom was a squeamish example of the art of proctology, a male version of birth induction. I held the glistening lump up to the light and exclaimed, "It's a boy!" Hang on, It's only 3.30 pm! What the fuck? Oh great. Now I feel obliged to venture out to eat and imbibe something. So I clutch a notebook and pen and head off.

Instinct leads me to some pseudo Belle Epoque brasserie stashed away in the unknown streets behind the D'Orsay Museum to my right. Where, sitting outside on the terrace, I work my way through a Croque Monsieur, complete with pommes frites, and a light dressed salad, plus a chilled half-bottle of Chablis. I've found that it's easier to eat out on your own in foreign cities if you have something to do with your hands when not eating or drinking, like reading a book or scribbling enigmatically from pen to paper. This way you seem to have a purpose rather than being seen as a slightly sad character reduced to solitary dining for whatever reasons. It seems to work, for my waiter, when not balletically weaving with tray aloft from table to table, asks me tentatively in that weird and fractured Franglais now so usefully prevalent in France if perhaps I am a writer? I shrug modestly and in the same new language say that: "Oui, c'est vrai, and I'm here to write a book about Charles Baudelaire." He now calls upon that magnificent Gallic gesture of shoulder and arms which, coupled with a throaty repertoire of: "Aah, Encroyable!" and "Oh, Baudelairrrre uh?".

"Form-i-da-ble!" suggests he's impressed. I wish I could convey this exchange succinctly but due to the non-visual and non-audio limitations of the written word I'll have to leave it up to you to imagine. After a Crème brûlée, a large café noir and the shedding of twenty Euros for the bill, I sidle down to the embankment of the Seine to peruse the wares of the myriad second-hand booksellers strung out along that stretch of the Left Bank. Ancient and modern tomes of all shapes and sizes nestle against lots of Lautrec posters and cards from the Moulin Rouge period. The bored vendors of these collections bathe in the après lunch sun, their corpulent bums wedged into the type of folding metal and plastic chairs that you'd take on a picnic. Suddenly to my joy I spy a Jim Morrison poster! It's a classic and features two police mugshots of an unrepentant and bemused Jim from his arrest in New Haven, Connecticut, in October 1967. Displayed beneath the pictures are his fingerprints and the arrest sheet. This is too good to pass up. I shadow over the slumbering gent and excitedly gasp, "Monsieur? Pardonez-moi. Mais, Je veux acheter cette affiche là!" gesturing towards the needed article. The stallholder starts awake, his peculiar dream of two blonde German soldiers wearing fishnet stockings fading as he squints into the white glare of the afternoon sun. He rises reluctantly to his feet, detaching the gripping arms of his seat from his weighty thighs, rolls the poster into a tube and wraps it in white paper. "Merci. Au revoir!" I cheerfully exclaim whilst handing him a 10 Euro note. It's a good omen. Why? Because I have a notion that Jim Morrison was Charles Baudelaire reincarnated. But that's another story.

Back at the hotel, cramped into the brightly mirrored and un-comfortably small elevator destined for my floor, I catch a glimpse of a haggard Max Von Sydow staring at me from the unforgiving glass opposite. "Jesus!" I spasm. Then, realizing that I'm only looking at a ghastly down-lit image of myself, I turn quickly away with relief. Now is not the time for me to be engaged in a lengthy game of chess with the Grim Reaper or suffering the demonic manifestations of a pubescent girl with a head that rotates through 360 degrees. The room door hisses shut behind me and I exhale a hiccup "Fuck!" under my late lunchtime breath as I start to get serious about my forthcoming escapades. I feel like I'm spaced-out already but I haven't even started yet. Placing my Walkman headthings into my ears, I sit on the bed and listen to a few of my Baudelaire tracks to re-focus myself on what I'm doing here and why. Soon afterwards I go over to my own bottles ranged across the top of the mini bar (I'm sure I heard a whimper of frustration emanate from within but I ignored it) and unscrew the top of the Absinthe.

After momentarily cradling this container of mythic displacement, I open the veneer door of the refridgerated bar and extract three glasses of differing size and shape. Glancing briefly into the smug interior, I spy the familiar triangular wedge of Toblerone, a packet of un-flavoured potato chips and a vacuum-sealed plastic bobble of spitefully small peanuts. I pour a suitably decadent measure of the opal-hued liquid into the smallest of the glasses and top it up with water from the bathroom tap. Now, I know we're supposed to dissolve a cube of sugar into the alcohol along with the H2O and then slowly imbibe it, but I can't be arsed. Let's cut to the chase. Mmm, that's hitting a few spots. The alcohol's taste is subconsciously flavoured with the sound of ear-slicing 19th Century artists laughing hysterically whilst pressed against the barren walls of an asylum or brothel. What time is it? God, it's just six in the evening and the day is still blazingly bright. I open a window and lean against the warm metal balcony and stare at the river. Inhaling the humid Parisian air with the warm sun in my face, I ignore the incessant swoosh of the cars speeding along the Quai below me and try to imagine Baudelaire standing here one hundred and forty six years ago. It's not too difficult actually, as the view across the river probably hasn't changed that much. The Tuilerie gardens, the Jardin du Carrousel, and the Musée and Palais du Louvre are as they were in the 1850's. I sigh at the beauty of it all, say "A tout à l'heure!" to the light bejewelling the water and close the curtains. A dark night is about to begin.

I place one of the bath towels against the bottom edge of the door to the corridor in order to contain within my room any illicit or confusing smells and I take off my clothes. I run a bath, discharge the contents of one of the small plastic bottles of bath foam into the water and slide under the balmy waves of strange content. I feel horny and watch my semi-tumescent cock turning indolently left to right like a basking shark cresting perfumed waves. Half an hour later, I clamber from the once foam-filled tub and now, dried and perfumed, slink myself into my new Selfridgian gown of delight, turning this way and that in front of the full-length mirror on the back of the bathroom door, and finally feel adequate and capable. I repair to the bedroom to sit, stare and ponder.

Without invocation, a Banquo-esque and vintage Keith Richards from 1976 suddenly appears, in the midst of my moveable feast, and slurs that I really ought to place scarves across the open tops of the two bedside lamps in order to create the ultimate cerebral shag-palace. I concur with his advice and, from the detritus of the closet, retrieve two of the silk Liberty numbers and proceed to drape them in accordance with Keef's wishes. He's right. They do cast an exotic ambience over the room.

Well, I don't know how he used to do it (or still does in those stoned moments) but five minutes after my adornment, both scarves started to smoulder and then caught fire. Please don't let the smoke alarm go off, I'm a 52-year-old man wearing only a dressing gown at 8 p.m.! I can't be caught this early into the game! The old 'towel in front of the door' trick restrained my embarrassment and, after a brief flurry of wet-flannel-beating, the baby flames diminished into a sour-whiffed silence. Into the bin, charred ones! Fuck, that's £20 down the chute already.

I lit a stick of Sandalwood incense, placed it in the wooden receptacle and positioned that on the top of the desk well away from any combustibles. OK, Tim. Relax. Breathe deep and drain that glass. That's better. I draped one scarf over the body of the television set, covering up that unholy eye. I must be strong, I am here for a purpose, and that is not to gawp inanely at MTV, Canal Plus or *The Simpsons* in French. I check my watch. It's now 9 pm. According to Artificial Paradise, Baudelaire's treatise on hashish (a copy of which is now spread-eagled upon my eiderdown) the drug should be taken on an empty stomach. Well, I ate about five hours ago so that should mean that I'm ready. Here's a little quote from the preface of said book: "Common sense tells us that the things of this world / Have very little reality, that true reality exists only in dreams. / In order to digest natural happiness We must have the courage to swallow it down / As with the artificial variety."

After all my rearrangements in the room it's no longer possible to ring for room service to bring me a pot of coffee, so I make do with the en-suite facilities. Those harsh sachets of Nescafé and small envelopes of tasteless sugar. I chew off a large sliver of the hash with my teeth and dribble it into a waiting teaspoon. With my cigarette lighter, I heat up the resin until it's soft and malleable and, once the plastic kettle has boiled, I tip and stir the murky residue into the cup along with the instant caffeine and sugar highs. I leave it to imbue for a couple of minutes.

I'm like a dark Nigella Lawson forced into slavery by her shameful and previously unrequited inner needs. Around the room, safely placed on their Ikea coasters, are six lit candles. I've made sure that anything in their vicinity is free from potential immolation. The scene is set. The time is now. Do it! I swallow the gritty infusion. Urrgh, it tastes like a molten Mesapotamian burial site (Max Von Sydow would be pleased) but I down the entire cupful in one go. Take your medicine, you bad boy! I lie back on my quilted launch pad and wait for the countdown...

Thirty minutes later. I decide to top up my abuse level with a glass of Remy Martin. I'm not a big brandy drinker, although I'm pretty large on everything else. I feel my heartbeat starting to accelerate. Nothing to be alarmed about, it's normal in this situation. I haven't swallowed hashish for a couple of decades. Smoked it consistently yes, but not taken it like this since I was a much younger man. I think the last occasion was back in '79 when my girlfriend of the moment and I chewed and swallowed a small quantity each and then decided to go and see *Alien* at the Empire cinema in Leicester Square. Bad choice. She spent most of the duration of the movie with her eyes behind shielding fingers, and I was tossed twixt irritation, concern, and horrific involvement in the plot. It was either before or after the film that we found ourselves in a small basement wine-bar in the square watching the other customers' faces and bodies morphing into different types of animal or bird. With our pupils like small spherical chocolates we got the giggles in a major way and lurched from the zoo out into the streets before we got ejected by force.

The room looks good. The candles and incense have given it a mellow timeless quality and, because the furniture is of an historic, albeit fake, style it looks pretty convincing as the sort of environment in which Baudelaire would have created his dark poetic visions. I'm lying on the bed now and have spent God know's how much time either staring at the involving patterns of light playing across the ceiling, or at the speckled teeming internity when my eyes are closed. Now I open them slowly like the drawbridge of a very ancient citadel. I feel every sinew and neuron in that part of my head straining to achieve this action smoothly.

I hear a bar of music by The Shangri-La's from the '60's, only now it's not *Da Doo Ron Ron* it's Da Neuron Ron. That sounds like a Teutonic Techno trio. I am aware of the blood coursing through my body, feeding and nourishing this fleshy collection of cells, memories and energy. It feels like I'm inside that miniature submarine from *The Fantastic Voyage* travelling within my own body. I hurl myself upwards from the bed, loom to the desk, and retrieve my black notebook and a pen. I can't do Laptop stuff when I'm this far out. I scuttle back to the raft-like eiderdown with relief. I smoke one of many cigarettes. Breathe. Focus. Breathe again. Look at that flame! Look at the possibilities! Look at the hissing passage of nothingness. No! Wait! It's not nothing, it's different. "I'll be alright won't I?".

"Hello? Is there anybody out there?".

My feet look ugly. Look at them! Stuck like the appendages of some hybrid creature on to the ends of my legs. You will surpass the humming. It's like I'm holding onto one of those mechanical Bucking Broncos that men in stetsons and plaid shirts seem to like so much in the Mid-West or dodgy Western theme pubs in Tottenham. The wilful steer is my torrid imagination and streams of thought, and it's fucking hard work to keep in the saddle. Maybe I should let go? Stop trying to be in control of myself and just go with it. Is there a God who can look without judging?

Am I my in own footsteps or someone else's? How could I have lived so long with hands this ungainly? I mean, stare at that skin, those prehensile bones! Does it all look normal to you? Of course it doesn't. You've woken up inside the wrong body. Colin Wilson (that most humane, concise and intuitive writer) once said, when talking of J. W. Dunne's theories of time: "He assumed that therefore it is possible to see the future in some way, that therefore in some sense the future has already taken place. That life may be rather like a roll of film, and if you could, sort of... as it were, 'pop' from one frame out into the next level, you would actually see what would happen in the future."

That is exactly what I'm feeling is imminent at this moment. If I did wake up inside someone else's life, would I then feel that everything I had experienced up to that point was just a dream? A kind of déjà vu? Is that how it works? I exhaled so deeply, so comprehensively, that I felt like a silhouette against the dawn of a new level of consciousness. "What is that music? Why do you swarm inside me?".

I didn't think that. That was Charles. Just for a flash I felt him coming through me. Yes! This is the point of all this. Do you see? Imagine that within this same building, but so long ago, Charles is in the same state of exploration as I am now. But he sees and feels me and my life coming back through time to him. Would he be scared or exhilarated? Get control over your rocket-fuelled heartbeat. I am a weather balloon floating above myself in a room of strange choices. Will I crash, burn and plummet down into the dusty and unsolvable plains of Roswell? Have I become an X File?

For me, true 'ART' is simply the ability to creatively use the recognition that there are many others embarked upon the same journey. I just thought of that. I'm glad I managed to write it down. Along with this: "Now breathe out.

Breathe out the demonic choir
The machinery of boredom
Self-loathing
And despondency.
Beg down and look at yourself.
Yes you!
Your prayer mat has shrunk
To the size of a postage stamp.
How are you going to fit yourself onto that magic carpet ride?
Mummy and dead skin.
Why do you look so angry?
You must be at peace now.
Come with me. I am not dangerous. Just disturbed and lonely,
Another needy recipient
Of your timeless seed."

Now, Charles didn't write that. It was me. But it was me thinking that it was Charles who was writing it.

"Enough already! Go and take a piss why don't you!"

The bathroom is tiled, harsh and brutal. Angular and cold. I hate it. I wish I could just wear silken nappies and piss or shit like babies do, wherever and whenever they need to. Actually, I do need a shit. So I'm going to have one right now. It's all right, you don't have to watch or listen, just turn away and think about the meaning of paisley or something for a few minutes. Lowered, warm and tactile arse kisses chilly and unforgiving plastic. And from my suddenly Biblical anus pour forth the twelve tribes of Israel! What the fuck? How was I restraining the multitude for so long? The Red Sea of my bum cheeks part and a download of mythic magnitude strikes the waters of the bowl. That's why Baudelaire stated one should do this on an empty stomach! Several ounces lighter, wiped and washed, I stand at the sink and see that Max is back in the mirror. Off goes the light quickly. I launch myself once more onto the bed. I say:

> "The water from the cistern
> In the hotel bathroom
> Sounds like the breath
> Of an angry dog."

Charles might have phrased it like this:

> "Canines with fearsome temperament Disport and exhale the sour fume
> Of soiled and indolent water.
> Once contained within
> The leaden pipes of guilt
> And shadowed sorrow."

Tonight I have gone to a place of creative symbiosis. Keep my place please, because I'm coming back very soon. Back on the reassuring and quilted bedspread, the effects of the drug slowly slowly dissipate I think of Vic Damone and Ann Blyth, singing that exquisitely melancholic yet profound ballad *Stranger In Paradise* from Kismet and decide, right there and then, to try and go to sleep. Before I finally do (after remembering to extinguish the candles), I am suddenly and inexplicably infused with the most wonderful sensation of supreme comfort. I see my mother standing on the roof of a building opposite me. Her hand is outstretched, gesturing me to join her. I close my eyes and slowly drift away.

"From our two hearts, two vast torches will pour the reflection of their double flames on our two spirits." From a letter from Baudelaire to his mother.

I awoke around 9 a.m. the next morning, strangely rested, and feeling quite pleased with myself that my little initial experiment had produced something workable. It's that old 'Whatever gets you through the night' syndrome. Some might say that a truly creative mind should be able to access all areas without recourse to re-creations or stimulants; others (including Baudelaire himself in his poem Get Drunk) would say that whatever it takes, whatever works for you, is the course that you should follow. Not only do I relate closely to this man's work, but also to his personality and emotions. His strengths and his weaknesses are present in my own character, although within me they suffer from being shack-led to a middle-class sense of restraint, a 'Politesse' of being too concerned about what others might think. That's why, to truly liberate myself, I do need some kind of push, a sense of hazard and disclocation even if it's only temporary. There's guilt by the side of the road, along with regret, boredom, frustration, anger, sorrow and fear. And the only way to curtail the activities of these nasty little demons is to bludgeon them into a creative act. Any act. It makes you want to lash out at something, anything within range. Your life feels like it's slipping away through your knotted fingers like dark abrasive sand. It gets dangerous then because the incubus who lives in the bottle or the needle or the spoon will attempt to inveigle you with promises of relief and anaesthesia.

Do you ever have those nights when, reeling under a surfeit of the drug or belief system of your choice, you long to wake up to find that the world has somehow shifted on its axis? That from this moment on, things will be brighter, more joyous and therefore easier? Yes, we all have. But it never seems to happen does it? That's because you have to work at it, consistently chip away at the coalface until we find the Dylan song in the demo pile. That's the bad news. The good news is that by pursuing some kind of dream, some kind of new thought, it will eventually lead you somewhere better. I have never really been a full-on "Hello trees, hello flowers" kind of poetic or pictorial devotee. That doesn't mean I don't appreciate depictions of natural beauty. Of course I do. Despite my sporadic faults of character I am as prone to joyful sentimentality as the next cynical romantic.

That's why I like the works of J. M. W. Turner for example. When you look at his paintings you get a sense of what it feels like gazing at a sunset or a misted dawn in Venice. Van Gogh? You can almost taste the torment; the passionate need to scream "YES!" fleeing out from his oily canvasses.

Pure reality is too mundane. People crave enigma, excitement and involvement. The same criteria apply in writing, I don't want to read: I looked out of the window and it was getting dark." I want: "Wiping the blood from trembling fingers, I gazed at my pallid reflection in the glass. Through it I saw darkness devouring the sky. I was alone now, nervous but perversely relieved that it was all over. A black car with no headlights hisses to a halt underneath my window. The door nearest to me opens and a man's prosthetic legs swing into view…"

What? Where did that come from? I have no idea, but I'm going to keep it for later use in something. I draw back the curtains, and, as a Nosferatu still wearing last night's dressing gown, reel back under the onslaught of fiery daylight. Windows are flung open and, like a scene from *Raiders of the Lost Ark*, I watch impalpable streams of nocturnally imprisoned spirits of booze, smoke, stale stuff and perfume hurtle past me, sighing as they scatter out into the nullifying Parisian air. I attempt a lungful of it. "Jesus!" That stuff's a killer if you're not used to it! I phone down to room service and order an early breakfast: A large pot of coffee, orange juice, scrambled eggs with ham, and two croissants. I quickly disguise any obvious remnants of illicit activity, which also includes stashing away my booze bottles and the candles on their waxy coasters. The Hotel proprietors musn't know that they have a deranged artist in their midst. But an eccentric, Gallo-friendly Brit with literary aspirations? Bien-sur!

I've always fantasised in hotel rooms about a young, tumescence-inducing, nubile room maid delivering my breakfast on a tray. She'd bend to place it on the table, her short black skirt would rise a few inches up her firm thighs to reveal just a peak of stocking- top. Then she would straighten and stand there with a coquettish smile on her pretty face, as if waiting for something extra. But dubious actuality decrees that it's always sadly going to be a sallow, slightly unsure, boy with bad skin. I turn away as he bends to place the tray but afterwards swivel back to slip him a five Euro note for his service.

Hopefully, tonight things will be very different and a lot more expensive within this room. Once more I shall draw darkness, scent and intoxication around me. I pour some cognac into my second cup of coffee, light a cigarette, and place myself at the desk and boot up the Apple Laptop. Here's the initial chord of 'Welcome!' music that Macs are prone to. The one that, to me, always sounds like the intro to Roy Orbison's *In Dreams*. You know, the song that starts: "The candy-coloured clown they call The Sandman, tiptoes to my room every night." Stephen King might well have based his whole literary oeuvre on those two lines.

Okay, I've got work to do. I tap out through the keyboard and onto the screen the first parts of the crazed notebook scribblings. After deleting errors of spelling and coherence I sit back, skin- up and read my story-so-far outloud. Yep, I'm pleased with this. It's flowing as I hoped it would. There's a line in a '70's song by Joni Mitchell wherein she says: "Chasing the ghosts of Gable and Flynn." Well, that's what I'm doing for real in Paris. Chasing Charles Baudelaire. I slither out into the sunlight for another lunch followed by a whisk through the Musée D'Orsay. I returned to the room, smoked another spliff, and stared across the river at Parisian history for a while.

Suffice it to say that I repeated the experiment that night and thrust myself even further out in inner space. I wasn't nervous or disconcerted this time; the trajectory was familiar and almost comfortable. But after careening around the void for who knows how long I found myself thinking about Jim Morrison more and more. Right movie! Wrong star! This was confusing in my swarming state, as it seemed like Jim was somehow pushing Baudelaire out of the way in his eagerness to be first through the door that leads into my head. I sat up, lurched to the desk, scrabbling for pen and notebook. Something's coming. Not wicked, but powerful and urgent and I had to somehow set it down before the portal slammed shut once more.

Jim is looking down from a high vantage point at a deserted stretch of road that seems to run parallel with the River Seine. He knows roughly where he is because he can see the silhouette of the Eiffel Tower over to his left. It's late at night, witching hour stillness. He sees ugly concrete and harsh sodium lights, bleak as only an unlovable section of urban underpass can be. The illumination is cinematic, greenish and cold, like a French film director's vision or an assassin's stare captured on cheap videotape. The black and indolent river water is barely moving, save for its repetitive and somehow sexual slapping against the thighs of the embankment. The wind against his face is that of a dying summer, melancholic with the imminent breath of early September. The air smells of hot chrome and rose petals.

Suddenly, from his right peripheral, a car approaches at great and dangerous speed as if in flight. Its colour is dark blue and its shape and design unrecognisable. In that strange clarity with which dreams are woven, he can see in sharp focus the manufacturer's insignia on the bonnet. Mercedes. He zooms into the car's dim interior - he can see four people: the driver and a passenger in the front seat staring straight ahead, and a young, elegant blonde woman on the back seat sitting next to a Middle Eastern-looking man. The woman's eyes are wide and fearful in close up, her face pale and imploring. She turns her head and looks straight through the window at Jim, who can powerlessly do nothing but observe. She opens her mouth as if to mutely cry for help, her elegant white-knuckled fingers clasped desperately together. A sudden series of strobe-like flashes of blinding white light are followed by the dreadful cacophony of colossal impact. Metal screams in death agony against unforgiving stone.

A dripping layer of silence now descends. Dark, shattered and conspiratorial, empty save for the passing sighs of departing souls, thrust brutally upwards and outwards. Blood fills his vision and tastes like sour copper in his mouth. He helplessly swims in tragic blackness. After a while, through the dense, thudding void he hears the keening sounds of grief, fading up like a tuneless orchestra in purgatory, a vast cacophony of bewilderment and sorrow.

Now Jim is walking in slow motion through an endless sea of picked flowers. Bouquets of every size, colour and perfume are accumulating to his left, right and in front of him, as far as his eyes can see. His splayed fingertips brush past silent and motionless people clasped together in suffering's unique tableaux. Sad legions of hollow-eyed strangers united for a brief moment by the siren song of inexplicable and unexpected loss. After another room service breakfast I read through the maze of words written in hasty flow onto the pages of my book. This is good stuff! The work of my imagination in full flight, and uncensored by daytime practicalities, inhibitions and distractions. The script itself was completely unlike my normal scrawl. Barely legible and veering off at strange angles, it looked as if I was writing over my own shoulder, or that someone else was guiding my hand. I felt exhausted. It's no wonder that true artistic vision causes the host body to burn out at a young age. That rare gift is a heavy burden to carry.

Prior to packing up to go home that afternoon I sat by the window and ruminated upon how uncomplicated it actually is to tune into something if you're focused and prepared. What I learnt and experienced from my brief Parisian jaunt was that I must never ever be afraid to go where my heart and my muse lead me. After all, what's the worst that can happen?

Chapter 32 – Tokyo II The Return

April 2005. Here's a scene for you to cut out and keep in your imagination. It takes place in Electric City in Tokyo. On the sidewalk outside a vast emporium, blazing with neon, that sells every conceivable hi-tech toy you could ever possibly need, a small Japanese man, who looks like a Nipponese Harry Potter, is engaged in a conversation of sorts with someone who is wearing a flesh-coloured rubber Dome Head mask, black sunglasses, white cotton gloves, and a long grey rubber Macintosh. They are being observed by another Dome Head from a few feet away and the conversation goes something like this:

Japanese Man: "Prease, you must come to Night Crub now and do show."

Dome Head 1 (voice muffled behind layer of latex): "No, we don't have a show. Sorry."

JM: "But it is good Crub. Many people waiting to see show."

DH 1: "We don't have a show."

JM: "PREASE! Come to Crub and meet rots of people. Nice people. Rove Engrish artists!"

DH 1 (getting more cross by the minute): "Look, I've said we can't do a show, because we don't have one. Okay?"

Suddenly, JM wilts like a dying flower down onto the pavement and kneels there, sobbing gently like a tragic Victorian heroine. He raises his head with a voice now tearful and tremulous: "Prease…"

DH 1 (now looming over the fallen one) raises his voice: "WE DO NOT WANT TO DO A SHOW IN A FUCKING NIGHT CLUB!"

Dome Head 2 now steps between them, helps the crumpled man to his feet, makes that 'OK, OK' raised palms gesture that signifies it's time to call a halt to this interlude and removes his mask. He says to JM (in a way that he hopes will placate him and thus prevent some kind of ritual disembowelment gesture of failure): "We'll come to the club and meet whoever you want us to meet, all right? We can't do a show because we don't have anything suitable. We need a proper stage and proper rehearsal, but Ronnie and Reggie Dome can certainly do a little something to show people. That's the best we can offer." JM throws his arms around DH 2 with fresh tears flowing down his cheeks, but this time they're ones of relief and gratitude. "Thank you. THANK YOU! You are my best artists ever!" It's hugs all round.

DH 2: "Now let's just go to the fucking club! Whoops, sorry."

Sean and I had longed to go back to Japan since our first visit as Tik & Tok back in 1982. We never thought we'd have a chance to be paid to go back again, so imagine our joy, after reconvening as T&T twenty three years later, to be contacted by a Japanese promoter asking if we'd like to come out for a week's worth of autograph signings and fun. We noticed that several fellow *Star Wars* guests at Conventions had been waxing rapturously about Japanese visits and we were envious. We said yes immediately and a few weeks later found ourselves in the Japan Airlines Club Lounge at Heathrow airport. We'd blagged our way into that by schmoozing an impressionable young girl at the check-in desk and giving her a couple of signed pictures. This could be a new form of global currency, I mused. For example, imagine going into your local branch of Marks & Spencer, filling up your basket with all manner of goodies and going to the checkout: "OK, sir, that'll be three Whiphids and half a Mon Calamari, please." "Sure, shall I make them out to M&S, or to you personally?"

Before we left home it was agreed between 'A' (our Promoter) and Sean and myself that Tik & Tok would do a live performance of two numbers as part of a *Star Wars* presentation at Kanda University in Tokyo. It transpired that 'A' teaches there and that would be a good opportunity for him to show the principal his acumen in bringing to Japan these special guests. It would be the first time that we had performed together in any context since October 1984, so it was quite a challenging but exciting notion. We'd decided to reform T&T the previous autumn to make some new music, and had reasoned that it couldn't do any harm to appear live and hopefully generate some interest. Two talented Electro musicians, Geoff Pinckney and Pete Steer, a duo named Alien 6, had already re-worked our old 1980s stage favourite *Vile Bodies*, into a much darker and heavier take on the song, quite Marilyn Manson-esque in its power. We were sure it would grab an audience's attention. We asked ourselves what's the most visually stunning thing we could do on stage as the first part of the act? Ronnie and Reggie Dome? Nah, too cute, too funny. Puppets? No power.

The only answer was to do The Robot routine once more. We'd vowed to lay that cash cow to rest after coming off Gary Numan's *Warriors* tour in 1983 and milking it for it was worth. But twenty-three years later we reasoned that being on the other side of the world, even if we fucked up, no one back home amongst our small but loyal fan base would ever know. Let's go for it! I crafted five minutes of brutal and rhythmic Techno/Electro for us to work to and, after we were both in agreement, I burnt the two tracks onto CD and we were good to go. Shit, we forgot to rehearse! Oh well, we'll do that when we get out there. Trust your instincts. That was always the Tik & Tok way and it got us through everything.

We'd bought white pancake face make-up and eye and lip stuff a couple of months ago for our new publicity pictures; we had the white gloves, black suits, shirts and shades. That was all we needed. So, at the University over two evenings, Richard and

Hans would be giving a slideshow presentation of their cut-away artworks of *Star Wars* spacecraft; Christine Hewitt would demonstrate the art of catwalk modeling (which was what she did in the 1960s) and Rusty 'Ewok' Goffe would play the piano and sing in a kind of old-fashioned English Music Hall style. ("Cor blimey, Guvnor, that's a well eclectic Bill, innit!"). We got the train out to the University. Sean and I were silent and introspective through- out the journey. Not an unusual state for dear shy and retiring Sean, but a pretty rare one for me. "Are you OK, Tim?" This was to be our first live performance for TWENTY-ONE YEARS. Therefore there's a certain degree of nervousness involved.

The two Cutaway Dudes and Rusty had given their presentations the previous day to a good reception and now it was our turn. We had a comprehensive sound and lighting check with the technicians in the medium-sized lecture hall. We wanted only green and blue floor lighting for our act, to give it a kind of spooky Sci-Fi look and they managed that to our satisfaction. And when they ran the CD through the PA, the sound was enormously loud, clear and powerful. I wondered how those in the front rows were going to react. It wasn't something they'd forget in a hurry, that's for sure. I was going to be singing live over my own pre- recorded voice on *Vile Bodies*. Once the levels were right, we returned to the dressing room to get ready. Then came that feeling again, that little excited but apprehensive worm in the gut I remembered so well from all those years ago. We'd bought along a bottle of Southern Comfort and we poured two generous measures into plastic beakers and toasted each other just as we used to do back in the day. On goes the white pancake, the smell of which triggered many memories. It took me right back to my very first professional mime performance back in 1977. Isn't it strangely wonderful how something as simple as an aroma can instantly recapture a moment from so far back?

We did some warm up exercises once the make-up was completed then we got into the suits. Shit, we forgot to rehearse! Oh well, we'll busk it like we always did. Deep breaths, a smile and a shake of Sean's hand, then I'm off round to my side of the stage behind the curtains. Once in position, with the black shades and gloves on, I look across at Sean on the other side and it is EXACTLY the same feeling, the same energy that we had on the Warriors tour in 1983. Tim and Sean have gone now. This is Tik & Tok.

The lights in the hall fade down to black and the intro music starts with its deep outer space drone and FX and we glide out in perfect unison to centre stage. The floor lights come up as the rhythms kick in and there's an audible intake of breath from the audience as we start to move, followed by cheers and whoops led by Hans and Richard at the back of the hall. God, this feels good! My movements are sharp, strong, and more mechanical than ever before. The Japanese love robots and have done for a long time (think about the whole Transformers phenomenon), so this was like a fantasy come to life for them.

The robot music ends, and the *Vile Bodies* intro crashes in. We rip off the jackets, shades, gloves and ties, throw them behind us and pick up the two previously positioned radio mikes just in time for verse one. Boy, am I going for it BIG TIME! I'm outside of my body observing myself and I'm thinking: "This looks pretty fucking amazing!" The audience are transfixed. I throw in to the pot every bit of Physical Theatre that I've ever loved, from Lindsay Kemp, to *The Rocky Horror Show*, to Marilyn Manson. Yes, it was completely and shamelessly over the top and I revelled in every moment of it. It was probably my last chance to ever do this again, because if Tik & Tok reform in another twenty-one years, I'm going to be 74 years old and I'll be doing The Robot behind a zimmer frame, connected by tubes to a drip with a nurse standing by in the wings. Not a happy picture I think you'll agree. My toothless mouth will look like a large walnut with a hole in it and my incontinence pants will be filled with the excitement of it all. Oops, there goes the spittle straight into the front row! The song ends, we bow and walk off to pretty much rapturous applause by Japanese standards. We are both wet through with sweat and the make-up is dripping off my face, but what a rush that was!

A few days later Sean, Hans and myself decided to wander out and find somewhere amenable to have a male bonding session over several drinks. About two blocks out from the hotel, we spy a little discreet doorway that says 'bar' in English and so we enter. Pushing through a curtain we find ourselves in a small dimly-lit room containing some serious Karaoke equipment, a well-stocked bar and about half a dozen Japanese men nursing glasses of booze. A female hostess approaches us and we explain that we'd like to have a drink. She leads us to comfortable sofas behind low tables. We order Suntory whisky and beers for the three of us. She's an attractive girl in an ugly sort of way (if you know what I mean) and is very professional and courteous. She's wearing the kind of pastel blue floral printed mini dress last seen in England in about 1973. Her name is Mikki and she brings us a full bottle of whisky (uh-oh) and three large bottles of Sapporo lager. She kneels gracefully by the side of our table and proceeds throughout our stay to refill our glasses the moment that they are emptied.

A middle-aged man is standing up and singing along to the lyrics on the Karaoke screen. We take in our surroundings after we've knocked back the first of what will be far too many whiskies and it's pretty weird. There are large plaster relief depictions of lithe young couples having intercourse in a kind of Karma Sutric way on each of the flesh-coloured walls and the lights are low and somehow sinister. Everything is lit by the cathode glow from the TV screens. The man is singing a Japanese pop ballad that sounds exactly like My Way slowed down and sung backwards. It is a total David Lynch moment. One of the men makes it understood that it is now our turn to sing. We decline politely but he insists. We decline again, but then he sways upright, takes one of the radio mikes from the rack and thrusts it into my hand. Some sort of vocal pissing contest is about to take place and it's really the last thing that we wanted to get into this night. We're handed a book of Karaoke songs the size and weight of a telephone directory and we stall for time, leafing through it and trying to decide what on earth might be suitable as we sink another glass of whisky. I opt to perform Bowie's *Ziggy Stardust*.

The anaemic and nowhere near loud enough backing track kicks off and I launch into the first line: "Ziggy played guitar, jamming good with Weird and Gilly and the Spiders from Mars." Fuck! It's in a different key to the original and therefore beyond my range and is faster too. And the lyrics are badly translated! I back down gracefully when the high notes come in on the line: "So where were the Spiders, while the fly tried to break our balls?".

"Ha! Round one to us," thinks the businessman. He slides into another song identical to his first and we proceed to get seriously wasted. Now it's our turn again. Hans (in a brave but foolhardy moment of derring-do) decides to inflict upon them *Bohemian Rhapsody*. Bad call. It starts off manageably, but when it moves into the "thunderbolt and lightning, very, very frightening me" section and everything that follows it (except for the final verse), it's time to get your coat. The weird thing about Karaoke is that, even though you know your chosen song by heart and have done so for decades, as soon as you try to follow the timing of the lyrics on the monitor you lose it completely. We did. The bill when it arrived in Mikki's fair hand was actually very reasonable considering we'd drunk three quarters of a bottle of whisky and nine beers. We resolved to come back the next night with Richard and 'A' and force the punters in the bar to listen to our take on *Hey Jude*. On the way back to the hotel, in that rubber-legged style of motion that sudden exposure to fresh air after lots of booze bestows upon you, we look across the street and see two stark naked men lying flat on their backs outside an open supermarket. As we stare transfixed one of them rises gracefully to his feet, scratches his balls and walks casually into the shop.

Chapter 33 - Dream Orphans and a Celebration

In early 2006, after our Tokyo jaunt, Sean and I felt the time was right for a modest bash at Tik & Tok Mark II. We'd recorded half of an album of new material, all created on my G4 PowerBook and using Logic Pro 7. Some of it was ambient; other tracks were pretty funky; culminating in a full on anthemic guitar and synth track called *Time4Us*, which borrowed intentionally from *Show Me Something Real* from our 1984 *Intolerance* album. In February, we released a four-track EP called *Slightly Deranged* through a wonderful American company called CD Baby. You pay a small set-up fee, send them four physical cds and they distribute them as either physical discs or (more popular these days) as a digital download. It still sells modestly to this day in fact, through iTunes and other outlets.

I wanted the full album to be like a journey or at least the soundtrack to going on one; a conscious decision to avoid the perils of me trying to write commercial pop songs that I was prone to back in the '80s. We used Peter Steer and Geoff Pinckney again to co-produce five tracks and they gave them a more upbeat and contemporary sound. A character named Zag (probably not his real name) wrote in an online review: "The album has an uneasy undertone that makes you feel uncertain, unsure of what's coming next. I don't know why but I feel slightly dirty after playing it, probably the sweaty bits in the middle! ... Kraftwerk meets Vangelis, fondles Numan and gets a good kicking from the Prodigy, all with a modern dance style and plenty of the T&T tartiness we all love." Well, I couldn't have put it better myself! That's exactly the effect that I was hoping to achieve. Although Sean wasn't active in the actual playing of the music his contribution was invaluable in his 'Out of the box' approach to it all. His suggestions, his likes and dislikes, and his sense of fun and adventure, meant I could tailor it to both of our needs. We called the album *Dream Orphans* and readied it for release in early 2007. That's actually the name of a font I have but I thought it fitted the sound and feel of this new music so well that I pinched it. Sorry!

In April 2006, Frank, a promoter of electronic music events in the UK, contacted us and asked if we'd like to do a special guest appearance at a large all-day gig called Elektrofest. There would be eleven other acts performing and we would be on bang in the middle. In a nicely circular and historical twist, the venue for the event was what used to be The Camden Palace back in the early '80s. It was Steve Strange and Rusty Egan's biggest club after Blitz took off and the whole New Romantic thing spread out from London. Tik and Tok did a PA to promote *Summer in the City* there in 1982. For a couple of years, we used to hang out in the upstairs bar. It was now called Koko. Twenty-four years after our last performance there we were again treading its sticky stage and waiting in the same slightly shabby dressing rooms and corridors. We said we could only do two numbers and luckily he agreed. Anymore would be impossible because of the constraints of Sean's working patterns. He was only available in the evenings.

In my living room, we managed to rehearse for a couple of hours each evening in the week before the gig. Sometime earlier we'd bought two Monkey Boy masks from Carnival, Camden's joke and novelty shop, and here was the perfect opportunity to put them to use. Actually they looked more like a completely bald Keith Richards after a spectacularly out-of-it week. They were made from a lightweight flesh-coloured latex and, we discovered to our joy, that you could actually articulate the mouth by grasping it lightly with your gums. We thought they were amusing and very us! We wore black t-shirts and black suits under the long dark grey rubber macs we'd found in Muji, the Japanese shop in Whiteleys in West London. The addition of the old white gloves completed the outfit. We worked out some fast-moving and strangely abstract movement to a track called Stimula from our *Slightly Deranged* EP that seemed to involve two simian-type aliens adrift on a tube train and suffering the effect of Earth's gravity in a somewhat unexpected manner. At the end of it we'd rip of the masks, the gloves and the macs, and launch into *Time4Us* from the forthcoming album. That's pretty much what happened actually. The only slight glitch was that there was no MC on the night, which meant that none of the acts were actually announced. We had an enthusiastic throng who rushed to the front once they knew it was us on stage but to be honest, neither of us felt the gut-wrenching and exciting energy we thought might flood through us if we stuck our heads over the parapet once again. It was more like: "Was that it? Twenty-two years later and we've only got a throng? Hmm..."

A young lady named 'Zed' seemed to be impressed though. She wrote on MySpace: "I've watched roughly four hundred bands in my lifetime and theirs was by far the most surreal performance I've ever seen...' She called it 'terrifying... super-charged... emotional" and wrote that "the sparse crowd swelled and the cameras came out. They both sung a nifty Numan-esque song with one repeated line, something to the effect of 'We're leaving now'. Then, good as their word, they threw a bunch of fliers at the audience and walked off... I was deeply impressed." Bless! 400,000 more reviews like this one and we'd be back for good and quite probably ruling a small country in Latin America populated only by Electro-loving over made-up young things with black hair and extraordinary clothing. Naturally, none of us would ever emerge in the harsh light of day but we'd all dance the nights away to the sounds of synths and sequencers a go go!. Luckily we do have the Koko PA on YouTube for posterity viewing. Considering how long we'd been out of action (nearly a quarter of a century!) it was pretty amazing that we managed to create anything at all. I think that a little part of both of our heads and hearts thought that just maybe we should have let the past carry us to the future and to not do something again. After all, we'd defined some- thing so well back then how could we seriously hope to compete with that? But hey, if there's any opportunity anywhere why not grab it? Life can be so dull without those little unexpected moments.

In April, Sean and I did finally release *Dream Orphans*. With our usual sense of irony and humour we said in the press release, posted on our own website and other fan sites, that we'd just nipped out for lunch in 1984 and it had taken a bit longer than we thought to get back! We spent what available money we had on having 500 copies manufactured for us. I designed the sleeve artwork using pictures I'd taken in Tokyo two years earlier for the cover and the back. Inside was a double-page pic of Sean and me at a Convention in Germany the year before, being manhandled by a rather well-built young lass clad in black PVC with a long leather serpent's tale attached above her bum. She works as a fetish model under the name Dark-WingZero. We continue to sell the album through our official Tik & Tok website and it has recouped our initial outlay a couple of times over, which is pleasing but not exactly the scintillating return to the public domain, with all our previous sins forgiven, that we'd hoped for. And as the old cliché goes: 'Nostalgia ain't what it used to be'.

Another little platter of musical retroactivity appeared out of the blue in the summer of 2007. A gent named Peter Parnell, who runs an Indie label called Angel Air Records, located Georg Kajanus and me and asked if we'd be interested in granting him an official release for our Noir album *Strange Desire*. Naturally we weren't going to refuse as our home-mastered version had been languishing on our hard drives since 1997, emerging sporadically only as sold CDs through our personal websites. Angel Air deals solely in re-releases of albums by artists from previous decades, an eclectic melange of rare recordings by UK groups such as Nazareth, Bad Company, Sailor, Mott The Hoople, Atomic Rooster, Third Ear Band, Stackridge, etc. Hopefully my life will teeter onwards in a slurry fashion without ever having to hear another note from the Third Ear Band. I saw them at the two free concerts in Hyde Park in '69, before Blind Faith and The Stones, and they were ball-curdlers of the first order! Meandering, atonal, imageless, bill-fillers with no definable or remotely human image, who provided the soundtrack to an acid trip you never quite got over. Anyway, good old Mr. Purnell popped our *Noir* album out on his label (it had achieved vintage status by being all of ten years old!) and all the loyal Sailor and Tik & Tok fans bought it. G and I are grateful that someone with a record label had faith in our unique musical creation to release it, a wonderfully unique musical and poetic journey that started with two stylish gents who both owned black and white brogues.

Of course, 2007 also saw the introduction in the UK of a ban on cigarette smoking in all public places apart from designated areas. A ruling which, as a smoker since the age of thirteen, might have induced a sense of fear and resentment in one so hardened to the perilous joys of inhaling continuous amounts of a toxic substance. But instead it left me in some way strangely relieved, as if deep down I knew that it would facilitate my eventual move to quitting completely five years later.

Chapter 34 - Art Reconnection

By 2007, I'd become somewhat creatively disenchanted. I was concerned by the lack of opportunities for me as a producer of digital photographic art. I felt I was treading in similar waters to a lot of other people who shared a penchant for surreal and sensual imagery. Come with me please as I momentarily take you back a few years:

Back in the mid '90s I was active in the area of hand-distressed photographs. I gleefully explored new techniques both in and out of the darkroom, I showed finished work in exhibitions here and there; images were published hither and quite often thither, and the feeling in my head was that I'd discovered a real voice in a previously unexplored medium. Then out comes a wondrous application called Photoshop and I, and everyone else could achieve, with ease and speed, so many of the effects I used to create by hand in the darkroom. All those hours of burning in, dodging, toning, bleaching, sanding, inking of newly developed photographic prints were now negated by several simple clicks of the cursor and a basic understanding of this new technology. I took to it like a digital duck to water. Now I could seamlessly montage and collage images together without the need for scalpel blades, spray glue and vast amounts of expensive photographic paper. It was wonderfully liberating and satisfying. My hands no longer smelt of foul and noxious chemicals, I worked now in daylight, and could easily nip off for a piss, a coffee or a glass or two of wine, without fear of exposing valuable paper to the light. I could talk on the phone; pander to the girl cat's occasional needs, and do all the other things that were denied to me in the dank, odorous and solitary confines of the red-lit darkroom. But sadly I could no longer have spontaneous sex in various parts of the flat with a ready and willing female co-habitant when the mutual mood struck. Now we'd just email each other instead and my own hand would have to do the necessary relief work. Dull yes and frustrating too. BUT have you seen this picture I've just created? Wow, it kind of makes it all worthwhile doesn't it!

In February 2007, Robert Pereno (yep, he was back in my life again, for one of those irregular sojourns that have occurred every decade since 1981) invited me to an exhibition of Holographic Art called *Lust For Light* (loved that title!) that was taking place on a Thursday night as a Private View at a gallery named 286 in Earl's Court Road, West London. The gallery is situated on two floors of a grand Victorian town house owned by a very erudite and charming gentleman named Jonathan Ross. No, not the cheerful floppy-haired TV host. That one's a bit younger. This immaculately moustachioed aesthete is long-term collector of holograms and lenticular prints and has devoted many years to the promotion of the work of artists he admires. The ground floor space (and indeed the majority of the house) retains all of its original fixtures and fittings - the fireplace, tiles, flooring, cornices, architraves etc. and the walls are decorated in a chalky and somehow classical red-coloured paint, which is ideal for displaying artwork and paintings of a more colourful nature. Whereas downstairs the large basement room had been converted into a pure white area, more suitable for photographic or modernist creations.

On this night, elegant, stylish and charmingly eccentric-looking people populated both gallery spaces. They stood in small clusters, quaffing complimentary wines of two colours (or juice and mineral water for those of a 'drying out' disposition) whilst chomping discreetly on crispy nibbles and chattering earnestly to each other about the displayed art. I felt drawn towards the environment and these interesting types, whom I construed as being sadly missing from my current social life.

Robert had given me a few VHS tapes (gosh, remember them?) that he wanted me to copy onto my computer as digital files. Needless to say, in my excitement at finding myself somewhere new and stimulating, I put them down on a table and then promptly forgot all about them. The next morning I realized my negligence and phoned Jonathan to ask if I could come over when convenient and retrieve them. On the Saturday, I returned to the sanctuary of 286 Earl's Court Road to pick up the tapes and I also enjoyed a jolly banter with Mr. Ross. Then, after she emerged, apron-clad and flour-dusted, from her kitchen, I met Jonathan's beautiful wife, Camilla Shivarg, a lady of many talents. Not only is she a sculptress with a rare gift and vision, she is also a devoted and passionate creator of gardens and an exceedingly talented cook of fine and hedonistic food. It became clear to me on that winter's afternoon that I'd stumbled into the presence of two wonderful people and I hoped that somehow we'd become friends. To my joy we did.

Flashing forward several months, past my attendances at more Private Views by other artists and being the recipient of some splendid wining and dining at 286, Jonathan asked me if I'd like to contribute some work to his annual Christmas show in the gallery. I said 'Yes!' immediately and came home and thought about what I could bring to the table. My imagined current shortcomings as a visual artist slid into my forebrain as I recollected just how good, skilful, daring, vibrant and innovative a lot of the work was that I'd seen in the gallery's eclectic shows. I certainly

didn't feel that my current oeuvre of surreal and well-executed Photoshop montages was really quite up to par.

On an impulse I searched for and located, stashed and coated with dust behind the door of the spare room I romantically called my Studio, a folder left over from my Art School days. Inside it was a selection of the hand-distressed original pieces I'd created back in the '90s. Amongst them were three naked female Angels; the portrait of Georg Kajanus entitled *Le Sophiste*, for which I'd won a prize in the John Kobal portrait competition in 1994; and portraits in hand-made frames of two girls from The Mediaeval Baebes. A day or so later, I whizzed over to 286, showed them to Jonathan who loved them and said he'd show all six! In fact, he was so enamoured of one of the images that he made it the front cover of the A5 invite for the 2007 Christmas Show! It's a portrait of a bare chested, androgynous looking, and cigarette smoking Angels that I'd entitled *Wings Of Desire*. To my joy, a small selection of his more prudish or old-fashioned female patrons found it slightly offensive when ripping open the envelope containing the invitation. Which put a smile on both our faces! Was it the proudly erect nipples on display or the noxious white cylinder of death drooping in a louche fashion from full red lips that disturbed their delicate sensibilities the most? I mounted the images on textured art card, signed, numbered each image, (1/1, as they were all absolute one-offs), fixed them into pre-bought simple 24" x 20" black frames, as they didn't need to be further embellished, and took all six over in a large suitcase.

The day of the first Private View of the show, now subtitled 'A Wicked Christmas' (Oh yes!), arrived on December 11th. I'm there promptly at 6.30pm in my vintage black Rock-A-Cha 1950s suit and open-collared shirt spread over the lapels of the jacket, nervously necking down a couple of glasses of the complimentary red wine for starters and smiling inanely at any stranger within my sights. At about 7pm, a well-dressed and elegant lady of mature years stands in front of me and *Wings* and declaims to no one in particular: "Oh my God! That is so beautiful! I'm buying it right now!".

"Erm, hello!" I move to her side. "I'm the artist and I'm very glad that you like my picture! Thank you so much!".

"It's beautiful. You're very talented. It looks just like a painting. Fabulous! Now, where's that Mr. Ross?". She moves away to locate the gallery owner whilst extricating a heavy and sizeable chequebook from a handbag that in all probability cost more than my entire outfit. The deal is done and shortly afterwards a coveted red dot is stuck on the wall next to my picture. I can't tell you how pleasing that moment was! It was an affirmation that once upon a time I did do something unique and it hasn't dated and it is still sexy, beautiful and collectable. An hour after Lady One completed her purchase, Lady Two appeared from nowhere and re-enacted the exact same scenario with another 'Angel'. Crimson dot Number Two - Come On Down! That was it for me that night. Total gratification and a reawakening of the fact that I still had something to offer even though the work was thirteen years old.

At Sunday's Private View I sold my portrait of Georg to an independent documentary filmmaker who happened to be a huge fan of Sailor and Mr K's music. Three red dots in the opening week! Vindication and joy-a-go-go! The combination of cash and confidence got me through the purgatory of Christmas and the New Year with a degree of comfort for the first time in a few years. I have shown and sometimes sold work (some new and some old) in every Christmas show at Gallery 286 ever since. High Point, Star Bright!

Chapter 35 – Unexpected Connectivity

A large part of 2008 was enlivened momentarily here and there by little treats such as removing my own testicles incrementally day by day with judicious tweezer usage and applications of Deep Heat. It had become apparent over the last few months that I would no longer be needing them! I also devoted a considerable amount of time and energy to perfecting my dark and somewhat 'Dry' sense of humour.

I had a very brief flirtation with Neuro Linguistic Programming, at a massive three-day seminar held at Excel in London's Docklands and run by a very charismatic American guy and his cohorts. But I found the whole experience to be unbearably Evangelical, with its Hollywood suits, teeth and hair; thunderous rock and dance music; prancing and syncopated girls like cheerleaders: radio headsets, Botox faces and embarrassing exhortations to stand up every hour or so and bellow: "Whoooooooh Yeah!!" whilst flinging our arms upwards and grinning inanely at our neighbours. When that wasn't happening we were constantly being sold the idea that by the culmination of Day 3 we'd all be transformed and enlightened human beings whose troubled lives would now be firmly back on the right track but, of course, with a bank balance several thousand pounds in the red overnight. Luckily I was given a freebie ticket by a girlfriend to satisfy my curiosity so my penurious state remained at its consistent level. The flatline remained unbroken! It's quite possibly true to say that my natural cynicism did get in the way of potentially achieving some kind of wished for breakthrough but the ludicrous and relentless showbiz display of the practitioners nuked it for me. It was like some ghastly demonic mash up of *We Will Rock You*, an advert for the best cosmetic surgery money can buy, and an open casting call for walk-ons in a remake of *The Stepford Wives* directed by Scientologists.

In March, Sean and I found ourselves caught in Travel Purgatory on our way to an autograph convention in Dallas, Texas. It's an amusing-only-in-retrospect tale of how one valiantly tries to cope with a night spent huddled on a stone bench in an open alcove opposite a branch of McDonald's in JFK airport, waiting fully awake through the interminable hours until dawn when we might be able to get a flight to Dallas at 7.30am. Why were we there? Because of this: Halfway through the connecting flight, as we're flying over the endless and bland Mid-West, and I'm looking out of the window and musing on just how many serial killers there must be in this area of the States alone, I am interrupted: "This is your pilot speaking. We've had reports of a snow blizzard affecting the landing of all planes at Dallas, Fort Worth. It has been strongly advised that we now turn back to JFK to wait for the storm to blow over and await further instructions. Otherwise we'll be in a holding pattern above Fort Worth for about six hours and we cannot land as the runway is now under two inches of snow and therefore unsafe. On behalf of 'Scrote Bag

Airlines', I sincerely apologise for any disruption to your journey. Arrangements will be made to ensure your ongoing comfort."

Naturally, this dialogue is spoken with a reassuring Texan accent that is virtually impossible to replicate in the written word, but ahm sure y'all git the ideah? Snow in Dallas? That's like being told that there's a tropical heat wave in Manchester or a tsunami is on its way to Cardiff. Such things just do not happen. Nonetheless, as we absorbed the news, we began curving our way back towards JFK.

Sean and I have no friends or relatives in the city and not enough money for a hotel. Hence the stone bench. The grim eternity inched past with sporadic distractions like avoiding conversation with a Bible reading, gently rocking, elderly woman humming hymns as she sat for five hours on spread newspapers; smiling in a "Hello, we're English!" kind of way at a sauntering pair of fully-armed NYPD cops giving us the inquisitive look which often precedes the "Step away from the vehicle, Sir" moment; and resolutely not making eye contact with an obviously totally out of his tree Ghetto Kid with a portable computer, on which he repeatedly played Rap videos at a loud volume. At about 2am, to place the jewel in the crown of our weary discontent, an elegantly dressed middle-aged lady entered our enclave, looked around in a state of some confusion and then proceeded to hurl from her mouth, and in every direction, the entire contents of her stomach. It was a Jackson Pollock moment I can tell you!

Nina, my long time friend, muse, lust object and romantic love lady from the early 1970s (from the Jimmy Cagney In White Face chapter) died of a stroke in her isolated little Almshouse in a quiet part of the Surrey countryside in July. The loss of her was the first of several coming around time's unknowable corner. I felt bad because we'd had very little contact over the preceding two decades. She'd become a recluse and had severed ties with virtually everyone from her past except for her two grown-up children. Our last exchange was by letter, which contained no desire for a visit from myself, and I felt it best to keep my memory of her sacred somehow, by remembering her as a beautiful, intelligent, sexy and creative woman who undoubtedly changed my life. Her ashes were scattered underneath the pair of tall pine trees that she loved so much on the crest of Redhill Common.

I'd succumbed to Facebook's siren call sometime in 2007, that addictive and in turns fascinating, trivial, stimulating, masturbatory and occasionally REALLY irritating vehicle for daily self-display. A year later, I was utilizing its networking facilities to the best of my ability and, yes, sometimes even I felt the need to post cute pictures of my two girl cats. It meant I could now draw together fans from the work I'd done in the '80s and direct them towards buying Tik & Tok CDs both old and new from our official site, and the Shock DVD/CD I put together and sold from my own website. Suddenly, large numbers of *Star Wars* fans and followers of other work I'd done, like *Father Ted*, *Xtro* and *The Tenth Kingdom* now had a vehicle for communication too and they could seek me out and interact. And Lo! All of a sudden we could all display with ease photos, videos, links to other websites, what we had for breakfast, the shape, colour and texture of our bowel movements (for those thus inclined), our fave movies, books and music and much more. The possibilities were suddenly endless.

So anyway, in the early Autumn of 2008, I'm chumming away with real friends, new 'Friends', and a great many sundry others on a daily basis when, out of the blue, pops a friend request from South America from a man I had had no contact with at all for eighteen years. Mo Blackford. A guitarist of unique talent whom I had first met back in '84 when he was playing 'Mick Ronson' to Beki Bondage's 'Bowie' in her four-piece group, Ligotage. They'd signed to EMI and were being groomed for something big that could combine a Punk sensibility lyrically with the musical and vocal energy of say Van Halen or Pat Benatar. Mo's stage name was MoMo Sex, which should give you the heads up about his off-stage interests. At that time I was embroiled in a live-in relationship with Ms BB so I gradually got to know Mo as a tight-trousered new friend with talent, a sense of humour, perfect blond hair and a wickedly elfin face. And he owned a vintage Fender Strat and a Marshall stack too. He and I would drink a lot, inhale whatever was on offer or affordable, and invariably fall over giggling together in the nefarious rock 'n' roll hang outs in central London. The usual suspects back then being the Marquee, the St. Moritz, the Intrepid Fox, the Bat Cave, The Embassy and Camden Palace.

Anyway, things changed, mutated, inverted and diverted but, against all odds, Mr. Sex and I did make some interesting music together. We liked each other and admired what we both brought to the table. I last saw Mo shortly before I got married in June 1990. That was it I thought. But, via Facebook came the mutual messages: "Hey! Where the fuck have you been for the last eighteen years? How the hell are you? How's your life? Blah, blah, blah!" It transpired that he was coming to London very soon, having left his habitat in Rio de Janeiro. He arrived and, after a day or two from him to recover, we have coffees in a chain-place in Covent Garden. Fuck, he looks good: pumped, short hair but still wicked! I feel old but hopefully still retain an air of elegance and possibly of accumulated wisdom. We talk for three hours plus about EVERYTHING! Proof that time really is no obstacle when it comes down to true friendships. Just before we almost tearfully part company at Tottenham Court Road tube, I say off the top of my head: "Look, I know you're not going to be here that long, but if you've got any time at all do you fancy maybe trying to make some music together?"

"Oh man, I thought you'd never ask! Yes, of course I'd love to, you bastard!"

A couple of weeks later, after a trip to Germany, he came to my place carrying with him a hand-made Brazilian acoustic guitar, a beautiful instrument created from love that, under his fingers, sounds like a dream. I have the software and the computer. He plays the chords. I craft some kind of rhythmic backing in a subtle electronica style and add it to what he's laid down to a click track. Now something's cooking. Something new, unexpected and totally original. For me it's a bizarre moment because I am not, by any stretch of anyone's imagination, a natural musician. Plus, I had made a set in stone decision after completing the *Dream Orphans* album, the wonderful Noir experience, and the 'Baudelaire poetry set to my own music' experiment, that my personal involvement with, and the need to create, music in any shape or form had moved far beyond its sell by date. So, what the hell was I embarking upon now then? You see? "Never say never". Well, unless self-mutilation, a diet of celery and rhubarb, torture by Rap music or sex with reptiles are on offer.

Then it's a pretty safe bet that I will be uttering the 'N' word repeatedly and with great emphasis.

We finished off the backing track over a couple of days and in a rush of creativity, I wrote all of the lyrics in a couple of hours. I called the song *Somewhere*. It's a message of hope for the lost and lonely in need of comfort. I had my niece Gena Dry specifically in mind, as she had just landed back in England having been thrown out of the States for not servicing her Visa. Poor love. She'd sold everything she owned to move out there and make a career as a singer/songwriter and now, for various reasons, she was back penniless and homeless and very, very disturbed.

Mo came over a day or two later and we hugged each other in a brotherly way as we realised that we'd created something new and different to anything else around. He was adamant that after years of decibel excess in the '80s he never wanted to play electric guitar again. That suited me fine as I too felt I'd explored enough of its sonic possibilities. So, now we're a duo? It is strange that, having come to accept that my duo days had gone forever, they were back in a completely un-looked for way. How bizarre and exhilarating life can be some times! Thank you Facebook! You see? It can have its uses. How could I have possibly found out Mo's whereabouts without it? I'd long ago jettisoned any contacts in my cathartic early '90s clear out and, to be honest, I'd consigned our friendship to the file marked Whatever Happened To?

So, what to call ourselves then if we're going to make a go of it? Our brains were wracked but nothing seemed to encapsulate us, so as a temporary measure we opted for TIMANDMO. In caps. Stunning in its raw simplicity don't you think? It might well mean something in some obscure language but we never discovered what that might be. And we never did find a better name either. Not a good sign if you think about it. We did briefly contemplate The Why but dumped it as being too slavish a retro homage.

Unfortunately, the fickle finger of fate then decided to give us the sit and swivel gesture as it became apparent that Mr Blackford's tenure in the UK was going to be short-lived. A complete lack of work opportunities here decreed he would have to accept a job teaching English in a private school in Colombia! What? You've got to be kidding! No, I'm not. Bollocks! A date was set for the first week of November, so we could we got together and lay down the bare bones of another track to which I would later add my stuff. The day before he left, we roped in Mo's sister to film us, with her DV Cam, on the roof of my building singing and playing Somewhere, and with the facilities of Final Cut Pro and my imagination, I was able to create a fairly presentable little video showcase for the song. Yes, it's on YouTube! If I could only train my two cats to do Robotics they'd get three million plus hits and I could monetize the video and retire gracefully to the South of France.

So Mo and I were faced with an interesting challenge, namely, is it possible for two people on opposite sides of the planet to continue to make music together? The answer was yes. Through the wonders of email we sent each other bits and pieces of song ideas. He would hire some cheap local musicians in Cali, go into a studio and lay down a backing track of say, acoustic guitars, upright bass and live drums and percussion. He'd then send those audio files to me. I'd import them into Logic and add what I wanted. How unutterably cool was that! Of course we had our occasional spats and tiffs over each other's choices, and a few harsh emails whizzed around the planet, but on the whole it was a very gratifying and exciting venture. All in all we created eight original songs, and one cover version of a Bowie track, and put them on-line as an album called *Happy Accidents*. Still available to purchase from the usual outlets. Oh, come on it's all about self-promotion these days in whatever form, don't try and tell me it isn't! Everyone's Twittering away 24/7, from the biggest to the smallest, like a vast cage full of avians on crystal meth!

When Mo came back after being paroled from the college, we played four live gigs in cool and intimate venues like London's The Troubadour and The Bedford. They were okay from our point of view, and well-received by the small but vociferous audiences, but I've got to admit that my heart wasn't really in it, much to Mo's surprise and confusion. I just don't feel comfortable these days standing on stage with just a microphone. It seems somehow... ungainly for me. I feel I'm too old for that now. I did all my stagecraft a long time ago and no longer have any desire to do it again outside of a film or TV role. Maybe the truth of the matter is that I no longer have a mask or make up or an act to hide behind in a live situation? There's only me left...

Chapter 36 – Carry That Weight

Some years start off exceedingly well and inexplicably end in disaster of one degree or another. 2010 was the inverse. It started with a devastating and ghastly event and somehow, over the following eleven months, evolved into a somewhat better place for me. The older I get the less I seem to understand the workings of life. I mean, I'm in my sixties and do feel, at this advanced stage, that I really should have achieved a satisfactory degree of wisdom. Surely by now I must have created, through a lifetime's experience of so many things, a patina of acceptance and recognition of the balance inherent in all living things? Have I fuck!

Some days I don't feel that I'm any further down the road of knowledge than I was when I was eighteen. That's a somewhat depressing realization for someone who's always striven to better themselves. Quite often, in my many private moments, I feel somehow like a Dinosaur, the remnant of a once-proud species still vainly fighting with scaly resistance against evolution's better-equipped and younger army. Or the lone Japanese soldier who endlessly circles, stranded and mad on that forgotten island waiting for the enemy, not knowing that the war is over. I always imagined that by this time of life I'd be calm of temperament and focussed on the here and now. I would have perfected the ability to gently tug, with thoughtful strokes, at my long grey beard whilst enticing those in front of me to be ever deeper into the mystic blue whirlpools of my enlightened eyes. My calm and measured voice would sooth the neophytes in my circle into a state of utter relaxation wherein I would intone the secrets of time, space, life, experience on every sensual level and how to programme the timer on your DVD recorder.

I'm stalling. Covering my tracks. Steeling myself. Faking it and charming it as usual. Lulling you into a state of calm with my customary humour before I display, with brutal honesty, the shattering emotional fallout still descending like black snowflakes to this day from the heartbreaking events of February 11th 2010. Which incidentally was my late father's birthday.

> *MYSTERY surrounds the tragic death of a former indie music star whose body was found on rail tracks 30 miles from her home in Angel.*

The smashed and broken body of Gena, my gifted and beautiful niece, was found on the railway tracks outside of a station named Burnham in Buckinghamshire mid-morning. I knew something was wrong. Only weeks before, she'd told me she'd contemplated jumping from a train. I never thought that she would do such a thing. I talked to her and counselled her as best I could. I understand depression, believe me. I try my hardest to deal with it. It's a minefield. People who do not know better will often dismiss these frightening emotions as just being self-indulgent or pop out that sickening cliché, "Oh, pull yourself together. It's not that bad." How the fuck would you know?

> *Transport Police are appealing for information after Gena Dry, who lived in Liverpool Road, was discovered near Burnham station in Berkshire just before 11.30 a.m. last Thursday.*

Throughout the course of 2009, I'd watched Gena gradually regain her confidence, her social skills and her creativity, and thereby find the motivation to surmount her situation. She'd also started coaching people in singing and expressing themselves vocally for modest but vital fees, as well as finding a small but comfortable flat to rent in Islington. A part of London with which she'd long felt a kinship.

> *It is believed that she may have boarded the 10.25am service from Chippenham to London Paddington. Ms. Dry, 46, was a former member of Colour Noise, and was the A&R manager for Virtual London, part of the online virtual reality world, Second Life. Police are treating her death as unexplained but not suspicious.*

Gena and I spent a lot of time together during the year before her death. We became even closer than we were before she'd left for the States, almost like brother and sister, as the age difference between us was not that large. She started to blossom and it was a wonderful butterfly-like metamorphosis to witness. Her relationship with her estranged parents was still somewhat difficult though and, in many ways, she was closer to her father, my half- brother, David, domiciled in Andalucia, than her somewhat insular Hungarian mother sequestered in Wiltshire.

Gena and I shared the 'Dry' sense of humour, which more often than not involved fart jokes, vast intakes of cheap red wine, crude tales of sexual misconduct on both our sides, and a general disrespect for authority and conventionality. Georg Kajanus asked Gena, after hearing her backing vocals for one of my *Baudelaire* tracks back in 2001, if she would sing the lead on a song called *Oh Johnny* for his extraordinary *Sailor - The Musical* project. She leapt at the chance, as she was a fervent admirer of Mr K's talent. The song she'd been given is a highly charged emotional piece that very few trained singers could handle. It involves death, love in its purest form, and annihilation. They recorded it in my tiny studio at home whilst Barbie and I sojourned to the nearby Prince Edward pub for foodies and refreshments. When we returned a couple of hours later, Gena emerged exhilarated, flushed of cheek, and damp with perspiration. Georg had the benign and enigmatic smile on his face that he wears when something pleases him greatly. It is a truly heart-rending performance and I hope with all my heart that one day it will be heard in the way that it so strongly deserves. Gena's image towards the end of 2009 incorporated her wearing a white sailor's cap in homage to Georg's enormous success with his group, Sailor.

Gena left me a message on my answer machine in the afternoon of the day before her death. "Tim, hi it's Gena. I need to come over and talk to you. It's important. Call me back".

To my eternal regret I was not at home to personally take the call. When I couldn't reach her by phone on her landline or on her mobile that night, or repeatedly during the following morning, on some instinctive level I knew what she'd done, and when, in the afternoon, I received the news from her mother that Gena's body had been found, a chilling sense of despair and loss of terrifying intensity swarmed through me and remains there in my heart to this very day. It will never leave me whilst I'm alive. I know that. I don't have the guilty thoughts that so many of the bereft are plagued with because I know I was there for her when she needed someone. We shared each other's pain and fears often and were able to give each other comfort. But for those poor people cursed with the disease of bi-polar disorder even that is not enough.

Her funeral was held two weeks later on a suitably bleak, grey and rain-soaked morning in the Islington Crematorium. A small gathering paid tribute and said their tearful goodbyes. It was a scene worthy of a Victorian melodrama filmed in misty black and white. Her mother fell to pieces. Her father chose not to attend but instead held his own farewell ceremony in the bright sunlight of southern Spain. After my initial anger at his absence had abated, I envied him his own belief system with its desire to embrace Gena's soul into the light with joy and not with grim sorrow into the turbulent, dark and bruised skies of London. The inquest was in June in Windsor. Her mother did not show. I knew she wouldn't. I doubt if any parent would want to hear the ghastly details of their child's demise.

> *Yesterday's inquest, at Windsor, heard that Miss Dry, from Islington, north London, charted her suicidal thoughts in a diary on her computer. An entry from August 2009 read: 'I bought a knife and I stood on a railway platform and contemplated if I could throw myself from a moving train.' Miss Dry killed herself on February 10 after visiting her mother in Chippenham, Wiltshire from a high-speed train from Chippenham to London at 10.25 a.m.*

She was seen leaning out of a window by a passing train driver, and was found dead by another soon after. Her uncle Tim told the inquest: "She was cold, tired, frightened and confused. She probably tried to have a cigarette at the window and just in that moment she thought, "I can solve this right now". Recording a verdict that Miss Dry took her own life, Mr Bedford said: "I am satisfied that the only logical conclusion for Gena coming out of the train is that she threw herself out." He added: "I very much accept the opinion of the family that this was a spontaneous act."

Goodbye darling. I'll love you forever.

Chapter 37 – Shafted by the Sunset Kid

Robert Watts is well-known for his work as a producer on the three original *Star Wars* movies and the Indiana Jones trilogy, but his CV also includes production credits on movies like *Who Framed Roger Rabbit?* Alive and more esoteric fare such as *Meetings With Remarkable Men*. Since re-meeting Robert at Celebration Europe at Excel, London, in 2007, we've become friends. I told him I was writing a memoir called 'Continuum', a collection of my experiences filming *Return Of The Jedi*, and the mad world of Conventions twenty-plus years later. He gave me an enigmatic smiley look, scrawled an email address on a scrap of paper and handed it to me saying: "If you need any help, drop me a line. I'd love to read it too". Once I'd finished the book, I sent him a PDF copy and, in a moment of brazen cheekiness, added that I would be really pleased and flattered if he'd consider writing a foreword. To my joy he loved what I'd written (oh, praise indeed!). Over the next two weeks, he crafted a nicely flattering, amusing and honest intro to my collection of odd tales.

Robert comes to London on occasion and when he does we'll meet up and he'll invariably stay over at my place. I think there's an ulterior motive at work here and it involves absolute love for, and a need to bond with, my girl cats, Stella and Luna. Once they're finally asleep, he'll tell me stories of nefarious dealings and rampant egos in the movie biz. There's a spectacularly amusing one involving Steven Segal but, unfortunately, libel laws permit me from sharing it. Upon our return from one of the many restaurants adjacent to my London pad we continue to chat whilst we get high on left-over catnip and Whiskas cat milk laced with Jack Daniel's. Let's face it, it's not every day you get to hang out with a Hollywood player in your own home is it? However, there's a lot more to Robert than Tinseltown title-tattle. There's a lot of history there. He's a very wise and indeed a very mystical man who is well-embarked upon his own journey to the light.

In April 2010, Robert called me and said he'd been contacted out of the blue by a guy he first met way back and who had now inherited his own small publishing company based in Vermont. He suggested they might be interested in publishing *Continuum*. I emailed this character (who can only be written about under an assumed name) and, after an enthusiastic reply, I send him the MS of the book. He's hooked. He reads it in three days and says he wants to put it out on an imprint of his publishing set up called 'Cowboy Press' (not its real name, in fact, if you hadn't already guessed). It's not big and to be honest it's not clever. They print globe-bestriding titles like: *Vermont - Where Is That Exactly?*, and *A Concise History of Maple Syrup*. I'd been rejected by a few publishers in the UK but Robert, my handful of loyal fans, and myself, felt there was life in the old wordy dawg yet. So I agreed to let them publish it. To be truthful I was not exactly Mr. Overjoyed of London Town, there was no slo-mo skipping through Hyde Park with arms outstretched and my grinning face held up to a sky suddenly full of rainbows and pink fluffy cherubs giving me the thumbs up. No, it was more like: "Oh well, it's better than nothing". Naturally there would be no advance, so the longed-for trip on the Orient Express with an elegant and voluptuous female companion hit the back burner once more. But one day, somehow, I shall make it so. Cut to a few months later:

An agreement had been signed between 'Saddle Sore Joe' and myself. A lot of pimply hyperbole had been flying across the Atlantic in my direction over the weeks but we didn't seem to be that much closer to a definitive date for publication. Little tiny, tiny bells of gentle alarm begin to tinker ever so quietly somewhere in my consciousness but I dismissed them as being a subtle manifestation of my long abhorred cynicism and self- doubt. Then the Chap Wearer states in an email further to the agreement that "The entire cost of the book project will be somewhere in the region of $30,000". I started to wonder if he was planning on having the whole book printed on some rare and exotic plant pulp that is only harvested by hand once every twenty five years by naked female virgins in the depths of the Peruvian jungle. I mean, $30,000 for a limited run of a mostly words only book with a few pages of black-and-white photographs? Tinkle, tinkle Vermont Tzar, how I wonder who you are?

May saw the announcement that Lucas Film Ltd were organizing *Star Wars* Celebration V in Orlando, Florida. Naturally, Jerkalong Cassidy thought this would be a great opportunity to get some books printed and flogged. Fine and dandy because I can sell my signed pictures of me as well so we can both come up smelling of horseshit and stardust. The slight snag is that I have not actually been invited as an official guest. So what does our Man Who'd Dearly Love To Wear A Stetson Full Time do? He goes to dear old Robert Watts (unbeknownst to me) and asks him to lend him the money to get me out to Florida. Oh, and he says that he needs the funds to pay his son's school fees. I know nothing of this, so thinking that the Sundance Adolescent is funding it all, I gaily ask for a per diem of $100 cash on top of meals, hotel and return flight and transport to and from...

I arrive in Orlando sometime on the 12th of August. I meet my chums from previous shows and the movie itself, and we hang out in the hotel's open-air bar during the nights. But there's a nagging sense of me somehow not being legitimate at this particular event and therefore not belonging. It's not coming from my compadres that's for sure; it's more like I haven't been invited to go on the coach trip with them all. Robert W. is there and he's as bemused as I am by the bizarre physical countenance of my apparent host. Did I mention he was a Mormon? No? Well, that's easily done isn't it! Somehow he looks like a badly Photoshop'd Klaus Kinski auditioning for the part of a door-to-door salesman in the TV version of a lesser known Stephen King novel set in a small town in Vermont. He's just... wrong. Here's the cut up: Day 1. Interior massive and densely populated Conference Center. No books. When? Uh, tomorrow? Phone the printers you twit! I go to the bar. Find cool young lady dispensing vehement Margaritas for $5. I love it here. I'm staying! Day 2 in the am. No books. Where are they? They'll be here this afternoon. Really? Fuck it. Margarita time yet again. 2p.m.

Two boxes arrive. I rip them open with glee. Yes! It's ME! IN PRINT! Look at the cover! COOL! Turn book over - the spine is blank. Huh? Turn book once more - the back cover is completely wrong. It has the text from the back of the publicity postcard but NOT my artwork. How many books do we have? 75. 75? Tell me you haven't paid for these right? Erm... How much did you pay for them? $17 per book. You've paid $17 for a book that has no spine and the wrong back cover? Yes. Ok.

How much are you planning on selling these mutants for then? $24. Twenty-four dollars? Are you out of your bible-snogging mind? Well, if you sign them and then maybe Robert signs them too I reckon people will go for it. Really? Good luck! Hi, yes one of your finest Margaritas please. And so on.

The upshot of all of this is that I become very disillusioned with the publishing capabilities of the tarnished Rhinestone Cowboy and, over the course of the next year, I slowly but surely extricated myself from his clutches. Reasons? email after email from him each full of false and vague promises of potential reprints, eBooks and even movie rights! Missed phone calls galore, bullshit excuses based on his or family illnesses. Robert telling me how much he'd actually given him for me to go to Orlando, a good friend of mine being ripped off to the sum of £2,500 and so on and on. I know that I'm cynical and I know that I do have a tendency to be wary of people in business but this time I managed to suspend those faults for a while at least in order to furnish a possibility to the best of my ability. I was proved wrong. Oh, the irony! In September 2011 court proceedings were instigated against The Beige Coloured Kid for his deliberate defrauding of fifteen authors as part of an elaborate Ponzi scheme. In April 2013 he was sentenced to six months in jail and a further year under home confinement. His wife and kids must be so proud of their Pa as he slopes of into a sunset entirely of his own making. It's all so sad really, as he's fundamentally a nice man who obviously loved the idea of being a publisher but got in way over his head. Such a shame. I was lucky as I escaped financially unscathed. Robert W. unfortunately did not.

Chapter 38 – Son of Nosferatu

Several years back, my friend David Rose, who in 1980 directed the promo video for Shock's first single *Angel Face*, told me of a notion he had for a short film. It involved the comical adventures of a homeless and hapless vampire who is in fact the son of Nosferatu himself. Would I be interested in playing him? Do Popes shit in the woods? YES! Count me in. When do we start? What shall I wear? Whoa, easy tiger! It's just an idea at the moment. Oh, ok. I mentally unpack my suitcase and get on with what I've previously written about for five effing years! Suddenly it's 2010 and we're in a definite go mode. Are you still up for it he asks? YES! Is the bear a Catholic? Showbiz, don't you just love it?

David had crafted a good and amusing script. The movie will run approximately twenty minutes and is now called *SON of Nosferatu*. Why caps for 'SON'? No idea, sorry. I went down to David and Kathy's house in Sarf Lundin, one day in early August, for a read through and a bit of a casting session for the teenagers needed for various roles. The synopsis of the film is this: Nosferatu died penniless, so his SON (who was never given a real name) is homeless and reduced to selling *The Hot Issue* on street corners and, as a consequence, has lost his mojo... Melanie is looking for a good cause and when SON tells her that he is the last Vampire on Earth, she thinks that by helping an endangered species she will get back into the Fairy Ring. So SON and Melanie set out to find a way to ensure that he is not the last ever Vampire...

We sat in the garden; I drank a glass or three of chilled white wine, smoked and looked on in admiration, and a degree of envy, at this gaggle of bright young things before me as they excitedly read the parts they'd been allocated. Or hoped they'd be given. One girl stood out instantly, Sophie Sumner, a professional model, eighteen years old, blonde, pretty as hell and the owner of a sharp and intuitive mindset. In other words she's a natural and perfect to play Melanie, the naughty fairy with a good heart. I'd yet to find my voice for the character so, on this day, I opted for a kind subsonic and cancerous husk, like that of the guy who does the voice-overs for every movie trailer. It territfied the youngsters admirably but wasn't really sustainable. I ended up using my own tones. They've served me well so far.

A week or so later, I did a screen test with Sophie in David's sitting room and the chemistry was absolutely spot on. Wonderful! Having reluctantly given up on the concept of being an actor, or more truthfully having had acting give up on me over the last ten years, I was suddenly aware that, just like an alcoholic or any addict, the drug still lurks in your DNA however successfully you think you've buried it. It only takes one sniff of a performance (or a glass or a pipe) to bring it out to the surface once again. But this time I took it for what it was; just a harmless piece of fun, nothing more and nothing less. Not a triumphant return to the bright lights, the glamour, the Hollywood parties, and countless lurid exposes in gossip rags as I'm captured by Paparazzi stumbling wide-eyed and legless from nightclubs all over the globe. Followed inevitably by a contrite and charming appearance on the Jonathan Ross TV show after rehab sojourn number five. No sirree! Those days were way, way behind me. After all, I'd become a father of healthy male twins, landed in a secure marriage at last; I was glowingly clean and sober, marvellously reinvented as a pillar of society and mega rich as the owner of health clubs in Mayfair, Chelsea and Notting Hill. Oh, hang on; I drifted into being someone else for a moment. Bugger!

Mr. Rose somehow blagged everything we needed. Either he had some very heavy friends that he kept quiet about or he just called in favours with charm and a great script from those he knows in The Biz. We shot on the fly on High Definition Digital using a portable camera. God, how brilliant! How very modern darlings! Imagine all the palaver and humping around of vanloads of kit this would've entailed if we were still in the 1980s? It re-minded me of our little Euro jaunts as Noir doing our inserts for Channel 4's *Feast* way back when. That was a kind of guerrilla film making too. We had a beautiful Russian make up lady named Olga; fellow actors like the wonderful Rula Lenska and Ed Kingsley; stylists; wardrobe personnel; sound and lighting geezers and a good little collective of Background Artistes.

I opted to wear my black Rockacha '50s style suit with black brogues, a white shirt and a black-and-white polka dot cravat. I didn't want to go into some kind of period style presentation so chose an elegant and timeless look that could fit in to any environment. We filmed on the streets of London; in Olga's sumptuous penthouse apartment in Victoria, and a lot inside Tony Moore's wonderful music venue in Balham, South London called The Bedford. This is a great building with an interesting history. Back in Victorian days, it was a large hotel and then a high-class brothel. It fell into a state of disrepair in the 1950s and became a venue for live music in the late '60s. It's un-modernised from top to bottom, panelled in dark wood with grand staircases and has, as its main feature on the ground floor, a circular music area fashioned after the Globe Theatre. Fantastic acoustics. I should know as Mo and I played there before SON was filmed. Sophie and I filmed one scene in the back of a bright red Bentley driven by a very camp black chauffeur wearing a vivid crimson leather suit and cap. It's that kind of movie. And like everything else (for better or worse) it can be found on YouTube. A certain Madame Noir on IMDB wrote a review, "*SON Of Nosferatu = fun, frolics and fangs*" and called it "refreshingly inventive ... unpredictably hilarious. Tim Dry and Sophie Sumner shine in their roles ... and writer-director David Rose helms the flick with imaginative flair."

I'm very pleased with my work in the film, even though I'm only really playing a slightly exaggerated version of myself, just as I did in Berkoff's *Harry's Christmas* all those years ago. I think I carried it off with a degree of aplomb (I love that word and never really find enough opportunities to use it), charm and humour. Who knows what it may lead to? It's quite probably the only time I'll ever have a part specifically written for me. We had an invitation-only screening in the private cinema at the delightfully decadent Sanctum Soho Hotel in The West End in November. The demand for seats was so great we had to have two showings and it went down a storm! It was one of those absolutely magical moments. I got just a little Tired and Emotional at dinner afterwards, much to the irritation of a very, very good friend of mine. She'll never understand it and I can never truly explain it.

Incidentally the following year, the delightful Ms Sumner went on to win the very prestigious and high-profile event America's Next Top Model. She's now working all over the world, bless her. She'll be unaffordable if we ever make a sequel.

June 2011 saw me in Indianapolis at a Convention called *Days Of The Dead* hosted in the Wyndham West Hotel and one of the big Horror autograph Fests which take place worldwide every year. It was the first to feature me as a signing guest. The enterprising organizer thought that because of my role in *Xtro* I'd be a viable attraction. Hey, you're paying for it and therefore I'm not going to argue!

And I have to say that it made for a pleasant change of scene after eight years of the world of *Star Wars* shows and their oh-so-familiar questions and imagery. Don't get me wrong; I'm not biting the hand that feeds. I'm just looking forward to a change of scenery.

Sometime in the late afternoon of day two, I was sitting behind my incrementally diminishing stack of photos and watching the actions of a well-known film actor newly released from 'Dr Fuck-wits Globally Syndicated Rehab' TV series. He's across the aisle from me and is getting more and more bored and distracted. He sweats a lot. I can almost see those thought bubbles circling like little dark zeppelins above his troubled head as they ask: "Why? Why? Why?" He goes back to his hotel room several times to change his T Shirt. Meanwhile I'm thinking how is it that I'm selling more pictures of me as my two *Star Wars* characters than those that depict me as a most horrible and slimy *Alien* who rapes an innocent Page 3 girl in her isolated country cottage? There goes the 'I'm on vacation from Episode VI notion. Suddenly, I'm interrupted by the very loud voice of a woman berating someone in her vicinity by shouting at him or her: "Dwayne! Be careful with your chainsaw!" I look up, head a-swivel, body startled but poised for immediate evacuation and/or fight. Sharpie pens, empty plastic cups and 10x8s of me in movies fall in slow motion to the carpeted floor as I rise to my feet with adrenalin pounding through my jaded veins. But what do I see? Nothing but a tearful six year old boy clad in a blood-spattered butcher's apron, standing only a few feet away from his hysterical Mom, clutching a mini-sized and obviously plastic replica of the main weapon from a major cult horror film of the 1970s. I sink back to my seat relieved and disturbed in equal measure.

At the end of the first day, it's time for a serious amount of drinkage of cheap, nasty, but nonetheless free red wine from the bar in the hotel's function room, as there's some kind of aftershow party going on. It seemed to mainly consist of tattooed stocky lads from merchandising with a spindly spliff tucked behind each ear leering at moderately attractive young ladies in short and very tight dresses. Who no doubt had won their non-speaking parts in films like *Human Centipede II* or some such by dint of their talent alone. The boys circled them whilst drinking prodigious amounts of beer in between hurling themselves in an epileptic fashion around the dance floor to loud Death Metal music. At some pre-arranged signal they all swarmed as one to a corner of the room and, with guttural roars of primeval delight, started eating from greasy boxes of White Castle mini hamburgers nicknamed 'Sliders'. Having tried a couple out of morbid curiosity, I discovered a couple of hours later in the privacy of my bathroom, the exact cause of their sinister nomenclature.

Whilst observing the goings on, as is ever my wont, I found myself sitting at a table with a lovely and equally bemused gent named John E. L. Tenney. John's an archivist and researcher into the paranormal. We had a most entertaining and invigorating conversation. I told him my Magic Hour experience (as detailed earlier in this book) and he nodded knowingly. When we tired of having to converse by shouting into each other's ears we decided to blag a couple of plastic glasses each of the acidic wine and move outside to a wooden bench on forecourt of the hotel. I was gagging for the first of many hand-rolled cigarettes and, with a sigh of relief from sparking up number one, I plumed upwards a graceful exhalation of fragrant tobacco smoke and we reconvened our mystical and enlivening chat.

About twenty minutes into our sojourn, the sky started to blacken and, from nowhere, a strong breeze began to manifest and grow increasingly more vehement. A couple of local dudes nodded their heads sagely at each other and said: "Yep, storm's a comin' in". I was rapt. Especially when the strength of the wind escalated and things like signs and waste bins started to be blown right across the parking lot. Small trees bent double under the onslaught. I could see lightning forking down through the inky clouds on the flat horizon line and the noise was becoming deafening. It was a Spielbergian moment for sure. I wished I'd brought my camera with me to try and capture some of it. Strangely enough there was no rain at all. Then, as quickly as it had arisen the storm was gone. Leaving a heavy silence and a fair amount of refuse in its wake. I could hear the thunder slowly rolling off into the distance. How brilliant! How very Mid-Western! Everything slowly clicked back into place and we continued to talk and drink what was left of our wine.

A red car starts to become visible way, way down the long drive-way leading up to the building. It slowly gets closer. The headlights are on. Now we can see that it's a vast stretch limo of the sort favoured by pimps and gangstas with zero taste. You know, the type that has the angled strips of lights on the edges of the three pairs of windows. It's an even more lurid shade of scarlet closer up as it silently glides to a halt right in front of us. The back door opens and out steps a portly man in a Santa Claus outfit complete with a full white beard! He strides nonchalantly into the hotel lobby followed by two young girls who've also exited from the limo. They are wearing bright red Cheerleader outfits and they're giggling and clutching on to each other for support it would appear. John and I turn to each other with that 'Did that just happen?' look of incredulity. What a deliciously surreal moment to cut out and keep. Especially as it's the height of the summer!

Chapter 39 – Death and Life

My brother David passed away after a lengthy battle with prostate cancer that had spread to his spine. Poor man. It's an ugly way to go and, to be honest, from what I'd heard of the massive indignities he suffered in his last few weeks, I'm glad that I didn't go and see him. That would have hurt me far too much, especially as it was only a year and a quarter after Gena's death. I owed him so much for introducing me to live music from the age of twelve and for telling me the real facts of life when I was ready. Also thanks are due in retrospect for his giving me several metaphysical clips round the ear when my self-indulgent whining got on his nerves.

He'd become a wise man over the decades and most definitely he was a brave soul who followed his heart wherever it led. Bless him. I've also lost two cousins, the female half of my acting Agency, and two female friends over the last couple of years alone. But these were all accidents of one kind or another rather than the result of old age and, I must admit, I have become increasingly aware of my own mortality and, subsequently, I've developed a sporadic fear of the future. I have virtually no family left now, no offspring, no savings, no belief system to fall back upon, no property and no partner. That scares me. So I have to keep busy, keep constantly creative to take my mind away from those worries. I'm also very much obsessed with how quickly time is now passing by for me. I recall an event and I think, oh that was just a couple of years ago. No, it was eight or nine or more! Huh? How did that happen? It's not just us 'Oldies' who are incredulously watching the years whizzing past, I've spoken with younger people and they're aware of it too. I think it's an adjunct of the speed of communication with which we are all living. Plus the ease of long distance travel and the pervasive screens of the media transmitting events and information almost the instant it happens wherever in the world it takes place. We want it all and we want it NOW!

I mean I sent them an email FIFTEEN minutes ago and the bastards haven't replied yet! When was the last time that any of us wrote someone an actual letter by hand? For me it was sometime in the early to mid-nineties. Getting a computer put paid to that long-winded palaver. I mean, not only undergoing the exhausting physical act of putting pen to paper and trying to make it legible but then having to go out and buy a stamp and find a post box and then wait a week for a reply. I mean, really! The only letters I receive these days are from creditors. I don't really miss the letter-writing thing that much, although I do love the smell of ink and paper. I have an old wooden box in which I keep selected letters from the past forty years, mainly from girlfriends but a few from male friends of my own age. The earliest one dates back to 1970 and is from my first proper love known to you as 'R' from earlier in this book. It's heart-warming to re-read that declaration of innocent teen love and affection.

I have found what I would define as a true creative voice twice in my life; an artistic passion or bliss to follow if you like. The first was the decision to move to London to study mime in 1976, which without a doubt was the best thing I have ever done. It's safe to say that every good thing that has happened to me was a result of taking that leap. The second was the discovery of photography as a means to express myself visually. So then, where does one go next on this strange journey along the peculiarly unmapped and somewhat speed-bumped road to artistic fulfilment?

After *Continuum* garnered favourable reviews for my writing style, I realized I could no longer procrastinate about creating my first work of fiction. I knew I had the imagination and the technical skills to be able to write in a way that was appealing. So I began to create a novella entitled *Ricochet*. I like the notion of a novella because it takes away the enormity of crafting an A to Z novel with its narrative arcs, huge numbers of pages and a satisfyingly dramatic but open-ended conclusion that could well indicate that an even more lucrative sequel might just be on the cards. No, a novella is cosy and gives you room to stretch out but not so much that you'll need a literary osteopath to put you back in shape. We're talking somewhere between 20 and 50,000 words. That's suitable and manageable for me. The book's tagline is: Reality Is Just A Fragment Of Your Imagination. There's a relatively new literary genre out there now and that is called Speculative Fiction. You can file me under that please.

Through Barbie Wilde I was put in touch with a literary editor named Dean M. Drinkel. He finds authors for short story collections, and he'd enabled Barbie to have two dark tales successfully published in horror anthologies, so I emailed him extracts from *Ricochet*. He liked them. A short while later he asked me to write a story of a maximum word count of 5,000 for an anthology called *Demonology*. It was an A to Z, as a lot of these collections are, and I was handed the letter 'N'. After a short Google search for an alphabetical Demon list I found an 'N' that grabbed me and off I went. What fun! It's wonderfully liberating to put yourself inside someone else's head. Especially if they're a mischievous and malevolent beast from Hell! Dean loved it and promptly asked me to write another for a book called *The Bestiarum Vocabulum*. A pervy story about a mythical beast that begins with 'O' slid into my consciousness and grew with the same ease of imaginative flow and freedom of thought as before. The more I let go and lose the fear the better it gets. I love it. I sense that quite possibly a third creative passion might have been slowly growing unrecognized inside me for a long while, it just needed the right midwife to assist with the birth.

For me the great thing about writing fiction is that I don't need anyone else to create it with and I don't have to employ cutting edge technology to do it. The bottom line is just give me a pen and some paper and I'll travel anywhere and craft a story for myself and thus for you. A third dark tale is on the go as I write this, for the *Phobophobias* anthology. So, three stories coming out and a novella to finish and get published. And that is just the beginning.

Chapter 40 – A Dream

I turn over in the single bed in my old bedroom in my parents' house on Christmas Eve and enter an exhilarating dream of flying. I launch myself out into space from a diving-board somehow suspended hundreds of feet above an anticipatory crowd clustered beneath and swim through the stippled air with ease and grace. It's the best feeling I've ever had. It feels so… right. I soar, I glide and I swoop. The distant throng way below adore me and applaud my skill. I look around me and see everything that is happening now and everything that has ever happened all at once. Random Access Memory.

Pure white snow, lush and nostalgically thick, had fallen gracefully during the bleak and inscrutable night before the dawn of Christmas Day. This hallowed and indigo time, when children sleeplessly wrap themselves in promises of gifts to come, sees 158,000 Angels dressed for bad weather and essential business, waiting in anxious ranks for their descent to the restless city.

Elvis, shrouded in '50's cashmere and manly cologne, leaves the Theatre from a hidden exit and hunches out into the night, his dyed but still luxuriant hair flecked with wistful flakes of adoring snow. He sings quietly to himself under a breath perfumed by chicken fat and teenage pussy. James Dean, with collar up-turned, and the frown of permanent Teen angst causelessly tattooed on his tragically beautiful face, shoulders past the King on a silent white and deserted street corner and mutters a few words of resentful seasonal cheer. Jimmy is late to meet Liz Taylor in a diner of the sort painted by Edward Hopper and fears her strident anger at being kept waiting. She's okay at the moment, unusually placid, and in the first whoozy flush of intoxication. As she sits with her ankles crossed under the bar-stool, Liz drinks elegantly and dreams of Richard Burton in full Roman costume slowly and with acned empirical grace, raising the hem of his toga to reveal the proud and straining extent of his Celtic passion.

Four Victorian urchins dressed in rags but with rosy and optimistic faces, press themselves up against the antique glass of a bow-fronted shop window, and gaze slack-mouthed at the displayed small dulled-glass jars containing the skin-cells, DNA and body fluids of recently deceased and now forgotten pop and movie stars. Somewhere inside the clammy, mucus-coloured fog of the East End, a tall man with a doctor's bag, charmed-up and deadly, turns into a shrouded alley off Berners Street. On the West side of town, in a large flat in a Gothic apartment block recently relocated to the Guggenheim Museum, John Lennon turns away from the sight of Mick, Marianne, Damian Thorn and Mia Farrow entwined like sea-horses (so very wetly enjoying each other) and slips into potent memories of Macca on all fours and the Maharishi with a DigiCam.

Inside a stable in the heart of Somerset, safe from incessant warfare and the magnet of CNN, the infant baby Jesus is re-born for the umpteenth time. Through metaphorically gritted teeth he winces once more at the endless pangs of reincarnation and steels himself for the onslaught of relatives bearing gifts he outgrew several thousand years ago. Three Kings on Harley Davidsons, wearing piercings and ebony leather, miss the Motorway turn-off to Compton Dundon and decide instead to head to a Fetish party in Kennington. They roar regally past Charlie Chaplin locked in a frosty clinch with Alfred Hitchcock on the corner of the Peckham Road. Radios endlessly chime the carols created by machines for needy greedy supplicants. The Temple is full but the churches are bare. The clubs are chocka. Bouncers with faces like mallets deny Marilyn and John F. Kennedy entrance to their own party. A birthday cake (autographed by Richard Harris) melts in a slushy gutter just to the left of Norma Jean's goose-fleshed bare legs. JFK reaches bemusedly up to repeatedly scratch two incipient bald spots on the front and back of his head.

Silently, like a multitude of Bruces desperate to die hard wearing only a singlet, the Angels gracefully land in the almost deserted Metropolis and de-wing themselves. Some rub celestial hands and await a mini cab to Hoxton. Others fret about entrance to 'SitCam' (a celebrity blood-bath club for has-beens). Still more remember their actual purpose here on Terror Firma and consult the A-Z on their mobiles, dial in their co-ordinates and set off by foot or by Dirigi-Cab to Knightsbridge and eventually, Upton Park. One Dark Angel, whom most others either avoid altogether, or beg autographs from, consults his own battered agenda, laughs and rises majestically into the night sky, heading silently but inevitably towards the riverside home of an ex-Tory MP currently writing the sequel to his prison memoirs.

In a room in Hazlitt's hotel in Soho, Charles Dickens raises his damp face from between the thighs of Kylie and has a blinding flash of an idea for a new novel. Oscar Wilde, in a fetching cat-suit fashioned from lizard skin and sequins, furiously buggers Joe Orton in his shabby bedsit in Islington and stares at the blood-spattered illustrations from library books that decorate the walls. A five-foot high snowman erected by two scabby-kneed boys in long grey shorts from the 1950's melts in tearful dissaray in the gardens of Leinster Square, watched by a shivering solitary Fairy clad only in gossamer-thin clothing designed by Arthur Rackham. She tilts her weary head and imagines George Clooney dressed as a frisky Santa brushing himself down and grinning irresistibly as he emerges from a barren fireplace in a room in the St. Giles Rookery.

Two young lovers with flushed and excited faces furtively kiss on a maroon velour chaise longue in a candle-lit corner of the Grill Room in the Cafe Royal in 1927. Screams echo through the fog-dampened streets of Whitechapel. 2.5 million laptops simultaneously and without warning decide to display only the closing moments of *It's A Wonderful Life* as a looped Quick Time movie. Bing Crosby links hands with Danny Kaye as they step off the Millenium Bridge and plummet down into the oily, chilly waters of sluggish and benign Father Thames.

Bohemian Rhapsody plays distantly on a thousand neighbours' sound systems. Then my dream shifts into me dying and waking up somewhere different. Then I really do wake up and I realise that I am definitely somewhere very different now and that things can never be the same again. It's alright though; I am at peace with the past and ready for the future.

Chapter 41 - A Clue

I was never really a fan of The Grateful Dead, even in the depths of my spaced out and brief tenure in Brighton in the early 1970s. Sure I pretended to listen deeply when in the company of others, whilst sitting cross-legged and with enlarged pupils, gazing in awe at their beautiful album artwork. But to be honest I found their music meandering, unspecific, unresolved, tonally ungainly, lyrically lacking and, above all, aurally unsexy. I surmised that life as I knew it then would actually continue to go on even if I hadn't spent what felt like 24 hours listening to yet another seemingly endless version of *Dark Star* on side three of yet another live album. But one little sliver of cosmic definition contained within one song of theirs, somehow filtered down through all of the murk and fermented a kind of emotional and synaptic connection. Just a simple four-line refrain that resonated then and still does today. Back then it was a romantic notion of some kind of suburban ersatz outlaw life but now it hits home hard as an actual definition of the reality of my life. It's this:

"Sometimes the light's all shinin' on me Other times I can barely see Lately it occurs to me What a long, strange trip it's been."

From the song *Truckin'*. © 1970. Garcia, Hunter, Lesh, Weir.

Ricochet

Ricochet was published in March 2015 by an imprint of Spectral Press named Theatrum Mundi. To date I have short stories in five anthologies edited by Dean M Drinkel: *The Thirteen Signs, Phobophobias, The Grimorium Verum, Demonology and The Bestiarum Vocabulum*. I also have a story entitled *Inside* in an anthology called *47-16: Short Fiction and Poetry Inspired by David Bowie*. All the proceeds of which go to Cancer Research. I have co-written a photographic novel/screenplay called *Detroit Rising* with filmmaker Thomas Eikrem. I also play a wine-loving arms dealer in his movie *Le Accelerator* (2017) I had two short stories printed in Forbes Magazine and I wrote an article about *Xtro* for *Film Rage* magazine.

In 2014 I grew a goatee beard to play an unpleasant gangster in a short film *Pier Pressure* that was released in 2016. I've kept the facial accoutrement as I feel that it adds a certain gravitas to my countenance! I'm still appearing at Autograph Conventions here, there and everywhere. There's life in this mature tomcat yet, believe me. Stay tuned!

The Nutshell

Answers to real questions sent in by fans to the Tik and Tok website.

Favourite Colour? Black, black and yes, just a little bit more of that dark stuff. Silver (is that a colour or a state of grace?). And red wine seen through a glass held up to the light. Stained glass windows. Red lipstick on the full mouth of a beautiful girl.

Point in the day? Sunset, somewhere warm and sexy. Dawn, as seen from the window of an aeroplane flying over the Alps. The first fall of snow in London in the quiet early morning. The smell of autumn in the country (can only take so much fresh air before my lungs give out!).

Quote? "The future is a mirror without any glass in it." Xavier Forneret
  "Consistency is the last resort of the unimaginative." Oscar Wilde

Female Singer? Kate Bush, Joni Mitchell, Madonna (Ray of Light), k.d. lang, Ella Fitzgerald, Lisa Gerrard. *Male singer?* Bowie ('71 to '80), Jim Morrison, Lennon (in Fabs days), early Elvis, David Lee Roth (Van Halen), early Sinatra, David Sylvian, Serge Gainsbourg.

Pair of shoes? A pair of black & white co-respondent brogue shoes bought from Rock A Cha in London in 1995. A pair of pointy black ones from Robot (like Brothel Creepers, but without the big soles) in '98. Deck shoes in the summer. The Kung Fu slippers we used to wear in the early '80's. My feet are unsightly monsters.

Food? Thai for taste, spice and variety. Italian for full-on passion and waistline trauma. A really good American burger the size of your head in NYC or one or two places in London now. A selection of Tapas in a small Spanish village. A tiny Chinese restaurant in Boulogne in Northern France that does a dish of sizzling scallops in spicy sauce. Anything that has taste and sensuality, so sadly no German or Dutch food let's face it!

Drink? (To refresh): A Margarita cocktail, in a salt-rimmed glass, sipped with infinite relish in a bar in any major city. A glass of chilled Pinot Gris in a restaurant that I can't possibly afford to actually eat in. A tall, cold glass of beer in a dusty roadside bar in Spain or France. *To get pissed with?* The quickest way for me is a large Jack Daniels (no ice) and a Kronenbourg lager to follow. Three of those and you're all my best mates, ever. Or, a bottle or three of some fruity, virulent red wine and no lunch. Champagne doesn't thrill me at all, cocaine makes me ravenous for everything that I want but can't achieve so I try (yeah, right) to avoid it at all costs when I'm able. Let's face it; I'm a cheap date. If you pour enough of anything down my throat I'll become the abusive clown that you wish you'd never invited to your party, and your shocked friends will talk about me for days (sometimes weeks) to follow. But then again at other times I'll be the best company you've ever had!

Book? *The Shining* (Stephen King), anything by Bill Bryson, *A Criminal History of Mankind* (Colin Wilson), *To Your Scattered Bodies Go* (Phillip Jose Farmer), *Alice In Wonderland* (Lewis Carroll), *The Infinite Cage* (Keith Laumer), *Naked* (David Sedaris), *Revolution In The Head* (Ian Macdonald), *The Ascent of Man* (Jacob Bronowski). Oh and about 3,000 more that I can't spring to mind at the moment.

Film? *Amelie, Withnail & I, Performance, Gladiator, Laura, Don't Look Now, Blow-Up, Pulp Fiction, The Ring, Ben-Hur, A Clockwork Orange, True Romance, 12 Monkeys, Nikita, Blade Runner, if...., Vertigo,* etc, etc.

Comedian? Erm... God! Let's face face it, who's got a better sense of humour than that guy? And also: The late Bill Hicks, then Bill Bailey, early Richard Pryor, certain Eddie Izzard moments, *The Office, Fawlty Towers*, bits from *The Fast Show*, etc.

TV Commercial appeared in? After Eight Mints, Guinness Enigma, Ford Fiesta (Germany) and Rene Lezard (Germany). I rest my case. These are the fruits of my advertising loins. To paraphrase Morrissey: How strange is now?

Tim, What do you think of the way music has evolved from The New Romantic scene, early 80's, to the pop music of today? There are probably a lot of cool and talented people working underground. I hope.

Sports? No! Neither to watch or in which to participate Apart from gym attendance, and stuff at home, my main exercise is trying to control an over-active imagination.

Possibility of us not being alone in the Universe? Come on, where do you think Tik & Tok came from?

World Politics and our fight for World Peace? How can you *Fight* for Peace?

Fashion. Compared to early 80's and the trendy things Tik and Tok and Noir wore? What fashions? Everybody wants to look like everybody else. Dull and shapeless.

Cats or dogs? Cats definitely. But dogs are essential if you live in the country or somewhere isolated.

Do you do Martial Arts? No. I did Wing Chun Kung Fu for a year back in '85. And then I thought, if some over-enthusiastic sparring partner breaks my nose.... it's all over! The level I achieved was possibly: 'Do not fuck with me'. I hope I still carry that with me.

Did your size cause you any problems while training? My colossal penis did get in the way sometimes, but with the aid of Gaffa tape and generous trousers I was able to bypass this potential stumbling block!

How often do you paint the town red / do you see many live acts? Funnily enough, I do sometimes sneak out from my sleazy West London Palace of Fun late at night, wearing my Ronnie Dome mask, armed with only a large paintbrush and a 2 litre can of Blood Red emulsion, and do a bit of re-decorating where it seems apt. I do not go out and see bands on a regular basis any more, unless they're friends of mine or there's some connection. I saw the best back then and I'm happy with those memories.

Do you have or keep to a strict daily schedule or just take the day as it comes? My daily schedule! The most effort involves un-corking another bottle of red wine and aiming it at the nearest glass and then pointing it mouthwards! I do, in all seriousness spend a huge amount of time in front of my Mac perfecting pieces of writing, music or imagery. Everything revolves around a degree of satisfaction with a day's creativity. I read a lot and I do watch a great many DVDs and the occasional bit of TV. I have two or three female friends who force me out for walks or to visit interesting places in town whenever they can.

Tim, could you please tell us 10 things you'd like to see happen?
1. Time travel. But backwards only. The future scares me.
2. A strange but welcome re-growth of my cranial hair.
3. Fundamentalist Islamic and Christian beliefs seen by all to be as utterly reprehensible, destructive and pointless as they have shown themselves to be.
4. Women finally recognised as being more important than men.
5. The death of Rap music. And football no longer being seen as a call to arms or indeed as anything remotely important outside of the playing field.
6. Alien intervention before it's too late.
7. The total banishment of those ridiculous 'low level' jeans that make you look like an Inmate of a prison or an asylum.
8. An end to dumbing down and the beginning of wising up.
9. Cats as the true inheritors of the earth.
10. And the re-instatement of the belief that everyone is an open-minded individual with an infinite capacity for change and betterment.

INDEX

Adam Ant 92, 94
Adamski 67
Alice in Wonderland 35, 38, 241
Alien 15, 149, 205, 233
Amélie 241
Dante 36, 44, 48
Marc Almond 75, 183, 185
Dave Ambrose 117-118
Amsterdam 84-85, 154-155
Jon Anderson 66
Ann-Margret 161-163
Steve Ausden 89

David Bailey 102
Ginger Baker 23, 25
Martin Baker 66
Long John Baldry 23
Bangkok 69-71, 78
Barcelona 154-157
Syd Barratt 25
Jean-Louis Barrault 53
Alan Bates 29
Robert Bathurst 166
Charles Baudelaire 141, 197, 199, 200-210, 224, 227
The Beatles 18-20, 24, 25, 52, 63, 72, 82, 104, 110, 132, 141, 150, 159, 179, 185
Samuel Beckett 173
Patti Bell 74
Rrussell Bell 94, 97, 100
Pat Benatar 224
Steven Berkoff 10, 11, 13
Martine Beswick 195
Biddie and Eve 66
Christopher Biggins 11
Ronnie Biggs 60
Bird 135
The Bitch 65
Black Sabbath 25, 33, 169
Mo Blackford 224-226
Blade Runner 102, 162, 241
Katharine Blake 148-149, 197
William Blake 36
Blow-Up 56, 241
Blue Mink 16
Ann Blythe 87
Bohemian Rhapsody 126, 215, 239
Simon Le Bon 102, 104
Beki Bondage 117, 184, 224
Jorge Luis Borges 54
Bow Wow Wow 75
Angie Bowie 48-50
David Bowie 34, 36, 39, 46, 48, 49-52, 58, 59, 67, 72, 75, 77, 86, 89, 92, 94, 97, 110, 118, 141, 145, 191, 194, 215, 224, 226, 239, 240
Boy George 75
Marlon Brando 26, 121
Braveheart 122
Jacques Brel 185
The Bride of Frankenstein 78
Brighton 10, 14, 36-46, 48, 185
Arthur Brown 24

Jack Bruce 23, 39
Frank Bruno 195
Richard Burgess 73, 79, 87, 88
Richard Burton 237
Kate Bush 58-59, 67, 78, 86, 94, 141, 240

Cabaret (film) 159
Cabaret Voltaire 75, 86
Cabinet of Dr. Caligari 13
James Cagney 51, 59
James Cameron 177
Joseph Campbell 196
Capetown 127-128
Carole Caplin 77-82, 86-89
David Carradine 195, 196
Martin Carthy 21
Caterham 27, 143
Robin Chaphekar 119
Charlie Chaplin 77, 238
Chicago 188-193
Citizen Kane 121
Nicky Clarke 14-15
Eric Clapton 19, 23, 65, 119
Classix Nouveaux 80, 151
Peter Clifton 50
A Clockwork Orange 52, 241
George Clooney 238
Close Encounters 14, 15
Alma Cogan 18
Anne Collingham 18
Jackie Collins 65
Joan Collins 10-13, 122, 144
Billy Connolly 54
Continuum (book) 229, 236
Steven Cook 5, 185
Cool Running 96-97, 110, 116
Cornwall 32
Cosmic Colouring Book 48
Elvis Costello 62
Ken Cranham 137
Sean Crawford 5, 16, 64, 67-69, 71-75, 78-79, 82-90, 92-120, 125, 137, 158, 188, 190-197, 212-217, 222-223
Cream 23, 27, 39
The Crimpers 74
Carl Crompton 148
David Cronenberg 41, 182
Bing Crosby 238
Janice Crotch 140
Russell Crowe 66, 176
Aleister Crowley 34, 60

Maryam D'Abo 16
D.A.F. 75
Salvador Dali 70
Timothy Dalton 48
The Dam Busters 195
The Damned 60
Vic Damone 87, 208
Anthony Daniels 195
Dawn of the Dead 195
Thomas de Quincey 200

James Dean 237
Roger Dean 47
Death Wish 3 5, 164
Claude Debussy 87
Decadence (film) 10-13
Étienne Decroux 53
Demonology (book) 236, 239
Depeche Mode 75, 80
Charles Dickens 238
Bo Diddley 97
Die Hard 238
Dirty Harry 70
Thomas Dolby 96
Donovan 21, 24
Ray Dorset 127
Kirk Douglas 47, 189
Dream Orphans 215-217, 224
Dean M. Drinkel 236, 239
Gena Dry 5, 197, 225, 227-228, 235
David Dry 5, 21, 23, 30, 45, 194, 227, 235
Dublin 95
Dune 38
J. W. Dunne 206
Duran Duran 75, 94, 102, 104, 109, 117
Bob Dylan 21, 208

Shirley Eaton 195
Rusty Egan 72-74, 79, 80, 88, 216
Vince Eager 18
The Eagles 51, 52, 59
Eclection 25
Paul Edgley 116
Britt Ekland 195
Eminem 127, 169
Brian Epstein 72
Eraserhead 59
Esbjerg 67
Kenny Everett 119
The Exorcist 205

Facebook 223-225
Faces of Death 71
Marianne Faithfull 49, 140, 237
Famous Names 76-77
The Fantastic Voyage 29, 206
Steve Fairnie 77
Mia Farrow 237
Father Ted 223
Dave Fenton 60
Nicholas Ferguson 92
The Fifth Element 188
Peter Firth 137
Carrie Fisher 90, 192
Simon Fisher-Turner 49
Fleetwood Mac 24
Florida 230-231
The Flying Pickets 115
Peter Fonda 26
The Fool 24
Harrison Ford 90, 192
Nina Fortune 48, 51, 223

243

Charles Fox 80
James Fox 54
Freddie & The Dreamers 19
The French Connection 186

Fad Gadget 68, 87
Serge Gainsbourg 152, 240
Liam or Noel Gallagher 23, 48
Paul Gascoigne 195
Antonio Gaudi 155, 157
Mel Gibson 122
Gilbert & George 151
Glastonbury 15, 141, 155
The Glitter Band 72
Jean-Luc Godard 120
The Godfather 121
Godley and Creme 119
Peter Godwin 80, 94, 135
William Golding 176
Gong 51
Kevin Gould 116-118
Graham Bond Organization 23
Hugh Grant 62, 189
The Grateful Dead 239
Larry Grayson 119
Greece 166-168
Greenslade 47
George Grosz 146
Alec Guinness 31

Nina Hagen 67
Daryl Hall 27
Leslie Halliwell 16
Hamburg 10, 129-132, 145, 148, 149, 154, 159, 160
Mark Hamill 90
MC Hammer 202
Hammersmith Odeon 19-20, 82, plays 110
Lal Hardy 117
Jean Harlow 121
Richard Harris 238
George Harrison 54
Noel Harrison 189
Rex Harrison 189
Rula Lenska 232
Rutger Hauer 161-163
Nazia Hassan 102
Hellraiser 5, 15
Jimi Hendrix 220
Herman Hesse 37
Christine Hewitt 213
Benny Hill 53, 148
Steve Hillage 34
Alfred Hitchcock 238
Adolf Hitler 182, 190
Hokusai 99
Hong Kong 101-102
Anthony Hopkins 156
Edward Hopper 237
Nick Hornby 54, 60
Hot Gossip 63, 66, 69, 119
The House of Wax 46
Joe Hubbard 110, 111, 116
Kate & John Hudson 72
Human Centipede II 234
The Human League 65, 75, 79, 116
Humble Pie 60

The Idol 56
Billy Idol 135
if... 241
Iggy Pop 109, 119, 184
Indianapolis 233-235
Intolerance (LP) 104, 118, 215

Jack The Ripper 186
Michael Jackson 141
Mick Jagger 54-55, 72, 138-142, 144, 179
Danny John-Jules 195
Sandy Johnston 166
Brian Jones 23
Desmond Jones 53, 58, 59, 65, 67, 90, 171
Grace Jones 75
Howard Jones 99
Paul Jones 24
Jane Kahn 74, 96, 99, 102, 104, 105, 107
Kajagoogoo 94
Georg Kajanus 25, 51, 94, 128, 137, 149-160, 217-218, 221, 227, 228
Lindsay Kemp 52, 58, 65, 214
Ross Kemp 125
John F. Kennedy 238
Kill Bill 195
Stephen King 209, 230, 241
Ed Kingsley 232
The Kinks 182
John Kobal 221
Kraftwerk 51, 72, 75, 97, 216
Stanley Kubrick 56, 86, 112, 174

Elsa Lanchester 78
Landscape 54, 73, 79, 86, 87
k.d. lang 240
Led Zeppelin 33, 50, 141
Christopher Lee 11
Lemmy 119
John Lennon 24, 82, 141, 159, 169, 237, 240
Rula Lenska 232
Victor Lewis-Smith 165
The Liberated Lady (shop) 62, 78
Lightning Bear 195
John C. Lilly 38
Dai Llewellyn 76
Federico Garcia Lorca 87
Peter Lorre 49
Lover Come Back To Me 92-93
The Lovin' Spoonful 92
Lowri-Ann (Shock) 62
George Lucas 90-91, 190, 192
BarBara Luna 193
David Lynch 59, 158, 215
Roy Lynes 60

Barbara Machin 92
Scott McKenzie 190
Doug McClure 193
Francis McGee 197
Nikki McKevitt 197
Keith Macmillan 67
Mad Max 2 106, 113
Madonna 121, 240

The Magus 38
Malaga 10, 169
Manfred Mann 23
Jayne Mansfield 68
Marilyn Manson 169, 212, 214
Marcel Marceau 53, 167
Marilyn 75
Marquee Club 21-23, 224
Glenn Matlock 72
John Mayall 24
Linda McCartney 25
Paul McCartney 25
Malcolm McClaren 32
Mediaeval Baebes 149, 221
Metropolis 169
Mezz 74, 76, 87
Bette Midler 66
Midnight Express 71, 86
Milan 127-129
Pete Miles 21, 40-41
Frank Millard 28, 36, 37
Henry Miller 29
Joni Mitchell 209
Tony Mitchell 80, 104
The Monkees 30
Marilyn Monroe 87, 140, 200, 238
Monty Python 53
Keith Moon 25
Michael Moorcock 38
Tony Moore 232
Georgio Moroder 72, 86
Desmond Morris 171
Morrissey 106, 241
Jim Morrison 7, 141, 199, 203, 210, 240
Mott The Hoople 89, 218
Don Mousseau 94
The Move 24
Mungo Jerry 127
Caroline Munro 195
Simon Napier-Bell 102
Nausea (Sartre) 179
New York City 82-83, 99, 161
Anthony Newley 11
Tessa Niles 118
Steve Niner 34-38, 43-46
Noir 134, 149-154, 158, 217, 218, 224, 232, 241
David Niven 126, 190
Gary Numan 4, 72, 85-88, 94, 107, 109-113, 116, 118, 119, 212, 216, 217
Terry O'Neill 50
Hans Werner Olm 147
Laurence Olivier 115
Ray Orbison 147, 209
Joe Orton 238
The Osric Tentacles 185
The Outer Limits 158
Robert Palmer 52, 86
Anita Pallenberg 54
Paris 51, 53, 54, 120, 150-155, 168, 169, 182, 193, 197-211
Larry Parnes 18
Peter Parnell 217
Maxfield Parrish 14
Louis Pauwels 38
Harold Pendleton 23

Robert Pereno 62-63, 65-74, 78, 78-89, 219
Performance 53-54, 56, 140, 241
Perfume 202
Anthony Perkins 170
Edith Piaf 185
Pablo Picasso 155
Wilson Pickett 86
Geoff Pinckney 212, 216
Pink Floyd 24, 25
Robert Plant 141
Plastic Bertrand 169
Roman Polanski 82, 121
Ted Polhemus 76
Jackson Pollock 223
Cole Porter 135
The Poseidon Adventure 172
Predator 149, 181
Elvis Presley 18, 26, 141, 162, 164, 237, 240
Vincent Price 46
Prince 135, 141
David Pritchard 151-153
David Prowse 195
Richard Pryor 70
Psycho 126

The Queen 48, 60, 169

Arthur Rackham 238
Raiders of the Lost Ark 209
Basil Rathbone 9
Red Dwarf 195
Redhill 14, 20, 25-35, 46-48, 59-60, 113, 178-179, 223
Reigate 14, 32-34
Oliver Reed 29
Jean Reno 152
Repulsion 121
Return of the Jedi 90-91, 95, 188, 190-191, 229
Revolution 164
Nick Rhodes 94, 177
Rhyl 84
Cliff Richard 18
Keith Richards 140, 184, 204, 216
Frank Richmond 94
Ricochet 4, 236, 239
Roland Rivron 66
The Rizzo Brothers 74, 99
Nic Roeg 53, 54, 165
The Rocky Horror Show 52, 214
Rollerball 192
The Rolling Stones 23
Ronny 80, 97
David Rose 78-79, 102, 231-33
Rosemary's Baby 82
Rosie 11, 13, 125-126, 133, 136-138, 144
Jonathan Ross 219, 221
Jonathan Ross (TV host) 232
Dante Gabriel Rossetti 20
David Lee Roth 141, 240
Ken Russell 4, 29
Teresa Russell 54
Marek Rymaszewski 96

Bev Sage 77
Sailor 25, 51, 94, 149, 157, 218, 221, 227
Peter Sarsted 190
Leo Sayer 119
Ryuichi Sakamoto 75, 97, 99
Jean-Paul Sartre 169, 179
Rat Scabies 60
Scanners 182
Martin Scorsese 82, 193
Ridley Scott 102, 121
Sebastian Scott 121
Screen Me, I'm Yours 79, 97, 106, 109, 160
Pete Seeger 21
Kenichi Segawa 99
Jules Seifert 183
The Sepia 183, 184
The Shangri-Las 206
Gerry Shephard 72, 78
The Shining 112, 241
Camilla Shivarg 219
Susie Silvie 16
Frank Sinatra 141, 193
Grace Slick 48
Slightly Deranged (EP) 215
The Small Faces 24
Paul Smith 201
Robin Smith 105
Soft Cell 75, 185
The Song Remains The Same 50
Karen Sparks 63, 68, 70, 72, 80
Harry Dean Stanton 172
Star Trek 137, 164, 192, 193
Star Wars 4, 90, 168, 171, 188, 189-197, 212, 213, 229, 230
Pete Steer 212, 216
Steampacket 23
Steely Dan 47, 51, 119, 178
Peter Steer 336, 341
The Stepford Wives 129, 166, 222
Pamela Stephenson 54
David Stewart 34
Rod Stewart 23
Stoke-on-Trent 107-113
Steve Strange 72, 80, 216
Strange Desire (LP) 217-218
Falcon Stuart 151, 154
Donna Summer 112
Summer in the City 92, 94-95, 97, 99, 101, 106, 109, 216
Sophie Sumner 371-373, 375
Peter Süskind 202
The Sweeney 171
Swinbrook 136-137
David Sylvian 240
Max Von Sydow 203, 205

Talking Heads 75, 87
Jimmy Tarbuck 19
Elizabeth Taylor 58, 237
Techno Twins 77
John E. L. Tenney 234
The Terminator 177
Hunter S. Thompson 94
TIMANDMO 225-226
Richard Todd 195

Tokyo 99-102, 211-213, 215, 217
Tomita 87
Tommy 25
Felix Topolski 102, 103
Pete Townshend 21, 23, 25, 34
Spencer Tracy 193
Transformers 215
The Trial 170
Freddie Truman 195
J. M. W. Turner 209
Simon Fisher-Turner 49
12 Monkeys 241
Twin Peaks 142
2001 A Space Odyssey 49, 86, 102, 183, 186

U2 77
Ultravox 75, 80
Midge Ure 72

Van Gogh 20, 156, 209
Van Halen 224
Vangelis 66, 75, 97, 115, 216
The Vanishing 126, 154
The Vapors 60
Rod Vass 109
Gene Vincent 26
Jack Vetriano 10
Vice Squad 184
Vile Bodies 96-97, 109, 212-214
Visage 86, 87
Von Daniken 37

Christopher Walken 11
John L. Walters 89
Robert Watts 90, 229-230
Burt Weedon 21
H. G. Wells 186
Vivienne Westwood 62, 92
Dick Whittington 179
The Who 23, 25
Wiesbaden 125
Barbie Wilde 5, 58-59, 63, 65, 67-73, 76-89, 119-120, 135, 137, 149, 151, 153, 157-159, 227, 236
Oscar Wilde 75, 96, 238
Bruce Willis 238
Stevie Winwood 23
Carl Wayne 24
Pete Williams 77, 82
Colin Wilson 38, 206, 241
Wind in the Willows 35
Winnie The Pooh 35
Johnny Winter 60
Withnail and I 37, 241
Trevor Wooldridge 48, 51
Women in Love 29

The X-Files 145
Xtro 15-17, 223, 239
The Yardbirds 19, 23
Yello 97
The Yellow Magic Orchestra 75
Yes 25

Frank Zappa 48, 143

www.ingramcontent.com/pod-product-compliance
Lightning Source LLC
Chambersburg PA
CBHW060353080526
44583CB00012B/293